Terry McInturff
3311 20th Street
Lubbock, TX 79410

WHO DECIDES?

WHO DECIDES?

STATES AS LABORATORIES OF CONSTITUTIONAL EXPERIMENTATION

Jeffrey S. Sutton

OXFORD
UNIVERSITY PRESS

OXFORD
UNIVERSITY PRESS

Oxford University Press is a department of the University of Oxford. It furthers
the University's objective of excellence in research, scholarship, and education
by publishing worldwide. Oxford is a registered trade mark of Oxford University
Press in the UK and certain other countries.

Published in the United States of America by Oxford University Press
198 Madison Avenue, New York, NY 10016, United States of America.

Library of Congress Cataloging-in-Publication Data
Names: Sutton, Jeffrey S. (Jeffrey Stuart), 1960– author.
Title: Who decides : states as laboratories of
constitutional experimentation / Jeffrey S. Sutton.
Description: New York, NY : Oxford University Press, [2022] | Includes index. |
Identifiers: LCCN 2021009439 (print) | LCCN 2021009440 (ebook) |
ISBN 9780197582183 (hardback) | ISBN 9780197582206 (epub) | ISBN 9780197581704
Subjects: LCSH: Constitutional law—United States—States. |
Constitutional amendments—United States—States. |
Constitutional history—United States—States.
Classification: LCC KF4530 .S889 2022 (print) | LCC KF4530 (ebook) |
DDC 342.73/042—dc23
LC record available at https://lccn.loc.gov/2021009439
LC ebook record available at https://lccn.loc.gov/2021009440

DOI: 10.1093/oso/9780197582183.001.0001

1 3 5 7 9 8 6 4 2

Printed by LSC Communications, United States of America

To my parents, David and Nancy Sutton

CONTENTS

—————≫◆≪—————

Part IV Federalism Within Federalism

Part V The Amendment Process

PREFACE

<hr>

When the pioneers prioritized what to take with them when they settled the Northwest as it expanded from Ohio to the Dakotas to what became Oregon, a well-stocked legal library did not lead the list. Life was too hard to allow it. No one earned an invitation to the Oregon Trail based on the size of the library they could bring with them.[1]

Which prompts this question: What happened when they reached the end of the Trail and it came time, eventually, for the people of the Oregon Territory to apply for statehood and to write their own constitution? Where did they look for guidance? Some states had assistance from knowledgeable scholars, it's true. Thanks to funding by railroad interests and unbeknownst to the people of North Dakota at the time, James Bradley Thayer, the celebrated Harvard Law School professor, was a co-author of its constitution, and Thomas Cooley, the renowned Michigan Supreme Court justice, spoke during the debates over it.[2] But not every state had such assistance. And it's difficult to believe that the blacksmith-lawyer or woodsman-lawyer filled the Conestoga wagon with resources they could use as a model for drafting a new constitution. And yet they had something. Maybe some serendipity entered the picture, the happenstance that a settler from Indiana brought a copy of his state's charter, prompting the first Oregon Constitution to share similarities with the Hoosier State's Constitution.[3]

In writing about state constitutions, I sometimes have felt like the blacksmith-lawyer and the woodsman-lawyer, knowledgeable about some features of state constitutional law but worried, eventually certain, there was plenty more to know and too little time to sort out every mete and bound. To my luck, several scholars have helped me along the way. Dependable guides all, they have suggested which mountains to climb, which rivers to cross, what parts of the journey to leave to others.

51 Imperfect Solutions: States and the Making of American Constitutional Law focused on the liberty and property protections that our state constitutions guarantee. This book shifts from individual rights to structure, to how our state constitutions allocate power within each state, all while comparing the state experiences with the federal experience. Constitutional structure is a daunting topic, making me grateful for the considerable scholarship already undertaken in some of these areas. In contrast to the drafters of many of our state constitutions, I have had access to shelves of books and articles written by dedicated scholars.

In speaking to bar associations, students at law schools, and fellow judges about *51 Imperfect Solutions* over the last three years, I have learned a lot, including how much more there is to say about state constitutions. Conversations generated during these speaking events, plus discussions with students in my state constitutional law classes, made me realize how many questions remain unanswered, some about individual rights, others about the role of constitutional structure in promoting liberty, still others about the balance of power between the national and state governments. That explains why this book picks up where the last book left off and why a few parts of the book, mainly in Chapter 4, borrow in places from *51 Imperfect Solutions* and elaborate on points initially made there. The same is true of a few other parts of the book, mainly in Chapter 6, which borrow in places from *State Constitutional Law: The Modern Experience* (3rd ed. 2020).

Several young lawyers and law students have helped me with research. Michael Lemanski offered considerable assistance with the research for Part I of the book, dealing with the state courts and their experiences with judicial review, judicial elections, and territorial courts. Helpful throughout were John Acton, Giebien Na, Drew Hamilton, Rebecca Hill, Joe Jakubowski, Sam Lioi, John Macy, Zachary Nallen, John Sutton, and Nathaniel Sutton. Several former law clerks kindly read drafts of the book and gave me useful feedback: Justin Aimonetti, Kyle Grigel, Will Hall, Ben Harris, John Kendrick, Elizabeth Nielson, John Rockenbach, and Sarah Welch.

Commenters included three federal judicial colleagues, Eric Murphy, Bill Pryor, and Chad Readler. Several state court judges kindly looked at drafts—Randy Holland, Erin Lagesen, and Fred Nelson—as did scholars Zaki Anwar, Niko Bowie, Erwin Chemerinsky, Sanford Levinson, Jason Mazzone, and Miriam Seifter. So did friends Tom Barnico, Jim Garland, Steve McAllister, and Dan Schweitzer. John McGuiness offered helpful comments on the chapter on state courts and judicial review. Aditya Bamzai, Kristin Hickman, Aaron Saiger, and Chris Walker did the same for the chapter on administrative law, as did Richard Briffault for the chapter on local governments. Sixth Circuit librarians Owen Smith and Jane Underwood offered considerable help in tracking down difficult-to-find books and other resources.

The Oxford team has continued to be highly supportive and helpful. My editor David McBride offered perceptive insights and suggestions and provided reassurance when I needed it. Jeremy Toynbee, Patterson Lamb, and Emily Mackenzie have been terrific in helping with the editing and marketing of the book.

Then there's my indispensable family—Peggy, Nathaniel, John, and Margaret—without whom this book would not have been started or finished.

Introduction

FOR BETTER, FOR WORSE, or for more of the same, this is a sequel. After writing *51 Imperfect Solutions*, I learned two things. I needed to mention other ideas for protecting individual rights under our fifty-one constitutions, many of them learned from engaging state court judges and lawyers about our state charters. And I needed to tell the other half of the story, the role structure plays in the state and federal constitutions in protecting freedom.

Everything in law and politics, including individual rights, comes back to divisions of power and the evergreen question: Who decides? Do the states, the federal government, or both have authority over the matter? Within each government, how does the relevant constitution delegate power to the legislature, the executive branch, and the judiciary? Our state and federal constitutions give surprisingly different answers to many of these questions and to the control the people retain over public policy decisions and the officials who make them. But who would know? For too long, American law has taken a one-sided view of these questions, focusing on the US Constitution's answers to these questions and rarely considering, sometimes not considering at all, our fifty state constitutions' answers to them. A true understanding of American constitutional law requires attention to both. A focus on just one side of the balance not only slights the role of our state constitutions in American government, but it also obscures an encompassing view of each system.

Structure and Individual Rights

51 Imperfect Solutions told stories about state and federal individual rights, as judicially enforced by the state and federal courts—stories about equality in educational opportunity over the last fifty years, about limits on the police to investigate crimes under the exclusionary rule over the last 120 years, about prohibitions on involuntarily sterilizing individuals at the height of the eugenics era in the early twentieth century, and about protecting the rights of minority religions and dissenting voices in the midst of the patriotic fervor needed to get us through World War II. These stories and others like them cover the most resonant of constitutional rights, the music-to-our-ears rights. Past and present, these guarantees speak to us as individuals, to what we expect the legislative and executive branches of government will do for us and to what we hope the courts will protect if these other branches of government let us down. Because individual rights are the easiest to understand—they protect *us* after all—they are the ones most often taught in our schools and thus are the most recognizable constitutional rights.

They're important, too. "In the compound republic of America," Madison reminds us in *Federalist* No. 51, "a double security arises to the rights of the people"—the protection of liberty by the state and federal governments as well as the separate state and federal courts. All individual constitutional rights, federal and state, have the potential to protect us.

Pull back the lens, however, and it should become clear that individual rights are the least important, the least reliable, constitutional guarantees. Forced to choose between a constitution that identifies ample individual constitutional rights and one that firmly separates powers among the various branches of government, every citizen should opt for the latter. Divisions of power offer the ultimate protection of freedom by subtraction and addition—by cutting back on the power of each branch of government and by aggregating multiple protections from many branches of government. Learn from Madison once more in *Federalist* No. 51: "Ambition must be made to counteract ambition," demanding "partition" of the branches of government. Power checking power is a far better guarantee of liberty than the hope that any one government (federal or state) or any one branch of that government (executive, legislative, or judicial) will be there when you need it.

Think about balance of governmental power in the context of individual-rights guarantees in a constitution, such as the bills of rights found in all of our American constitutions. It's easy to put down on paper that all individuals in a country are entitled, say, to a trial of their peers before the government may convict them of a crime. That ink-and-paper guarantee becomes real only when the country has independent courts to enforce the guarantee without risk or reward from the executive branch that implemented the law or the legislative branch that wrote it. That's a trickier proposition.

Ask the people of Russia and North Korea. Their constitutions protect all kinds of rights on paper: freedom of "speech, of the press, and of assembly, meetings, street processions and demonstrations";[1] the right to criticize the government without fear of persecution;[2] the right to form political associations and to vote in elections;[3] freedom of conscience and of religion;[4] and the inviolability of the person and of the home.[5] "Wonderful stuff," as Justice Scalia liked to say.[6] The same points could be made about the constitutions of Cuba, China, and many other countries.[7] But these constitutions are not enforced by independent courts. Because these countries' *"real constitutions . . . do not prevent the centralization of power in one man or one party,"* their individual-rights guarantees are easy for the government to ignore.[8] Even the most exalted rights come to naught if there is no place to honor them. A "bill of rights has value," Justice Scalia reminds us, "only if the other part of the constitution—the part that really 'constitutes' the organs of government—establishes a structure that is likely to preserve, against the ineradicable human lust for power, the liberties that the bill of rights expresses."[9] Otherwise, a government's bill of rights is a Potemkin Village, nice to look at, not free to live in. Individual rights mean little without independent courts willing to enforce them.

Structure, Rights, and Balance of Power

But judicial independence sometimes creates problems of its own. True separation of power requires separation in every direction. Even federal and state judges can trespass across inexact boundaries into places they don't belong. If some countries do too little in enforcing individual rights through their courts, other countries run the risk of doing too much. Just as it's essential to ask whether a court system is willing to check the political branches, it's essential to ask whether the courts have colonized areas traditionally handled by the elected policymaking branches. Today, the American risk runs in the second direction. No country in history has embraced judicially enforceable rights more than ours. It's easy to criticize countries with lavish individual rights and no place to enforce them. But beware the possibility that knowledge-able citizens in those countries might return the favor by reminding us how we tend to resolve some of our most intractable policy debates: through US Supreme Court decisions that the people cannot realisti-cally change, issued by life-tenured justices whom the people cannot replace. We may have some planks in our own eyes when it comes to the social contract.

This is not new. Shifting imbalances of power run the gamut in American history. Some branches dominate one era. The next gen-eration corrects those faults and, like a never-ending game of Whac-A-Mole, generates faults of its own. The constant in each cycle is an American people suspicious of *any* branch of government having too much power and *any* group of people having too much influence. What's not constant, what's largely forgotten, what needs renewed attention is an appreciation of the role of our state constitutions in navigating these repeated recalibrations—and a reckoning of the balance-of-power risks and rewards arising from all of our constitutions when it comes to promoting freedom.

To test the waters on how separation promotes freedom as well as in-novation and good government, consider how fifty-one distinct sources of power operate in the context of civil and criminal laws.

Structure and State Innovation

In 1932, in the throes of the Great Depression, Justice Brandeis dissented from a decision about Oklahoma's regulation of ice, of all things. "It is one of the happy incidents of the federal system," he observed, "that a single courageous State may, if its citizens choose, serve as a laboratory" and "try novel social and economic experiments without risk to the rest of the country."[10] Little did he know that "laboratories" of democracy would not be a metaphor one day. As a nationwide crisis, the COVID-19 pandemic is an unlikely candidate for illustrating how federalism works in some ways. It's not a parochial problem with parochial effects; it's an existential threat to everyone, all people, all American governments. And it's a problem that does not respect borders.

But it's a problem in which borders add tools and flexibility for fixing the problem. Putting all hands on deck benefits everyone. The question on the table is not whether the national *or* state governments should engage in fighting a national problem. It's whether roles exist for both. In national crises, the role of the federal government frequently grows, usually appropriately so. But consider the ways in which fifty-one governments hold the potential to benefit the country.

Not every crisis brings an Abraham Lincoln into the presidency or a governorship. Our structure of government assumes as much. No president or governor has exclusive authority to answer the challenges of a pandemic. Whether as a matter of power or capacity, presidents cannot address every component of the emergency. Cooperation is the order of the day, with Congress, governors, and state legislatures. Governors may have considerable power over a local quarantine, but they cannot exercise control over neighboring states. Their power to prohibit people from entering the state has limits. So too are there limits on their power to provide near-term economic subsidies to those in need or to coordinate the development of a vaccine and distribute it nationwide.

Then there are the many unknowns in dealing with a new virus. What kind of health risk does it present? How effective are various precautions in slowing its spread? What treatments work best with infections? What impact do stay-at-home orders have on students' educations, on people's mental health, on their spiritual health? How does all of this affect the public welfare in another sense—people's jobs, the local economy, the national economy? And who supplies income for people unable to earn it?

What leader, what government had answers to all of these questions and resources for all of these problems at the outset? Trial and error was all there was, frustrating though that may have been. In a country of 330 million people covering 3.5 million square miles of utterly distinct land, a singular guess at answering all of these unknowns could have caused more problems than it solved. Imagine if one person had the power to pick one set of solutions for this problem at the outset. How many elderly men and women would have been moved from crowded hospitals to nursing homes? Would all in-class learning in all schools have been shut down for the year? Would we have had the same lockdowns in all parts of the country, whether rural or urban? The state and federal Framers had other ideas. Better, as it turned out, to allow different governors to try different approaches and to watch the results in real time—and to allow the president and Congress to provide support and to learn from the give and take along the way before nationalizing some remedies over others.

It's true that it was the same virus affecting all Americans. And it's true that uniform answers to uniform problems often work best. But that's only when the answers are known. That wasn't the situation at the outset.

Structure and a National Backstop

Interests in uniformity call to mind another modern challenge— the persistence of racism—one rooted in a downside of federalism, in truth a downside of government. State governments, like all governments, can do courageously good things and cravenly bad ones. None of our fifty-one constitutions perfects human nature or fixes the ever-falling problems that go with it. States no doubt have been trailing protectors of individual rights at various stages in American history. We have a national government and a national constitution for an overriding reason. Some rights are not up for negotiation or discovery through trial and error. But even national protections do not cure all nationwide problems. That means there's still a role for state legislatures, state governors, state courts, and mayors to play. If a problem seems to defy a national solution or Americans become impatient in identifying one, that leaves considerable room for local innovation and leadership.

Structure and Liberty

Now look at division of powers from a different perspective: a criminal conviction and sentence, the most extreme deprivation of liberty a society can impose. The states are the key place to look. In 2017, there were 17.4 million state criminal cases and only 82,000 federal criminal cases.[11] With over 200 state criminal cases for every one federal criminal case, the states are where most of this liberty gets lost or preserved, where the rule of law exists or does not.[12] Why, one might ask, do the states have the primary responsibility for enacting criminal laws? Answer: separation of powers. Because the US Constitution makes Congress one of limited and enumerated powers under our federalist system, it does not have a general police power to enact criminal laws.[13]

Only the states have that power. How does division protect liberty at the state level? There must be a criminal law before there can be a criminal prosecution. Separation of powers in the legislative branches ensures that the states do not casually or lightly criminalize conduct. Two legislative houses in all states (save Nebraska) and the potential for gubernatorial vetoes slow the impulse to criminalize, together with many process-based limitations on state legislatures unique to state constitutions. Even if a legislature enacts criminal laws, it may not enforce them. That falls to the discretion of a separate branch: the executive. Here we have a little-appreciated contrast between state and federal criminal prosecutions. One person stands at the headwaters of every federal criminal prosecution, the president of the United States. But no such unitary executive exists at the state level, where the state constitutions usually empower independently elected attorneys general and local prosecutors, and occasionally governors, to handle law enforcement. Once arrested and in state court, individuals have criminal procedure rights under the federal *and* state constitutions to preserve their freedom. Some of these rights apply to the investigation, some to the trial, some to the sentence. At each stage, two shots beat one in a dual republic when independent state courts stand ready to enforce them.

In the last analysis, if liberty, security, and good government are the goals, structural protections often are the best ways to advance them, as a hypothetical criminal prosecution, the history of Jim Crow, and a real pandemic illustrate. Fifty-one approaches offer diverse ways to structure a government, permit variation when variation is due, generate a healthy competition for the best models, allow other sovereigns to import winning approaches when they suit their circumstances, and ultimately permit national solutions to nationwide problems.

Structure and Variation between the State and National Governments

Even as all fifty-one American constitutions prioritize balance of power in government, they do so differently. The key variation is not among the states; it's between the states and the national government. A step back from the present confirms the remarkable gap that has arisen between the ways in which the states and the national government have come to arrange their governments.

What do the constitutions of California, Colorado, Florida, Illinois, Mississippi, Montana, Ohio, and Oklahoma have in common? They are one in differing from the US Constitution when it comes to many of the most fundamental choices in allocating and limiting power. Take in this sample of differences:

* All eight states permit the election of justices for a term of years to their high courts, and in several instances have age limits. But federal judges have life tenure after the president selects, and the Senate confirms, them.[14]
* All eight states have a plural executive branch, in which the people may vote separately for, say, a governor and an attorney general, and in which each official exercises separate power. But the federal side has just one chief executive, the president, who oversees the entire branch.[15]
* These states all place limits on the power of executive-branch agencies, either by denying them deference over the meaning of laws they implement or by refusing to permit the legislature to delegate unconstrained policymaking power to them. But that has not been the case on the federal side.[16]

* These states have adopted a range of constitutional limits on the use of legislative power: clear-title provisions, single-subject rules, public purposes clauses, balanced-budget requirements, among many others. But no such limits on Congress appear in the federal constitution.[17]

* All eight states authorize direct democracy—the authority of the people to initiate constitutional amendments on their own. And they permit those changes to the constitution, along with those initiated through the legislature, to pass with a mere 51% vote. But neither option exists under the federal constitution.[18]

How could that be? How could the constitutions from these diverse states not be representative of the choices the American people have made for their one national constitution? How could the people of Mississippi and California, for example, both want the same things for their states but then not join forces to create something similar for their national government? This gulf in reality understates the point. What's true for these eight states is true for most states. All fifty state constitutions are far easier to amend than the US Constitution, usually requiring just 51% electoral support as opposed to the formidable requirements to alter the federal charter, support from three-quarters of the states. With a set of state constitutions that facilitates amendment, the American people have not hesitated to voice different preferences for structuring their local governments throughout history. On the state side, the key structural trend is the people's desire to have a say over who is in power and what they may do, constantly finding new ways to limit the power of their public officials. All that changes are the manifestations of this "democracy principle," as Jessica Bulman-Pozen and Miriam Seifter put it, every generation or so.[19] By contrast, the difficulty of amending the US Constitution has given the people few opportunities to insert these ever-more-democratic impulses into the structure of the federal government. Exploring these differences, taking in lessons from the comparison, is a key undertaking of this book.

As a structure of its own, the book has five parts. Part I deals with the judicial branch. Chapter 1 discusses an acutely American dilemma, a fear that the courts will do too little in enforcing constitutional rights and a fear they will do too much. Chapter 2 begins a search for insights in resolving the dilemma by looking at how the state courts innovated judicial review and how they initially exercised it. Chapter 3 covers judicial selection, the rise of judicial elections in the states, and the impact of different selection systems on judicial review. Chapter 4 addresses an under-explored aspect of many states' histories, their years as territories with territorial courts. Why, the chapter asks, did the local-control preferences that prompted the territories to seek statehood not lead to lasting local-control preferences in interpreting their own constitutions? Attention to when and how the federal *and* state courts exercise judicial review, particularly with respect to our most difficult-to-define constitutional rights, holds promise as a way to address our current imbalance, a country in which we may be asking the federal courts to do too much and may risk politicizing them in the process.

The second part of the book looks at current issues facing the executive branch in the state and federal systems. Chapter 5 compares the unitary executive at the federal level with the plural executive at the state level. Unlike the federal system, in which the attorney general, the secretary of the treasury, and other members of the cabinet all report to one person, the president, the states usually divide this power into separately elected offices. The rise of the state attorneys general as a source of local and national power offers one illustration of the modern salience of the plural executive. Chapter 6 looks at an aggregation-of-power issue in the executive branch, the growth of administrative agencies. Few at the founding contemplated this utility-player branch, which consolidates executive, legislative, and judicial powers over a single subject in one agency. The states have not hesitated to mark their own paths in this area. In contrast to the federal courts, state courts frequently prohibit their legislatures from delegating policymaking power to agencies and frequently curb the power of agencies to interpret state laws or altogether reject the *Chevron*-deference model used by the federal courts.

The third part of the book deals with the legislative branch. Chapter 7 explains the myriad restrictions that state constitutions place on state legislatures—single-subject rules, public-purpose clauses, uniformity clauses, among the most prominent examples—and the kinds of problems that prompted them. The US Constitution does not place comparable restrictions on Congress. Chapter 8 takes on the thorny challenges of drawing legislative lines and of resolving recurrent fights over voting rights, all while comparing the federal and state treatment of these perennial quandaries.

The fourth part of the book, all in Chapter 9, takes vertical separation of powers one step further: federalism within federalism. It explains the division of powers between state and local governments and chronicles disputes that have arisen between them. If, in modern America, like-minded people increasingly gravitate to similar states, the same is true within states, whether in congenial cities, suburbs, or rural areas. Home rule and other local allocations of power sometime allow people in these overlapping communities to express their distinct political preferences and to live under them, too.

The last part of the book, Chapter 10, addresses the ultimate recourse of liberty, the freedom to change. Having ratified the structure and rights in our fifty-one constitutions, the people retained authority to alter them. In juxtaposition to the near-impossible amendment process at the federal level, the people may readily amend their state constitutions, usually with a 51% vote, often with citizen-initiated petitions. The differences between these models for change raise the possibility of state lending and federal borrowing in some instances and power-checking, freedom-securing separation in others.

PART I
The Judicial Branch

Why start with the judicial branch? Most books about federal constitutional structure start with the legislative branch, the key source of policymaking power at the founding. But almost every one of the state charters *begins* with a declaration of rights in Article I.[1] Judicially enforceable rights come first in the state constitutions in contrast to the US Constitution, which did not add a Bill of Rights until 1791. The state courts over time have become the key forum for vindicating state constitutional guarantees. A persistent theme in American history, moreover, has been the *decline* in state legislative power and the increasing limitations placed on it by state and federal constitutions, by state and federal courts. In the zero-sum world of changes to American domestic power, the courts have been the net winners, the state legislatures the net losers, so far. An examination of how this happened and what to do about it offers an apt place to begin.

Four chapters take on these topics: the American dilemma of too much or too little judicial review; the origin of judicial review in the state courts and the lessons it offers for today's state and federal judges; the rise of elections as a way to select state-court judges and the impact of judicial selection methods on judging; and the experiences of the territorial courts and how that history has, and oddly has not, influenced today's state courts. The constant throughout is to look for insights about the proper role of judges in American government, the proper balance between state and federal judicial power, and the opportunities for the two systems to work together in the distinctly American phenomenon of identifying new judicially enforceable rights.

I

Umpiring and Gerrymandering

IN AMERICAN GOVERNMENT, NEARLY all roads lead to the courts. Little did Alexis de Tocqueville know in 1835, when he observed that there is "no political event in which [one] does not hear the authority of the judge invoked" in the United States,[1] how pin-pointed that description would become.[2] The growth of judicial power started as a way to curb corrupt and over-reaching state legislatures and manifested itself in allowing the judicial branch, as opposed to the other branches, to resolve more disputes over contracts, property, debts, and other distinctly nineteenth-century problems. For the last seventy-five years or so, however, something else has propelled its influence: the growth of constitutional review at the federal level, the power to invalidate state and federal civil laws and executive branch actions as well as state and federal criminal prosecutions. But trees don't grow to the sky, and anything that can't go on forever usually won't.[3] The state courts offer several useful ways to alleviate the balance-of-power issues that have arisen with the growth of judicial review in the federal courts.

Let me set the stage by pulling together two things usually thought of separately: judicial umpiring and political gerrymandering.

Chief Justice Roberts compared the role of a judge to the role of an umpire during his confirmation hearing. Like umpires, he said, judges call "balls and strikes,"[4] a job so modest that "nobody ever went to a ball game to see the umpire."[5] As someone who has run the gauntlet of the confirmation process myself, I admire the analogy, its easy-to-understand way of capturing what judges do—by invoking America's favorite pastime no less. No one notices umpires in a well-called game because they merely say which pitches come within the strike zone and which do not. Sounds a lot like the good judge, dressed in sartorial black for good measure.

Some have criticized the metaphor as too simplistic on the ground that judges have a lot more discretion to identify new claims than baseball umpires do in defining the strike zone. Maybe so. But most good analogies are meant to simplify. Plus, the chief justice might respond that his critics do not give enough credit to the difficulty of umpiring a baseball game. Televised games now mark the accuracy of every call by showing the not-so-neutral fans the actual dimensions of the strike zone after each pitch—the fixed space above home plate and the fluctuating space between each batter's knees and the midpoint of their torso. Umpiring is not a job for the timid, and that's not unlike the situation the Court faces after it issues landmark decisions and the second-guessing commences.

But I bring up the umpire analogy for a different reason. It calls to mind a more perilous problem for the judiciary. Every baseball game involves two teams. The referee, unaffiliated with either team, is a neutral arbitrator who calls balls and strikes. In that respect, umpires are just like judges. They have no stake in the game. But think about what happens when a litigant asks the US Supreme Court to decide a new federal constitutional claim. Each time the Court decides that the US Constitution's strike zone covers a new claim, if you will, the Court becomes a player as well as a referee in the contest at hand, to say nothing of future contests managing its scope.

Suddenly three teams, not two, take the field. Consider a dispute between the president and Congress over the meaning of a constitutional provision. If the Court decides that the matter is ripe for judicial resolution, as opposed to a political question unsuitable for the federal courts to resolve, the Court becomes a player. Why? The next time the president and Congress tussle over who gets to do what, they will have to account for the position of the US Supreme Court and where it will draw the lines of power. Or take an individual-rights dispute over a new liberty claim. If the Court decides that the matter is ripe for judicial resolution, it becomes a player in the definition and enforcement of that right in that case and future cases.

Who really thinks that only the citizen and the challenged branch of government have a role to play in those disputes? Who wins the contest at hand may turn on who decides it. And who wins the next contest will turn not just on the meaning of the Constitution but on an interpretation of a prior decision of the Court—the last decision of a new player in the dispute.

A consequential development in American history has been the growth of federal judicial power over the last seventy-five years through the expansion of the strike zone of the US Constitution. Try to put to the side whether you think these decisions are good or bad in terms of the individual rights or structural guarantees they protect or the interpretive methods that identify them. If you can't do that, you have plenty of company; few people can these days. As with most Americans, that probably means you like some decisions and not others—and reserve a special intensity for some decisions that resonate with you. What also unites Americans and what seems undeniable about this increase in judicial power is something else: its impact on our shared perception about the role of the federal courts in American government. Does anyone think that American citizens interested in limits on presidential or congressional power, interested in identifying new individual liberty or property rights, or interested in preserving existing constitutional strike zones have no interest in who our judicial umpires are? Just ask any federal judge or justice who has gone through the confirmation process in the last three decades. A lot of American citizens now watch what the courts do, pay attention to White House nominations, and obsess over United States Senate confirmation hearings because *they care more about who the umpires are than who the players are*. Exhibit A is the 2016 presidential election, which turned, by too many accounts to deny, on a sufficient number of Americans treating a vote for president of the United States as a proxy to fill one seat on a nine-member Court, the vacancy left by Justice Scalia's death. We have come a long way since 1776.

One signer of the Declaration of Independence was Elbridge Gerry, who accomplished a lot in his life. He was in the room at the convention, a representative from Massachusetts in the First Congress, the vice president for President Madison, and one of three participants in the Constitutional Convention of 1787 who did not sign the Constitution (in his case because it did not contain a Bill of Rights). Having done all that, luckless Elbridge Gerry remains remembered first and last for gerrymandering, attributed to him because he helped to redraw state senate district lines in 1812. Fairly or unfairly, Gerry is connected to something that few people publicly support today.[6] With the use of computers, voting records, and scads of demographic data, both political parties have turned gerrymandering into a highly effective political tool for creating safe districts for state and federal elections. So effective is the tool that citizens of both political parties have filed claims in the state and federal courts in recent years to the effect that gerrymandering violates an assortment of state and federal constitutional rights, the right to vote and the right of association being the most frequently raised. In 2019, in its most prominent decision of the Term, the US Supreme Court in the *Rucho* case rejected by a one-vote margin the claim that the US Constitution permits the federal courts to resolve partisan gerrymandering cases. Some state courts, most notably courts in Pennsylvania and North Carolina, have taken a different tack. Unlike *Rucho*, they have granted relief in the face of similar claims under their state constitutions.

I will return to these cases in Chapter 8. What interests me at the outset is not whether extreme gerrymandering violates the federal or state constitutions. It's this unabridged truth: *No one defends gerrymandering as a matter of policy in its most far-reaching forms today*. All agree that it has been poisonous for American government. It warps democracy for one thing. By allowing the governing officials to choose who elects them, gerrymandering dishonors the principle that "the voters should choose their representatives, not the other way around," in Justice Ginsburg's words.[7] And it warps deliberation over complex policy issues for another. If we make nearly 90% of congressional districts safe for one political party or the other, that makes the party primaries nearly the only elections that matter, elections that occur long before the first Tuesday after November 1. The same is true for state legislative districts. All safe districts stay safe only as long as incumbents do not make themselves vulnerable to a primary challenge by someone from their own party. Because elected officials fearful of losing office face only the risk of being outflanked by candidates from their own parties, they will err in the direction of that party's preferences. That's fine for them in terms of keeping power. Just look at your political party's top-ten wish list and hew to each of them, the more forcefully the better.

But this is not good for the country. Making democracy more un-democratic undermines confidence in government. Gerrymandering is especially pernicious for a country desperately in need of more compro-mise, not less. Compromise requires elected officials to look in the op-posite direction—to the opposing team, not the home team. How else to find common ground, areas with room for give and take? No one publicly says that we need more gerrymandering, and vast majorities think we need a lot less of it.

So what connects judicial umpiring to political gerrymandering? Too much, I fear. Power too often is about getting what you want. Gerrymandering is designed to help parties, the people who support them, and interest groups get what they want—all the better without having to earn the majority support usually needed to get it. The most successful form of gerrymandering in this country is not bending elected districts to improve one party's chances of obtaining power it does not deserve. It is making the state and federal elected districts *irrelevant* by giving power over selected issues to a Court whose individuals all have life tenure and whose decisions, realistically, cannot be overruled by the people. That's quite a trick. That's especially a trick with respect to is-sues that the US Constitution does not mention by name and that the American people thus never voted for in the original Constitution in 1789, the Bill of Rights in 1791, the Fourteenth Amendment in 1868, the Nineteenth Amendment in 1919, or in any other amendment.

Yes, some democracy plays a role in the membership of the Court: Only elected presidents select the justices; only elected senators by a majority vote confirm them; and only five members of the nine-member Court can identify new rights. But those democratic constraints, however meaningful, surely lapse over time, particularly in a world in which justices on average serve for twenty-five to thirty years. Traditional po-litical gerrymandering by contrast requires a re-ordering every ten years after each decennial census. Redrawing those lines every ten years, by the way, never affects the composition of the Court because the district lines do not affect presidential elections or US Senate races.

Judicial review in its most extreme forms may be the greatest kind of gerrymandering ever known. Which creates this puzzle: Why is it that Americans are contemptuous of electoral-district gerrymandering yet continue to embrace having judges make ever-more-important decisions that the American people never approved? If Americans perceive one form of gerrymandering as problematic, should they not be skeptical of a more undemocratic form of it? It's a question surrounded by exclamations. If I had to identify one risk to the state and federal judiciary over all others, it's this: The American people are catching on. Imprudent though they may be in the short term, they are not imprudent in the long term. They are slowly, fitfully, resentfully, coming to appreciate how large the footprint of the federal courts on American government has grown—and how much larger it is than anything the Framers ever could have imagined. Sad to acknowledge, the typical American, I fear, has come to think of judicial interpretations of our constitutions as another form of gerrymandering—another way, perhaps the most extreme way, for one group or another to get what they want at the expense of their political opponents—and at the expense of large swaths of the American people.

Ask what Niccolo Machiavelli, no mean observer of power, would say about the modern reach of the federal courts' power to override the other branches of government based on interpretations of the US Constitution, especially interpretations of "unenumerated" rights. He might have devoted Chapter 1 of *The Prince*, his shrewd descriptions of how people acquire and maintain power, to the topic. What method of acquiring power is better than constitutionalizing the key priorities of a political faction and prohibiting anyone from changing the rule other than by doing the impossible (getting three-quarters of the states to overrule it) or preying on the unpredictable (hoping to replace life-tenured members of the Court with justices of your liking).

Let me shift from umpiring and gerrymandering to offer two concrete ways to illustrate the stakes of judicial review and the difficulty of sorting out the right answer to the role of the state and federal courts in America today. One turns on recent history; the other turns on personal history.

The year 1987 was eventful in American constitutional history. After the retirement of Justice Lewis Powell from the US Supreme Court that year, the United States Senate rejected President Reagan's nomination of Judge Robert Bork to fill his seat by a 42–58 vote and eventually confirmed Judge Anthony Kennedy to the seat by a 97–0 vote in 1988. In political terms, this was a win for the Democratic Party and a defeat for the Republican Party. In policy terms, it was a win for some interest groups and a loss for others. In terms of constitutional interpretation, it was a win for flexible methods of interpretation and a loss for more formal approaches to deciding cases, such as textualism and originalism.

At the risk of opening old wounds, I want to look back on that event with a different scorecard: the federal judiciary's role in American government. During his thirty years on the Court, Justice Kennedy was the most likely justice on the Court to apply the US Constitution to disputes between the individual and the government or between two governments.[8] What would have happened with a Justice Bork? Who can know for sure? But I suspect he would have been the least likely justice during that time to invalidate a law or stop a criminal prosecution based on the US Constitution. Plenty of data points support that suspicion. One of Judge Bork's problems as a nominee was that he had written extensively as a law professor about the proper role of the federal courts in performing judicial review. Those articles all pointed in the same direction: He was the leading advocate of judicial restraint in the country.[9] On top of that, he had shown in his six years as a judge that he practiced what he preached.[10] In 1986, one year before his nomination to the US Supreme Court, Judge Bork upheld a provision of the DC Code that prohibited protestors from displaying near embassies signs that tended to bring that foreign government into disrepute. He explained the need for judges to show restraint in cases touching on foreign affairs, especially so when faced with a law that "both Congress and successive Presidents have declared to be necessary to fulfill our obligations under both customary international law and a treaty,"[11] and even when the claimant asserts a constitutional right. The US Supreme Court reversed the decision two years later,[12] making it the only time the Court reversed one of his decisions. More to the point, Judge Bork's reasoning underscores his conviction that "courts ought not to invade the domain[s] the Constitution marks out for democratic rather than judicial governance."[13] After his failed confirmation and after he retired from the court of appeals, he wrote *The Tempting of America*, which confirmed that he was a skeptic of using the federal courts to identify

new constitutional rights not enumerated in the document. In the face
of this evidence, it's fair to think that a Justice Bork would have been
one of the least likely, probably the least likely, justice during that time
period to identify new constitutional rights.

What a difference that would have made. And it's the kind of difference we Americans need to think about more critically. I say this not
because I would prefer one justice to the other, any more than I would
prefer one of my two bosses, Justice Powell or Justice Scalia, to the
other. That's like being asked whether one prefers a mother or a father.
I admire Justice Kennedy and Judge Bork, both of whom consistently
adhered to their theories of judging throughout their careers. I ask the
question for a different reason. We tend to focus on individual rights
outcomes (what was decided), not the structural integrity leading to
them (who should decide them). In that sense, we are eminently pragmatic, perhaps too pragmatic. If we can get relief from a legislature, we
will take it. If from a state court, we will take that too. So also for the
US Supreme Court. But at some point, we should ask what's the best
vehicle for making these critical decisions—particularly if we start to
place one institution (the US Supreme Court) at risk by relying on it
too heavily to referee the most intractable disputes of the day.

The American people, through their 100 senators, decided in 1987
and 1988 that they did not want a restraint-driven justice. And perhaps
that view was wise if we think of the US Supreme Court as a Court of
Outcomes. Think of some concrete 5–4 cases over that thirty-year period. We know where Justice Kennedy stood. During his tenure, he was
the key vote in decisions protecting abortion rights (*Casey*), establishing
same-sex marriage (*Obergefell*), protecting free speech in political
campaigns (*Citizens United*), and recognizing an individual right to
bear arms (*Heller*). Would a Justice Bork have recognized each of these
rights? His written record, decrying substantive due process, makes it
unlikely he would have supported *Casey* or *Obergefell*.[14] He also wrote
that the Second Amendment protected only a collective right in light
of the Court's *Miller* decision.[15]

But a Justice Bork probably would have agreed with Justice Kennedy
on the outcome in *Citizens United*, though perhaps not all of its reasoning. Before becoming a judge, Judge Bork believed "constitutional protection should be accorded only to speech that is explicitly

political."[16] One data point suggests he would have thought the First Amendment protected money expressly used for political speech. As solicitor general, he authorized, extraordinarily, three different briefs on behalf of the federal government in *Buckley v. Valeo*, a case involving a First Amendment challenge to the Federal Election Campaign Act or FECA, in which Congress placed limits on campaign contributions and expenditures. Years later, Judge Frank Easterbrook described the situation. The opponents of the law had little "difficulty persuading Solicitor General Bork" that the law "was unconstitutional root and branch."[17] Bork, Easterbrook says, "kept referring to the issue involved in this case, the constitutionality of the FECA, as the 'fecal matter.' He was not in favor of this statute. Defenders insisted that the law represented a 'narrow' regulation of politics. And his reaction was, 'Yeah, it has been narrowed right to the core of the First Amendment.' What to do? Well, in the end he authorized the filing of three briefs; he came to the bold conclusion to do everything."[18] While it's an open question whether a Justice Bork would have joined in all of the reasoning of *Citizens United*, it's fair to think he would have voted the same way as Justice Kennedy did in the case and would have agreed that the regulation of a film criticizing a presidential candidate violated the First Amendment.

All of this suggests that three (though probably not four) of these 5–4 rulings would have come out differently if we substitute the most libertarian justice for the least. It's possible all four would have been written differently. And it's likely that this substitution would have altered the outcome of many other constitutional debates. That's highly consequential from the perspective of the Court's footprint on American government. For individuals who care deeply about any of these rights, it's an easy call which justice they would support. So also for the interest groups who support the individuals who care about those rights. But for the political parties, it's well to ask, who won? Which political party won over the next thirty years by having the Court, rather than traditional democratic processes, resolve so many significant issues in American government? The Democratic Party was the key critic of Judge Bork, and the Republican Party was his key supporter. Ask yourself which political party benefited the most by having these issues resolved by the Court as opposed to the political process. It's easy to wonder if the Democratic Party lost some political benefits they might have gained from airing these disputes in the state legislatures and state courts and in some instances in Congress—and the Republican Party won some benefits by being able to protest the Court's decision to take these issues away from the voters while freeing themselves from having to take a political stand on some of them.

Wrong or right about that guess, resolution of many of the key issues of the day by the US Supreme Court is not consequence free. It sometimes prompts backlash in presidential elections. It sometimes short-circuits the possibility of developing a deeper consensus over an issue. It always removes the stabilizing force of political compromise.

Comparing Justice Kennedy and Judge Bork and this one seat on the US Supreme Court that the political parties fought so intensely over filling—echoed later with the fight over filling Justice Scalia's seat in the presidential election year of 2016, to say nothing of comparable fights over Justice Kennedy's and Justice Ginsburg's replacements—highlights the impact of different approaches to judicial review. Justice Kennedy favored a more engaged use of it, and Judge Bork favored a more re-strained view of it. The two options mark a lasting difference in how we come to grips with shifting norms, new technologies, and other changes that potentially intersect with constitutional rights.

Try this experiment to add perspective on the issue. If you lean to-ward liberal outcomes on constitutional rulings, find a friend who is conservative. If you lean toward conservative outcomes on constitu-tional rulings, do the same in the other direction. Let each person iden-tify the five federal rulings that they would most like to see overturned. To simplify things, stick with decisions over the last seventy-five years that invalidate state or federal laws on federal constitutional grounds. Now ask: Would you take the trade? Would you eliminate the five worst federal constitutional rulings over the last seventy-five years in return for giving someone with a different worldview the chance to do the same? In practical terms, this would mean taking ten of the most controversial issues constitutionalized by the US Supreme Court and returning them to the democratic process, whether at the state level or the federal level, or returning them to the state courts. In one sense, it's a rational trade. It's fair. Each person gets five things they like in return for five they don't. It's not permanent. Each side gets second and third chances to vindicate its perspective on the issue. Having removed the federal constitution from the equation, the individual or group can vindicate itself through the democratic process or seek relief from a state court under its state constitution. One might think people would have the courage of their convictions on all ten issues—that they would see themselves as in the right about all of them and would be able to convince neighbors, fellow citizens, state legislatures, and, if need be, state courts to see it that way. When I propose the test to law school students or bar groups, however, most people tend not to take the trade. There are two exceptions. Some will take the trade if there is one constitutional ruling that dominates their perspective. They would get rid of that decision in return for losing nine others, maybe even more. Some judges see the benefit of the trade, perhaps because they see the risks of using the federal judiciary to resolve so many of our most intense public-policy disputes.

This thought experiment suggests two possibilities. One is distinctly American. People won't take the trade because they think they will ultimately win—full control of the US Supreme Court, that is—and will be able to win all ten issues there. Over time, they will convince the Court to overrule the decisions they don't like and preserve the ones they do. Perhaps it is this kind of spirit that makes America distinct, that helps it persist in ways that have helped us win so many wars, defeat pandemics, and overcome other challenges. But it's well to remember who your opponents are: other Americans. They are not going away. Sticking to the calf's path in our evenly divided political culture most likely preserves a world in which half the time the Court rules your way and half the time it doesn't. Do the people want that with respect to the ten most significant constitutional issues of the *future*, having no say over how they get resolved and having to follow the rule of five justices on the Court in all of them? That seems less likely. Still less likely is the possibility that the people want the Court to use substantive due process—the authority to innovate individual rights unmentioned in the US Constitution—to handle future contests over the most controversial policy matters of the era. Least likely of all is the idea that the federal founders would have wanted us to resolve many of our most significant political debates through the federal courts.

The other possibility is that we don't take the trade because the Court victories we would give up are ones we never thought we deserved in the first place. The anxiety is that they were gerrymandered victories from the start. And what one does not deserve one is not likely to get at the ballot box or in enough state courts to matter.

Now let me be solipsistic, not for the first time, and mention my shifting thoughts on judicial review since becoming a lawyer. If, in Emerson's words "there is properly no history[,] only biography,"[19] lots of biography is assuredly autobiography. Charting my own evolving views of judicial review highlights some of the difficulties of identifying a best theory of judicial review. In contrast to Justice Kennedy and Judge Bork who consistently applied their theories of judicial review, I have not been of one mind.

I started out favoring judicial restraint. That had something to do with my first key job, as the solicitor general of Ohio. Where you stand on issues, they say, often turns on where you sit. In my capacity as a state lawyer, I had the duty of defending the constitutionality of many state laws and state criminal prosecutions from attack under the Ohio and United States Constitutions. At that point, I took the view as a lawyer, and I came to think as a citizen, that the state and federal courts should hesitate to enter the fray and should err on the side of leaving unclear or difficult constitutional questions to the political process and to the elected branches that usually control it. That's the Judge Bork view.

But I saw the matter differently when I represented states in another type of litigation—challenging federal laws that trespassed on state authority under the US Constitution. My first encounter in that area came in *City of Boerne v. Flores*, in which I argued that Congress could not apply the Religious Freedom Restoration Act to the states. In an opinion by Justice Kennedy, the Court invalidated the act as applied to the states. That decision led to other like-framed challenges to limits on federal power on behalf of my clients.[20] At that point, no doubt influenced by the parties I represented and the claims we pursued, I had a different insight about judicial review. How, I came to wonder, could there be a presumption against invalidating state and federal laws under the US Constitution? Every case presented a zero-sum problem. Think about a fight between Congress and the president over the lines of power between them under Articles I and II of the US Constitution. How could the Court presume that the Constitution preferred one side to the other in that debate? The same was true about fights between the national government and the states over the constitutional lines between federal and state power. And the same, it seemed to me, must be true about contests between an individual and a state over the meaning of the Fourteenth Amendment and other federal individual rights. One way or another, the Court had to interpret, sometimes even articulate, the Constitution's lines of power, leaving no room for presumptions in favor of the individual or the state, one government or another. Someone had to determine where power began and where power ended for each government. Who better to do it than the courts? That left no room for presumptions either way, whether in favor of invoking the Constitution to curb a government's action or not. All that mattered was that lines needed to be drawn and preserved, just the sort of things the courts had long done. That's the Justice Kennedy view.

Then my views shifted again, perhaps because where I sat changed again. As a federal judge for nearly twenty years, I've had to do what I say. That means seeing firsthand the implementation of prior decisions I wrote, seeing colleagues of different perspectives work with the same issues, seeing the US Supreme Court handle the issues, and seeing how difficult it can be for anyone to apply constitutional innovations about structure or rights in a fair and even-handed way.

Before any of that, the confirmation process created a jolt. It's said that receiving the president's nomination for a federal judgeship is like being struck by lightning. That seems about right, particularly if you add that the Senate confirmation process requires the nominee to survive the lightning strike. Throughout a two-year confirmation odyssey, I felt like a bill going through Congress. In one way or another, most federal judges, especially appellate judges, have had similar experiences over the last twenty years, whether Republican or Democratic presidents nominated them. In that time, it's hard to deny a pattern, a growing politicization of the selection and confirmation process for federal judges.

The most depressing part of the modern confirmation process is that it's rational. Federal judges are exercising considerable power, which explains why the people want a say in who they are. It's hard to deny the premise, and it takes a good advocate, it seems to me, to avoid the conclusion. We federal judges can't have it both ways. We can't make so many critical decisions about American policy yet expect the American people to look the other way when the selection process calls our name.

Understandable though the political intensity of the selection process may be, this pattern creates a problem. We have reached a point in which US senators vote almost 100% along partisan lines for virtually all judicial nominees, especially US Supreme Court nominees. In the face of those votes by US senators, how can the people they represent not see judges and justices in political terms? We judges can say and do all kinds of things to head off this reaction. At the courts of appeals across the country, for example, we have unanimity in roughly 90% of our cases, no matter which presidents nominated the three judges on each panel.[21] The US Supreme Court has unanimity in 30% to 40% of its cases—and the most difficult cases at that, as they review only cases in which the courts of appeals themselves disagree.[22] Forced to choose between believing what the judges say and what their elected politicians say, however, the American people inevitably will come to side with their political representatives. We judges are outmatched in political debates and always will be. Once the American people perceive the federal judiciary as another political branch of government, the time of reckoning has arrived. They will wonder why one political branch (the judiciary) is permitted to check other political branches (the president, Congress, state governments). That undermines confidence in judicial review and dims the luster on one of the crown jewels of American government.

If the confirmation process affected my views about judicial review, the experience of judging changed them, too. It's not an easy job. The constitutional provisions that lead to many of our hardest cases are written in the most general terms and thus prompt tar-covered questions. What process is "due"? What searches are "unreasonable"? What punishment is "cruel and unusual"? When is speech not "free"? When is the exercise of faith not "free"? Where are the rarely specified lines of horizontal and vertical separation between the different branches of government? Each time we federal judges add a protection to a general guarantee, moreover, we create the possibility of still more debates about still more lines to draw. The more judges do, the easier it is to ask them to do still more. As someone who prefers to think that judges are more like referees than players, I find myself more and more inclined to the view that the US Constitution does not answer every question—or at least does not answer it in a way that federal judges deserve the final say. Some disputes about the meaning of the US Constitution, I have come to appreciate, aren't for judges to resolve. They either are political disputes solely for the elected branches to sort out or are constitutional disputes that lack articulable guidelines for judges to identify and fairly enforce. Otherwise, as modern American politics has come to reveal, judges increasingly become conspicuous players in the game, too often the most conspicuous players in the game. That has me somewhere between Justice Kennedy and Judge Bork—and wondering about something else.

Maybe there's nothing wrong with having slightly different views of judicial review at different times—slightly erring in one direction or another across eras though not within them. In thinking about the right theory of judicial review, maybe there's no need to decide whether every Warren Court decision was right. Past isn't always precedent. What we really need is an acceptable theory for our time, one that appreciates the lessons of the past and one that accounts for the growing balance-of-power risks to the federal judiciary of delegating too much responsibility to it to identify new constitutional rights. In this respect, I am reminded of the charitable and sage advice that Justice Thurgood Marshall gave Justice Clarence Thomas. Justice Marshall had the kind of career that could generate a lot of wisdom. He was the first African American solicitor general of the United States, and he became the first African American to sit on the US Supreme Court when President Lyndon Johnson nominated him in 1967. After his retirement, he met his replacement, Justice Thomas. During the meeting, he said: "I did in my time what I had to do. You have to do in your time what you have to do."[23]

Perhaps that's not a bad way to think about it. In our time, is it possible that, if our legal system paid more attention to our state courts and gave them more opportunities to lead when it comes to the development of individual and structural constitutional guarantees, the country would reap the benefits of judicial review and curb some of its risks? I will return to the right theory of judicial review for our time, and a way to balance state and federal court involvement, after looking at how we got here.

2

Judicial Review

Democracy and Duty

The conventional account of judicial review starts with a US Supreme Court case, *Marbury v. Madison*, and Chief Justice Marshall's memorable line that "it is emphatically the province and duty of the judiciary to say what the law is."[1] A division-of-powers, a checks-and-balances, idea emerges before long in traditional explanations of why we have judicial review—that the US Supreme Court performs a counter-majoritarian role when it enforces the individual-rights and structural guarantees of the US Constitution against the elected branches of the state and federal governments.

This account confirms the peril of reducing American constitutional law to a single story.[2] Judicial review in truth starts with the state courts and the state constitutions, not the US Supreme Court and the US Constitution. Before the US Constitution existed, the state courts established American judicial review and were the first courts to wrestle with the ineffable complexities of exercising it.[3] Judicial review also is foremost a structural story, not an individual-rights story. The delegation of power to the judiciary to decide the meaning of our constitutions laid the groundwork for the growth in power of American courts—especially the federal courts, which have become the go-to answer for so many who-decides questions in American government over the last seventy-five years.

Our single account of judicial review often neglects to deal with the possibility that, without a sound theory for deciding when to check the other branches of government, judicial review runs the risk of aggregating power in the judicial branch, not preserving a balance of power among the branches of government. The standard account frequently leaps over the question of when and how courts may second-guess the actions of the political branches of government—and above all how much deference, if any deference, they should give to other branches when they interpret constitutional provisions. It's a tricky business to aspire "to the end" of being "a government of laws and not of men," in the words of the 1780 Massachusetts Constitution,[4] and yet place final interpretive authority of our constitutions in the hands of small groups of men and women. The early history confirms the point many times over. Separation-of-powers considerations gave birth to judicial review, and separation-of-powers considerations may pave the way for judicial review to emerge intact from its mid-life crisis.

The point of this chapter is to look at the origins of judicial review and to consider how the first courts to use it, the state courts, practiced it at the outset. The harder a problem, the more useful it can be to scavenge the past for insights. What's complicated today was complicated then.

Initial State Choices About the Judicial Branch

When the American colonies split from England in 1776 to become self-governing states, they had to decide what these new governments would look like. A system of three branches of power was not as inevitable as it now seems. Our conventional account of judicial review, in Jack Rakove's words, "makes it easier to exploit, for introductory pedagogical purposes," the idea of a "classic Montesquieuian framework of three kinds of power" and to make students think it was all pre-arranged.[5] But there was little destiny about how to divide power at the founding.[6] Much of it was improvisation, on-the-spot innovation to account for the political realities the state and federal founders faced, most especially the paradox of trying to create several sovereign states within a single sovereign nation. Among many choices, the judicial function might have stayed in the executive branch, as it did in some states for a time, or it might have resided in the legislative branch, as it did in the House of Lords in Parliament.

One explanation for a separate judicial branch that could interpret constitutions was the choice to commit them to writing. "The written constitutions of 1776 and 1777," Gordon Wood notes, "gave revolutionary Americans a handle with which to grasp this otherwise insubstantial fundamental law. Suddenly the fundamental law and the first principles that Englishmen had referred to for generations had a degree of explicitness and reality that they never before quite had."[7] A related explanation, offers Philip Hamburger, arises from an established judicial duty, long existing in the colonial courts and English legal system, to apply the correct law to the case at hand.[8] Still another influence on the road to constitutional review, says Mary Sarah Bilder, was the English practice of limiting corporate ordinances, including the royal charters for each colony, from violating the laws of the nation.[9] No matter the precise combination of explanations for a separate court system, the early state charters generated trial-and-error judicial experiments with ideas that have become constitutional mainstays today: separation of powers and an independent judiciary. These innovations, eventually placing judges on somewhat equal footing with legislators and executive officials, created the conditions that made it possible for judicial review to emerge as an accepted feature of our constitutional system. Gordon Wood again: "Redefining judges as agents of the sovereign people somehow equal in authority with the legislators and executives fundamentally altered the character of the judiciary in America and deeply affected its role in interpreting the law."[10]

Debates about how a government of separated powers works present elemental questions: Who resolves which policy questions? How and on what grounds? Which branch, if any branch, has the final say over what each constitution means? How do we ensure that the interpreters of constitutions do not transform us into a government of men and women rather than a government of laws? At the founding, several choices about how to allocate power to decide constitutional questions shaped the development of judicial review in the states and the nation. But one thing "everyone knew" for sure: "setting aside legislative acts could be no ordinary matter."[11]

Juries or Judges?

We don't think of using juries to resolve constitutional questions or any legal questions for that matter. But that's not as unusual as it sounds, at least for the founding generation. It was the people who ratified the state constitutions and eventually the US Constitution. And the people not only distrusted the Crown and Parliament, but they also distrusted government in general. The closest proxy for the people in American government is not the legislature, a governor, or a court. It's the jury. If the people ratified the relevant constitutional provisions, why not let juries interpret them in individual cases?

Supporting this intuition was skepticism of judges. Early Americans did not trust judges and preferred that their liberty and other rights rest in the hands of their peers or what was then perceived as the next-best option: legislatures.[12] During the colonial era, most Americans saw judges as beholden to the royal governors.[13] They feared that judges would look after the interests of the Crown, not their interests, and they had reasons for thinking that way. In most of the colonies, British officials had the final say over the selection and removal of colonial jurists.[14] When the American Revolution forced these judges to pick sides, most of them "sided with their king."[15] "In ten of the thirteen colonies, the sitting chief justice or his equivalent chose George III over George Washington."[16] Juries, on the other hand, represented a cross-section of the community, a group of fellow Americans with an interest in preserving the rights and the liberties they shared. "The people themselves," emphasizes Akhil Amar, "had a right to serve on the jury—to govern through the jury."[17]

Little surprise, the early state constitutions enshrined the right to trial by jury. The right appeared not only in the section that secured individual rights (usually Article I) but also in the sections that set forth structure.[18] Even in the states that did not initially adopt new written constitutions, Connecticut and Rhode Island, the right to trial by jury was elemental and eventually judicially enforceable.[19]

The preference for juries extended beyond the right to a jury trial. Americans entered 1776 with a legal system in which "juries rather than judges spoke the last word on law enforcement" in many instances.[20] Save in equity cases, which the colonists distrusted anyway, "judges could not enter a judgment or impose a penalty without a jury verdict."[21] Juries often heard arguments from counsel about the law as well as the facts, and sometimes they had the final say on both.[22] Even after the early state constitutions vested the appointment of judges in officials elected by the people, many states did not permit judges to overrule juries.[23]

Massachusetts

Anyone doubting the power of juries in early America should take stock of how Massachusetts by one measure became the first state in the country to outlaw slavery. An African American woman, Mum Bett (later named Elizabeth Freeman), and an African American man, Quock Walker, spurred the development, and in each case juries and the state's constitution played lead roles.

Mum Bett was born into slavery and became the property of Colonel John Ashley. After hearing revolutionary pleas that "all men are born free and equal, and have certain natural, essential, and unalienable rights," she argued she should be free, too.[24] In 1781, her attorneys argued to the Berkshire County Court of Common Pleas that Bett was not John Ashley's property and should be freed. The jury of "Jonathan Holcomb Foreman & His Fellows" agreed in two ways.[25] It ruled that Bett is "not and [was] not at the time of the purchase of the original Writ the legal Negro Servant[] of him the said John Ashley during life."[26] And it ruled that Ashley had to pay thirty shillings in damages and the cost of the suit.[27] Ashley initially appealed. But he assented to the ruling soon after another jury ruled the same way, this time in disputes arising from Quock Walker's efforts to obtain freedom.[28]

Walker's case became several cases. Walker had escaped from enslavement only to be tracked down and brought back to his master, Nathaniel Jennison, and beaten by him.[29] Several lawsuits ensued. Walker filed a claim for assault and battery against Jennison. Jennison sued another family for inducing Walker's escape. And the state brought criminal charges against Jennison.[30] All three cases ended up with judgments in Walker's favor and recognized, at least implicitly, his freedom.[31] The arguments for Walker included references to the Massachusetts Constitution, natural law, and the Bible.[32] The clearest indication of Walker's freedom under the Massachusetts Constitution came in the 1783 jury verdict against Jennison in his criminal indictment: *Commonwealth v. Jennison*.[33] Before the state's highest court, the Supreme Judicial Court of Massachusetts,[34] Jennison argued that Walker was merely a runaway slave, giving Jennison the right to capture and reprimand him as a fugitive from justice. But one of the jury instructions given by Chief Justice Cushing noted that slavery was repugnant to the Massachusetts Constitution of 1780.[35] On these arguments and with these instructions, the jury chose to convict and fine Jennison.

The jury verdict does not deserve all of the credit for the ruling. The jury charge of Chief Justice William Cushing, one of several charges given by the different appellate judges to the jury, is given acclaim for interpreting the Massachusetts Constitution and instructing the jury that "*all men are born free and equal*; and that *every subject is entitled to liberty*."[36] In context, the charge looks more like informed dicta than judicial review. This was just one judge's interpretation of the law on a panel of five.[37] But the jury retained the final decision over whether slavery could exist under the Massachusetts Constitution.[38] And Massachusetts juries historically exercised a highly discretionary decision-making role.[39] "While the judges interpreted the constitution and explained its relation to the cases at bar, Massachusetts veniremen had in the past and would again ignore the wishes of the bench in interpreting and applying the law."[40] The jury, a group of white male landowners, thus remained capable of acquitting Jennison and of treating slavery as legal. But that did not happen.

Although jury verdicts like these did not naturally lend themselves to precedential declarations of the meaning of constitutions, their significance extended beyond the fate of the individuals involved. In one case, the slave owner had to pay damages to Bett. In the other, the slave owner was criminally convicted. Ask yourself how many slaveholders in the Bay State felt comfortable keeping slaves after that. That explains why many credit these decisions with effectively ending slavery in Massachusetts.[41] Some historians minimize the impact of these decisions, noting that slavery technically remained legal in Massachusetts for several years.[42] But the acclaim of the decisions at a minimum spurred changing public perceptions of slavery[43] and left slaveholders like Colonel John Ashley with an unmistakable message: Purported authority to own another human being was no longer a reliable defense in Massachusetts courts.[44]

Georgia

The Georgia Constitution of 1777 shows how far a state could go in delegating authority to juries. The charter made juries finders of law and fact, prohibited directed verdicts by judges, allowed judges to give only advisory opinions (at the request and for the benefit of the jury), and devised an appeals procedure that empaneled a second appellate jury. Amendments to the state constitution in the late 1700s and early 1800s brought it closer to today's constitutional mainstream,[45] but the state did not have a supreme court, in the sense we use the term today, to hear appeals until the 1840s.[46]

The 1777 constitution created a "supreme court," composed of different judges for nearly every case, to hear all lawsuits except admiralty cases and small claims.[47] This supreme court, in fact these supreme courts, "consist[ed] of the chief-justice, and three or more of the justices residing in the county" where the case originated.[48] The state thus had only one statewide judicial officer who rode circuit to attend court in all of the state's counties.[49] The other judges and the jurors came from the local community.

Instead of appellate courts, the constitution provided litigants disappointed by a jury verdict with the right to "demand a new trial by a special jury."[50] The special jury consisted of twelve jurors drawn randomly "out of a box provided for that purpose" from a pool of eighteen—six selected by the appellant, six by the appellee, six chosen from the general jury pool.[51] Ordinary and special juries were "sworn to bring in a verdict according to law, and the opinion they entertain of the evidence; provided [that] it be not repugnant to . . . this constitution."[52] Special jurors also had to swear that their verdict would not be "repugnant to justice, equity, [or] conscience."[53] The idea of jury review of legislation was widely discussed and accepted at the founding,[54] even though it was considered a "supplement" to judicial review, not a "substitute" for it.[55] With its constitutional provisions preventing judges from acting on their own or overruling juries, Georgia delegated considerable power to juries, perhaps more than any other state, as confirmed by the reality that the state placed the power of jury review in its constitution.

How foreign this sounds to modern ears. Whether one considers Massachusetts or Georgia or the other early states, it's strange to conceive of lay citizens on juries as having *any* role to play in deciding the meaning of laws, especially the paramount laws in our state and federal constitutions. But perhaps the idea should not be foreign, particularly when it comes to the definition of unenumerated rights in our state and federal constitutions. As to those rights, particularly when we think of identifying values in an unwritten constitution, as renowned scholars already claim judges do,[56] it's not fanciful to think of the people, as constituted in juries, as no less equipped than judges to identify them. Nor is there any reason to think that the people, through their participation as jurors, will necessarily do a bad job in protecting rights. How informative that the first decisions to make slave owners outlaws in this country emerged from a panel of fellow citizens, not a panel of judges.

Juries also responded to a problem inherent in constitutions. It's fine to create superior laws. But it doesn't fix anything if the interpreters of them are no more trustworthy than the authors of the underlying laws. If "a power above law" is perilous and if constitutions operate "to deny a power above law to any part" of the policymaking branches "of government," as Philip Hamburger writes,[57] juries were an understandable first place to look in deciding what constitutions mean. Juries were not a feared part of government. They were the very people these parts of government were meant to represent, freeing the law (and constitution) to report to them, not to report to someone over them.

The modern growth of the initiative process in the states may reflect a return to this instinct. More and more states, more and more citizens, have come to rely on these statewide votes of the people as a way to identify new constitutional rights or second-guess ones identified by their courts. The initiative also solves the problem that juries could resolve constitutional questions only in the context of one criminal or civil case at a time, with a new jury empaneled for the next case. Having started with an assessment of constitutional decision making through the people, the book ends with a return to this topic in Chapter 10, the last substantive chapter.

Judges or the Other Branches of State Government?

The decades after 1776 were not friendly to this experiment of allowing the people, through independent and separate juries, to decide the meaning of the rights in their state and federal constitutions. But the experiment facilitated the development of another third-branch option already in play: judges. "Judicial review," Jack Rakove explains, "could only become possible after influential segments of the American political community moved away from the belief that juries were competent triers of law and fact alike."[58] The country became increasingly comfortable with empowering judges to resolve constitutional cases and with perceiving them as trustworthy agents of the people.

Even by 1776, American judges had the legal tools they needed to interpret constitutional texts as law that governs the other branches of government. American lawyers, trained in English common law, understood the difference between superior and subordinate sources of law. The colonial laws were themselves policed by colonial courts, the Privy Council, which heard judicial appeals from the colonies, and by Parliament itself for conformity with applicable English law, including the colonial charters. Whether a law was "repugnant" to a superior source of authority had meaning to colonial lawyers and judges, just as it did to their English counterparts.[59]

With state charters reduced to writing, the question was whether the common techniques for interpreting statutes[60] could be extended to constitutions. That took more of a leap than it might seem. The English constitution's unwritten customary character and Parliament's status as a legislative court precluded ordinary courts of law from reviewing acts of Parliament in those terms.[61] When Parliament passed legislation in the English system, it "in effect declared that the constitution permitted such an act."[62] That was harder to do with the *written* state charters. Explaining why judges should decide what's constitutional became a task for the early state courts. Courts were aware that legislators could just as easily read the new constitutions and decide for themselves whether a bill under consideration complied with the constitution, and decline to enact those that did not. The judicial branch's approach to defending constitutional review thus called as much for mutual respect and conflict avoidance as it did for assertions of power by a distinct arm of government. Judges in the early Republic had to combine the commonplace (reading fundamental law like ordinary law) with the unusual (establishing a hierarchy between constitutions and laws) to make judicial review work.

But this task generated another question. Do judges or elected officials decide what the constitution requires in uncertain cases? The early state court judges were all appointed by governors or legislatures.[63] None was elected.[64] The risk of unelected judges seizing power over questions best left to legislatures existed at the outset. Whether a decision should rest with the branches closest and most directly accountable to the people or whether it should be more removed from the political processes puzzled lawyers then no less than today. Some states eventually hedged their bets by electing their judiciaries, a partial solution that generated challenges of its own. But in the early years of the Republic, before the advent and growth of judicial elections, judges had to establish their legitimacy and explain why they, not elected legislators or elected governors, had the final say over the constitutionality of laws sought to be enforced in the cases that came before them.

None of the early state constitutions—before Kentucky in 1792—explicitly authorizes judicial review by making laws contrary to the constitution void.[65] But some of them, by expressly dividing and limiting each department of government, seem to imply it—at least at a first glance. The 1780 Massachusetts Constitution offers a good example. Authored by John Adams, it prohibits the legislature and executive from "exercis[ing] . . . judicial powers."[66] That seems easy enough. Only the judiciary decides what the constitution means because only the judiciary may exercise judicial power in the cases that come before it. But then one has to account for two other realities. The same provision says that "the judicial [branch] shall never exercise the legislative and executive powers,"[67] suggesting that judicial review is legitimate only if it respects the prerogatives of the other branches, a grueling task in cases about generally worded guarantees.[68] In addition, some of the history behind these provisions suggests they were mainly designed to separate personnel, not powers—to prevent "dual officeholding" in the form of a judge, say, serving at the same time in the legislature.[69] Not so easy anymore.

Virginia

In 1782, Virginia's highest court helped to launch judicial review in this country. In the *Case of the Prisoners*, John Caton, James Lamb, and Joshua Hopkins faced execution for treason during the Revolutionary War. The Virginia Constitution of 1776 vested the governor with the pardon power but separately allowed the legislature to transfer that power to the House of Delegates, Virginia's lower house.[70] A complication arose when the legislature enacted the Treason Act, which said that treason pardons needed to receive the assent of both houses. Noting that a resolution pardoning them had passed the House, the prisoners insisted they should be spared because the Treason Act, requiring the Senate's assent, violated the state's constitution.[71]

The participants appreciated this early test of judicial power.[72] A who's who of founding-era luminaries, the lawyers and judges in the case were worthy of the occasion, and the occasion may even have helped to make them. On the Commonwealth's side was Edmund Randolph, Virginia's attorney general, who would become a delegate to the Philadelphia Convention, where he introduced the Virginia Plan that formed the basis for deliberations, a signatory of the resulting US Constitution, and the attorney general and secretary of state of the country he helped to create. On the prisoners' side as a friend of the court, known as an *amicus curiae* to lawyers, was St. George Tucker, who later sat on the Virginia Supreme Court of Appeals, edited the American edition of Blackstone's *Commentaries*, and became a prominent legal scholar. George Wythe, one of the judges, was the first Virginian to sign the Declaration of Independence. Sometimes called America's first law professor, he earned the title given his roster of students: Thomas Jefferson, John Marshall, Henry Clay, and Tucker.[73]

Randolph conceded the principle of judicial review in his arguments to the Virginia Supreme Court of Appeals, now called the Virginia Supreme Court. He acknowledged that the court had authority to declare the law unconstitutional under Virginia's constitution, and he did so even while representing the state.[74] But he sidestepped the conclusion that might follow from that confession, insisting that conflicts between statutes and the state constitution ought to be avoided and that, if the constitution's "spirit opposes the exclusion of the Senate, its words [suggesting the opposite] must be free from ambiguity . . . or cannot have the supremacy."[75]

On the other side of the case, Tucker argued that it is "uncontrovertible" that "the power properly belonging to the Judiciary Department[] is[] to explain the Laws of the Land as they apply to particular cases."[76] That made judicial review consistent with a tripartite separation of powers and the judicial oath, and it implicated a distinctly legal function, deciding cases according to legal rules.[77] Tucker made a concession against interest as well. He admitted that he had to show that the constitutional provision and statute clearly conflicted. It is "the touchstone" of judicial review, he acknowledged, that, "if any Act . . . shall be found absolutely and *irreconcilably* contradictory to the Constitution, it cannot admit of Doubt that such act is absolutely null and void."[78]

The prisoners lost the case. The formal practice of publishing opinions did not exist at the time, leaving murky the reasoning of the judges and requiring the use of several sources. According to Chancellor Edmund Pendleton's notes, two judges ruled for the prisoners and six against. Their reasons varied. George Wythe endorsed the power of judicial review but upheld the statute anyway. Peter Lyons declared himself against judicial review. And Pendleton struck a middle ground by adopting Randolph's saving construction of the law. James Mercer would have held the Treason Act unconstitutional.[79]

Pendleton's opinion reflects caution about invalidating democratically enacted laws along with an insistence that he will do what judicial duty commands, capturing the competing attitudes of the times.

> But how far this Court in which it has been properly said the Judiciary Powers of the State are concentrated, can go in declaring an Act of the Legislature void, because it is repugnant to the Constitution, without exercising the Power of Legislation, from which they are restrained by the same Constitution[] is a deep, important, and, I will add, an awful question; from which, however, I will not shrink, if ever it shall become my duty to decide it: at present I am happy in having no occasion to make the decision.[80]

While George Wythe also ruled against the prisoners, he embraced constitutional review as part of the judicial office, which he saw as deciding all questions submitted to the court "to the best of [his] skill and judgment."[81] Wythe also thought judges had a special responsibility to clarify the lines of authority between different branches:

> It is equally m[y duty] to protect the one branch of the legislature, and, consequently, the whole community, against the usurpations of the other: and, whenever the proper occasion occurs, I shall feel the duty; and, fearlessly, perform it. . . . Nay more, if the whole legislature, . . . should attempt to overleap the bounds, prescribed to them by the people, I, in administering the public justice of the country, will meet the united powers, at my seat in this tribunal; and, pointing to the constitution, will say, to them, here is the limit of your authority; and, hither, shall you go, but no further.[82]

How did the prisoners lose? The constitutional guarantee goes one way and the statute seems to go another. The shared assumption that the prisoners had to show a blatant conflict between the two had something to do with it. Wythe and Pendleton apparently took the view that the Virginia Constitution established the House of Delegates' consent as a necessary but not always sufficient condition for legislative pardons, leaving authority to add a requirement of Senate approval.[83] Randolph acknowledged in a letter to Madison that his position "would appear unintelligible" to anyone "but lawyers."[84] Wythe added that the House of Delegates alone could pardon impeachments that it prosecuted, but the legislative pardon power required approval by both houses for all other pardons.[85]

One last thing. The prisoners lost the skirmish but won the war, at least if they had a taste for war. The Senate pardoned them later that year on the condition that they leave Virginia or join the revolutionary army for the remainder of the war.[86]

In 1793, more than a decade after the Virginia Supreme Court of Appeals decided the *Case of the Prisoners*, the Virginia General Court, the Commonwealth's highest common-law court, heard *Kamper v. Hawkins*.[87] The seriatim opinions in the case show judges growing comfortable with enforcing the constitutional guarantees, even while emphasizing different themes in doing so. The case involved a matter of concern to Virginia's judges. The legislature gave equity jurisdiction, previously reserved to the Chancery Court, to lower district courts, where judges did not have to be appointed in the same way or have the same removal protections.

The Virginia General Court held the arrangement unconstitutional, with all five judges deciding the case on constitutional grounds. Judge Roane made two essential points: American legislatures are not sovereign but subordinate to the people; and where legislation affects the judicial branch, the judges should "distrust their own judgment if the matter is doubtful, or in other words require clear evidence before they decide in cases where interest may possibly warp the judgment."[88] Passages of Judge Roane's opinion reverberate in Chief Justice Marshall's opinion in *Marbury* ten years later.[89] That Judge Roane, described as "Marshall's greatest judicial antagonist,"[90] saw judicial review as Marshall saw it suggests that support for judicial review spanned the Federalist-Republican divide that polarized American politics at the turn into the nineteenth century.

Judge Tucker began by noting that the Virginia Constitution, unlike ordinary legislation, "derived its existence" from "a power which can supersede all law . . . namely, the *people*, in their *sovereign, unlimited,* and *unlimitable* authority and capacity."[91] It was thus "the first law of the land," binding on all branches of government, including the judiciary.[92] Tucker explained that judges could "resort to" the law of the constitution whenever "it becomes necessary to expound *what the law is.*"[93] "This exposition," he continued, "is the duty and office of the judiciary to make. . . . [H]ow can any just exposition be made, *if that which is the supreme law of the land be withheld from their view?*"[94] "The *judiciary* are *bound* to take notice of the constitution, *as the first law of the land,*" and anything "contradictory thereto" is "*not* the law of the land."[95] That did not make the judiciary supreme over the legislature; it simply required each branch to perform its function within the constitutional limits set by the people.

In addition to requiring a clear conflict between the statute and constitution,[96] Judge John Tyler invoked his duty of independent judgment:

> To conclude, I do declare that I will not hold an office, which I believe to be unconstitutional; that I will not be made a fit agent, to

assist the legislature in a violation of this sacred letter; that I form this opinion from the conviction I feel that I am free to think, speak, and act, as other men do upon so great a question; that as I never did sacrifice my own opinions for the sake of popularity in the various departments I have had the honour to fill, however desirable popular favour may be, when obtained upon honorable principles.[97]

Judge Nelson shared the view of his colleagues that "an act contrary to the Constitution . . . is *no* law" and that judging the constitutionality of legislative acts implicates the judicial task of deciding "whether an act of the legislature *be in force* or *not in force,* or in other words, whether it be a *law* or *not.*"[98] In a conflict between the constitution and a statute, he explained, "the prior *fundamental law*" prevents the later statute from "*coming into existence* as *a law.*"[99]

Judge Henry echoed Judge Roane's observation that, unlike British Parliament, the state legislature is neither sovereign nor "*omnipotent,*" that it is bound by limits on its power and by "certain and permanent" procedural limitations from which it is not free to depart.[100] But he ultimately rested his decision on a narrower ground. Because the constitution gave the legislature the power to choose judges and did not prohibit it from appointing the same man to two judicial offices, he reasoned, one part of the law was not clearly unconstitutional. Even so, he added, another part of the law could not stand because it gave district judges the chancery court's powers without following "the [manner of] appointment and commission prescribed by the constitution" for those judges.[101]

Kamper may be the most illuminating case from the era. The five opinions emphasize slightly different themes, some focused on structure, some focused on text, all requiring a clear conflict, and all confirming the novelty of the task. As Judge Roane aptly foreshadows, courts sometimes have to be careful about developing a stake in the allocation of power at hand—the legislature's regulation of the courts in that instance, the legislature's regulation of other matters, including judicially identified rights, in later instances.

North Carolina

Bayard v. Singleton, a 1787 decision of the North Carolina Supreme Court,[102] also accepts the legitimacy of judicial review and uses it to invalidate a state law. During the Revolution, North Carolina confiscated the land of British loyalists who refused to pledge allegiance to the new state and sold the land to fund the war effort. After the war, the North Carolina legislature passed the Confiscation Act to prevent the former property owners or related claimants from getting it back. The statute "required state courts to dismiss any suit in which the ownership of property was at stake if the defendant submitted an affidavit that he held the property pursuant to a purchase from the state's commissioner of forfeited estates."[103]

The daughter of a British loyalist, Elizabeth Bayard lost her land during the Revolution and sought its return. She sued Singleton, who purchased the land after the state took it. Many lawyers of substance worked on the case. Representing Bayard were future US Supreme Court justice James Iredell and two future governors of the state, Samuel Jonson and William R. Davie. Singleton also was represented by prominent, if less appreciated, lawyers. Former governor Abner Nash was one. The other was future US Supreme Court justice Alfred Moore, whom David Currie describes as deserving "a high place in the ranks of the insignificant."[104]

The North Carolina Constitution, like all founding-era state constitutions, contained a jury-trial guarantee. "In all controversies at law respecting property," it said, "the ancient mode of trial by jury is one of the best securities of the rights of the people, and shall remain sacred and inviolable."[105] If the state court judges had power to invalidate a law under the Tar Heel Constitution, the Confiscation Act offered a good vehicle for proving it.

The official reporter of the North Carolina Supreme Court suggests that the justices did not relish the duty of constitutional review and sought to sidestep it:

> The Court then, after every reasonable endeavor had been used in vain for avoiding a disagreeable difference between the Legislature and the Judicial powers of the State, at length with much apparent

reluctance, but with great deliberation and firmness, gave their opinion separately, but unanimously for overruling the aforementioned motion for the dismiss[al] of the said suits.[106]

Realizing there was no way around the conflict between the state law and the state constitution, the justices took comfort in "the obligation of their oaths":

> The duty of their office required them in that situation, to give their opinion on that important and momentous subject; and that notwithstanding the great reluctance they might feel against involving themselves in a dispute with the Legislature of the State, yet no object of concern or respect could come in competition or authorize them to dispense with the duty they owed the public, in consequence of the trust they were invested with under the solemnity of their oaths.[107]

"By the constitution," the court explained, "every citizen had undoubtedly a right to a decision of his property by a trial by jury," and no law "could by any means repeal or alter the constitution, because if they could do this, they would at the same instant of time, destroy their own existence as a Legislature, and dissolve the government thereby established."[108] The court rejected Singleton's motion to dismiss the case.

While it fell to opponents of the American Revolution, the family of Elizabeth Bayard, to lay a cornerstone for judicial review in this country, she did not profit from the victory. The trial court held the trial that the Confiscation Act denied her. After the evidence was in, the trial court instructed the jurors that, under English law adopted in North Carolina, Bayard's father could not have owned the land to which she now claimed title. The jury, likely composed of some members unsympathetic to loyalist Bayard, obliged. It ruled against her.[109]

New York

Rutgers v. Waddington involves a taking in the other direction—an American citizen, Elizabeth Rutgers, trying to get paid for the British occupation of her brewery during the Revolutionary War. New York's favorite son, Alexander Hamilton, stood on the British side of the case and sought judicial review of the legislature's efforts to infringe his client's rights. The case starts in New York City in February 1784, when Rutgers sued Joshua Waddington, the agent for two British merchants. Her claim: They owed £8,000 in rent for operating her brewery during the British occupation of the city from 1778 to 1783. "*Rutgers* to the man in the street became a melodrama the plot of which involved an aged Patriot widow who was done out of her property by two prosperous British merchants."[110] Rutgers fled advancing British forces in 1776, leaving behind her brewery in Maiden Lane, near the site of the Federal Reserve building today.[111] For five years, the British merchants profitably ran the brewery. When she reclaimed the property in 1783, all that was left were ashes from a fire started two days before the British left the city.[112]

Joshua Waddington cut a sympathetic figure, too. He did not make any money from the brewery. He was just the agent for his uncle Benjamin and for Evelyn Pierrepont. Rutgers did not sue the two merchants directly, as they had left New York for England.[113] It's not apparent that Benjamin and his partner behaved badly anyway. When the men received the keys to the brewery from the British Commissary General in September 1778, two years after Rutgers abandoned it, they found a brewery in "shambles" and "stripped of everything of any value."[114] The merchants spent £700 to get it going.[115] Then, in 1780, the British military ordered that they pay £150 per year in rent on the property.[116] When the British prepared to leave New York City in June 1783, the military commander ordered Benjamin and Pierrepont to begin paying rent to Rutgers. They agreed to comply and asked about the rent going forward. Greeted by silence and a demand for back rent, the merchants tried to settle matters by returning the improved brewery to Rutgers. "In reply, they were told that they would be expected to leave the fixtures in addition to paying £1200 in back rent."[117]

Rutgers sued Waddington under New York's Trespass Act. Enacted in March 1783, the act was one of several measures the legislature passed to punish supporters of the Crown.[118] The act gave patriot New Yorkers a cause of action against anyone who occupied their property during the war and barred defendants from pleading official authorization as a defense.[119] With this act and the earlier Confiscation Act, locals expected "that many Loyalists would be stripped of their last penny."[120]

Eminent lawyers took up both sides of the case. Egbert Benson, New York's attorney general from 1777 to 1789, represented Elizabeth Rutgers. Hamilton represented Joshua Waddington.[121] "In view of the existing tensions, the trial must have been a highly dramatic occasion distinguished by performances by some of New York's most brilliant and colorful lawyers under the sharp, surveying eye of Mayor Duane."[122]

Dealt a difficult hand under the act—the inability to plead military authorization as a defense—Hamilton saw an opportunity in customary international law and in the Treaty of Paris, which provided a limited amnesty for "those injuries . . . done in relation to the War."[123] The linchpin to both arguments was judicial review. "Underlying all," says Gordon Wood, "was the basic question whether the court had the right at all to refer to any other source of law in order to control the authority of the legislature which was supposedly the supreme lawgiving body of the state."[124]

Hamilton invoked Article 35 of the New York Constitution of 1777, which said "that . . . the common law of England . . . shall be and continue the law" in the state provided it does not conflict with the constitution. Because the law of nations was part of the common law and because the law of nations permitted the use of property captured in war, Hamilton argued that the legislature could not confiscate Waddington's defense.

One problem. Article 35 allowed the legislature to amend the common law by statute. Hamilton responded (1) that the law of nations formed a fundamental part of the common law that states could not alter through positive legislation; and (2) that the Declaration of Independence and the Articles of Confederation gave the power to conclude peace treaties to the Union, not to the states, binding New York to the amnesties granted by the Treaty of Paris and made part of national law.[125] The argument comports with Hamilton's later answer to critics of the proposed US Constitution that "it can be of no weight to say that the courts, on the pretense of a repugnancy, may substitute their own pleasure to the constitutional intentions of the legislature. This might as well happen in the case of two contradictory statutes; or it might as well happen in every adjudication upon any single statute."[126]

Choosing the right law to apply in a particular case, Hamilton argued, is the courts' bread and butter; it's what they customarily have done.

Mayor Duane's decision did not adopt Hamilton's arguments but ruled in part for his British client. He started by expressing unease at the complexity of the task. Keep in mind that the mayor's court was a third-tier court, with appeals available to the New York Supreme Court, then to the Court for the Trial of Impeachments and Correction of Errors.

> It were to be wished, that a cause of this magnitude was not to receive its first impression from a Court of such limited jurisdiction, as that in which we preside[]—from *Magistrates actively* engaged in establishing the police of a disordered city, and in other duties, which cut them off from those studious researches, which great and intricate questions require. If we err in our opinion, it will be a consolation, that it has been intimated to be probable, whatever the determination that it will probably not end here.[127]

This warm-up should have prepared readers for Duane's pivot. He escaped the conflict between the statute and the Treaty of Paris by invoking the British equity-of-the-statute canon,[128] what might be called today an extreme form of constitutional avoidance.

> When a law is expressed in *general words*, and some *collateral matter*, which happens to arise from those general words is *unreasonable*, there Judges are in decency to conclude that the consequences were not foreseen by the Legislature; and therefore they are at liberty to expound the statute by *equity* and only *quoad hoc* [with respect to this] to disregard it.[129]

Under the court's split judgment, Joshua was liable to Rutgers for rent between 1778 and 1780, when Benjamin and Pierrepont occupied the property rent-free with the permission of the British Commissary General. But he would not have to pay Rutgers for the period between 1780 and 1783, when the commander-in-chief had made them pay rent.[130]

That the British agent obtained any relief did not sit well with the public. What difference did it make that the court sidestepped parts of the act through the equity-of-the-statute canon as opposed to declaring parts of the act void through a ruling of unconstitutionality? Not much, as many New Yorkers saw it. "A storm of indignation followed . . . [and a]n association of citizens formed to have it reversed."[131] Leading citizens condemned the decision as an attempt by the court to "assume[] and exercise[] a power to set aside an act of the state."[132] The State Assembly voted on a two-part censure resolution. The first part, which passed 25 to 15, expressed the legislature's dismay that "if a Court instituted for the benefit and government of a [municipal] corporation may take upon them to dispense with, an act in direct violation of a plain and known law of the state, all other Courts either superior or inferior may do the like."[133] The second part, which would have called on the state's Council of Appointment to replace Mayor Duane, failed 31 to 9.[134]

Not everyone criticized the decision. Mayor Duane sent a copy of his opinion to George Washington. Washington responded that, although "he [did not] pretend . . . to be a competent judge of the Law of Nations, or the principle & policy of the Statute," he believed "that reason seems very much in favor of the opinion given by the Court, and [his] judgment yields a hearty assent to it."[135] Rutgers and Waddington eventually settled the case, leaving Mayor Duane as the last word in the first case of judicial review in New York.[136]

Early Judicial Review and Modern Judicial Review

The Early State Court Cases Reveal a Consensus About Several Aspects of Judicial Review

A consensus, *first of all*, emerges relatively quickly in the bench and bar about the legitimacy of judicial review.[137] The judges and advocates largely accept this judicial authority and the premises that undergird it. State constitutions amount to fundamental law. When a state statute and a state constitution conflict, the fundamental law stands. And judges have the authority, indeed the obligation, to determine the meaning of fundamental charters and to apply them rather than a conflicting statute in cases properly before them.

Perhaps the consensus emerges from the British common law tradition by which superior laws trumped inferior laws and from the judge's duty to honor the superior law. "Common law judges frequently had to determine the lawfulness of various subordinate laws, including local customs and corporate by-laws," as Philip Hamburger shows and Mary Sarah Bilder supports as well.[138] Once people accept the idea of a hierarchy of laws, it's a small but consequential step to accept that constitutions amount to superior laws.

Perhaps the consensus emerges from the longest-lasting legacy of the Revolution: the American people's distrust of power. Even if the state constitutional founders placed most of their confidence in legislatures, that did not mean they trusted them or anyone else in power. That's why they divided power in so many ways, and it's one reason they would create a separate "judicial power." There had to be some place to go when the inevitable happened—when the legislature as agent did not serve the people as principal—and the courts, sworn to uphold the law as a matter of duty and equipped to ascertain the law as a matter of calling, were a natural place to look, at least after a few experiments with juries.

Perhaps the consensus emerges because the early judges exercised this power sparingly and with restraint. It's a lot easier to accept a proposed assumption of power when the proponent invokes it infrequently.

Whatever the reason, most likely reasons, it's before 1803 and *Marbury*, not after, that American judges and lawyers develop judicial review and American citizens come to accept it.[139] Put another way, even if Chief Justice Marshall had not been born, even if the election of 1800 had come out differently, even if the political fight underlying *Marbury v. Madison* had never occurred, this country still would have adopted judicial review—and the federal courts still would have followed the state courts' lead in doing so.

Second, there is little discussion about special rules for discerning the meaning of words in constitutions as opposed to terms in other laws or legal documents. Modern debates about the application of judicial review tend to generate sharp division, a stubborn back and forth over whether originalism, pragmatism, living constitutionalism, or some refinement of these schools of thought is the correct way to interpret a constitution. But this absence of debate in the early state courts should not surprise. Why debate whether a constitution has a fixed or evolving meaning when the people just ratified it? Because the constitutions hadn't yet had time to develop, if develop they could, there was no reason to debate whether their meaning could grow or shrink or stay as is. Why, too, debate whether the meaning of a *state* constitution is fixed when the document can be easily amended (usually by a simple majority) and when the people regularly convened state constitutional conventions after 1776? The Jeffersonian approach to constitutional amendment—that a convention should be called every twenty years so that each generation could govern itself—assumes a fixed meaning of constitutions. Why else amend them on a regular basis? Because the state constitutions preserved a straightforward method for ensuring that a constitution keeps up with the times—amendment—there was no reason (or pressure) to debate whether their charters could evolve through interpretation.

To the state and federal Framers, living constitutionalism would have resembled an idea they rejected, the British model of parliamentary sovereignty with respect to an unwritten constitution. Instead of leaving it to the members of Parliament to update an unwritten constitution by enacting new laws of the land, the American people would have delegated authority to update America's written constitutions to judges. But that would have been revolutionary in its own way. Whether in 1776 or in 1789, whether in the states or in the new national government, no one claimed that unelected judges should be in charge of updating the new American written constitutions to account for evolving circumstances.[140]

All of this left the state court judges (and eventually the early federal court judges) with a quotidian job: trying to figure out what the written words mean. With few special rules for construing constitutions, they resorted to the same tools for interpreting statutes, the same tools colonial lawyers and English lawyers had long used in construing legal terms. As John McGinnis illuminates, the early judges shared many perspectives when it came to interpretation—that the law was discovered, not made, that it was a legal science that relied on the interpretive canons for determining the meaning of language that Blackstone and others had invoked.[141] Even when the state court judges in these early cases disagreed, sometimes spurred by the custom of issuing seriatim opinions, they tended to be of one mind about method and about the value of using these canons of interpretation. While discerning the meaning of language hits roadblocks from time to time, lawyers of the age shared many conventional tools for undertaking the task.[142]

Third, if the early lawyers and judges held a shared perspective on how to identify the meaning of all laws, one might have expected judicial review to turn into a pure conflict-of-laws inquiry for each judge. First identify the best reading of the statute. Then identify the best reading of the constitutional guarantee. Now look for a conflict. If one emerges, the duty-bound judge must honor the paramount law, not the subsidiary one. But this is not what happened in the early state court cases. What did happen offers lasting lessons.

It takes two—a statute and a constitutional guarantee—to have a constitutional clash involving the legislature. That leaves two ways to resolve the conflict short of declaring the government's handiwork unconstitutional, something early state court judges remained reluctant to do. Option A is to construe the law to comport with, rather than to contradict, the constitutional command. Option B is for judges to demand clarity in the meaning of the constitutional guarantee before they feel obliged to follow it rather than a properly enacted statute. State court judges invoked both options in handling early constitutional cases.[143]

Start with *Option A*: benevolent interpretations of laws to avoid the conflict. Consistent with common law canons designed to harmonize potentially conflicting laws, the state judges frequently narrowed the coverage of a statute to eliminate the conflict, often based on the assumption that the legislature would not lightly enact an unconstitutional law or one inconsistent with the reason of the common law or one inconsistent with natural law.[144] The early cases frequently invoke the principle. State court judges also had an even more aggressive tool at their disposal, the equity of the statute. The idea was to "cut back" statutes in spite of their plain terms "to avoid inequitable results that did not serve the statutory purpose."[145] But as Dean John Manning forcefully points out, this more aggressive form of constitutional avoidance likely did not survive the founding and the separation-of-powers imperatives installed in the first American constitutions.[146] "The sharp separation of legislative and judicial powers was designed,

in large measure, to limit judicial discretion—and to promote governance according to known and established laws,"[147] thereby eliminating
the most "charitable"[148] avoidance interpretations. At some point after
all, there is little difference between equitably cutting off the limb of a
statute and refusing to enforce that limb as unconstitutional.

Option B involves another area of state court consensus: that judges
did not lightly decide that the meaning of a constitutional guarantee
conflicted with the lawmaking prerogatives of the legislature. Even
when early judges and early advocates could not steer away from a constitutional problem by a narrowing interpretation of the statute, they
still spoke and wrote in deferential terms about the threshold showing
for invalidating a law under a constitution.[149] It's a striking feature of
the early state court cases, which may have a lot to do with the general
acceptance of judicial review early in American history. One reason
judicial review would seem uncontroversial at the outset was that the
state courts infrequently invalidated laws under it. Just a few handfuls
of state constitutional law cases in the first three or four decades of our
history invalidate state laws or executive branch actions. In handling
these cases, the state court judges showed a reluctance to second-guess
the handiwork of the other branches, and generally did not second-
guess them when it came to the ruling in the case. Talking about judicial review in deferential terms and rarely invalidating laws became a
good way to legitimate it, and perhaps would be a good way to preserve
it today.

But what did deference in construing a constitution mean? We have
considerable help from scholars in sorting it out and more than one
perspective to consider. In *Law and Judicial Duty*, Philip Hamburger
helpfully explains that the roots of constitutional review are deep,
spring from the soil of the English common law, and ultimately turn
on a judge's oath-bound duty to apply the right law to the case at hand.
That duty started with the assumption that the judge would apply the
statute. But if the meaning "of a statute or a constitution could not be
discerned, it could not be obligatory" and if "a statute was not manifestly contrary to the constitution, the statute simply retained its obligation" of enforcement.[150]

Hamburger's work sets up the scholarship of John McGinnis, who
says in an equally incisive article, "The Duty of Clarity," that the early

decisions and the lawyers' arguments in them show a consensus about a founding understanding of judicial review: that judges deployed conventional tools of interpretation in construing constitutions and would invalidate a statute only if a clear conflict arose between the two. That's what it meant when courts and advocates said there had to be a "clear" conflict,[151] a "repugnance,"[152] an "evident" inconsistency,[153] an "absolute[]" contradiction,[154] or a "plain" and "manifest" conflict between the statute and constitution.[155] And that's why the early state courts, in applying judicial review, did not invalidate laws in "doubtful" cases.[156] Only when there was an "irreconcilable variance" between the statute and constitution, in the words of Alexander Hamilton in *Federalist* 78,[157] did the court have a duty to refuse to enforce the statute. Without a clear conflict between a statute and constitution, the judge remained bound by the statute.

Early US Supreme Court cases require something similar, a clear conflict between the law and the constitution, even as they did not issue a constitutional ruling. Some examples: the Court ought not to invalidate the act of a co-ordinate branch "but in a very clear case,"[158] "to pronounce any law void, [there] must be a clear and unequivocal breach of the constitution, not a doubtful and argumentative implication,"[159] and "the presumption . . . must always be in favour of the validity of laws, if the contrary is not clearly demonstrated."[160] So too of Chief Justice Marshall in *Marbury*. "An act of the legislature[] repugnant to the constitution[] is void," writes Marshall,[161] keeping in mind that "repugnancy" required that a subordinate law "flatly or absolutely contradict[]" a superior one.[162] No less than David Currie confirms that, even "before 1801," the US Supreme Court established a "lasting principle[] of construction": "doubtful cases were to be resolved in favor of constitutionality."[163]

William Treanor says that the most significant factor in the early state court cases was their subject matter. Judges, he claims, seemed to be most comfortable using judicial review to invalidate laws when a case concerned judicial matters: court authority, the role of juries, court-related processes. He observes that the earliest state cases show that judges hesitated to exercise judicial review unless "the challenged statutes affected the jury trial right or judicial matters, whereas the one challenged statute that did not fall into these categories was upheld, despite a strong tension between the statute and the relevant constitutional provisions."[164] Whether the subject matter of the early cases is the reason the early judges acted the way they did remains a contestable matter, but there is considerable overlap between invalidated laws and court-related functions.[165]

Larry Kramer takes a different tack. He says that early "judicial review was a substitute for popular action," something judges exercised "as the people's faithful agents."[166] Political rather than legal circumspection convinced judges that it was "a power to be employed cautiously, only where the unconstitutionality of a law was beyond doubt."[167]

Whatever the best explanation from these impressive sources, one thing is clear: The early state courts rarely declared laws unconstitutional.[168] What the courts said and what they did, whether in construing the statute to avoid the problem or in demanding clarity in the meaning of the constitutional guarantee, conveyed a reluctance to invalidate legislation.

How should this perspective work today? Can it work today? Many state and federal cases of the past seventy years or so do not remotely convey an attitude of deference when deploying judicial review. Is it too late to embrace these lessons? Does the judicial oath leave room for deference anyway?

What do the early state court cases tell us about how to exercise judicial review today? How does a judge convey deference to another branch of government's assessment of its authority under the constitution without shirking the judge's obligation to assess that authority under the same constitution? Two competing approaches, two difficult choices, seem to exist. One way of thinking about it is that judicial review is simply a conflict-of-laws problem. Judges are oath bound to enforce the superior law, and there's no room for deference in deciding what that law means. In a conventional conflict-of-laws problem, the parties might debate whether one state's law or another's applies to a dispute. No one much worries about judicial accretions of power in that setting. All the court needs do is to pick the right law to govern the situation. Something similar is going on with judicial review, one could argue, and as a result no imbalance-of-power anxieties should arise there either. Everyone accepts that the constitution, say, the Wyoming Constitution, is a superior state law, and everyone accepts that it controls in a conflict with a subsidiary law, say, a statute enacted by the Wyoming legislature. The conflict-of-laws question simply turns on a judicial liquidation of meaning of each law and a judicial assessment of whether they conflict. Even if courts have authority to construe a *statute* to avoid the conflict, they have no authority to construe a *constitution* to avoid the conflict as a way of deferring to the legislature. That seems especially true when one accounts for the judicial oath: to perform all duties under the constitutions and laws of the state and country.[169] If the constitution applies to a dispute, how could an oath-abiding judge not respect that reality? And how could a duty-bound judge uphold the inferior law? That seems all the more true when it comes to constitutional debates about constitutional structure, the division of powers in a government? How strange if judges could sidestep the duty to ensure that each branch of government colors within the fundamental lines of its power, diluting one of our sturdiest guarantees of liberty along the way.

But there's another side to the debate. We started out with a representative government, and we continue to aspire to have one. In a democracy, there's a lot to be said for encouraging the legislature to be the lead policymaker in handling difficult policy debates and for making it the rare enactment that a constitution prohibits. That sounds deferential. And shouldn't courts be mindful of the reality, call it a compound-interest principle, that every time judges decide the constitution applies to one dispute it becomes easier to say it covers the next dispute, raising the risk that courts become pivotal policymaking players in government. How can we ignore, moreover, what the early judges, all oath-bound too, were saying and doing? Their words conveyed deference over and over, requiring "clear" conflicts, "repugnancy," or an "irreconcilable variance" between ordinary law and the constitution, and calling for judicial forbearance in "doubtful" cases. So did their actions. They rarely invalidated laws, handling their work in restraint-driven and deferential terms. An unvarnished oath-driven, conflict-of-law perspective also would not allow for a salient technique at the founding for resolving these cases short of invalidating the statutes—construing statutes to avoid the conflict. That's not the technique of a purist focused on conflicts or not, adherence to duty or not.

The Thayer approach has much to commend it but ultimately is not the right way to handle the problem. Roughly halfway between the founding and the present, James Bradley Thayer, an influential Harvard Law School professor, offered his influential take on the proper method of judicial review. His 1893 article, "The Origin and Scope of the American Doctrine of Constitutional Law,"[170] explained that the early cases show that judges, in view of "the remarkable peculiarities of the situation,"[171] should not invalidate statutes absent proof "beyond a reasonable doubt" that the law and constitution conflict. In his telling, any "rationally permissible" justification for upholding a statute would do.[172]

There's something to Thayer's advocacy for deference, particularly if one adds to the mix the risk of politicizing the courts and of losing sight of one of his on-the-mark observations: that a community of people who turn to the courts for answers to difficult problems will never learn how to answer problems for themselves. He rightly debunked the idea that "the judicial power" is "our only protection against oppression and ruin."[173] He closed his article by lamenting that

> our doctrine of constitutional law has had a tendency to drive out questions of justice and right, and to fill the mind of legislators with thoughts of mere legality, of what the constitution allows . . . [;] the safe and permanent road towards reform is that of impressing upon our people a far stronger sense than they have of the great range of possible harm and evil that our system leaves open, and must leave open, to the legislatures, and of the clear limits of judicial power; so that responsibility may be brought sharply home where it belongs. The checking and cutting down of legislative power, by numerous detailed prohibitions in the constitution, cannot be accomplished without making the government petty and incompetent. . . . Under no system can the power of courts go far to save a people from ruin; our chief protection lies elsewhere.[174]

Thayer also is not someone to dismiss casually. He looked at the problem closer in time to the founding than our sight permits. And his assessment was influential, prompting Justice Holmes, Justice Frankfurter, Judge Hand, and other luminaries to perceive the judicial role as limited when it came to invalidating acts of the legislature. Before going on the Court, Frankfurter echoed Thayer's warning: The "real battles of liberalism are not won in the Supreme Court"; for "only a persistent, positive translation of the liberal faith into the thoughts and acts of the community is the real reliance against the unabated temptation to straightjacket the human mind."[175] Long after being on the bench, Learned Hand reflected on the point: "I often wonder whether we do not rest our hopes too much upon constitutions, upon laws, and upon courts. These are false hopes. . . . Liberty lies in the hearts of men and women; when it dies there, no constitution, no law, no court" can "save it" or "even do much to help it."[176] Time also has vindicated Thayer's concern that non-deferential review runs the risk of transforming judges from referees into players, from interpreters into lawmakers.[177]

Much as there may be to his arguments, the Thayer view of deference was implausibly one-sided. His plea for deference applied only to federal-court review of federal laws, not to federal-court review of state laws. Thayer thought that the federal government had a "duty in all questions involving [its] powers . . . to maintain that power against the States in its fullness," and that judges thus ought to give the US Constitution "nothing less than its just and true interpretation" when the actions of a State are put up against the "supreme law of the land."[178] In fairness to this idea, I should note that Justice Holmes promoted it as well. "I do not think the United States," he observed, "would come to an end if we lost our power to declare an Act of Congress void. I do think the Union would be imperiled if we could not make that declaration as to the laws of the several States."[179]

But Thayer, it seems to me, does not account for a few things. Does anyone realistically think that the US Constitution would have been ratified if it had permitted the US Supreme Court to review the validity of state laws but not federal laws? At the core of the anti-Federalists' demands for a Bill of Rights was a checks-and-balances concern that arose from the states' distrust of the new National Government, what many feared would act like a foreign government based (eventually) in Washington, DC. The Thayer perspective loses sight of the equally salient horizontal *and* vertical divisions of power created by the US Constitution. This view also takes the US Supreme Court off the field when it is the *only* court available to correct an overreach. Most challenges to state laws are susceptible to two challenges, under the state and federal constitutions in the state and federal courts. Not so for federal laws.[180] No doubt, federal judicial review of state laws became an essential tool for creating a union of states and preserving it. But that shows only that federal judicial review of both types of laws—state and federal—ought to exist. Equivalent principles of review for each kind of law also balance out judicial predispositions, whether tendencies in a national or federalism direction.[181]

Overlooked by Thayer are the ways vertical separation of powers secures liberty. Just one frame of reference illustrates the point. Think about the 155,000 or so individuals who reside in our federal prisons for lengthy, sometimes too lengthy, criminal sentences.[182] Many of them would not be there if the federal courts had picked just one area—criminal law—to impose judicially enforceable limits on congressional power. The power of the federal courts to declare Acts of Congress constitutional, it is well to remember, can be no less potent than its authority to declare them unconstitutional, as the anti-Federalists well appreciated, allowing the national "judicial imprimatur" to "burn away the fog of doubt surrounding the scope of congressional authority and clear the way for more aggressive exertions of national legislative power."[183] Recall also that the power to regulate is the power to preempt. Every time the federal courts permit Congress to regulate a new area, they allow the national legislature to take over the field—to prohibit any state from enacting any laws in the area, whether that state law advances freedom, offers a useful insight to a policy problem, or amounts to a useful experiment in a difficult area. States' rights can indeed be individual rights. It may be hard to resist Thayer's call for an approach to judicial review that combines "a lawyer's rigor with a statesman's breadth of view."[184] But if breadth of view permits the removal of one of the key structural guarantees of liberty—some judicially enforceable division between national and state power—one can fairly worry about what other constitutional values this breadth of view shortchanges.

Thayer's "beyond a reasonable doubt" formulation also takes an evidentiary form of proof and awkwardly gives it a linguistic task. Meaning is not determined by proof. It is determined by context and conventional tools for interpreting language. It falls to judges to use those tools to determine what contested words and phrases mean and to ascertain whether they apply to the controversy at hand. Some readings bear fidelity to the text, and they deserve credence as a result. A beyond-a-reasonable-doubt approach to interpretation seems to ignore all of this and generates what might be called a dying-constitution approach to the meaning of state and federal charters. Each time a court defers to the legislature, each time it asks whether there is a plausible basis for upholding the law, it narrows the scope of the protection.

Compare use of the beyond-a-reasonable-doubt formulation in the place for which it was designed (jury findings of fact in criminal trials) and the place for which Thayer deploys it (judicial interpretations of a constitution). When a jury decides to acquit under this formulation, it does not set a new standard for application of that criminal law to future criminals. It just establishes that, in that case, the government did not meet its proof. But if a constitution has a range of meaning, or worse a shifting range of meaning, that applies only when proof beyond a reasonable doubt establishes its application, wouldn't that alter its scope over time? Not for all provisions, I acknowledge. The approach still would allow for judicial enforcement of highly specific constitutional provisions, such as the electoral college, Senate elections, a 35-year-old-age requirement for the presidency. But it would run the risk of shrinking the meaning of generalized guarantees, such as due process, equal protection, unreasonable searches and seizures, free speech, and of shrinking still more the meaning of our structural guarantees of liberty—the vertical and horizontal separation of powers.

Every decision upholding the law creates the risk of a diminished data point, a new binding precedent that expands the world of plausible explanations for upholding still more laws. Just as a pure conflict-of-laws approach can exponentially increase the domain of a constitution, so a beyond-a-reasonable-doubt approach can exponentially shrink it. The Thayer approach gives away too much. The inaction of courts over time permits legislatures to enact more dubious laws. Each non-invalidation of an unconstitutional law makes the next exercise of lawmaking power easier to withstand the supposed scrutiny of judicial review. Just as the general terms of our constitutions do not constitutionalize everything, they do not constitutionalize nothing.

If Thayer deference does not work but if his concerns about unbridled judicial review have been vindicated, what does work? Even if Thayer overshoots, something remains to his restraint-minded attitude, and

renewed attention to the early state court rulings offers a way to capture it. Before doing that, it's worth remembering the stakes. Neither
a deference model nor a pure conflict-of-laws model, when fairly applied to *all* structural guarantees and *all* individual rights, inherently
favors one set of policy outcomes over another. Neither restrained judicial deference nor unapologetic judicial engagement dictates what
happens with tomorrow's disputes. They just tell us who will make the
calls, legislators or judges. History locks in the point. In more recent
decades, it's true, the courts have been inclined toward more progressive outcomes in construing constitutions. But 100 years ago, closer in
time to Thayer's writing, the opposite was true. Courts were known for
using judicial review in ways that favored conservative outcomes, what
came to be known, fairly or unfairly, as the discredited *Lochner* era.[185]
Either way, if the American people decide they trust judges more than
legislators to make key policy choices for them, they will relentlessly
ensure that our judges are their kinds of people. That doesn't tell us who
will win; it just tells us who gets to decide. How, then, to tailor Thayer's
concerns to today's state and federal courts?

First, one still-relevant lesson from the early state court cases is that
the constitutional-avoidance canon remains a legitimate way to honor
the benefits of deference while refusing to ignore true conflicts between
laws and constitutional guarantees. Most judges today agree that they
may not rewrite laws to sidestep constitutional conflicts under the "equity of the statute." But they tend to accept that a genuine ambiguity
in a law should be construed to mitigate, not exacerbate, potential
conflicts with a constitutional guarantee. Some state and federal judges,
it is true, have grown skeptical of the constitutional-avoidance canon.
If their point is to critique aggressive uses of the avoidance canon, to
critique equity-of-the-statute-type rulings, that's fair. If the point of
these skeptics is to eliminate the canon, however, that's a more hefty
lift. Anyone promoting that approach must counter the evidence that
constitutional avoidance was an accepted feature of how the early state
judges handled judicial review, must explain why the state and federal
founders and the public would have understood the "judicial power"
to be exercised differently, and must explain why the constitutional-
avoidance canon died at the founding. Another source of skepticism
about the constitutional-avoidance canon turns on a fear that it has

become a duty-avoidance canon—that it tempts judges to engage in wholesale surgery of clearly worded statutes to escape invalidating laws they do not want to invalidate or to avoid constitutional questions at all. But as with many things, this is a question of degree. So long as judges are not re-writing statutes to suit their preferences but fairly construing true ambiguities to avoid constitutional clashes, they seem to be operating within a long-accepted culture of interpretation.

Second, the early state court cases suggest that the right balance between restraint and duty is not deference at the outset. Just as "where there's a will there's a way" is not a useful attitude for a judge to take in invalidating laws, it's not a useful attitude for a judge in upholding laws. The judge should instead start with the attitude that all laws, including constitutions, usually have a discernible meaning, and conventional tools of interpretation offer a way to capture it. Only after that task ends, unweighted by any thumb on the scales, does deference come into play. At that point only, the judge asks whether the statute conflicts with the clearly discerned meaning of the constitution. If the meaning of the constitution is not clear, democracy controls through the representative branches of government. If the meaning is clear, the constitution controls.

As John McGinnis shows, the early state court cases (and the federal cases to boot) required judges to use the traditional techniques of interpretation to reduce the language of constitutional guarantees to meaning. A clear-conflict requirement, he explains, was a background principle that explained the arguments of advocates during the era and the rulings of judges. The abundance of clear-conflict language documented by McGinnis in this era[186] suggests that an understanding of constitutions as legal texts with discernible meaning that could establish "irreconcilable" differences between superior and subordinate law traced back to the English legal concept of "repugnancy" and shows that lawyers and judges accepted existing assumptions about compatibility between superior and inferior laws.[187] If, in undertaking this inquiry, judges can identify a clear meaning of the constitutional provision and if that clear meaning renders the statute invalid, then judges should, indeed must, so rule. If not, they must exercise the restraint of our early judges and leave the matter to democracy's domain.

Third, a clear-meaning approach mitigates a modern problem with judicial review. What was difficult then hasn't gotten any easier over time. If the right way to interpret a constitution was difficult to figure out in the late eighteenth century, when the early state court judges wrote these decisions, or in the late nineteenth century, when Thayer wrote his influential piece, think of the challenges today. It's difficult for lawyers and judges, non-historians in the main, to determine the meaning of guarantees written long ago, sometimes centuries ago. Search data bases and new tools, like corpus linguistics, have alleviated some of these difficulties for sure.[188] But it's hard to deny the challenges of fully understanding the historical context of a two-century-old provision. One possible solution is this:

> The best way to ensure that a Constitution written for all time is useful for all time is to construe it, when the application of the historical understanding of a provision to a modern dispute is unclear, to allow for democratic innovation, empowering various federal and state laboratories of democracy to answer the thorny questions raised by this or that policy debate.[189]

These two problems—identifying the original meaning of constitutional guarantees and making sense of the language of deference from the early state court judicial review decisions—can be cured, it seems to me, in one stroke. A clarity imperative becomes a principle for then and now. As to the past, it honors what the judges said they were doing (only invalidating statutes that clearly conflicted with the constitution) and what they did (rarely invalidating statutes). As to the present, it respects the critique that it can be difficult to size up centuries-old guarantees against a recent law. If the historical evidence is unclear about the meaning of the guarantee, after deploying all of the pertinent tools of interpretation, including tools like corpus linguistics, that means the people of today must resolve the problem through the normal recourses of legislation or through amending the relevant constitution. This approach also mitigates a paradox. Our courts rarely exercised judicial review in the first forty years after our constitutions took root and our knowledge of them was fresh, and our courts regularly exercise it today when the meaning of many of those documents tends to be harder to understand.

Fourth, a clarity requirement navigates the competing intuitions of judicial-restraint deferential review and oath-driven conflict-of-laws review in another way. In thinking about the duty of judges to apply the superior law to a dispute, it's useful to go back to the oath that, in one form or another, all state and federal judges must honor. Many duties go with being a judge, and there's a lot to be said for a theory of review that makes it easier to honor those duties: to "administer justice without respect to persons," to "do equal right to the poor and to the rich," above all else to discharge those duties "impartially."[190] Appreciation of the oath is the only way that a premise of judicial review makes sense, that does not reduce everything to political judging, and that honors the distinction between judgment and will. So long as judges exercise neutral, law-driven judgment, not policy-driven will, it makes sense to give them the final say about the meaning of constitutions in the context of resolving cases and controversies. But if judges unleash, or cannot resist, their will to find any satisfying way to resolve a dispute, one premise of dividing these powers collapses and the idea that judges and "the judicial [branch] shall never exercise the legislative and executive powers," in the words of the 1780 Massachusetts Constitution, is hard to take seriously.[191] There's also little explanation for using the judicial branch, once it becomes a political branch, to check other political branches over the meaning of our foundational charters. Why would one group of politicians deserve this privilege over another?

A clarity requirement offers a realistic way for national and state judges to honor the duty of impartiality. Every judge has individual predispositions. Their life experiences, worldviews, theories about judging, and policy prejudices all naturally lead them to react favorably or unfavorably, at least initially, to fact patterns in cases.[192] What else should we expect of sentient beings, particularly those who have had substantial careers in government or practice before joining the bench? An obligation of clarity in construing a constitutional guarantee helps to wash out those predispositions by requiring the judge to identify a clear legal rule before invalidating a law.

The setup of our state and federal appellate courts respects the same insight and offers a comparable way to mitigate it. All appellate courts sit as collegial bodies, in groups from three up to roughly nine judges, who decide cases as a body of potential wills, not as a single potential will. A clarity imperative simultaneously helps to honor the judicial duty of impartiality and makes it easier for the neutralizing benefits of collegial decision making to take hold, as a majority of the court seeks agreement over whether there is a clear constitutional meaning, and whether that meaning applies to the law before them, not over whether there is a best meaning. The requirement improves the odds that judgment, not will, that legal reasoning, not intuition, will carry the day.

A duty of clarity also advances the ideal of impartiality in the context of cases in which the judiciary is particularly at risk—disputes that affect their own turf or prior decisions identifying new rights. Recall that Judge Roane in *Kamper v. Hawkins* said that judges must "distrust their own judgment if the matter is doubtful, or . . . require clear evidence before they decide in cases where interest may possibly warp the judgment."[193] He was concerned that, in constitutional disputes affecting the judicial power, judges would be tempted to over-protect their authority. "Though a judge is interested privately in preserving his independence, yet it is the right of the people which should govern him, who in their sovereign character have provided that the judges should be independent."[194] That's especially so in cases asking the courts to take sides on the social issues of the day. Judges have no more experience-generated expertise in that setting than any fan pulled from random out of the stands of a baseball game, and traditional principles of interpretation rarely answer those questions with any degree of confidence about legal outcomes.

A clarity requirement helps judges when they face the greatest risks of becoming players rather than referees. Take measure of the idea in terms of self-restraint, not judicial restraint, as a judicial attitude for each judge, not a one-sized rule for all. That frame of reference reminds me of the attitudes of two former colleagues, now deceased. When I joined the Sixth Circuit, I had the fortune of learning from Judge David Nelson, whose seat I filled, and from Judge Cornelia Kennedy, who paved many paths in understated ways. They were uncommonly self-aware judges, alert to their own prejudices and predispositions. When they made mistakes, if they did make mistakes, I thought it was because they were so afraid of imposing their will on a constitutional case that they pushed too hard in the opposite direction.

Think of how few lawyers would describe the federal and state judiciary that way today. Think of the odds of getting a judgeship if the nominee was known for trying to resist his or her policymaking impulses. And think of how few citizens want judges who think that way today. No one seems to want judges who will rule in close cases *against* their policy preferences, unless of course an opposing political party nominated them. A duty of clarity helps judges, whether they have the built-in navigation systems of a Judge Nelson or Judge Kennedy or not, to find the safe harbors of neutral judging.

A clarity requirement, last of all, calls to mind one of Justice Scalia's lasting insights, that rule-based judging improves the odds of neutral judging.[195] The one thing judges usually know for sure about judicial review is that they don't know what the next case will look like, a veil that advances the goal of impartiality in resolving today's *and* tomorrow's cases on neutral and consistent grounds. A duty of clarity increases the odds that the interpretive inquiry, whether at the state or federal level, will produce a rule of sorts to govern that case and the one after that. Absent clarity, the dispute is not for judges to resolve. With clarity, judges must tie themselves to a seen clear rule come what may in future unseen disputes.

3

Judicial Selection

How to Use Democracy to Select Individuals for a Non-Democratic Job

Difficult though judicial review may be, the state courts' innovation of the power to invalidate legislation did not generate controversy in the main, and the federal courts followed the path marked by these decisions with decisions of their own in *Marbury* and the like. But if judicial review generally was accepted in the abstract, that did not mean it was accepted in the concrete, and that did not mean Americans would refrain from wanting a say in who their judges are.

Judicial selection follows an arc of its own. The first state constitutions used appointments to select judges. The only debate was whether to delegate the responsibility to the legislature, as most did, or to the governor, as some did. Consistent with the state practices, the US Constitution adopted an appointment power, which vested nomination in the president and confirmation in the Senate.

The federal appointment model, like its life tenure provision, has stayed fixed since 1789.[1] The state practices have not.

Who selects the judges and how long they serve became recurring questions in the states, especially from the founding to the Civil War. A range of developments prompted the inquiries. A few state court decisions that invalidated popular legislation generated controversy, prompting efforts to rein in the judges. Cutting in the other direction were over-reaching and occasionally corrupt uses of legislative power, by what was originally seen as the most trustworthy branch of government, prompting efforts to curb *its* power and generating a thirst for *more* judicial review. That led to efforts to build up the authority and prestige of the judicial branch. A judiciary that owed its selection and tenure to the people, many thought, would serve both goals, and steel it to check the other branches of power, whether in division-of-powers disputes or individual-rights disputes. The Jacksonian era's extension of the franchise generated political pressure to use it more often. These developments set the base for seventeen state constitutional conventions between 1846 and 1861.[2] Nearly every state in the mix changed its constitution to select judges through elections for defined terms.

Judicial review and judicial selection are inseparable. The more a court engages in the former, the more scrutiny it can expect in the latter, whether that scrutiny is tied to debates over the next election/appointment or to debates about changing the selection and tenure methods. This chapter ties the two together and looks for insights about the proper balance of state and federal judicial review today.

Early State Practices

Before 1776, British colonial governors largely chose judges in the colonies, the two exceptions being Connecticut and Rhode Island.[3] The posts tended to go to men loyal to the Crown. The colonial governors were reluctant to cede control of the appointments to the colonial legislatures, which along with colonial juries became centers of imperial resistance.[4]

After 1776, the power to choose judges generally shifted to the state legislatures. Early state constitutions conveyed distrust for executive power, which the new country associated with colonial rule. The new states thus erred on the side of giving legislatures extensive supervisory powers. "The Americans knew," says Gordon Wood, "they had among themselves 'tyrants enough at heart'; and although their governors would now be elected periodically by the people or their representatives, so intoxicating and corrupting was the power of ruling that an elected magistrate was actually no less to be dreaded than an hereditary one."[5] The people in the first states feared that allowing governors to appoint judges, as they had in the colonial governments, would foster an unhealthy "dependence . . . on executive caprice" that in time would undermine liberty.[6] The only exceptions were Massachusetts, where the governor made the appointments, and New York, where that responsibility fell to a Council of Appointment composed of the governor and a group of senators.[7]

Few saw judges as a threat to representative government at the outset. Perhaps that was because colonial judges did not have the kind of independence that their English cousins had won during the Glorious Revolution a century before.[8] Or perhaps that was because the framers of the state constitutions thought it would be a subservient branch. While the States separated power in three branches, the framers of the state constitutions in practice asked *which* elected branch should control the judiciary, not *whether* one should.[9] Americans at the founding knew whom they trusted to choose and supervise state judges and other government officials: state legislatures.

Early "efforts to separate the judges from their customary magisterial connection eventually set the judiciary on a path toward a kind of independence in American constitutionalism that few in 1776 ever envisioned."[10] Structural protections like tenure "during good behavior" furthered this transformation, insulating judges from executive and legislative interference.[11] The adoption of these reforms in the 1780s and 1790s underscores that Americans designed the judicial branch on the assumption it needed more independence, not less.

Courts in the revolutionary era by and large did not exercise power in ways that would warrant turf-war anxieties from the legislature or who-do-you-think-you-are sensitivities from the people. Recall that judicial review was still in its infancy in the 1770s and 1780s. Courts weren't even the only public bodies to exercise judicial power at that point. State legislatures passed private bills granting relief to litigants and some even revised court judgments by statute.[12] Special tribunals composed of legislators or executive officials in some states sat as final courts of appeal in the state court system, a continuation of colonial practices.[13] The first juries, as noted, also had considerable authority over the meaning of laws.

By the mid-1780s, legislatures had largely shed their judicial role and courts gradually asserted their power to review legislative acts. Because the state assemblies often legislated in response to specific requests, producing a body of law that was "confused and piecemeal," judges exercised more discretion "to make sense of the legal chaos."[14] When legislatures tried to limit this newfound discretion by directing the outcome of a case or the rule of decision to be applied in a particular controversy, judges began to push back. In Massachusetts, the legislature repeatedly tried to stay judicial proceedings or to single out particular cases for a new trial, a procedure it soothingly, if pointedly, called "restoring men to their law."[15] The Commonwealth's judges held firm, refusing to subject their courtrooms to legislative control or to surrender their best judgment to politicians. By the late 1780s, the Massachusetts legislature grudgingly "concede[d] some authority to the courts" to decide when new trials would be appropriate, though it continued to grant them for some time nevertheless, a sign of the incremental pace of change.[16] By the late 1780s, Alexander Hamilton, writing in *Federalist* 81, would criticize the state practice of vesting final appellate jurisdiction in political bodies. "The members of the legislature will rarely be chosen with a view to those qualifications which fit men for the stations of judges," Hamilton observed, creating a danger that they will be "deficient in [the] knowledge" needed for judicial decision making and that "the natural propensity of such bodies to party divisions . . . [will] poison the fountains of justice."[17]

Increasing the power of state courts and taking away legislative tools for reining them in sparked political confrontations. Both developments, together with brush fires over specific cases, created pressure to obtain greater control over the power to select and to remove judges. Two stories, one early in our history, one almost fifty years after the founding, illustrate the intensity of these contests. Some thirty-seven years apart, both controversies (and others like them) set the people on a course of seeking two different things: independent judicial review by their state judges and more say over who they were.

Rhode Island

On the eve of the federal constitution's framing, Rhode Island's legislature held a leash on its judges, selecting them for renewable *one-year* terms. Annual legislative appointment was not unique to Rhode Island; it was one of two colonies to select judges that way.[18] And it was not unique after independence; at least two other states did the same.[19] But the state's populist politics, the absence of a written state constitution, and the legislature's strength, even by the standards of the time, all meant that judges in Rhode Island were more dependent on the legislature than their counterparts in other states.

Trevett v. Weeden puts a case caption on the point. The dispute arose from one of many economic crises that followed the Revolutionary War. A shortage of hard currency (gold or silver) meant that residents of the state had a difficult time paying debts and taxes even as their farms or trades prospered. Paper money issued during the Revolutionary War was worthless and by decree of the state legislature no longer legal tender. The liquidity crisis hit farmers and rural landowners the hardest, leading to farm foreclosures and livestock seizures.[20]

The state legislature passed a paper-money law in May 1786 that called for printing new banknotes and making them legal tender. Merchants treated the new paper money the same as the old and refused to take it. Because the statute made it harder to collect debts in hard currency, all "trade practically ceased."[21] Intent on enforcing the law, the legislature punished merchants who refused to take the depreciating paper money: a £100 fine for the first offense, disenfranchisement for the second. But this deepened the crisis and provoked a food shortage in the state, as butchers, grocers, and other merchants closed shop rather than risk the fines. Undeterred, the legislature enacted a new law directing violators to be tried without a jury.[22]

It fell to John Trevett and John Weeden to bring this brinksmanship to its end.[23] In September 1786, Trevett sued Weeden, a Newport butcher, for refusing to take paper money for this one man's meat.[24] It's not clear which party was more luckless. Trevett lost an eye and injured a foot while a captain in the American navy during the Revolutionary War. Back home, he took up cabinetmaking and, "like many other men of limited means, he struggled . . . to avoid hunger."[25] Weeden had little in common with the "prosper[ous]" merchants and commercial interests whom the paper money laws targeted.[26] "Only two weeks earlier," observes Philip Hamburger, Weeden "had been 'an object of charity in the streets of Newport.'"[27] How, he must have thought, could a law force him to operate his business at a loss and threaten him with fines if he did not comply?[28]

Weeden caught one break. Though "excessively poor and unable to pay counsel," his case attracted the attention of James Mitchell Varnum, a general in the Revolutionary War, a leading attorney, and a future territorial judge in the Northwest Territory.[29] "Eloquent" and "vigor[ous]" in his advocacy, Varnum put those qualities to the test in arguing that a state law was unconstitutional in a state without a written constitution.[30]

When the justices of the Superior Court set the case for a jury-less trial, Varnum argued that "the legislature could never make a law contrary to the principles of the constitution," written or unwritten, "because the principles of the constitution 'were ordained by the people anterior to . . . the powers of the General Assembly.' "[31] Judges, by virtue of their oath to "truly and impartially execute the laws . . . to the best of their skill and understanding,"[32] were duty-bound "to measure the laws of the legislature against the constitution and the rights of the people."[33] Even without a written constitution that spelled it out, Varnum insisted, the right to trial by jury was beyond legislative reproach. Rhode Island's Royal Charter and a colonial statute—providing that "no freeman shall be . . . deprived of his freehold or liberty, . . . nor shall be passed upon, judged or condemned, but by the lawful judgment of his peers, or by the laws of this Colony"[34]—"memorialized an earlier, inexplicit compact of the people" that rose to the heights of fundamental law.[35]

The five judges decided that they did not have jurisdiction over the lawsuit, handing Weeden (and Varnum) a victory.[36] An account in the *Providence Gazette* says that three of the five judges agreed that "the penal law [was] repugnant and unconstitutional."[37] The remaining two ruled without opinion that Trevett's lawsuit could not proceed.

The legislators were not happy. They denounced the "unprecedented" decision as likely to "abolish the legislative authority."[38] That authority, they thought, was "Supreme" over the courts even as to matters of constitutionality. Upset that the judges refused to enforce its paper-money law, the legislature summoned them to explain themselves. The purpose of the hearing was to decide how best to proceed to "reestablish the Supremacy of the legislative authority."[39] "In a state without a constitution," Philip Hamburger observes, the legislators could "be excused for [their] astonishment that some of the judges had held a statute unconstitutional."[40]

Three of the judges appeared before the legislature, while the other two declined the invitation based on illness—ill from what was left unsaid. Here's how the healthy judges defended their decision and independence. Judge Howell, "the youngest justice" on the court, "spoke for over six hours against the legislative interference."[41] He claimed that judges "were not accountable to the Legislature" and could not be made to answer for their opinions.[42] Judge Tillinghast noted that, in view of the "trifling" benefits of their office and judicial salaries "not worth mentioning," the only reward that they could expect from the job was a clear conscience that they had done their duty and got the law right.[43] While Judge Hazard expressed his support for the Assembly's paper-money policy, he explained that "it was not possible to resist the force of conviction" about the jury trial right.[44] All three judges invoked judicial duty and the judicial oath as an explanation for their power to declare laws invalid.[45]

The judges insisted that the legislature lacked the power to remove them without process and "an opportunity to answer to *certain and specific charges*" of criminal wrongdoing.[46] The legislators referred the question to the state's attorney general, who said it would be improper to "suspend[], or remove[] [the judges] from office, for a mere matter of opinion, without a charge of criminality."[47] Other counsel agreed that the legislature would need a trial-like process in which the legislature would need to "state the facts particularly upon which the impeachment is found."[48] Finding no available criminal charge, the General Assembly let the judges go, leaving un-withdrawn their displeasure with the ruling.[49]

That left the legislature to exercise a power it did have. Within the year, it declined to reappoint all but one of the judges after their one-year terms expired. Only Chief Justice Mumford, who did not give a reason for his vote in the case and pled illness when summoned by the Assembly, kept his job.[50] So ended the first experiment with judicial review in the Ocean State, which left judicial independence, if not judicial tenure, intact. Confirming the need for both, the state's courts would not pass on the constitutionality of a statute again until after Rhode Island's adoption of a written constitution in 1842.[51]

One legacy of *Trevett v. Weeden* is its effect on the tenure of *federal* judges. After the decision, Varnum published his courtroom arguments along with an account of what happened in a widely read pamphlet, described as "the most prominent discussion of judicial review" before the Philadelphia Convention.[52] During the Convention, James Madison lamented that "the Judges who refused to execute an unconstitutional law were displaced, and others substituted, by the Legislature who would be the willing instruments of the wicked and arbitrary plans of their masters."[53] The experience of the judges in Rhode Island likely encouraged the federal Framers to guarantee life tenure to federal judges.[54] And it likely encouraged Alexander Hamilton, in *Federalist* 78, to praise life tenure for judges as an "excellent . . . barrier to the encroachments and oppressions" of legislatures and "one of the most valuable . . . improvements in the practice of government."

Kentucky

Thirty-seven years after Rhode Island's encounter with judicial politics, Kentucky faced a lengthy controversy over its judges and their power. Between 1823 and 1826, the people of the state intensely debated in newspapers, pamphlets, and statewide elections whether, and under what circumstances, the state's judges could treat legislation as void under the constitution. The controversy, as Theodore Ruger chronicles, "demonstrates that significant pockets of opposition to judicial review persisted even two decades after *Marbury*, thirty-five years after the Framing, and a half-century after independence."[55] The issue that "convulse[d] a nation,"[56] Ruger explains, reflects a nuanced, sometimes contradictory, view of the judicial role—simultaneously "a limited endorsement of judicial review" and "a successful exercise of meaningful popular constitutional interpretation."[57] The controversy is as much about who the judges were as it was about how they decided cases, as much about the reality that judges dominated the headlines for three election cycles as it was about judicial review's final victory. By the time the controversy came to a close, judicial review in Kentucky had emerged "from the bottom up rather than from the top down."[58]

Like *Trevett v. Weeden*, the Kentucky controversy arose over debtor-relief laws enacted to alleviate economic stress for some (debtors) and compound it for others (creditors). This version of the debate, too, had local strands. It was a controversy of place, as Kentucky author Wendell Berry might say, given the many long-endured and hard-earned sensitivities that its residents had over land debts and land ownership. Kentucky became the fifteenth state in 1792, covering what had been the Kentucky District of Virginia. Through its first Constitution, Kentucky "was unusual in specifying within the text of its constitutional declaration of rights" that " 'all laws contrary thereto, or contrary to this constitution, shall be void.' "[59]

Before and after statehood, Kentucky was "shingled over" with overlapping land claims due to poor land surveying, often done long after the land was settled.[60] The legislature exacerbated the issue after statehood with a "liberal" land-grant policy that often resulted in two or more people "owning" the same piece of land. "In 1797, Kentucky's surveyor general reported to the legislature that existing grants totaled approximately twice the state's actual acreage."[61]

Those who kept their land often heavily mortgaged it to deal with fickle crop prices, leading to a spate of foreclosures after a severe recession in 1819. That development fueled resentment toward lawyers, who collected the debt, and toward the courts, which ordered foreclosure of the properties that secured it. To the people, it looked like "lawyers, clerks, sheriffs, [and] constables made great crops," while "most of [their own] were diminished" during this period of economic hardship.[62] "By 1821," observes Ruger, "a third of the state had been conveyed to banks or nonresidents through forced sales, foreclosures, or other forms of judicial process."[63] The rights of out-of-state landlords were aided by "the one-sided compact through which Kentucky had attained its separation from Virginia . . . [which] disabl[ed] the new state's sovereign authority in the critical area of land policy."[64]

The court side of what became known as the Kentucky Courts Controversy began after two state court cases held that the State's Relief Act of 1820 impaired contract obligations under the state and federal constitutions. The act tried to solve the twin problems of the state's liquidity and foreclosure crises by giving creditors "a choice: either accept payment in Bank of Kentucky notes, or undergo a two-year stay of execution."[65] But the decisions by the Court of Appeals, the court of last resort in the Commonwealth at the time, read the contracts clauses to prohibit this choice, a decision that "startled" the "state's majoritarian polity."[66]

As in New York in 1784, Rhode Island in 1786, and Georgia in 1815, the first port of call for Kentucky's legislators was a resolution. They condemned the decision and the court's assumption of authority to declare laws void. Also familiar was the gist of their criticism. The Court of Appeals had "wrested from the representatives of the people the power [to make and] to suspend the operation of the laws," a power not rightfully theirs.[67]

The legislators' next approach also followed a pattern. They tried to remove the judges. But the Kentucky Constitution stymied them. Unlike Rhode Island and neighboring Ohio, which had short terms of office before the leash of reappointment could be pulled,[68] Kentucky's judges served during good behavior and only "address" or impeachment by a super-majority vote of the legislature could remove them from office.[69] Address amounted to an alternative to impeachment found in many of the first state constitutions; it allowed legislatures, sometimes by simple majorities, to request that the governor withdraw a judge's commission and remove him from office.[70] It thus allowed legislatures to remove judges without the heightened finding of fault or process that impeachment required.[71] But this procedure did not work in Kentucky in 1823. The governor supported the court's decisions, and his opponents did not have the required two-thirds support in the legislature to remove the judges.[72]

"These were only temporary obstacles," Ted Ruger says, "for the election upcoming in August 1824 provided an immediate opportunity to strengthen the majority in favor of removing the judges."[73] The 1824 contest became perhaps the first general election in American history fought over who would decide constitutional cases and controversies. Signs at campaign events denounced the "three judicial tyrants" who invalidated the Commonwealth's debtor-relief laws.[74]

Opponents of the court won, securing 63% of the popular vote and electing their candidate for governor and a strong majority in both houses of the legislature.[75] But that did not suffice to remove the judges. Articles of address still fell short of the needed two-thirds support.[76]

The new legislature did not stop there. With the support of Governor Desha, the General Assembly dissolved the Court of Appeals and created a new "Supreme Court" in a late-night session on Christmas Eve 1824. Desha signed the bill on the House floor that night.[77] The new court came with a limitation on its power of judicial review, confining it to holding laws unconstitutional only when all four judges agreed. More important still was the chance to appoint new judges, men who could be counted on to resolve matters with deference to the legislature.[78]

The new state supreme court provoked an "immediate debate" over its "dubious constitutionality."[79] The Kentucky charter, then and now, does not provide a way for the legislature to change the high court. Although it permits the legislature "from time to time" to "erect and establish" lower courts,[80] it says nothing about authority to remove or change the high court. Supporters of the old court reminded everyone that Kentucky's constitution protected judges from removal unless two-thirds of both houses agreed on "cause" to do so.[81] Supporters of the new court responded that "law courts were no different from public grist mills, and if 'you build another mill that does not oblige you to employ in it the miller of the former one.' "[82]

The old Court of Appeals judges "refused to go quietly into constitutional exile."[83] They refused to recognize the dissolution, continuing to hear and decide cases for the 1825 term just as the new court did. That meant that in 1825, and then again in 1826, the Commonwealth had two supreme courts with two competing claims to the final judicial power of the state—and no process for resolving conflicts between them over state law. Each side accused the other of usurpation and each side "empanel[ed] [its] own grand juries in hospitable counties" to indict and censure the "wrong" court.[84] The more resourceful members of the Bluegrass bar, according to Ruger, saw a rare opportunity, "intrajurisdictional forum shopping" for a court of last resort.[85] Leave it to Kentucky, home in later years to some of the best college basketball in the country, to license its attorneys to take their cases to both state high courts, sometimes even in the same case, giving the two-shots option provided by state constitutions a meaning all its own.[86]

By 1825, the "new court" party's actions triggered a backlash. Many voters came to the defense of the old Court of Appeals, and the August 1825 election for the General Assembly shifted the balance of power back to the old-court party. But while old-court supporters now held a legislative majority, Governor Desha, with three years left on his term, could veto any attempt to restore the Court of Appeals. The fight between the parties over the competing supreme courts did not end until the 1826 election. At that point, the voters handed a veto-proof majority to the "old court" party, which restored the old Court of Appeals.[87]

National figures followed the controversy. Most supported the old-court judges. Chief Justice John Marshall, whose family had substantial landholdings in Kentucky, reported to his cousin that he "rejoiced a good deal at the triumph" of the "old court" party, which he believed to be on the side of "sound constitutional principles."[88] John Quincy Adams, Henry Clay, and Abraham Lincoln all said much the same thing, as did James Madison, though he chose his words more carefully. Thomas Jefferson, whose name new-court supporters invoked to create a more deferential form of judicial review, declined to weigh in. And the populist Andrew Jackson, then the governor of neighboring Tennessee, lamented the political divisions in Kentucky but otherwise did not take sides. Jackson later included two prominent new-court advocates in his cabinet, reflecting a shared anti-establishment political vision if not actual support for the court reorganization.[89]

While there is nothing old hat about the Kentucky Courts Controversy, it resolved around two familiar questions: Do the courts have the final say over constitutional rulings? And who selects the judges? By effectively putting the original judges on the ballot, Kentucky answered "the People" to both, paving the way for more debates about judicial review and judicial selection in other places.

Judicial Elections

Within six years of the end of the Kentucky controversy, one state would change its constitution to become the first to select judges for its high court based on direct elections. And within twenty years, a large group of states would begin to go down the same road. Today, roughly 90% of all state judges in the United States—spread across the thirty-eight states that elect all judges and several other states that elect some of their judges—must run in an election to obtain or retain a seat on the bench.[90] Judicial elections, perhaps more than any other feature of American government, have become a fixed and salient feature of the American judicial system. Virtually no other country uses them.[91] Then again, no other country embraces judicial review the way Americans have.

States began to experiment with judicial elections in the 1810s, when the states of Georgia and Indiana chose to elect some lower court judges.[92] In 1832, Mississippi became the first state to elect the members of its highest court through a constitutional convention that instituted judicial elections for all state court judges.[93] A swell of constitutional amendments followed in the 1840s and 1850s, led by New York's decision to vote for judges and leading to popular votes elsewhere to make elections the favored method for choosing state judges.

A few trends stand out. One is regional preferences. The original thirteen Atlantic states, excluding New York and Pennsylvania, do not use judicial elections.[94] Another is that all states admitted to the Union after 1789, save Maine (part of Massachusetts until 1821), adopted judicial elections of some sort. And most of the new states did so for all courts. A third is that all states that entered the Union between 1846 (when New York adopted judicial elections) and 1959 (when Alaska became the forty-ninth state) did so with constitutions that provided for judicial elections of one kind or another.[95] That 113-year run ended in 1959 when Hawaii's constitution provided that the governor would appoint judges with the advice and consent of the Senate.[96] A fourth trend, begun in the Progressive era, is the transition in many states to non-partisan elections for judges, usually indicated by the judges not running in connection with a political party and without the name of the party on their ballot identification. Roughly 20% of appellate judges (and 40% of trial judges) run in non-partisan elections.[97] Roughly 33% of appellate judges (and almost 40% of trial judges) run in partisan elections for their first terms.[98] The last key trend is the move toward retention elections after an initial appointment, started in the 1940s and continued to the present. Roughly twenty states now use retention elections—with just that judge on the ballot—to decide whether a judge, often appointed by a governor, should be retained.[99]

Mississippi

Mississippi became the first state to elect judges, including the justices of its supreme court, in 1832. More than a decade before New York's decision to hold judicial elections, Mississippi's early adoption of the practice did not sit well in all quarters at the outset. "Our constitution," lamented one former supreme court justice, "is the subject of ridicule in all the States where it is known. It is referred to as a full definition of mobocracy."[100] Other states that adopted judicial elections over the next twenty-five years apparently disagreed. Although New York is often cited as the wellspring of enthusiasm for judicial elections, Caleb Nelson observes that "other [states'] conventions tended to rely on Mississippi's experience as much as New York's."[101]

In the 1820s and 1830s, Mississippi was part of the Democratic heartland. Along with Alabama, Georgia, and Tennessee, the state firmly supported Andrew Jackson in successive presidential elections. Learned Hand, who blamed "the full tide of Jacksonian democracy" for the adoption of judicial elections in his native New York, chalked up Mississippi's reform to "a burst of democratic enthusiasm" in the Jacksonian tradition.[102] But the Magnolia State began putting its judges up for popular vote almost two decades before most of its neighbors began to do the same. Only Georgia, which had elected its inferior court judges since 1812 and began electing its superior court judges in 1835, had taken (timid) steps down this path. Even then, Georgia's 1835 constitutional amendment authorized *the legislature* to appoint judges to its high court.[103] "Democratic ideology and frontier culture were significant in Mississippi's adoption of judicial elections," according to Jed Shugerman, "but they were not decisive."[104]

Mississippi's turn to judicial elections grows in part out of a struggle between rural populists and the state's "aristocrats" from the area around Natchez, then the capital and a commercial center.[105] "The aristocrats of Natchez had dominated the state through their disproportionate representation under the 1817 constitution, and like good aristocrats, they monopolized the judicial appointment process."[106] Through the 1820s, as the Jacksonian movement won egalitarian concessions from the elites in other southern states, the Natchez elite held firm and even pushed back. "Nothing represented the power of the Natchez old guard and its overreach better than the courts."[107]

In 1818 and 1820, the Mississippi Supreme Court issued a pair of "remarkable" decisions that "undercut slavery's legal status" in the state.[108] In *Harry v. Decker and Hopkins*, the court declared that "slaves within the Northwest Territory became free men" based on the Northwest Ordinance and could "assert their legal freedom in the courts of this state."[109] Two years later, in *Mississippi v. Jones*, the court held that masters had a legal duty to feed and clothe slaves.[110] The two decisions suggested to some that "elite legal culture" in Natchez was generally "out of touch" with slaveholders throughout the rest of the state.[111]

The court's 1824 decision to invalidate a popular debtor-relief law provoked a stronger reaction. In *Cochrane v. Kitchens*, the Mississippi Supreme Court held that the law, which delayed enforcement of judgments in favor of a creditor for one year and limited sheriffs' collection powers, violated state and federal constitutional guarantees. "More stunning was the court's decision to fine a sheriff $100 for enforcing the statute."[112] Lawmakers "were incensed" and summoned the justices to explain themselves before the legislature,[113] demanding that they "show cause" as to "why they should not be removed from office."[114] "The House of Representatives," reports Shugerman, "questioned whether the court had the power of judicial review at all."[115] It was not lost on Mississippians that the case paralleled the Kentucky and Rhode Island court controversies. "Are we not gradually approaching to a Kentucky anarchy," one newspaper lamented.[116]

While Mississippi avoided the chaos that engulfed Kentucky, it did not avoid calls for judicial reform by populist Democrats. In 1828, backwoods legislators added a new seat to the state supreme court, intending the new justice to "represent the northern rural region" of the state. To their disappointment, "the legislature found a way, yet again, to appoint a Natchez lawyer for a rural judicial district."[117] The Natchez elite maintained control, with aristocrats holding onto four of five high court seats in 1831.

These developments primed the people for change. "In August 1831, the voters approved [a] call for a [constitutional] convention by a vote of almost four to one."[118] Representing the reforming spirit was a faction of populists called the "Whole Hogs,"[119] and judicial reform, especially judicial elections, was a "hot topic" at the convention.[120] The Natchez aristocrats argued for the status quo, while the "Whole Hogs" favored elections across the board, a first for any state. A smaller faction, the "Half Hogs," urged a middle course of following Georgia's and Indiana's lead by electing judges only to the lower courts.[121] The

"Whole Hogs" won when the convention approved judicial elections for all judges by a 26 to 18 vote of the delegates.[122] Through the convention, the state removed sitting judges from office and provided that the supreme court's justices would be elected by district rather than by statewide votes. Two of the districts were to be predominantly rural, thus guaranteeing a voice to long-ignored rural voters.[123]

Much as Mississippi's adoption of judicial elections seemed to be a victory for Jacksonian democracy, this "trailblazing" victory by the "Whole Hogs" came with two twists.[124] The convention delegates' enthusiasm for democracy had limits. As Caleb Nelson observes and Jed Shugerman concurs, "The same delegates who had argued passionately for the right of the people to elect their judges refused to allow the people to vote on the new constitution, despite the spirited objections of those who had favored appointment."[125] On top of that, the delegates' attempts to gerrymander the supreme court judicial districts did not produce the anticipated results. "Two of the three members of the nation's first elected court of last resort were Whigs, at least one of whom was 'strongly opposed to an elective judiciary.' The third, though a Jacksonian, also opposed the elective system."[126] To this day, the people of Mississippi continue to elect their state court judges.

Pennsylvania

With one foot planted in the East and one in the West during the first half of the nineteenth century, Pennsylvania offers a good example of a state that migrated from appointments to elections for its judges. From independence through the advent of judicial elections, Pennsylvania's approach to judicial selection and tenure followed accordion-like national trends.[127] The state's first constitution, in 1776, vested appointment of judges in its president, whom the legislature appointed annually, and his council.[128] Judges served seven-year terms and could be removed "for misbehavior at any time by the general assembly."[129] Over the 1780s and 1790s, attitudes toward legislative dominance changed, and so did the Pennsylvania Constitution. The 1790 charter gave judges tenure during good behavior, required a two-thirds majority of both houses of the legislature and "reasonable cause" to remove judges by address, and protected them from the diminution of their salaries while in office.[130] It also vested power to appoint judges in a popularly elected governor alone.[131]

In the 1800s, sentiment started to swing in the other direction. Jeffersonian Republicans criticized the state's judiciary "as a barrier to legitimate democratic and egalitarian aspirations within the state."[132] By 1801, commentators criticized the tenure during good behavior granted to judges just over a decade earlier. A leading reformist newspaper questioned "why judges and justices of the peace should be more independent of the control of a free people, than those who have the formation and execution of the laws entrusted to them."[133] Why, it asked, did the sort of good behavior tenure given to English judges "independent of the *king* justif[y] the making of [American judges] independent of the people"?[134]

In 1838, Pennsylvania abolished tenure during good behavior for judges and reinstituted fixed terms—fifteen years for justices of the supreme court.[135] The reform subjected courts to regular review, and one might have expected influence, by the governor and the state senate, whose concurrent approval was needed to appoint a judge. Yet the opposite appears to have happened as judicial review in Pennsylvania grew in the 1840s. Before 1840, the Pennsylvania Supreme Court had held a state law to be unconstitutional only once. In the decade that followed, it did so in seven cases, one of the highest rates of judicial invalidation of statutes in the country.[136]

Local sentiment turned against control of the judiciary by the political branches in the late 1840s. Commentators and politicians pushed for judicial elections as the best guarantee of judicial independence. The concern, Shugerman notes, was bipartisan, at least in a hypocritical sense: "When a Democrat was governor, Whig newspapers called for judicial elections so that judges would have more power and independence to check him. Then, as soon as the Democratic governor . . . was replaced by a Whig, Democratic newspapers adopted the same argument."[137] But there were some principled arguments for judicial elections, too. "Election always has and always will give us better men and better officers than appointment—more independent men," said one representative.[138] Said another observer: "When the Judges derive their authority immediately from the people, and can take an appeal to the same paramount power, the fear of removal . . . for resisting Legislative usurpations will no longer exist."[139]

The Keystone State also offers a good example of evolving perspectives about judicial review by one judge, John Bannister Gibson, during these years. Gibson was not a slouch. Roscoe Pound ranked him as one of the top ten federal or state judges in American history.[140] His career on the Pennsylvania Supreme Court captures what looks like a paradox to modern eyes: that the rise of judicial elections coincided with a rise in judicial review. Justice Gibson wrote an influential dissent against judicial review in *Eakin v. Raub* (1825), then ran on a record of favoring judicial review when Pennsylvania adopted judicial elections. If the people began electing judges on the strength of a Jacksonian impulse to restrain judges through closer popular supervision, why didn't judges back off from declaring legislative acts unconstitutional? And why did supposedly populist judges run on platforms of counter-majoritarian review?

Justice Gibson's career highlights the give and take. He joined the Pennsylvania Supreme Court as an associate justice in 1816 at the age of thirty-six and served for thirty-seven years until his death in 1853. He was the chief justice for twenty-four years. In 1825, nine years into his service on the bench, Justice Gibson questioned whether judges should oversee the judgments of the political branches: "The constitution of Pennsylvania contains no express grant of political powers to the judiciary. But to establish a grant by implication, the constitution is said to be a law of superior obligation; and consequently, that if it were to come into collision with an act of the legislature the latter would have to give way; this is conceded. But it is a fallacy to suppose that they can come into collision *before the judiciary*."[141] The "provisions of a constitution are to be carried into effect immediately by the legislature," Gibson explained, and they do not furnish any rule for *judges* to apply in individual cases.[142] "If the judiciary will inquire into anything beside the form of enactment, where shall it stop? There must be some point of limitation to such an inquiry; for no one will pretend, that a judge would be justifiable in calling for the election returns, or scrutinizing the qualifications of those who composed the legislature."[143]

Gibson, says William Nelson, saw "no basis for courts to question political decisions made by the people; for him, judicial review denied '*a postulate* in the theory of our government, and the very basis of the superstructure, that the people are wise, virtuous, and competent to manage their own affairs.' "[144] That view, however deep its support at the beginning, lost currency in the 1830s and 1840s, and "even Judge Gibson felt compelled by 1845 to recant his former views."[145] " 'Experience [had] prove[d]' to Gibson," Nelson says, "that the constitution was 'thoughtlessly but habitually violated,' " and judges had a role to play in fixing the problem.[146] As the state and times changed, so did Justice Gibson.

Through these changes, however, Gibson remained resolutely anti-populist. Gibson "strongly opposed" the state's turn to judicial elections,[147] and yet he narrowly won a spot on the party ticket. Said a biographer: "In one sense the nomination was a rebuke to himself. He had seldom lost an opportunity to express his want of confidence in popular action, and his disapprobation of every movement designed to enlarge the boundaries of popular power."[148] Apparently a poor retail politician and with little party support despite his long tenure on the court, he "rode the party machine to victory" without doing any campaigning.[149] His eventual views in favor of judicial review, premised on a counter-majoritarian distrust for elected officials, only became stronger after he took his seat on the now-elected court in 1851.[150]

Modern Judicial Selection Methods and Tenure Provisions

While nearly 90% of today's state court judges must run for election, not all judicial election systems operate in the same way, and the other 10% use a range of appointment and tenure approaches. Variation in tenure provisions also is a constant. Today, state court judges might run in partisan or non-partisan elections, run for election to obtain a seat on the bench in the first place, or stand only in an up-or-down retention election. Some states, like the early judicial-election pioneers at the turn of the nineteenth century, hold popular elections only for inferior courts and appoint judges and justices to higher courts.

Twelve states don't elect judges at all. Some of them allow just the governor to appoint, and the legislature to confirm, jurists; others use nominating commissions before the governor makes a selection, and still others combine two or more of these approaches. Ten of the twelve non-election states are from the East Coast. Appendix A categorizes the selection systems and tenure provisions in all fifty states.

Just one state, Rhode Island, has a selection and tenure system similar to the one created by the US Constitution. In each system, the executive branch nominates the individual, the legislature has a say in confirming the judge, and the judge has no age or length-of-service restrictions. There are two differences. In Rhode Island, a nine-member nominating commission submits three to five names from which the governor may make the selection. And in Rhode Island, both houses of the legislature must approve the nominee. All of this makes the tenure provisions for the largest and smallest American governments the same—and their selection methods largely comparable. Choices in selection and tenure provisions apparently do not correlate with scope of jurisdiction. Thanks to *Trevett v. Weeden*, it appears, federal judges have always had life tenure, and Rhode Island's judges have gone from having the least job security in the states to the most.

With so much variation in the selection process, it should startle no one that controversies over judicial selections present in many forms. At the federal level over the last three decades, it is the rare appellate judicial nominee, and the non-existent US Supreme Court nominee, who gathers consensus support. Paul Freund reminds us that selection battles over US Supreme Court Justices have been with us from the beginning.[151] Pick any era of American history, and you will find confirmation or appointment fights triggered by an assortment of reasons: party politics, petty inter-personal tensions, political payback, regional priorities, or ideology.[152] The same has been true at the state level.[153]

Modern selection fights nonetheless seem to differ in kind, not just degree. Maybe it's a function of the information age. Or televised confirmation hearings. Or the prominence of the courts in resolving many polarizing policy disputes. President Franklin Roosevelt, true enough, fought the Court and threatened to increase its size in the 1930s. And President Nixon, true also, ran his 1968 election in part as a protest against the Warren Court's criminal procedure rulings.[154] But 1987 set a new standard. Just the year before, Justice Scalia had won confirmation by a 98–0 vote. The same would not be true for Judge Bork, who lost by a 42–58 vote. More significantly, the personal nature of the attacks and the wide number of interest groups involved in them seemed to create a new paradigm of judicial selection fights, one that has lingered, sometimes intensified, since then and does not seem to be on the wane.

Less notably, but no less noteworthy, the states have had their share of modern political fights over judges. Even retention elections, considered the least political way of permitting the people to have a direct say in selecting their judges, have generated intense political fights. Start with a trio of retention elections for the California Supreme Court in 1986, in which the people voted not to retain all three justices. It occurred one year before the Bork fight and was no less intense, perhaps suggesting *it* paved the way for the federal fight the next year. Fairly or unfairly, Chief Justice Rose Bird has long been the historical face of this dispute, even though two other justices on the court, Joseph Grodin and Cruz Reynoso, also lost their retention bids that year. Before 1986, no appellate judge in California had lost a retention election.

Governor Jerry Brown appointed Rose Bird to be chief justice in 1977, making her the first woman to sit on the California Supreme Court.[155] At forty, she was young and had not been a judge before.[156] It did not help her cause that one of the prominent liberals on the court thought *he* should have become the chief justice. "Associate Justice Stanley Mosk still seethed from being passed over as chief justice, and he let Bird know immediately where he stood. 'I certainly cannot blame you for being here,' he told her by way of welcome, 'but I blame Jerry Brown for putting you here.' "[157]

Her first retention election, in 1978, was close. She won just 52% approval, "the smallest margin" of any California supreme court justice before.[158] By 1986, she had a record that was easy to pillory. The key statistic was that, in sixty-one capital convictions that had come before the court, she had yet to affirm a single one and often relied on the California Constitution in overturning the convictions or sentences. She not only appeared to favor just one side in criminal cases, but civil plaintiffs also "tended to fare exceedingly well on her watch,"[159] and a 1982 decision on a gerrymandering case was seen as blatantly partisan.[160] "Thus was born an alliance among Republican politicians, business leaders, law-and-order activists, and campaign consultants" against her and her colleagues.[161] Butcher-Forde, "an Orange County consulting firm, organized and ran the campaign" against her and used plenty of television advertisements in the process.[162] Conservative politicians and interest groups, including crime-victim groups, led the opposition, but even some Democrats quietly hoped that Bird would resign from office.[163] The *LA Times* estimated that the opposition spent over $10 million to defeat her.[164] She lost by a 2–1 margin.[165]

Whether Bird's defeat amounted to a referendum on specific issues (the death penalty or criminal law or business disputes) or as a more general verdict about the liberal tendencies of the court during her nine-year tenure, one reality could not be denied. The people of California wanted change. Retention elections gave them that option, and they exercised it. With three vacancies and a Republican governor in 1987, a course correction followed, and the California Supreme Court became less likely to innovate new rights under the state or federal constitutions. During that era, the people of California not only altered the composition of their high court in response to some of its decisions; they also chose to limit its power to innovate rights under the California Constitution. In 1982, the state's constitution was changed to prohibit the high court from innovating criminal procedure rights that went beyond what the US Constitution already protected.[166]

Iowa saw a similar story unfold in 2010. Three members of the Iowa Supreme Court faced and lost retention elections that turned on one issue. The issue was same-sex marriage, and the case was *Varnum v. Brien*.[167] On April 3, 2009, the Iowa Supreme Court unanimously upheld marriage equality under the Iowa Constitution. It was the first unanimous decision on the issue from a state high court, and it came from the heartland, showing that these claims did not resonate exclusively on the American coasts. The reasoning of the decision also had Iowa roots. The Iowa Supreme Court invoked its first published decision, one issued seventeen years before *Dred Scott* and eighty-six years before *Plessy*, that had refused to treat a human being as property and had refused to permit separate-but-equal laws under the Iowa Constitution.[168] And it invoked the state's decision in 1869 to become the first state in the Union to permit women to practice law, three years before the US Supreme Court allowed Illinois *to refuse* to do the same.[169]

Three of the seven justices, as it happens, faced retention elections one year later in 2010. Voter turnout jumped from a typical mid-60%

level for retention elections to 88%.[170] To one follower of judicial retention elections,[171] this was "an unprecedented increase. There's been nothing like it in the history of judicial retention elections in any state."[172]

It's not clear what the voters were for, whether to reject marriage equality or to reject the process for creating it. "We heard a lot of 'It may have been the "right" decision based on the Constitution, but I just don't like it. So I voted them out.' "[173]

Iowa adopted the "Missouri Plan" for placing judges on the bench in 1962. Under the system, a panel of fifteen individuals—seven selected by the governor, seven by the bar association, and one sitting state supreme court justice—interviews potential candidates for a nomination. The panel chooses three finalists, and the governor selects one of them for the position. Supreme court justices go on the ballot at the first general election after their selection and every eight years after that. Before 2010, retention elections in Iowa had generated little controversy. Only four lower-court judges had ever lost a retention vote, each time in the context of allegations of malfeasance. No supreme court justice had ever lost a retention election.[174]

The three justices on the retention ballot were Chief Justice Marsha Ternus, Justice Michael Streit, and Justice David Baker. A poll by the bar association "found that more than 80 percent of the membership approved of Streit's and Baker's performance and more than 70 percent were positive about Ternus."[175] Over $1 million was spent on the campaign against them, a lot of it from outside the state.[176]

The three justices chose not to campaign. They opted not to answer charges of judicial activism or to discuss the *Varnum* case in the media. " 'My view of the court,' Ternus said years later, 'is it should not be involved in politics and its decisions should not be based on politics. I simply believed we shouldn't try to influence politics by manipulating how the courts work. That's not our concern.' "[177] It would have been legal to campaign, but Baker later said that "had we chosen to form campaigns, we would have tacitly admitted that we were what we claimed not to be—politicians."[178]

The three justices each won just 46% of the vote.[179] They were not retained as a result, allowing the governor to select three new justices. The new Iowa Supreme Court, however, has not revisited the marriage

decision since then. Nor have the people. Having changed the composition of its high court in response to one of its decisions, the people
of Iowa did not proceed to change the decision. They did not amend
the Iowa Constitution to prohibit same-sex marriage. While just 51%
of the electorate must support an amendment to the constitution, any
proposed amendment may go on the ballot only after the support of
two successive General Assemblies. At the next retention election in
2016, only one justice from the *Varnum* decision was up for retention,
Justice David Wiggins, and the voters retained him with a 55% vote.[180]

Selection Methods, Tenure Provisions, and Judicial Review

There is no minoritarian way to select judges in a democratic republic.
But the longer a given tenure provision for a state's judges, the less majoritarian the underlying selection process becomes over time.

When the colonies broke from Great Britain, they left a system in
which officials, politically unaccountable to the people, selected their
judges. In declining to embrace that system for themselves, the new
states all required judicial selections to run through a majoritarian process at some point. Whether its selection was by elected presidents or
governors and confirmation by elected legislators, selection through
partisan elections, or selection and retention through a combination of
the two, there is no way around giving the people some voice in who
the judges in this country are. Unless one is nostalgic for hereditary
positions or royal prerogatives, we should be grateful. And that is so
even if one laments the current climate surrounding judicial selections
for the state and federal courts.

One other truth cannot be denied. The more power judges exercise,
the more the people will want a say in who they are. The key power
delegated to judges is judicial review, particularly at the federal level
because the US Constitution is nearly impossible to amend and federal judges have life tenure. If the people may not overrule the Court
and if they may not remove justices from the Court, they have just one
option: focusing any preferences for the Court on the next nomination and confirmation. Think of the process as trying to channel the
Colorado River through a backyard rivulet. The system is not designed
to handle that much pressure.

Is there anything about state and federal judicial selection methods that might help to alleviate this pressure when it comes to how the two court systems exercise judicial review, usually the centerpiece of these political fights?

First, to see how the rise of judicial elections plays into modern debates about judicial review, it's worth going back to the explanations for judicial elections and their growth. A common explanation associates the election of judges with Jacksonian populism. Election of judges under this view became a natural "extension of the prevailing theory of democracy" that "seemed to require the popular election of all possible officers of government."[181] But that does not account for all of the reasons legislators and delegates in the state constitutional conventions gave for the policy: concerns over legislative corruption; partisan revenge; the need to insulate judges from the influence of legislators and governors.

Caleb Nelson adds a nuanced perspective. Judicial elections were indeed "part and parcel of the larger democratic movement," he writes, "but the reformers were hardly simple-minded democrats."[182] To grasp all of what these reforms meant, you need to look not only at the relationship of judges to democratic politics but also to the other branches of government. "Those who supported the elective system in the state conventions aimed to strengthen the judiciary at the expense of the legislatures," says Nelson, even as "other reforms were curtailing the independent powers of judges themselves, in a concerted effort to rein in the power of all officials to act independently of the people."[183] The aim was to "weaken officialdom as a whole,"[184] not to weaken or strengthen any one branch or to recalibrate the balance of official power. This was not so much an invention of Andrew Jackson or his party as it was an impulse that had "its intellectual roots in the proud philosophical traditions of the Founding," which "fear[ed] that irresponsible power threatened the people's liberty."[185]

Jed Shugerman sees elections as an attempt to secure judicial independence. They were designed to ensure "free[dom] from political pressure and [the ability] to rely upon their own legal interpretations"— hence "independence from elected branches of government, and independence from party patronage machines and special interests, as well as independence from public opinion."[186] Judicial elections were needed "to rescue the courts from political capture and to empower a more independent judiciary to prevent further abuses of power and economic crises."[187] In this way, judicial elections had populist and structural components. Change proponents from each of the political parties "turned to judicial elections as part of a broader constitutional revolution against legislative power and in favor of limited government."[188] The "counterintuitive" result of having the same people elect governors, legislators, and judges was a "developing notion that judges had a unique and separate role in government."[189]

To Kermit Hall, judicial elections amounted to a reform led by lawyers and designed to strengthen the courts as a steely bulwark against corruption and to remove politics from the judiciary. Sticking with an appointment system "denied the judiciary its proper claim for support from the sovereign people" and left judges vulnerable to criticism that they were " 'little aristocrats' who 'legislated judicially despite the wishes of the people.' "[190] Direct elections avoided that problem. Hall thus suggests that judicial elections were a "thoughtful response by constitutional moderates in the legal profession to ensure that state judges would command more rather than less power and prestige."[191]

No one needs to pick sides when it comes to these helpful assessments of the rise of judicial elections. What matters for present purposes is their shared perspectives. Electing judges at a minimum served several lasting goals. It created independence from the appointing branches. It gave the people a direct rather than indirect voice in who their judges are. It had the potential to give each judge a mandate directly from the people. And it advanced the goals of Jacksonian democracy *and* the Revolution—distrust of government, whatever the branch, whatever the function.

Second, most observers see a chasm between the initial reasons for electing judges (more judicial independence) and what has happened with elected judges today (less judicial independence). But in the initial years, that was not the case. As shown, proponents of judicial elections were vindicated. A rise in judicial elections led to a rise in judicial review, what seemed to be more judicial independence from the other branches of government and more judicial willingness to act as independent agents of the people in construing their state constitutions.[192]

But in the longer term, the picture is more complicated, perhaps appropriately so. Modern studies suggest that judicial elections have led to less judicial review, not more. In one study, Neal Devins found that judges who must run for election tend to vote with public opinion in what he terms "high salience" cases, meaning they tend to vote to uphold state laws or actions by elected government officials. Not in all cases, however. A good counterexample from Devins's article involves eminent domain cases.[193] Other studies have found that judges running for re-election tend to be tougher on criminal defendants, even in "liberal" jurisdictions.[194] Another study suggests that judges up for re-appointment (by governors or by legislatures) tend to be more deferential to the re-appointing body—call it the *Trevett v. Weeden* effect.[195] Instead of promoting judicial review, judicial elections have done the opposite over the long term, at least as compared to the states where an appointment system exists and as compared to the federally appointed judges.

There is one way in which the availability of judicial elections has been consistent with the explanation for the innovation. It has allowed the people in some states to push back when the courts became too independent—too independent from the people, that is. The division-of-powers considerations that led to judicial elections sometimes have reined in judicial power. That's the pesky lesson of the California and Iowa backlashes.

After the California Supreme Court refused to enforce the death penalty, held that rape did not count as a "great bodily injury" under sentencing law, invalidated the state's "use a gun, go to prison" law, required the state to pay for abortions, and held landlords strictly liable for defects and dangers on their properties,[196] the people called for change, as American a response as there is. Sure, these responses irk the supporters of the California Supreme Court's decisions and lead to complaints that future judicial decisions will lose their counter-majoritarian force. But that fails to account for whether the supporters of these decisions had earned and thus deserved these victories or whether they amounted to loading the deck in the first place. There was no tradition of refusing to retain judges in California before these elections. It took a lot to earn the people's distrust. Having gotten too far ahead of the people, or at a minimum having failed satisfactorily to explain to them why these interpretations of their state constitutions were right, they got what American voters have a long history of dishing out for all branches of government: thumbs-down votes. What makes judges think they should be immune? That certainly was not part of the conversation during the selection debates over the first seventy-five years of our history.

Iowa concerned one issue and was more transitory. The people chose not to retain three justices of the Iowa Supreme Court one year after the court invalidated its same-sex marriage ban under the Iowa Constitution. Before that election, no justice had ever lost a retention vote in the state.[197] But it seemed to be a one-time, one-issue vote, and a vote that did not change the underlying decision. Just as norms shifted across the country about marriage equality, they shifted in Iowa, and the issue had no traction in the next election—not even with respect to the author of the opinion when he faced a retention election in 2016.[198]

Third, one way to consider the difference between judicial appointments and judicial elections is to compare the performance of the state and federal systems when it comes to judicial review. Convention suggests that the comparison does not cast a flattering light on the state judiciary in general or on judicial elections in particular. But I wonder. I am especially skeptical of that verdict if the goal of any court system is to ensure that over time it respects the people and the constitutions they ratified. Ask yourself which system—the federal or state courts— has done a more faithful job honoring the language of the constitutions they interpret. If I were to put each provision of the US Constitution on the left side of a page and the US Supreme Court's interpretation of it on the right, I am confident that many provisions by now have become unrecognizable. Taking cues from the children's game of telephone, many federal judicial innovations show a remarkable transformation from the language of a guarantee into one interpretation after another that eventually has little connection to the initial words of the guarantee. No doubt, the states have similar telephone-game examples of their own but they appear to be episodic and occasional, not routine. The norm in the state courts tends to be a greater correlation between language and interpretation.[199] And I suspect that, if state courts ignore that tradition in the future, as the California Supreme Court did during the decade or so before 1986, the people will tend to replace the judges and change the constitution to prohibit future like-minded innovations. I know of no study that says the opposite. If fidelity to the people through the words they chose to put in their constitutions is the test, the state courts by and large have passed it and judicial elections have not gotten in the way.

Maybe electoral accountability has even helped in some ways. Whether state judges have long or short terms of office, whether they face retention or adversary elections, it may not be the worst thing for them to remember that they serve someone beyond their own value systems. At a minimum, elections foster judicial humility. On whose behalf, it's well to remember and sometimes easy to forget, are we judges interpreting the constitution? Former California Supreme Court Justice Otto Kaus captured part of the dilemma. Acknowledging the temptation for a judge to think about politically sensitive cases before retention elections, he said, "You cannot forget the fact that you have a crocodile in your bathtub. You keep wondering whether you're letting yourself be influenced, and you do not know. You do not know yourself that well."[200] But there are two ways, not just one, in which elected judges may not know themselves that well, whether it's subconsciously steering decisions toward politically acceptable outcomes for the next election *or* in subconsciously steering decisions toward their policy preferences. That leaves two crocodiles in every elected judge's bathtub. If the judge cannot ignore one, he probably cannot ignore the other. Because the two considerations often push in opposite directions when it comes to judicial review, it may be that they help to balance each other out, making judicial elections more helpful than hurtful.[201]

Fourth, let me shift to a perspective on judicial review that applies to elected and appointed judges. Imagine asking a foreign lawyer, who knows nothing about American law, to write two papers about how American judicial review works.

In preparing the first paper, the visitor may consult just two sources: confirmation hearings for US Supreme Court justices and campaign speeches by state court judges running for office. That's an easy paper to write. The visitor would notice the same thing being said over and over. "The judge's duty is to interpret the law, not to make it." "Judges are not policy makers. They must interpret the law as it is, not as they wish it to be." Any nominee on record who disagrees with this modest view of the judge—say, by supporting judicial authority to invent new rights not mentioned in the Constitution—will run into unrelenting criticism during the hearing or the next election. Few successful candidates for a judgeship get through the confirmation or election gauntlet by saying they have authority to identify new constitutional rights to account for shifting policy preferences in American society as they perceive them.[202] From this isolated set of sources, the lesson would be clear: Formalism triumphed. And that, I suspect, is just what our visitor would conclude. It looks like a legal world in which originalism and textualism prevailed. With the judiciary as indeed the least dangerous branch, with no power of purse or sword, the people have to look to their legislatures (or constitutional amendments) for new rights or new laws to account for new societal norms.

Now ask a second foreign lawyer to answer the same question. In this paper, however, she must use another source of evidence about how judicial review works, just the *US Reports* and the *State Supreme Court Reporters*. That assuredly would lead to a different answer. The lawyer would report that some of the time formal methods of interpretation win the day, and some of the time they do not. Whatever we judges say about judicial review, there are many appellate cases showing that what we do sometimes differs considerably from what we say we are doing. That's because there are indeed many decisions that creatively interpret constitutional guarantees in ways that account for shifting societal values and show that judges often treat the meaning of these guarantees as more fluid than fixed.

Why such different answers to the same question? What do the differences reveal? The first answer shows that there is a politically acceptable norm in America for describing what judges do. It's the norm first taught to generations of Americans in middle school civics and that prevails to this day. We judges interpret law. We don't make it. And we don't enforce it. That's for the (more) politically accountable branches. That's why judges in the most intense political environment they will ever see—a confirmation hearing or an election—incline toward this answer.

That does not mean judges prevaricate when they speak in confirmation hearings or give speeches on the campaign trail. For my money, they are saying what they genuinely believe, that judges strive to follow the law where it leads. That my observation of judges (and them of me) perhaps does not always match that perspective shows something else. Hard cases make it difficult to know exactly where these lines are. And judges being people, they err in the practice of doing what they say even if they rarely err in saying what they are doing. There's a human tendency, particularly for attuned and acute minds, to say what an audience wants to hear. Interpretation is sufficiently complex that no one should be surprised when that impulse takes over.

Because interpretation of constitutions often is complex, another human tendency helps to explain the different answers. When a judge has a predisposed, even highly educated, will about how to address a policy problem, there's often a way to follow that instinct in identifying rights written in general terms and, most tempting of all, in non-enumerated terms. An intractable problem with judicial review does not turn on methods of interpretation; it turns on the human temptation to think that what is good is legally required. That problem predates constitutions, and Brutus warned us about it at the outset in the *Anti-Federalist Papers*.[203] Neither an appointment system nor an election system nor a life-tenure system has cured it or likely can cure it.

Fifth, if most judges are roughly the same—they try to work within the lines of their limited authority in construing a constitution but do not always do so—that becomes a compelling reason for placing state court judges and state constitutions on the front lines of judicial innovation. The people in the states have more room to respond to inventive rulings if the courts get too far ahead of the people. They can choose not to re-elect them or they can readily amend their constitution. In every state in the country, it is easier for the people to amend their constitution than at the federal level, and in every state in the country, save lookalike Rhode Island, it is easier to alter the composition of the courts than at the federal level.

In this context, only someone who embraces judicial gerrymandering could say that the federal courts should be on the front lines of judicial innovation. That's especially true for unenumerated rights. If I had my way, we would not have such do-it-yourself judicial innovations. Then again, if I had my way, our judicial visitor would see no difference between what we judges say we do and what we do. In a world in which some judicial invention is our destiny, it makes abundant sense to have that innovation done first where it is least dislocating (one state at a time), where it can be most easily corrected (state elections or state amendments) and where trial and error can produce the best unenumerated rights (fifty state court systems of trial and error). Only then, only after time has allowed the people and courts to see how these experiments unfold, would the US Supreme Court recognize new unenumerated rights, if such rights there must be.

Sixth, having perhaps been unfair to judges about what we say we do, let me take seriously whether elected judges should view interpretation differently from appointed judges. Speaking strictly for me, I doubt I would see constitutional interpretation differently as a state court judge. Whether adopted at the state or federal level, words in a constitution are still words. They have meaning. And that meaning is fixed, which is why we bother to put laws in writing in the first place. It makes no difference, through it all, whether those words govern a large or small jurisdiction. Else, California and Delaware judges would read the same words differently. Absent a clear indication in the history or language, I doubt that state or federal judges, elected or unelected judges, big-jurisdiction or small-jurisdiction judges have a greater warrant to second-guess the handiwork of their co-branches of government. How at any rate could a method of selecting judges affect the meaning of constitutional language? But that's one perspective among many.

Others assess it differently. Some elected judges may see more room for flexibility with judicial review based on the reality that the people elected them, they have a direct mandate from them, and the people can throw them out or amend the state constitution in response to decisions they dislike. Those are fair explanations. One modest pushback is that an impetus for living constitutionalism does not exist in the states. In contrast to a federal constitution that is nigh impossible to amend, thus placing pressure on federal judges to update it, no such problem exists at the state level. The state constitutions, generally speaking, are easy to update, and there has been no comparable problem with amending them to keep up with the times.

There is one substantial way, however, in which elections should affect state court judges. It should make state judges *less likely* to imitate the interpretation of the US Constitution when they construe their own constitutions, one of many topics that the next chapter explores.

4

Are You a Territorial Judge
or a Territorial Lawyer?

DEBATES ABOUT JUDICIAL REVIEW began with the state courts, and the first sustained debates about how to select judges, by election or appointment, began there as well. The early judicial review decisions naturally arose in the first states, the thirteen royal colonies that gained independence in 1776.

This chapter looks at a later phase of state court history, one that necessarily concerns a different group of state courts but ultimately relates to all of them. Unlike the states that first entered the Union, most of the other states experienced a different pre-statehood status, usually as a territory of the United States. That status and the political experiences that went with it fed populist and distrust-of-government attitudes that fueled the growth of judicial elections,[1] and helped to lay the political groundwork for popular constitutional initiatives that began in the early 1900s. Just as judicial elections were primarily a phenomenon of the states that began as territories, so the same would be true of popular initiatives.[2]

At the same time that the territorial experiences of over three-fifths of our states re-enforced local innovations that did not migrate to the national constitution and were rarely adopted by the original states, these experiences seemed to have little effect on the attitudes of locally chosen judges, at least not in lasting ways. In most states today, Oregon one of a few trail-marking exceptions, many state judges start with the assumption that the meaning of their own constitution parallels the meaning of the US Constitution, even when the wording of the relevant guarantees differs and even when the language of the federal guarantee originated in a state constitution. Sized up against the territorial experiences of these same states, that's a puzzling contrast. Territorial judges, all federal appointees, were no more popular in the territories than colonial judges, all royal appointees, were in the colonies.

Once the states, whether former territories or colonies, obtained authority to select their own judges and write their own constitutions, one might have expected local judges to have fierce pride about the independent meaning of their state charters. That's not what happened over time. While state politics has long tended to be local, state judging tends to be national today, even in states that elect their judges. The meaning of our fifty-one constitutions has become surprisingly one-sized over time, a phenomenon that this chapter explores and criticizes. Hence the question: Are you a territorial judge or territorial lawyer? History and judicial elections suggest the answer should be No. But too often it is Yes.

The chapter closes by explaining how the state courts' independent interpretations of their constitutions has the potential to facilitate a dialogue with the federal courts in interpreting the US Constitution, whether with respect to generally worded rights or unenumerated rights. An accounting of American constitutional law in full could go a long way to improving judicial review in this country and to preserving the separation-of-powers and balance-of-powers considerations that originated it.

Territorial Governments

In one way, the territorial states came of age in circumstances different from those of the colonial states. As federal territories, the post-1789 states began as federal enclaves and ended as states within the same government. They were American from the outset.

In another way, their pre-statehood experiences echoed the experiences of the first thirteen states. Noblesse oblige went only so far in the British Empire. Parliament did not treat the residents of its colonies in the same way it treated British citizens, often failing to heed their complaints, always denying them a way to protect their interests: the right to vote. That of course was the central complaint that triggered the Revolution, a lack of representation of the American colonies in Parliament and "the long train of abuses and usurpations" that resulted.[3] A comparable problem arose in the American territories. Instead of colonies of the British Empire, they became territories of an American Empire—often ignored, often frustrated by a lack of representation in the national government, a lack of local authority over their own affairs, and a lack of local understanding by the federally appointed officials who ruled them.

It's true that not all states after 1789 started as territories. At least two were carved out of the first states. Think of Maine (from Massachusetts) and Kentucky (from Virginia). One arguably seceded from an initial state. Think West Virginia (from Virginia).[4]

A few states, notably Texas, Vermont, and California, were not territories at all before statehood. Though hardly twins separated at birth, Texas and Vermont began the same way, as independent republics with their own constitutions and governments. Vermont broke from New York on the eve of American independence, complaining of "neglect" by a far-away government whose authority Vermonters found it "extreme[ly] difficult" to accept.[5] Residents of the area chafed against the attitudes of foreign New York judges.[6] In Texas, persistent cultural insensitivities from a distant regime in Mexico City pushed American colonists to declare independence and to establish their own laws and government in the Lone Star State.[7] There, too, skepticism of foreign courts motivated the residents to seek independence.[8] California also started as a short-lived republic, at least in the minds of its residents.[9] The 1846 Bear Flag Revolt prompted a handful of residents to create the locally proclaimed "California Republic," which was never a sovereign nation. That quickly gave way to a temporary military government set up by American forces during the Mexican-American War, which Congress did not replace with a civilian territorial administration before admitting the Golden State to the Union in 1850.[10] American settlers complained about the military's decision to leave in place unfamiliar Mexican laws and to concentrate legislative and judicial power in the hands of local *alcaldes*, or magistrates, perceived as unaccountable to the people.[11]

But these differences in the status of the pre-statehood governments—that Texas was a republic and Indiana a territory—do not alter the explanation for recounting this history. The chapter tries to come to grips with a paradox of statehood: (1) local-representation considerations prompted the residents of the territories (and republics) to push for statehood in order to write constitutions of their own and to choose judges of their own, and yet (2) most modern state courts presume that the meaning of the guarantees in their state constitution parallels the meaning of the counterpart guarantees in the US Constitution, even ones worded differently from their own guarantees. To the extent that some states had more independence than territories, as was true for the republics of Texas and Vermont, that makes the contrast in those states more riddling.

Territory status had a purgatory component to it. It was a rough-and-tumble transitional time in which the federal government had authority over the area but was not prepared to allow the territory to enter the nation as a state on equal terms with the existing states. The Northwest Ordinance inaugurated this underappreciated chapter in American history. It's two ordinances in truth, not one. The Confederation Congress enacted the first one in 1787, establishing how to govern the land obtained from England after the Revolutionary War through the Treaty of Paris of 1783.[12] With the creation of the new federal government, the first Congress re-enacted the law in 1789 and laid the legal groundwork for what would become six states: Ohio (1803); Indiana (1816); Illinois (1818); Michigan (1837); Wisconsin (1848); and Minnesota (1858).[13]

The Northwest Ordinance of 1789 deserves more credit than it gets. It established the early rules of governance for these six areas from 1789 to statehood, a block of land that 16% of the American population now calls home. And it established crucial individual rights in the territories. It was the first federal law to outlaw slavery,[14] a law-making power that cleared the path for a later effort to outlaw slavery, the Missouri Compromise, which the US Supreme Court went out of its way to invalidate in *Dred Scott*.[15] The ordinance also contained protections for religious freedom, education, private property, and jury trials, along with bans on cruel or unusual punishments, all consistent with prohibitions contained in the first state constitutions and setting the scene for guarantees included in later state constitutions and the federal

Bill of Rights.[16] As for structure, the ordinance cemented federalism into American government by allowing Congress to admit territories as states "on an equal footing" with the existing states.[17] And it became a guiding precedent for laws governing future westward territories.

All in all, the Northwest Ordinance belongs on a Mount Rushmore of American laws. While Mount Rushmore was completed in 1941, the Northwest Ordinance has occupied a similar pedestal, as least as far as laws go, since 1934. Since then, as Gregory Ablavsky points out, just "four 'organic laws' of the United States have prefaced the volumes of the U.S. Code: the Declaration of Independence, the Articles of Confederation, the U.S. Constitution, and the Northwest Ordinance."[18] That's good company, and it explains why Congress would say in 1935 that the Northwest Ordinance established " 'such a complete change in the method of governing new communities formed by colonization, that it will always rank as one of the greatest civil documents of all time.' "[19]

There's much more to say about the Northwest Ordinance and the Territorial Era that it commenced. The norm-setting influence on American local and national governments set in motion by it seems hard to overstate. But I want to focus on another feature of the Territorial Era, a largely forgotten frustration of the soon-to-be states and an aspect of governance under the Northwest Ordinance and later federal laws that did not sit well with residents of the territories.

Before statehood, each territory created after 1789 amounted to an enclave of the federal government. Under the Northwest Ordinance, Congress delegated power over the area to officials chosen by the president and confirmed by the Senate: a governor (three-year terms); a secretary who acted not unlike a lieutenant governor (four-year terms); and three judges (good-behavior terms).[20] The governor and judges also worked together as the territorial legislature, and once the territory had 5,000 residents the residents of the territory could elect a "general assembly."[21]

After that, male citizens of the Northwest Territory who met residency and property qualifications voted every two years for the territory's "house of representatives," the lower house of its bicameral general assembly.[22] These representatives in turn nominated a slate of candidates for selection to the "legislative council," the territorial legislature's upper house. Congress still made the final selections, and it also retained the power to appoint territorial judges and senior territorial officials.[23] The governor also continued to appoint inferior magistrates and civil officers in the territory, just as before.[24] The elected lower house was thus the "sole concession to self-government" under the ordinance, and hardly a potent one at that.[25] The general assembly, it is true, could "regulate[] and define[]" the powers of minor territorial officials appointed by the governor and "make laws . . . not repugnant to the principles and articles in th[e] ordinance."[26] But these laws required the assent of the appointed legislative council and of the governor, were subject to disapproval by Congress, and depended for their enforcement on officials who owed their position to the president or to the territorial governor, not to the people.[27]

In many ways, the Northwest Ordinance's "territorial government strongly resembled British imperial structures."[28] One key difference was the prospect of statehood and admission into the Union. This principle, notes Gregory Ablavsky, represented a "sharp break from British law" and won praise from James Monroe, otherwise a critic of territorial governance.[29] The promise of statehood, said Monroe, was a "remarkable & important difference" between the way America and Britain treated people on the peripheries of their respective empires.[30]

The Northwest Ordinance anticipated the creation of several states from the lands of the territory and preliminarily divided it into three future "states" with the boundaries that today separate Ohio from Indiana and Indiana from Illinois, running north to the Canadian border. Once the population of one of these "states" reached 60,000 free inhabitants, the ordinance promised them admission into the Union and the chance to "form a permanent constitution and State government."[31]

Before the territories became states with locally chosen judges, they thus had federally chosen territorial judges. Many of them. Six hundred eight judges received presidential appointments to territorial courts from 1789 to 1959, when Hawaii became the fiftieth state.[32] In making these selections, the president had no obligation to pick residents from the territories.[33] "Much to the dismay of territorial residents, who loudly complained of the baleful effects of carpetbagger rule," Kermit Hall writes, "presidents invariably used the judicial patronage to reward supporters in the settled states," not to support settled residents of the territories.[34] That was especially so in the nineteenth century. From 1829 to 1896, presidents filled over three-quarters of the territorial judgeships with individuals who did not live in the relevant territory at the time of appointment.[35] Even if it may overstate matters to say that these judges were " 'wandering frontier lawyers' who 'took jobs in one territory after another' "—in truth fewer than 5% took territorial judgeships in more than two territories—it's fair to say that the residents of the territories did not know most of these judges.[36] They certainly weren't neighbors in the main. As non-residents usually at the time of appointment, as job holders without the life tenure given to Article III federal judges, as individuals without knowledge of the area, the territorial judges also were restless. From 1829 to 1896, over three-fifths of them did not stay long, serving no more than two years, and over three-quarters of them served no more than four years.[37] Territorial judges did not even report to the highest federal court for the first sixteen years. Not until 1805 could a losing litigant in the territorial courts appeal to the US Supreme Court.[38] With little say over the judges and other federal officials who governed them, it's easy to see why observers drew comparisons between colonial status and territorial status. "Are not the people in this territory in a much worse situation," some wondered, "than the United States were, before the late revolution?"[39]

In 1803, as Ohio became the first territory covered by the Northwest Ordinance to obtain statehood, the national government bought land west of the Mississippi River from France. The Louisiana Purchase required more territorial legislation, laws that set the rules of governance for what became most of the rest of the United States. Much like the Northwest Ordinance, the new laws created similar offices appointed by the president for each territory: a governor (three-year terms); a secretary (four-year terms); and three judges (four-year terms rather than good behavior).[40] And like the Northwest Ordinance, the new legislation generated debates over how the governors in the East would treat the governed in the West. As Gregory Ablavsky ably shows, there was considerable debate within the territories and within the national government over whether the residents of the territories were citizens of the United States and protected by its laws and Constitution.[41]

In taking sides on the debate, John Quincy Adams complained that territorial rule set "a bad precedent,"[42] a view shared by other commentators on the ground that it prompted the "creation of an American Empire," and "revealed . . . the problematic constitutional status of the territories in a United States to be governed of, by, and for the people."[43] Like colonies, the territories could be taxed without representation and were denied other aspects of self-government. This was a government "from above" and beyond, not one built from the ground up and situated in place.[44] "The people governed by the Ordinance had no say in its creation or adoption: Congress enacted it without any process for ratification or assent, and territorial citizens lacked voting representation in Congress."[45] If there was a silver lining in all of this, it's that western white men had reasons to develop political sympathies with the underrepresented sooner than their brethren in the East. The territories were one of the few places where the law treated white property-owning men just like women, minorities, Native Americans, and non-property-owning men.

Rough and aloof justice characterized much of the Territorial Era for the states. "There, beyond the limitations of federalism or democratic accountability, federal officials and military officers enjoyed seemingly unfettered authority, at least as depicted by territorial residents."[46] "The territories directly raised the question of how the center could legitimately govern the periphery—the questions of imperial constitutional structure that had prompted the Revolution."[47] James Monroe and a territorial resident saw it the same way. Monroe: "It is in effect to be a colonial gov[ernmen]t similar to that w[hic]h prevail'd in these States previous to the revolution."[48] Territorial resident: "Ordinance Government" amounts to a "true transcript of our Old English Colonial Governments."[49]

With people rooted in one place governed by people rooted in another, friction emerged. Territorial judges became one flash point for this tension. It's not hard to find examples of frustration with territorial judges unaccountable to local residents and often dismissive of their concerns. Some thought little of the quality of the judges appointed through this system. The territorial courts, one critic said, "might properly be called law schools, where the Judges get a smattering of law at the public expense."[50] The justices of the high court met annually, another snidely remarked, merely to "affirm each other's errors."[51] Still other critics complained that territorial judges were reckless after watching one of them throw the Arizona Territory into chaos by invalidating the acts of the first two territorial legislatures, "leaving the territory virtually without either a government or a legal framework."[52] Others complained that the unaccountability of territorial officers imposed "upon the people a system of vassalage which is both offensive and burdensome."[53] Three years after obtaining statehood, the Nevada attorney general remarked that "Nevada became a State to escape the dead-fall of her Territorial courts."[54]

Tension between residents and territorial judges was the rule, not an occasional exception, as the above suggests and as the specific experiences of Montana, Utah, and the Dakotas confirm.

Montana

Montana was a territory between 1864 and 1889,[55] and eighteen territorial judges served the area during that time. Just three of them lived in Montana before their appointment to the bench, and only one of them was a true "native son" born and raised in the state.[56] The first territorial justices, appointed by President Lincoln, came from Pennsylvania, New York, and Connecticut. The proportion of outsiders appointed to the Montana Supreme Court was high even by the standards of the time. On average, three-quarters of territorial judges came from outside the territory to take the job. [57] In Montana, the number was closer to 85% and even that doesn't tell the full story. Of the six judicial nominees whom the Senate rejected or never acted upon, five were from the area.[58] Why curry favor with people who could not vote, the people of the Montana Territory must have feared?

The residents noticed the pattern. Rich with Atlantic sarcasm, the Butte *Inter-Mountains Freeman* observed that it seemed "Eastern people are better calculated to run the Western machinery than those who have been out here so long."[59] Less sarcastically, the Helena *Herald* denounced it as a "vicious practice" that turned the territorial governments into "a sort of lying-in hospital for political tramps."[60] Between 1868 and 1889, Montana's advisory delegates to Congress, who had the right to participate in debates but not to vote on legislation,[61] registered the same complaints and lobbied for legislation that would subject territorial officials to local election or limit appointments to territorial residents.

Persistence was not the problem. Congress saw eight local-election bills and four residency-requirement bills introduced. All failed.[62]

One episode captures the situation. By 1886, restricting territorial appointments to territorial residents was "gaining popular momentum."[63] Perhaps seeing what was ahead, the admission of six states into the Union over the next ten years, both parties embraced the principle as part of their 1884 election platforms. But when Montana's Democratic delegate to Congress tried to take advantage of this "momentum," a fellow Democrat in the House of Representatives "did an abrupt about face."[64] The reason? Now that his party controlled the White House, he saw no reason to worry about the president appointing the wrong people to territorial posts.[65] Just two years later, this turncoat Pennsylvanian "threw a clean shirt into his carpetbag and started for Washington Territory and his new post as chief justice."[66]

In the Montana Territory's early years, tensions between territorial residents and federal appointees became a function of party politics, which spilled into the courts. Montanans were predominantly Democrats, but the Lincoln administration played to type by sending Republicans to fill territorial posts. Trouble soon began, confirming a dysfunction of territorial government. Montana's first election for the territorial legislature, conducted according to rules set by Congress in the territory's organic act, returned a Democratic majority. Congress delegated to the first legislature the task of setting up elections under territorial law, which it did. But Montana Democrats couldn't pass up the opportunity to gerrymander the rules.[67] Governor Sidney Edgerton, a reputed "crank posing as a radical Republican,"[68] vetoed the bill before leaving the territory for home in Ohio, where he spent most of his term.[69] The legislature adjourned without passing a replacement measure. No law, territorial or federal, authorized future legislative elections in Montana, making it an open question whether the legislature could convene a second session. Nonetheless, with support from the new territorial secretary, General Thomas Meagher, a lone Democrat in territorial office, the territorial assembly opened a new session in March 1866.[70] The Democrats "proceeded to reorganize the judiciary as completely as possible under the organic act."[71] With Edgerton absent and Meagher on the Democrats' side, the territorial bench "was the last stronghold for the Republicans."[72] The new judiciary law "set forth in detail" the jurisdiction of locally controlled probate courts, jury qualifications, and the rules of civil procedure in the territorial courts.[73]

The new regulations irked members of the territorial supreme court, and Montana Republicans lobbied the judges "to make a formal statement" calling into question "the legality of the second legislative session."[74] Then, when at last "a case [raising the issue] came before [Judge Munson] on June 4, 1866, he declared all acts passed by this legislative session null and void."[75] Republican members of the Helena Bar Association "delighted" in the victory and asked the territory's newspapers to print the judge's decision in full, which two did.[76] The Republican Congress followed up with legislation nullifying all territorial legislation adopted in 1866 the following February. The territorial legislature retaliated against Judge Munson in one of the few ways left: by "redefin[ing his] judicial district [] to assign [him] to the most remote wilderness possible."[77] "Sage-brushing," as it was called, allowed elected territorial assemblies to diminish the jurisdiction of territorial judges they did not like and could not remove.[78]

Montanans also complained about the quality of their judges, alleging that "they were frequently men 'who could never earn a living in competition with the local bar.' "[79] The attack contains kernels of truth and overstatement. Some territorial judges were removed for chronic absenteeism.[80] And some led undistinguished careers after removing their robes. "Hezekiah Hosmer, Montana's first chief justice," who served a full term without incident, later "became a federal warehouse inspector on the Pacific Coast."[81] But some judges stayed in Montana after their terms expired and led successful law practices. Decius Wade, who served four full terms, and Hiram Knowles, who left the bench in his third term, "proved honest and talented men," and "as time passed [no one] thought of them in terms other than as Montanans."[82] But none of this adequately explains why they got the positions in the first place. Asks one scholar: "Was it accidental that Decius Wade, who served as chief justice from 1871 to 1887, was a personal friend of James A. Garfield, a nephew of [prominent Republican senator] Benjamin Wade, and a brother-in-law of Vice President Schuyler Colfax?"[83] Or consider another coincidence: "With a Democratic administration in Washington from 1885 to 1889, . . . there was a noticeable influx of [territorial officials] from more southern climes."[84] The new chief justice came from Tennessee and other new justices came from Texas and Louisiana.[85]

The new arrivals' unfamiliarity with the territory sometimes showed. Thomas C. Bach, a graduate of Columbia College and Columbia Law School, came to Montana in 1884 as "a typical New York Stater."[86] Born to a prosperous Brooklyn family, he practiced law in New York for several years before following his brother to Montana. Two years later, at the age of thirty-three, he became a judge through an appointment by President Garfield. "An athlete in his college days" and "a good dresser,"[87] Bach stood out among the rough-hewn miners who flocked to Montana's "instant" frontier cities.[88] Llewellyn Callaway, who came to the Montana Territory as a child when his father became territorial secretary, practiced law there for more than fifty years after statehood, and served as chief justice of the Montana Supreme Court in the 1930s, tells this story about a trial Judge Bach handled in Fort Benson.

> In early September, [Judge Bach] opened court and summoned a jury from the county. Men came in from the ranches and herds, of course. . . . Upon taking the Bench he delivered a homily on the deportment and duties of a juror, then called the first case and directed the Clerk to call a jury. As they filed into a box a juror appeared without a coat. The Judge said, "Mr. Juror, don't you know it is not proper to appear in court without a coat? Have you no coat?" "Yes sir." "Where is it?" "At home." "Get it." The juror left the court room in a hurry. The Judge said, "Mr. Sheriff, adjourn this court for ten minutes." But the juror hadn't returned in ten minutes, nor did he return during the next half hour. The Judge said, "Mr. Sheriff, where did that juror go?" The sheriff replied, with a twinkle in his eye, "The last I saw of him he was on his horse, said he was going home for his coat." "Where does he live?" "About 40 miles from town," the sheriff said.[89]

After Montana became a state in 1889, the president of the United States no longer had any influence over the Montana Supreme Court. Montanans also were free to write their own constitution, pick their own governor, and elect the members of their own legislature.[90] This transition led to the passage of laws with a Montana flavor and led to the election of state court judges with Montana roots. But the question for Montana judges, like all state court judges, is this: Did this experience re-enforce the value of relying on local traditions in construing their own constitutions?

Utah

The territory of Utah also faced many challenges in handling the disparity between the priorities of the people in the territory and those in the nation's capital. During its lengthy period of territorial government, lasting from 1850 until 1896, the state experienced a series of conflicts over laws and courts. The failure had many sources. One was practical; the residents settled a remote part of the country. Another was cultural; the residents held customs frequently in tension with American law and the will of territorial judges. Still another was religious; the national government was suspicious of the Church of Latter-day Saints, and the church returned the favor by developing suspicions of its own about territorial officials.

Mormons settled the Salt Lake Valley in 1847. The first conflict over the courts began soon after Congress organized a territorial government for Utah in 1850. By then, the territory already had institutions on which the people relied to order their affairs. Sensitive to this reality, federal officials initially governed with a light and respectful touch. President Fillmore appointed Mormon leader Brigham Young as Utah's first governor and sent just a handful of federal appointees to fill territorial posts.[91] Things did not go smoothly anyway. Two of the three territorial judges soon offended the locals, prompting Governor Young to demand they apologize. They instead fled the territory, taking with them important documents and territorial funds.[92] Others, like the "hard-drinking, free-speaking" postmaster, did not fit the settlement they served and did not last much longer.[93]

More serious conflict arose in 1852, when the territorial assembly, elected locally and authorized by Congress to pass laws on "all rightful subjects of legislation, consistent with the Constitution of the United States and the provisions of [the territory's organic] act,"[94] tried "to enlarge the sphere of home rule by local officers as against government by federal appointees."[95] The assembly expanded the jurisdiction of probate courts. Because Utah's organic act did not clarify the cases the probate courts could hear, the territorial legislature exploited the ambiguity and gave the probate courts "original jurisdiction both civil and criminal."[96] The decision "effectively deprived the federally appointed judiciary of jurisdiction over most civil and criminal matters," converting the federal territorial judges into titles without portfolios.[97] What Utah's residents opposed most of all was the imposition of laws they did not choose and in many cases had rejected.

From the perspective of officials in Washington, DC, the Utah Territory under Young's leadership "was practically claiming independence."[98] President Buchanan "felt justified in dispatching one-sixth of the United States Army to Utah in 1857" to reclaim control.[99] The military confrontation ousted Young from his position as governor and earned him a treason charge, later pardoned, but it did not quiet the dispute over civil government in the territory, especially when it came to the courts. Howard Lamar notes that "from 1859 until the start of the Civil War, long-standing, basic disputes over the local court system of Utah were continued by Young and the new federal judges."[100] Two circumstances intensified the conflict. The military expedition brought 2,500 soldiers and another 2,500 non-Mormon civilians to Utah. And the new federal appointees, once again, were hostile to Mormon leaders and did little to endear themselves to the locals. "The new chief justice of the territory, Delana R. Eckels, was determined to assert federal control at all costs."[101] That did not make it easy to hold court sessions and empanel juries, which often failed to show up or refused to convict. The judges thus began sitting at Camp Floyd and drawing jurors from among the federal troops and their community.[102] One judge persuaded the territorial governor to send 800 troops with him when he held a trial in Provo.[103] To the locals, that was "a military threat to force juries to convict those being tried."[104]

After the American Civil War, two issues dominated the relationship between Utah and the federal government: the probate courts and polygamy. Ongoing resistance to enforcing federal laws, especially in the probate courts, prompted calls for reform. Plural marriage irritated eastern sensibilities, too. In 1862, Congress passed the Morrill Act, which imposed a hefty fine and possible jail time on anyone engaged in polygamy. Trouble was, "the local probate courts and juries refused to use it to try and convict offenders."[105] Only one person was ever convicted under the act, and even that was a test case to challenge the law's constitutionality.[106]

In 1874, the territory suffered two blows to local control. In *Ferris v. Higley*, the US Supreme Court invalidated the local law that conferred criminal and civil jurisdiction on the probate courts.[107] The federal organic act for Utah, the Supreme Court held, limited the jurisdiction of the territorial probate courts to powers these courts traditionally exercised in the Anglo-American legal system: administration of wills and estates and family-law matters.[108] Then, later that year, Congress passed the Poland Act, which reorganized the local Utah courts. The act limited probate court jurisdiction to "the settlement of the estates of decedents, and in matters of guardianship and other like matters" but expressly denied to them any "civil, chancery, or criminal jurisdiction whatever."[109] It expanded the role and authority of federal marshals and the United States attorney.[110] And it reformed jury-selection procedures, requiring balanced juries of Mormons and non-Mormons. After the law's enactment, the territorial court empaneled its first jury in four years.[111]

That was not the end of Congress's regulation of the territory. The Edmunds-Tucker Act of 1887 further diminished the power of probate judges, vested their appointment in the president, gave federal marshals expansive law-enforcement powers, disenfranchised women, and dissolved the Mormon Church and seized its assets.[112] Designed initially just to "abolish polygamy," the act became "one of the most far-reaching pieces of legislation ever passed in peacetime."[113] Senator George Edmunds's initial proposal was so ambitious that before it could pass the House, Virginia congressman John Randolph Tucker—the grandson of renowned jurist and judicial review proponent, St. George Tucker—had to revise Edmunds's bill to remove provisions that were likely unconstitutional.[114] "To carry out [the act's] many provisions, hundreds of federal officers and men were eventually employed to deal with Utah."[115] Polygamy virtually disappeared from the territory by the 1890s, when the Mormon Church forbade the practice.[116] Still, as a condition of statehood in 1896, Utah had to include a provision in its constitution banning plural marriage, a condition required of three other states as well.[117]

Cultural differences between the residents of Utah and the rest of the country did not end after Utah became a state in 1896. When Mormon apostle Reed Smoot arrived in Washington, DC, to take his seat in the United States Senate in 1903, things did not go smoothly. The Senate resisted seating him and "a broad coalition of American Protestant churches . . . sought to expel Utah's new senator," alleging that his position in the Church of Latter-day Saints "made him a conspirator" in violating "the nation's antipolygamy laws."[118] Between 1903 and 1907, the Senate Committee on Privileges and Elections held hearings on the status of polygamy in Utah to determine whether Senator Smoot could serve in the chamber. "The four-year Senate proceeding created a 3,500-page record of testimony by 100 witnesses on every peculiarity of Mormonism," prying into every facet of church life and the lives of its adherents.[119] The Senate fell short of the votes needed to expel Senator Smoot, who went on to serve his State for thirty years in the nation's upper chamber. Smoot eventually won "the personal respect and, in some cases, affection of his Washington colleagues."[120]

One feature of the episode captures a hard-to-forget instance of senatorial hypocrisy. Consistent with the church's 1890 edict, Reed Smoot had one spouse and by all accounts was loyal to her and she to him. The same could not be said for many of the men prosecuting the case against Smoot. Senator Bois Penrose of Pennsylvania put the situation well. "As for me," he said, "I would rather have seated beside me in this chamber a polygamist who doesn't polyg than a monogamist who doesn't monog."[121]

Dakotas

Like Utah, the Dakota Territory experienced a lengthy territorial phase, from 1861 to 1889. When the states of North and South Dakota joined the Union, their "statehood campaign" was "seen in part as a reaction against territorial rule by the federal government, reflecting a kind of anti-colonial mentality among the people."[122] As in other territories, Dakotans did not warm to outsiders who filled judgeships on the territorial court, most of whom knew nothing about the area.[123] In some ways, the territory's residents were the lucky ones. "Historians have rated [the Dakota judges] as among the best the territorial system produced."[124] "Dakota judges 'as a rule were creditable and conducted their office with wisdom, dignity, and justice. The few exceptions only stressed the rule.' "[125]

In other ways, however, the Dakota Territory was not immune from the cronyism that generally plagued the territories. To spur development in the Dakotas, Congress "gave the Northern Pacific Railway a huge economic stake in the government."[126] The relative competence, even talent, of the territory's judges did little good in matters affecting the railroads and related businesses and left residents with no way to hold territorial judges accountable.

Consider the career of Chief Justice Peter Shannon, a member of the supreme court of the Dakota Territory. Shannon took the job from Pennsylvania. A friend of Presidents Lincoln and Grant, he played a crucial role in helping Grant win a close vote in Pennsylvania during the 1872 election. More to the matter at hand, George Cass, president of Northern Pacific Railroad, urged Grant to appoint Shannon to the Dakota bench.[127]

In the early 1870s, "the struggle to secure a railroad" was "a key and binding factor," one that gave "meaning to Dakota politics."[128] "The railroad issue," Howard Lamar tells us, "was often the most important issue."[129] Congressional land grants meant to incentivize the Northern Pacific Railway to build its line from St. Paul through the northern half of the territory left the company in control of almost a quarter of the land in present-day North Dakota.[130] "For years, the railroads and the people struggled for control."[131] The construction of two east-west railroad routes, one in the north and one in the south, that would eventually converge in St. Paul, is a reason we have two Dakotas today.[132]

When Chief Justice Shannon arrived in the Dakotas in April 1873, he took his seat in the northern part of the territory. In the southern half, a controversy loomed over management of the Dakota Southern Railway, a government-backed venture that connected the territorial capital of Yankton with Sioux City, Iowa. The lawsuit between the railroad company and the Yankton county commissioners drew the ire of the Dakotas' governor, John Burbank, one of the directors of the railroad company. When a lower court judge entered an injunction in favor of the county commissioners, Governor Burbank "threatened to reassign" him to another judicial district and to replace him with a colleague "more favorably inclined toward the railroad company."[133] The judge in turn threatened Governor Burbank with "arrest and punishment for contempt of court."[134] The case settled but not before generating enough ill will that local banker Peter Wintermute shot and killed territorial secretary Edwin McCook. "Wintermute and others seethed under the territorial system of appointed officials whose political fortunes depended more upon their connections in Washington, D.C., than upon local sentiment."[135]

A Yankton grand jury refused to indict Wintermute for murder. McCook's father-in-law, who took his place as territorial secretary, blamed the territorial judge who sat at Yankton, and as acting governor followed through on Burbank's earlier threat. In another act of sage brushing, he sent the judge to northern North Dakota near the border with Canada, and called Chief Justice Shannon to Yankton.[136] Uneasy with these developments, "Washington authorities directed the governor" to "restore the judges to their former positions."[137] That settled matters for a time. But soon a friend of Shannon's in the US Senate convinced executive branch officials that the Dakota Territory's chief justice ought to sit in the territorial capital. People in Washington, DC, backtracked and ordered that the reshuffle be restored.[138] Once back in Yankton, Shannon invalidated the grand jury proceedings in Wintermute's case and convened a second grand jury, which this time indicted the banker for murder. The jury returned a compromise verdict of manslaughter. Wintermute appealed to the supreme court and prevailed over a dissent by Shannon. The Wintermute case produced "the first published non-unanimous decision by the Dakota Territory supreme court."[139] The territorial government retried Wintermute. At the request of the defense, the trial took place in a different judicial district, and two years to the day after Wintermute killed Secretary McCook, a jury found him not guilty.[140]

While "the neonate Dakota judiciary took a giant step toward legitimacy" through the Wintermute cases,[141] Chief Justice Shannon does not deserve the credit. Over and over, it seemed, his view of the law aligned with the railroads' interests and with those of the territorial officials. Historian George Kingsbury's assessment of Shannon's tenure is scathing: He "had not been marked by that friendliness, respect and confidence that should exist between the presiding judge and the members of the bar practicing in his court, but on the contrary, there had grown up a feeling of distrust toward the judge, and an entire and a total lack of confidence in his official integrity."[142] Most lawyers in Yankton opposed his reappointment to a third term. Gilbert Moody, an influential politician and future judge, complained about the court to the US attorney general the year Shannon arrived in the Dakotas: "You pledged us that we should have good men and good lawyers sent to us as judges and we get to constitute our Supreme Court an ass, a knave, and a drunkard."[143]

Local Customs Influenced Early Statehood Experiences

The early experiences of the territorial states reflected what one would expect: local innovations in their constitutions and local pride in the interpretation of them by state court judges. Soon after the transition from territory status to statehood, many state courts, now filled by judges from the area and chosen by citizens from the area, issued decisions that respected those customs and traditions. An example from Iowa illustrates the point.

Iowa

During the first half of the nineteenth century, intense political sensitivity about free and slave states dominated statehood admission decisions by Congress. That history was not forgotten after these territories became states, as a case from Iowa demonstrates.

In 1867, Alexander Clark sued "on behalf of [his] 12-year-old African American daughter, Susan Clark," so that she could "attend Grammar School No. 2 in Muscatine, Iowa."[144] Alexander Clark was "a prominent businessman, property owner, and a leading civil rights advocate for black equality."[145] When Clark moved to Iowa in 1842, the territory maintained "Black Codes" that discouraged African American migration. Clark had to prove to a magistrate that he was a free man and post $500 bond for "good behavior."[146] He started several successful businesses in Muscatine and eventually "became one of the county's largest real-estate tax payers."[147] Grammar School No. 2 was located in the Clarks' neighborhood, while the "colored school" was located more than a mile away.[148] "The school board did not dispute that Susan Clark resided within the boundaries of Grammar School No. 2," and "was qualified for admission."[149] But it denied admission based on its segregation policy.

In explaining what happened next, I cannot improve on the description by Goodwin Liu, a justice on the California Supreme Court:

> An early victory for black schoolchildren was the Iowa Supreme Court's 1868 decision in *Clark v. Board of School Directors*. The court framed the issue of segregation not in terms of whether public sentiment was sufficient justification for the practice, but in terms of whether state law vested the school board with any discretion to segregate by race. Tracing the history of state enactments on the matter, the court discerned "three distinct phases of legislative sentiment": first, the total exclusion of black children from public schools under the original Iowa Constitution of 1846 and related statutes; second, an 1858 statute "provid[ing] for the education of the *colored youths* in separate schools," except where "the unanimous consent of the persons sending to the school" allowed blacks to attend with whites; and third, statutes enacted in 1860, 1862, and 1866 providing for "the instruction of *youth* between the ages of five and twenty-one years," with "no mention of, or discrimination in regard to, color." The legislature had enacted the latter statutes pursuant to a new mandate in the 1857 state constitution to "provide for the education of *all the youths of the State*, through a system of common schools."
>
> Against the backdrop of the prior enactments, the court read the 1857 constitutional provision and implementing statutes to mean "all the youths are equal before the law, and there is no discretion vested in the board of directors or elsewhere, to interfere with or disturb that equality." The court's use of the phrase "equal before the law" provided a direct counterpoint to [Massachusetts] Chief Justice Shaw's use of the same phrase in *Roberts* [*v. City of Boston*, 59 Mass. (5 Cush.) 198, 206 (1849) (upholding Boston school segregation)]. The court in *Clark* broadly declared that the school board had no authority under state law to discriminate by race, color, nationality,

religion, or economic circumstance. Such discrimination, the court said, would violate "the spirit of our laws" and "would tend to perpetuate the national differences of our people and stimulate a constant strife, if not a war of races."[150]

While the decision marked the end of the family's trial, it did not end the trail the Clark family marked. Susan's younger brother Alexander Jr. became the first African American to graduate from the University of Iowa's law school in 1879.[151] A few years later, their father, by then in his fifties, attended the law school and graduated with distinction.[152]

Do Modern State Court Judges Premise Interpretation of Their State Constitutions on Local or National Grounds?

Something happened. The wording and early interpretations of the state constitutions, influenced by the territory experience and other changes in the country after 1776, differ markedly from the federal constitution, both with respect to structural and individual rights guarantees. As a matter of structure, variation is the norm when it comes to a comparison to the US Constitution, whether it's the plural executive, line-item vetoes, constitutional initiatives, or election of judges. As a matter of individual rights, variation is the norm also. The state constitutions contain many more rights, often more delineated rights, than their federal counterparts.

It's not just that the two sets of charters differ when it comes to structure and individual rights. Quite often in American history, locally initiated variations generated national movements. State efforts began the march to the prevention of gender discrimination in voting through the Nineteenth Amendment[153] and helped facilitate the eventual end of racial apartheid with *Brown v. Board of Education*.[154] But this source of new ideas and innovation has not held true in the modern era or at least not as true as one might expect in view of the territorial and colonial histories of many states. Over time, state courts' interpretations of their own constitutions have gravitated more and more to the federal interpretations.

Stop and think about that anomaly. In the face of the history of all states, once skeptical of royal colonial judges, once skeptical of federal territorial judges, the proclivity of many state courts to start their analysis of the meaning of a provision in their state constitution with the presumption that it mimics the meaning of a counterpart guarantee in the federal constitution defies explanation, at least an easy explanation. Yes, instances abound where state courts have found that presumption overcome. Take the state court decisions before the US Supreme Court's decision in *Obergefell* about same-sex marriage or the state court decisions after the Court's decision in *Kelo* about property takings or after its decision in *Smith* about the free exercise of religion.[155] But the existence of any across-the-board presumption is surpassingly odd.

Reconsider this approach to interpretation of state constitutions, a presumption that they match the meaning of the US Constitution, from this historical vantage point. It amounts to a state court judge acting like a territorial judge, taking marching orders from Washington, DC, rather than from Cheyenne, Wyoming. Why else would a state court judge assume that what is good for the federal constitution must be good for the Wyoming constitution?

State court lawyers and constitutional law professors bear equal responsibility for this oddity. In my experience, state court lawyers often act like territorial (and colonial) lawyers, relying heavily, sometimes solely, on federal precedents in making arguments about the meaning of their state constitutions. Lawyers who invoke the state constitution to invalidate a state or local law, however, must use *its* text and history if they wish the state courts to take their argument seriously. And of course most constitutional law professors know only, and teach only, the territorial—the federal—law.

Perhaps the skeptic wonders how often, or for what reason, a state court judge could grant relief under a state guarantee. Once one starts on this topic, it is difficult to stop.

Virtually all of the foundational liberties that protect Americans originated in the state constitutions and to this day remain independently protected by them. In our federal system, nearly every state and local law must comply with two sets of constraints, those imposed by the federal constitution and those imposed by their state counterparts, as it is the rare individual-rights guarantee that appears just in the national constitution as opposed to most (if not all) of the state constitutions. When individuals seek relief from their state or local governments, they generally will not care whether the state or federal constitution, the state or federal courts, protect them.

State courts have independent authority to construe their constitutions. Nothing compels the state courts to imitate federal interpretations of the liberty, property, and structural guarantees in the United States Constitution when it comes to the provisions found in their own constitutions, even guarantees that match the federal ones letter for letter. As long as a state court's interpretation of its own constitution does not violate a separate federal requirement, it will stand, and, better than that, it will be impervious to challenge in the United States Supreme Court.[156]

So why might a state court grant relief under its State Constitution when the federal court rejected a request for relief in construing similar or even identical language in the United States Constitution? One answer is that it can. Our federal system gives state courts the final say over the meaning of their own constitutions. As a matter of power, the fifty-one highest courts in the system may *each* come to different conclusions about the meaning, for example, of free speech guarantees in their own jurisdictions.

The more compelling answer is that, as a matter of reason, not just power, explanations abound for interpreting the two sets of guarantees differently. State constitutional law not only regularly gives the client two chances to win, but the state shot also frequently gives the client a better chance to win.

Start with institutional differences between the two sets of courts. The scope of the United States Supreme Court's jurisdiction creates disadvantages relative to the state courts when it comes to defining constitutional rights and crafting constitutional remedies. Because the Supreme Court must announce rights and remedies for fifty states, one national government, and over 330 million people, it is more constrained than a state supreme court faced with an issue affecting one state and, say, 12 million people. The more innovative a constitutional claim, the more hesitant the United States Supreme Court may be about entering the fray. That dynamic disappears in the state courts. Innovation by one state court necessarily comes with no risks for other states and fewer risks for that state.

New constitutional rights not only require the articulation of a new constitutional theory. They also require the management of a new constitutional right. Most judges worry about the next case when they think about identifying a new constitutional right. But United States Supreme Court justices have more to worry about than state court judges in view of the scope of their jurisdiction, the enormous breadth of which ensures that it is "always raining somewhere"[157] and that any new right will face a bundle of varied circumstances. In some settings, the challenge of imposing a constitutional solution on the whole country at once will increase the likelihood that federal constitutional law will be underenforced, that a "federalism discount" will be applied to the right.[158] State courts face no such problem in construing their own constitutions.

Now consider local differences that make the state shot a truly independent one, often a more promising one at that. Start by taking five minutes to do something most Americans have never done. Open your state constitution and read Article I. Often labeled the Bill of Rights or the Declaration of Rights, Article I of most state constitutions[159] covers individual rights. That's an illuminating contrast in structure from the outset. With the federal constitution, almost all of the enumerated individual rights come after the 1789 Constitution, starting with the Bill of Rights in 1791 and supplemented by other amendments after that. The state constitutions, in everlasting contrast, start by protecting individual rights, perhaps because the states, unlike the national government, are not governments of limited and enumerated authority.

There's a quick takeaway from reading the individual rights in a state constitution. The norm tends to be state rights that are phrased differently from the language of the federal Bill of Rights and the Fourteenth Amendment. It's not just different words. Often there are more words. Whether it's free speech, religious liberties, criminal procedure, myriad other individual rights, or structural guarantees, the state constitutions often protect them more specifically. Different words often lead to different meanings, sometimes more rights-protective meanings.

State courts also have a freer hand in doing something the Supreme Court cannot: allowing local conditions and traditions to affect their interpretation of a constitutional guarantee and the remedies imposed to implement that guarantee.[160] Does anyone doubt that the Idaho

Supreme Court might look at property rights—and takings claims—differently from the New York Court of Appeals? Or that the Alaska and Hawaii Supreme Courts might look at privacy issues differently from other states or for that matter the United States Supreme Court? Might the regulation of weapons generate a different reading in a state supreme court with a large rural population than in one with a large suburban and urban population? Might the state courts of Utah and Rhode Island and Maryland and Pennsylvania construe a free exercise clause differently from other state courts given their histories? State constitutional law respects and honors these nationwide differences in culture, history, and geography by allowing state courts to account for local conditions in interpreting their own charters.

The United States Supreme Court has no such option. It cannot, at least it should not, base an interpretation of the national constitution on the local traditions, cultures, or history of one state, one region of the country, or an elite group of citizens.[161] State courts have a free hand to *customize* constitutional guarantees to account for regional circumstances, while the US Supreme Court may not.

A mistaken or an ill-conceived constitutional decision is also easier to fix at the state level than it is at the federal level.[162] Not only do state court decisions cover a smaller jurisdiction and fewer people, but the people also have other remedies at their disposal to correct them: an easier constitutional amendment process and judicial elections. State courts, like state legislatures, have more latitude to "try novel social and economic experiments without risk to the rest of the country"[163] than the United States Supreme Court.

In considering the comparative advantages of the state and federal courts, be mindful how often American constitutional issues do not lend themselves to a single solution.[164] Many of the most frequently litigated guarantees are open-ended and generate intensely difficult interpretive debates. So difficult are some of these questions that lawyers and law professors alike insist that there are no right answers to some of the questions and, worse, that policy preferences underlie the judges' answers to many of them. Some judges even say so.[165]

As to these vexing areas of the law, state courts remain free, I would think obligated, to adopt their own interpretations of similarly worded constitutional guarantees. When difficult areas of constitutional construction arise—administrative law, free exercise, voting rights, or property rights—why should we assume that the United States Supreme Court is somehow an Oracle of Truth? And why should we impose on the members of that Court the unfair and unrelenting burden of treating it as the only supreme court in the country capable of offering an insightful solution to a difficult problem? That's a recipe for decreasing, not increasing, respect for the United States Supreme Court. The more difficult the constitutional question, the more indeterminate the answer may be—and the more appropriate to accommodate many imperfect solutions rather than to insist on just one.

Different methods of interpretation offer another reason why state courts might resist the pull of US Supreme Court decisions. Treat the universe of federal constitutional opinions for present purposes as occupying two rough categories. On one side are formal, text-based, and fixed methods of interpreting constitutions. On the other side are informal, purpose-driven, and less fixed methods for interpreting them. If roughly half of all US Supreme Court constitutional decisions fall on one side or the other (a rough estimate no doubt), that means that *half the time* a state court judge should presume lockstepping—using federal precedents to determine the meaning of state constitutions—is inappropriate. Why? If a set of state court judges happens to take the formal approach to interpretation and the US Supreme Court precedent falls on the informal side, they should start with the presumption that the US Supreme Court is wrong by their lights. That indeed must be the case if they mean what they say about their theory of interpretation. So too in the other direction. Because most judges take methods of interpretation seriously, that means roughly half of the time they should find the relevant federal precedents *not* helpful.

In some cases, time has not been good to the federal precedents, deepening the mystery of why state courts and lawyers would casually import them into state constitutional law. Think about equal protection and the use of "tiers of review" by the federal courts to interpret the guarantee. That may be fine for federal law. What started as two tiers of review (rational basis review and strict scrutiny) became three (intermediate scrutiny), then four (rational basis with teeth). By now, one scholar says, we have seven tiers of review.[166] It sounds almost biblical. On the first day God gave us rational basis scrutiny. On the second day, he gave us strict scrutiny. On the third day, he gave us intermediate scrutiny. And so on. State lawyers and judges are free to consider the limits of tiers of review, the limits of slicing things too many times. As a lawyer-woodsman might say, you can't "cut a plank so many times that it has just one side."[167]

Why would a state court lawyer casually assume that tiers of review are presumptively the right choice for the interpretation of a state constitution's equal protection guarantee—particularly if they do not help the client? Something else might deserve a try. Perhaps just two tiers of review. Perhaps it's better to balance the government benefits of the classification against the costs to the individual, as Justice Stevens long advocated.[168] Or perhaps it's better to use the nineteenth-century "class legislation" approach as a way to address the foundational requirement that like people should be treated alike. It's useful to remember that the US Supreme Court's decision in *Buck v. Bell*, a decision most state courts did not follow, rejected the class-legislation model. By contrast, the state courts generally used the class-legislation model in addressing, and usually invalidating, eugenics legislation that required the involuntary sterilization of individuals with disabilities.[169]

Is the "tiers of review" approach the only constitutional doctrine embraced by the federal courts that time has not favored? I have my doubts. Any lawyer considering a state constitutional argument should ask this question: Does the controlling federal doctrine hurt their client and, if so, are there pitfalls with the doctrine that the state court can avoid?

It's easy to lament that the underdevelopment of state constitutional law flows from the absence of a course on the subject in the curriculum of many law schools.[170] But that omission does not explain why state court lawyers frequently assume that federal doctrines apply to state constitutional law disputes. The current methodology for teaching constitutional law, truth be told, should lead to the opposite instinct. The law schools' prevailing preoccupation with federal constitutional law, and the way most professors teach it, captures an ideal set of prompts for developing independent, much-improved, state constitutional law.

Consider how constitutional law often is taught and the silver lining that comes with this approach. Yes, the class teaches just half the story, focusing on the federal constitution, rarely mentioning, if mentioning at all, the fifty state constitutions. And yes, the class infrequently addresses the second shot offered by the state constitutions in challenges to state and local laws and state and local criminal prosecutions. But consider another feature of how many law professors teach the class.

The classes tend to follow a similar arc. Before class, the students read a few federal cases in a given area. The class begins with a student reciting the facts of a case. Then another student identifies the rule that comes from the case, sometimes with a little back and forth over the best way to characterize the holding. Then the pattern repeats itself with related cases. All of this is a windup for the key pitch: the ways in which the individual cases sometimes do not fit together. Using the (federal) case method to help students think critically about the definition and scope of the constitutional guarantee, the professor reveals the unexamined problems with each decision, often at the expense of the federal judge who wrote the opinion. How could I not notice?

Studying federal constitutional law often amounts to learning about the flawed doctrines and unconnected dots in federal constitutional law. No other class leaves more strings untied. But all of this is good news for state constitutional law. What is the one thing federal constitutional law teaches every student? A keen awareness of the pitfalls state courts could avoid if they sidestepped a doctrine here, modified a doctrine there, or rejected a doctrine in full elsewhere. State constitutional law is the ship federal constitutional law students long have been waiting to board. They can use their knowledge of the serial problems in federal constitutional law to steer clear of similar problems in interpreting state constitutions and to help their clients win cases they never could win under federal law.

The more one looks at the problem, the more odd it seems that *any* state court decision would mimic a decision of the US Supreme Court when it comes to construing its *own* constitution. Only someone who embraces lockstepping would want to return to the Territorial Era, a time and chapter of each state's history that most residents eagerly departed. Of course, it's not always, it's not even usually, the state court judge's fault. Too many lawyers act like territorial lawyers, raising the federal claims and rarely addressing in any detail, if raising at all, a counterpart state constitutional claim. State judges referee the game.

They do not play it, and they thus cannot rely on state constitutional grounds never raised.

Lockstepping and the Modern Election of Most State Court Judges

Maybe, the reader worries, this is an anachronistic observation, history for history's sake, about a long-ago era in our country. Maybe the local pride that fed the quest for statehood reflects attitudes of the nineteenth century, and that's all. And maybe those attitudes changed as the key phases of the Territorial Era ended and as the authority of the national government grew during the Depression, as the country came together to withstand two world wars, and as the fight for civil rights led to national court decisions (*e.g., Brown*) and national legislation (*e.g.,* the 1964 Civil Rights Act). Who can deny that these developments generated nationalizing tendencies in American government? But none of these developments explains why modern state court judges would presume federal judges know best.

Think about lockstepping from today's vantage point. As shown in the last chapter, 90% of state court judges are elected in one way or another. Many commentators say that this predominant feature of the state selection process makes state court judges less likely to be independent.[171] Here, again, is an underappreciated opportunity to liberate state constitutional law from the persistent tug of federal constitutional law. There are many ways in which the election of state court judges should make them *more* independent, not less, and much more likely to treat the state and federal constitutions differently.

Imagine a candidate for a position in Kansas's legislature. Let's say that after she gave her first stump speech someone asked this question: "How do you handle new policy questions that others are struggling to address, say, privacy issues arising from new technology, the opioid crisis, or a pandemic? Is there any one author you look to, any influential thinker, any spiritual source, or anything else you consult?" Think what would await our candidate if she gave this answer: "I always ask myself the same question: What would Congress do?" Awkward silence.

Shift to the executive branch. Imagine if she ran for governor of Kansas and gave a similar answer. "I always ask myself first. What would the president of the United States do?" More awkward silence.

On no day in Kansas history would that answer work for either position. On no day in the history of any state would that answer work. That answer would doom a career in elected office for anyone anywhere anytime. Local pride matters. No state has residents, or ever has had residents, who generally believe that the people in the national government have superior insights about what to do with their problems, their community, their place. No one expects their state legislator or state governor to resolve all policy questions by looking to what the people in the nation's capital have done. It's a function partly of local pride and partly of local realities. The people in a state are much more likely than anyone else to know what ails them, to appreciate what matters to prioritize, and to understand what's needed to fix those problems without compromising other local interests.[172]

Why are things so different for state court judges, especially for elected state court judges? Shouldn't they share the instincts of the elected legislators and governors? By and large, many don't for reasons that escape me. The honest answer that some state court judges must give to the hypothetical voter's question is not a politically acceptable one. If a state court judge takes the view that the meaning of a guarantee in the federal constitution is presumptively the meaning of a counterpart guarantee in the state constitution, here's the answer: "Yes, I must acknowledge, the first place I look in answering difficult state constitutional questions is to what the justices in Washington, DC, have to say about the US Constitution, not the text of my state's constitution, not our history, not our traditions, not the right method of interpretation." That does not seem like a popular answer.

Traditional local pride, witnessed for all to see in the Territorial Era, should make state court judges presumptively distrustful of ideas and doctrines that emerge from the outside rather than from their own laws, land, history, and culture. Whatever the source of this oddity, whatever the source of the transformation from the local-pride traditions of the Territorial Era, it does not turn on the election of 90% of state court judges. Elections should lead to more local pride, not less, and less lockstepping, not more.[173]

The Local and National Benefits of Independent Constitutionalism at the State Level

Two problems in particular vex American courts today. One is the difficulty of identifying an approach to judicial review that respects the people's separation-of-powers objective of removing some issues from the policymaking branches of government but that does not create trespass problems of its own. The other is the quest for a workable selection process that does not exacerbate these separation-of-powers problems and does not turn judges into political players as opposed to neutral referees. True independence in interpreting state constitutions helps on both fronts.

First, the election of most state court judges, together with the reality that all state constitutions can be amended more easily than the federal constitution, eases the separation-of-powers problems created by judicial review at the local level. Anyone unhappy with a local ruling has two powerful, relatively immediate options: pick different judges or amend the constitution to overrule the decision. The same is not true at the federal level. If we return local judges to the front lines of rights innovation and think of federal judges as a final bulwark, we minimize the risks of too much judicial review (due to the state corrective mechanisms) and minimize the risks of too little (due to the federal backstop).

The state selection processes, particularly judicial elections, need not stand in the way of fair-minded constitutional decisions. Judicial elections hold the potential to be a friend of innovation, not its enemy. Some supposedly counter-majoritarian constitutional issues are not counter-majoritarian at all when presented effectively to elected state-court judges. Just as there may be politically functional and politically dysfunctional issues in legislation, the same can be true in litigation. And the two do not always overlap. That may explain why some structure and individual-rights issues—separation of powers, non-delegation, limits on agency deference, school funding, property rights, religious liberties, criminal procedure—have resonated more with state-elected judges than with life-tenured federal judges.[174]

Even the most mundane electoral practicalities do not warrant distrust in the capacity of state court judges to construe their constitutions independently. Elections should make judges more down to earth, remind them where they are, remind them what the people of that state stand for. And they should lead to *more* state-court independence from the United States Supreme Court, not less. Aren't there many federal constitutional rulings that *increase* the scope of a protected right and with which elected judges in some states disagree? And with which a majority of the electorate in those states disagree? Aren't there many federal constitutional rulings that *decrease* the scope of a protected right and with which elected judges in some states disagree? And with which a majority of the electorate in those states disagree?

The answer will depend on the issue and the state. That's as it should be. Federalism offers a quilt full of options from which to work, even after accounting for state judicial elections. It might horrify some state court judges, for example, to revive *Lochner* or reject *Blaisdell* [175] in deciding the meaning of their state liberty-of-contract and due process guarantees. But for others, this would be a welcome opportunity as a matter of legal reasoning, and in many states electoral considerations would not get in the way. Some state court judges might be inclined to follow *Rucho*'s federal lead in deciding that challenges to the constitutionality of legislative districts infected by partisan map drawing exceed the competence of judges to resolve fairly.[176] But for others, this might present a welcome opportunity for asserting a state court's independence as a matter of legal reasoning or (for judges so inclined) local policy preferences. If there are going to be experiments of this sort, it makes eminent sense in a country of our size and diversity to conduct them in the states. Let one state (or a few) experiment with reviving *Lochner* or burying *Blaisdell* or *Rucho*. Then see what happens. The same goes for other cutting-edge matters. In view of the many questions that have arisen recently about administrative deference under *Chevron* and the related non-delegation doctrine at the federal level,[177] the state courts are in an excellent position, as are state advocates, to propose courses of their own. Most state courts have already charted distinct paths from federal administrative law in these areas.[178] I could go on and on with other examples, some that progressives would favor, some that conservatives would favor. In either direction, state judicial selection procedures do not prohibit the states from returning to the front lines of rights and structure innovation. Whether appointed or elected, state court judges should take pride in dignifying local guarantees, as one might have expected would happen after the Territorial Era.

Second, the structure of the US Constitution favors putting the state courts on the front lines of rights protection and innovation. Judicial federalism respects the initial design of the United States Constitution, and its carefully drawn, if difficult-to-preserve, balance of power. Neglecting this structure has not been cost free. While history and constitutional structure may not be everyone's cup of tea, they can provide useful checkups for whether we have lost our way. History is not always backward. As written, the United States Constitution was *not* designed to facilitate rights innovation, whether through Congress or the courts. The document contains one blocking mechanism after another, all quite appropriate given the potential breadth of power exercised by the federal branches. As written, the state constitutions were change incubators, governing smaller, often more congenial populations with shared worldviews.

How strange that we have converted the one constitution most difficult to amend (the US Constitution) and the judges most difficult to replace (federal judges) into the key change agents in our society. The United States Constitution is nearly impervious to change through amendment, generating pressure on the United States Supreme Court to alter it through interpretation *and* to make each change nearly unalterable. It might be easy to look the other way if all of this made up for a leading flaw in the 1789 US Constitution, that so few people participated in ratifying it. A cynic might even wonder if the federal founders made the US Constitution so difficult to amend because they were gratified by how few people participated in consenting to it. No matter, that is not the key problem anymore. Property restrictions on voting disappeared long ago, and the Fifteenth and Nineteenth Amendments removed race-based and gender-based restrictions on voting long ago, well before the amendment-by-interpretation approach commenced seventy-five or so years ago. Even if one wishes to ascribe some of the interpretive innovations of the last three-quarters of a century to completing the job left undone by the Fifteenth and Nineteenth Amendments,[179] that does not explain things.

Consider this predicament. The more representative American government has become over the course of American history, the more powerful the federal courts have grown. As political representation goes up, the influence of the federal courts does not go down, confirming that there is no Laffer Curve for federal judicial power. The growth in influence of the federal courts does not appear to be justified by concerns about political representation, at least if one thinks that more representation in government is better than less. Whatever one thinks of allowing shifting majorities of a nine-member US Supreme Court to make essential decisions about American governance, that centralization of power is assuredly not *more representative* of the many people who live in this diverse country.

The problem with modifying the United States Constitution by interpretation rather than amendment is that each change increases the gap between our foundational charter and its meaning. Over time, updating a constitution by interpretation runs the risk of skewing democratic government, cheapening law, and imperiling the body responsible for making the changes: the federal courts. It's not healthy for a legal system to leave the impression that some constitutional texts have come to look like hurdles to clear, not words to interpret, telling us more about the people who interpreted the document than about the people who ratified it. The process gives too many political factions in the country victories they don't deserve. It incentivizes beneficiaries of these rulings to stick to this increasingly well-worn path in taking on new problems. And it offers too many reasons for other political factions to throw up their arms in defeat—"If you can't beat them, join them"—and adopt the same approach for getting what *they* want.

Our American embrace of judicial review and the political incentives that go with it will not disappear soon. But at least at the state level, the effects of frequent judicial review are less jarring, less disfiguring to representative government. How can people feel disenfranchised by judicial decisions when they have a direct say in who the judges are, as is true in so many states? And because all state constitutions are easier to amend than the US Constitution, those critical of state court decisions have a readily accessible remedy. The design of each charter signals that the states were meant to be the breakwater in rights protection and the national government the shoreline defense.

Third, the most acute challenges of judicial review turn on efforts to construe highly generalized phrases or to identify rights nowhere enumerated in the constitution. If we must have such judicially enforceable rights, would it not make sense to have state courts identify them first? By allowing the state courts to be the first responders in addressing innovative rights claims, the United States Supreme Court can gain valuable insights useful to all schools of constitutional interpretation, whether deferential or not, whether pragmatic or not, whether originalist or living constitutionalist. The risks of error associated with a state-first approach are fewer. And the possibility of exporting ideas that work to other states and sometimes to the federal government is as promising when it comes to American constitutional law as it has been when it comes to other areas of law in which the state and federal governments have overlapping responsibilities: criminal law, contracts, property, torts. Time has a way of showing which individual rights have centrifugal tendencies and which have centripetal ones. A core feature of American government—federalism—works best if we encourage both halves of the equation to take seriously their responsibilities under it.

Constitutional rights nowhere mentioned in the federal charter—often called unenumerated rights or substantive due process rights—offer the best place to put this approach to work. There are long-term risks with the national judicialization of so many American policies unanchored in the terms of the US Constitution. A potential compromise in this area is to continue to allow the development of federal unenumerated rights but only after a meaningful group of state courts or state legislatures have identified them. That cures a legitimacy problem for the US Supreme Court. It's harder to criticize the Court for making up rights out of thin air, or worse to characterize it as just another political body, when it can point to a sustained effort in the states to protect those same rights before it recognizes them. Call it reverse lockstepping.[180]

Yes, that means some majoritarianism must predate the recognition of these new federal rights. And yes, that undermines one of the legends of *Marbury*, that it is the job of the federal courts to identify new counter-majoritarian rights, even those never ratified by the people. But there's no other way to do it, fairly. Any other approach is unvarnished gerrymandering. If the people never approved a right through the federal constitutional amendment process and if one thinks that five members of the US Supreme Court have authority to identify those rights when they wish, that is indeed giving factions of the country political victories they never earned and do not deserve.

Nor does this require us to revisit every federal constitutional ruling of the past. Even if one accepts that many of the Warren Court decisions were for the good as a matter of policy, and even if one assumes that the states brought this diminishment of authority upon themselves, that does not tell us what to do next. All essential constitutional questions come down to structure. And structure concerns who—not what—should be the leading change agents in society going forward, not looking backward. There's a lot to be said for shifting the balance back to the state courts.

Whatever the prospects for change through state constitutions and state courts may have been in the 1950s and 1960s, I have a hard time understanding why they remain inappropriate vehicles for rights innovation in the twenty-first century—and why they should not be the lead change agents going forward. When Justice Brandeis launched the laboratories metaphor for policy innovation, he used the plural, not the singular, signaling an interest in hearing how the states in the first instance would respond to new challenges.

A single laboratory of experimentation, headquartered at 1 First Street, Washington, DC, for fifty-one jurisdictions and 330 million people creates more risks than rewards. A ground-up approach to developing constitutional doctrine allows the Court to learn from the states. It is useful to pragmatic justices interested in how ideas work on the ground. It is useful to originalist justices interested in what words first found in state constitutions mean. It gives both sides to a debate time to make their case. And it places less pressure on the United States Supreme Court. The Court may wait for, and nationalize, a dominant majority position, lowering the stakes of its decision in the process. Or it may treat occasionally indeterminate language in the way it should be treated, as allowing for many approaches rather than just one.

Fourth, a from-the-ground-up approach not only facilitates the legitimate identification of new constitutional rights, but it also facilitates neutral efforts to decide which prior decisions to stand by. If you think it is hard to identify a workable theory of judicial review, try stare decisis—the custom of deference, though not abdication, to prior court decisions—which doubles the difficulty.

Problem one is whether a constitutional right exists. That topic implicates judicial respect for another branch of government, a problem ameliorated by looking at the origins of judicial review and by demanding the articulation of a clear constitutional right before the courts invalidate the handiwork of a co-equal branch of government. Problem two turns on the extent to which an appellate court should respect the work of the *same* branch of government at a different point in time, an earlier court that faced the same issue. Courts normally demand good justifications for overruling a prior decision, usually proof that it is clearly wrong and has clearly warped the legal landscape.

But a "clearly wrong" inquiry confounds on a few levels. Stare decisis comes into play only when the underlying decision is wrong. Else, there is nothing to worry about. But how wrong is too wrong? That does not readily submit to a judicial test or even verbal formulation. It's also not easy for the judge to apply. Even the most self-aware judge is apt to think that the prior decisions that chafe their worldview the most are the most clearly wrong. Also hard is group consensus on a multi-member court about handling such issues in an even-handed manner. Timeless features of human behavior, captured by what psychologists call attribution theory, should alert us that judges will have an excruciating time trying to be fair about equally respecting (or equally overruling) liberal and conservative precedents.

More difficult still is the lack of consensus about methods of interpretation. How can US Supreme Court justices identify clear reasons for overruling precedents when they can't agree on what they are looking for, when their different methods of interpretation turn on something as basic as whether the meaning of a constitution can change or not? An originalist justice's reason for preserving a precedent is not likely to captivate the frame of reference of a living constitutionalist, who thinks the meaning of guarantees sometimes evolves. And a living constitutionalist's reason for preserving a constitutional interpretation is not likely to captivate an originalist, who thinks it odd to lock in place a fixed meaning of a Supreme Court precedent rather than the fixed meaning of a constitutional guarantee. That looks like an unbridgeable divide. Anyone trying to understand American angst about federal judicial selection over the last several decades should remember that one of its key sources is not the goal of winning new constitutional victories; it's preserving old ones.

But here, again, the state courts (and state legislatures) offer a useful path. Why not look to the same place when deciding whether to undo federal constitutional decisions? As with identifying new unenumerated constitutional rights, so with overruling them. Ask first what the state courts have done with the guarantee. In a healthy landscape in which state courts independently construe their own guarantees, it's fair to ask whether they have agreed with the federal ruling or not. No doubt, we do not yet live in that world. But here's how it could work and here's why judicial elections need not be an impediment to it.

In 2010, the US Supreme Court decided *Citizens United*.[181] In a 5–4 ruling, the Court determined that the free speech guarantee of the First Amendment prohibited legislatures from imposing limitations on the use of money in campaigns. The federal prohibition on independent campaign spending by corporations is a "ban on speech," the Court reasoned, because it "necessarily reduces the quantity of expression, by restricting the number of issues discussed, the depth of their exploration, and the size of the audience reached."[182] Although "the Government may regulate corporate political speech through disclaimer and disclosure requirements," it continued, government "may not suppress that speech altogether."[183] A ban on independent spending thus cannot stand under the First Amendment because it is tantamount to an unconstitutional ban on political speech, which "does not lose First Amendment protection simply because its source is a corporation."[184] Right or wrong, the decision generated controversy.

One year later, the Montana Supreme Court faced a similar free-speech challenge to a campaign-finance regulation enacted by its legislature. In that decision, the court *upheld* the law. It relied heavily on Montana history, in particular the "copper baron" era when Montana-based mining companies used campaign contributions to influence state governors and legislatures to look the other way as they harmed two of Montana's treasures, its rivers and mountains.[185] "The Montana law at issue," the court said, "cannot be understood outside the context of the time and place it was enacted, during the early twentieth century."[186] These, the court continued, were "tumultuous years . . . marked by rough contests for political and economic domination" in which "examples of well-financed corruption abound[ed]."[187] In one case, a mining baron bribed the state legislature to the tune of $400,000—that's over $10 million in current dollars—to secure appointment as a US senator. When his corruption came to light, the Senate expelled him. But, "in a demonstration of extraordinary boldness," he returned to Montana and secured his reappointment, only to promptly resign when an outraged Senate threatened him with expulsion a second time.[188] Political reforms, including the challenged campaign-finance restrictions, followed "not long thereafter."[189] How, the Montana Supreme Court thought, could a free-speech guarantee prohibit Montana from heeding the lessons of that disfiguring chapter of state history? How could the federal First Amendment be so rigid that it could not account for this local history?

What you might think would happen next did happen next. The US Supreme Court reversed the state court decision. The First Amendment applies to the states and the national government after all. And the Supremacy Clause mentions state court judges by name, requiring them to follow federal law and amounting to the one clause in the US Constitution that seems to mandate judicial review.[190] The Court issued a brief decision without argument that overruled the decision. "The question" was simple: Does "the holding of *Citizens United* appl[y] to the Montana state law"?[191] So too was the answer: "There can be no serious doubt that it does."[192]

That did not have to happen. The Montana Supreme Court could have begun its opinion by acknowledging that two constitutional guarantees potentially prohibit the state law: the state and federal free speech clauses. It could have started with the state guarantee, as state courts like Oregon do.[193] Then it could have unearthed this revealing Montana history, confirming that it was implausible that the Montana free-speech guarantee *required* the state to continue to live under corporate rule. The Montana court indeed could have framed the issue by saying just what it did say, just in reference to the state constitutional guarantee: "The question, then, is when in the last 99 years did Montana lose the power or interest sufficient to support the statute, if it ever did."[194] The finishing move could have gone something like this: "In Montana, our free speech clause protects speech, not money."

Having done that, it could have switched to the federal constitution and analyzed it in one sentence: "So long as *Citizens United* remains good law (not for long we hope), we must follow it under the Supremacy Clause and thus invalidate the law."[195]

In one sense, it's true, nothing would have changed. The state still could not have enforced its campaign-finance law. But in another sense, the court would have registered a legitimate local objection, under its own interpretation of free speech, to *Citizens United*. And it would have set a precedent for other state courts to consider in addressing similar claims. Does anyone doubt that other state courts, perhaps many state courts, would have followed this path in the years since 2011 if the Montana Supreme Court had marked it? Does anyone think the selection of judges through elections in progressive states would have gotten in the way? Depending on the force of the reasoning of these decisions, it's quite possible they would have laid the groundwork for a legitimate overruling of *Citizens United*.

One wonders why something similar has not happened with the equally controversial abortion decisions: *Roe* and *Casey*. As with *Citizens United*, it's easy to imagine that a healthy number of state courts do not agree with the decisions, and perhaps do not even agree with substantive due process. In a highly functioning federalist court system, one would expect state court disagreement with national decisions to be a useful and neutral barometer, if not the only barometer, for ascertaining what national constitutional decisions should stand and which should not. Yet there is not one majority state high court decision, as well as I can tell, that rejects *Roe* or *Casey* under its state constitution. A case from North Dakota offers a split decision by its Supreme Court.[196] Two justices would have held that the state constitution protects a right to abortion; two would have held that it does not; and one justice would not have considered the state constitutional issue in light of the federal right.[197] Because the North Dakota Constitution requires four votes to hold a statute unconstitutional, the state abortion regulation was upheld. The only other case that rejects *Roe* and *Casey* on state constitutional grounds is *Mahaffey v. Attorney General*, a 1997 intermediate-court decision by the Michigan Court of Appeals.[198] Deepening the mystery, four states—Alabama, Arkansas, Tennessee, and West Virginia—have amended their constitutions to clarify that they do not protect a right to an abortion.[199]

Many wonder if it is true that state courts may interpret their own constitutions to provide *less* protection than the US Constitution offers. Yes, emphatically so. The Supremacy Clause just requires state courts to honor federal decisions in *construing the federal guarantee*. But the clause has no purchase when it comes to the independent meaning of a state guarantee, even one that matches the federal guarantee word for word. Justice McDonald of the Iowa Supreme Court put the point well:

> The conclusion that this court can interpret the Iowa Constitution to provide less or more protection than a parallel provision of the Federal Constitution is inherent in the federal system. The Bill of Rights, in and of itself, applies only to the federal government. The Supreme Court is the final arbiter of the meaning of the Federal Constitution. In contrast, the Iowa Constitution applies to the state government. This court is the final arbiter of the meaning of the Iowa Constitution. In determining the meaning of state constitutional law, this court has a duty to independently determine the meaning of the Iowa Constitution. This is true whether we interpret the Iowa Constitution to provide less or more protection than the Federal Constitution.
>
> [The] contention that the incorporation doctrine dictates the minimum required content of state constitutional law misapprehends the incorporation doctrine. Incorporation did not change the substantive content of state constitutional law; it changed the substantive content of federal constitutional law. . . . Pursuant to the Supremacy Clause, this court is bound to apply the Supreme Court's Fourteenth Amendment jurisprudence to resolve claims arising under the Fourteenth Amendment. The Supreme Court's Fourteenth Amendment jurisprudence does not dictate the substance of the state law or the remedy for any violation of the same.[200]

That leaves two ways in which state court federalism can help discern the meaning of the US Constitution. The state courts can be the lead proponents of change in addressing new problems, the experimenters in chief. Why adopt one approach at the outset, this consideration asks, when it's not clear what the best approach is? Independent of that role, the state courts, together with state legislatures, can help in identifying a national consensus about the need for the US Supreme Court to identify new federal constitutional rights or the need to discard old ones—what we might call a free-market approach to the issue. But there's no free market—it's a skewed market—if state courts innovate only in granting *more rights* under their constitutions. The only way in which state court federalism helps the country is when state courts engage constitutional rights in both directions, registering respectful disagreement with some federal decisions and creating prompts for new decisions.

Fifth, if all else fails when it comes to consensus about national rights, that leaves the possibility that in some areas we are better off with state-by-state variation. The more difficult it is to find a single answer to a problem, the more likely state-by-state variation is an appropriate way to handle the issue. Just as the intricacy of a problem might prompt different, even competing, answers, it might prompt state courts (and legislatures) to pace change at different speeds. In many areas of law affected by changing social norms, the most important question is not whether but when, not whether but by whom. Local variation is a useful long-term option for problems impervious to one solution and a useful short-term option for problems cured by trial and error.

Some object to this idea on the ground that constitutional rights should be uniform, that we should not have patchwork constitutional guarantees throughout the country. It depends. But I can promise one thing. No one always wants uniformity for all federal constitutional rulings. Would it have been preferable if *Buck v. Bell*, for example, were treated as the only way to address state constitutional challenges to laws that involuntarily sterilized individuals with disabilities? Doubtful. I know of no one today who objects to the state courts' independent authority to invalidate eugenics laws under their state constitutions.

An individual's preference for uniformity usually amounts to an ink blot test for that citizen's assessment of the value of the right, nothing more. The lead-up to *Mapp v. Ohio* and its aftermath illustrate the point. One of the central explanations for nationalizing the exclusionary rule, according to *Mapp*, was a desire to ensure that all citizens suspected of crime were treated the same way from coast to coast.[201] But there is more disuniformity today when it comes to search and seizure protections than there was before *Mapp* in 1961,[202] and no one who favors an exclusionary rule objects to it. That is because today's variation arises primarily from state court decisions that provide more protection, even if more balkanized protection, than the Fourth Amendment provides. Not all constitutional rights lend themselves to blanket enforcement. And not all protection of rights in varied, balkanized, or patchwork ways is problematic. Sometimes the end product is a colorful, well-shaped quilt.

PART II

The Executive Branches

Two misconceptions sometimes arise in thinking about the structure of state constitutions. One is to think that because all fifty-one constitutions in this country organize government into three branches, the federal constitution requires the states to follow its lead in how they organize their governments, distribute power, set limits on power, and establish terms of office. That is not the case and misreads the history anyway. The early state charters first embraced the structural ideas of Montesquieu, a French judge incidentally, whose *The Spirit of the Laws* recommended that governments divide power into legislative, executive, and judicial branches. When the US Constitution followed the states' lead and embraced this model in 1789, it did not require existing and future states to stand by any one method of organizing governments. The "separation of powers embodied in the United States Constitution," the US Supreme Court reminds us, "is not mandatory in state governments."[1] As Alan Tarr puts the point, "state governments are not merely miniature versions of the national government—or at least need not be."[2] Just as states can vary from the federal model by electing their judges, so states can vary from the federal model by dividing up executive-branch power into separately elected offices— a governor, an attorney general, a secretary of state, even a superin-tendent of insurance—and by giving their governors special powers, such as the line-item veto, an authority American presidents have long sought but never obtained.

As Chapter 5 reveals, these state variations have many implications for how executive power operates at the state level. A multi-head exec-utive at the state level weakens gubernatorial power, while the line-item veto strengthens it. Throughout, a government with many elected heads of state at a minimum complicates the exercise of executive power at the same time that it democratizes each mini-branch of it.

The other misconception is to think that when states share a model of exercising power—say, the use of executive-branch agencies to im-plement and enforce regulatory programs—that power and any limits on that power will work in the same way at the federal and state levels. Not true either. While a multi-volume treatise could cover the many differences between state and federal administrative law, Chapter 6 focuses on two consequential differences. Up first is the non-delegation doctrine's limit on legislative allocations of policymaking power to other branches of government, and the array of approaches to the issue at the state and federal levels. Up second is administrative def-erence, and the many shades of deference given and denied to state agencies in construing statutes they implement, all in contrast to the federal *Chevron* model that requires judges to defer to reasonable interpretations of such laws.

5

One Chief Executive or Many?

IF A TIME TRAVELER set out to understand American history, an understanding of the United States Constitution and the US Supreme Court's interpretations of it would take her a good way down the road given how often federal constitutional developments overlap with political milestones of each epoch. What would complete the trip, what in truth amounts to a superior measure of American history, emerges from a review of our fifty state constitutions and their evolution since 1776. There have been just seventeen amendments to the US Constitution since the Bill of Rights in 1791. The easily amendable state constitutions, in swift contrast, have constantly changed in the face of new circumstances, offering real-time public-record evidence of American history and the best evidence of changing American preferences for how to allocate power and shape government.[1]

Our American executive branches illustrate the point. The fifty state constitutions and the United States Constitution share a "surface similarity" in describing the authority of their chief executives: They both vest executive power in a governor or president.[2] "But when one proceeds below the surface," Alan Tarr observes, "one finds that these apparently analogous structures of government . . . quickly evaporate."[3]

At the national level, the US Constitution places all executive authority in one president. "*The* executive Power," it says, "shall be vested in *a* President of the United States of America."[4] The president controls the executive-branch officers through the singular authority to choose all cabinet members, whether it's the attorney general, the secretary of defense, the secretary of state, the secretary of the treasury, the secretary of health and human services, and on and on. What's called a unitary executive largely is one, given the president's authority to hire and fire these executive branch officers. In separation-of-powers terms, we have a concentration of executive power in one place, a single target any time the people want change, and a single target any time the legislative or judicial branches push back on uses of executive power.

Contrast the state side. In response to the unhappy colonial experiences with a monarch, many of the first state constitutions created weak executive branches. All but one of the original state constitutions also mandated that the governor (sometimes called a president) work alongside an executive council.[5] As Gordon Wood puts it, these councils made the early governors "little more than chairmen of their executive boards."[6] The notoriously weak president of Pennsylvania presided over a council that made group decisions.[7] Even the governor of Massachusetts, the "most muscular" of the early state executives,[8] needed the consent of an executive council for many actions.[9] The early constitutions also divided the executive branch as another way to tame it. Each of the original states provided for the independent selection of an attorney general.[10] In some cases, the attorney general was appointed by the governor (with the consent of his council), and in other cases the office was filled by the legislature or, in the case of Rhode Island, by popular vote.[11] Some of the early state constitutions also included other independent constitutional executive offices—secretary, treasurer, auditor—whose occupants were selected by someone other than the governor, often the legislature.[12]

While the unitary federal executive has remained unaltered, the state executive branches have continued to evolve. The states not only departed from the federal model from the beginning, but they also often borrowed from other state models and sometimes innovated on their own. The idea of creating separate executive branch officials chosen by someone other than the governor continued into the early nineteenth century. The Indiana Constitution of 1816, for example, created a treasurer and auditor selected by the legislature.[13] At roughly the same time that some states began to select their judges through elections, some states began to select many executive branch officials through elections.[14] Similar considerations often drove both developments, the spread of Jacksonian populism at the top of the list.[15] Facilitating these changes, they often occurred in the same state constitutional conventions in the mid-nineteenth century that launched the election of judges.[16] Before long, separate elections for many separate executive branch officials became prevalent for new states entering the Union. In retrospect, a government that chose to allocate a valued right of citizenship—voting—parsimoniously at the outset should not have been surprised when more citizens wanted the right and wanted to use it for more and more government positions.

Today's stateside norm is separate statewide elections for numerous officials other than the governor. The approach to state attorneys general illustrates how removed the state experience is from the federal one. Forty-three of them are separately elected, and forty-eight of them are free from the governor's control.[17] The Maine legislature still selects its attorney general, and the Tennessee Supreme Court selects its attorney general.[18] The governor appoints the attorney general in New Jersey, New Hampshire, and Hawaii but cannot remove the attorney general at will.[19] That leaves Alaska and Wyoming, where the governor selects the attorney general and may fire him at her pleasure.[20]

A helpful survey by Miriam Seifter tallies the other state offices separately elected: thirty-seven states elect a secretary of state, thirty-four elect a treasurer, twenty-four elect an auditor, and twenty-two elect either a superintendent of public instruction or members of a board of education.[21] That's not the last of it. States elect many other officials, too. Nine states elect a commissioner of agriculture, and two elect members of a corporation commission.[22] Some states have unique elections, with Hawaii electing a board of trustees for the Office of Hawaiian Affairs,[23] Louisiana an election official,[24] and South Carolina an adjutant general.[25]

Just three states still stand by the federal model and elect a sole leader of the executive branch: the governor. That's Maine, New Hampshire, and New Jersey.[26] Note that every state after 1820, when Maine obtained statehood, has embraced the plural executive. In deciding how plural to make the executive branch, some states seem limited only by their imagination. Five states share the title for most elected executive officers, coming in at eleven.[27] They are Florida, Idaho, North Dakota, South Carolina, and Washington. In 2002, the average number of elected executive officers was 6.7, an increase from 6.0 in 1977.[28] Jacksonian populism continues to thrive in the states.[29]

Why divide up the state executive branches, but not the presidency, in this way? Keep in mind that the Framers of the US Constitution were aware of the option of creating more than one executive. The Roman Republic had tried it, and so had some of the early states. Alexander Hamilton became the foremost proponent of a unitary executive. The plural model would not work, he argued in *Federalist* 70, because "energy in the Executive is a leading character in the definition of good government," and one of the "ingredients" for "energy in the executive" is unity. Accountability also is at risk with a divided executive. *Federalist* 70 again: One of the "weightiest objections to a plurality in the Executive" is "that it tends to conceal faults and destroy responsibility." So: "Where power and responsibility is spread, it often becomes impossible, amidst mutual accusations, to determine on whom the blame or the punishment of a pernicious measure" should rest—permitting blame to "shift[] from one to another" and leaving the public "in suspense" over the source of the problem. According to Akhil Amar, the "vesting of such broad appointment power in one man"—to appoint an attorney general and a secretary of state, for examples—"contrasted sharply with most state constitutions, which located far more power in the legislature or some subset thereof, and with the Articles of Confederation, which had vested these personnel decisions in a multimember, quasi-executive proto-Senate."[30]

But time has shown some virtues of adopting a plural model, at least at the state level. One telling difference between the federal and state situations is the lack of a foreign-affairs or war-power imperative at the state level. The best justification for a singular, efficient, ready-to-go executive branch does not exist at the state level. That leaves the kinds of arguments that congenitally appeal to Americans. If in doubt, Americans prefer to check and divide the leaders to whom they delegate power and to vote for more, rather than fewer, of them. And if in doubt, they prefer to vote for both sides of the balance. By dividing the executive branch, a state constitution creates new restraints on power beyond those already provided by separate legislative and judicial branches. It forces the governor and secretary of state to account for each other on voting issues, and it forces them each to work with the legislature in enacting new laws or funding existing programs. The resulting coordination and cooperation curb the risk of abuses of power and potentially improve the power exercised. Separate elections of state officials allow citizens to train their political priorities on specific matters by subject rather than dilute them with one vote for one executive leader. A voter might prefer a governor with views that are congenial in general with the voter's preferred political party, a secretary of state with a preferred agenda on election matters, and an attorney general with an agenda of her own on consumer protection and other regulatory enforcement. Separate votes permit customized votes.

But what happens as a matter of governance when multiple state officials exercise executive power unsupervised by the governor and beyond her control? Few problems would arise if each state official exercised a silo-like power, did not compete for finite resources from the same legislature, came from the same political party as the other state officials, and had no ambition for higher office. But how often does that happen? Plenty of complications, political and otherwise, arise from separately elected stations. A secretary of state not only must obtain the support of the legislature in altering the voting laws, he also must convince the governor to sign the bill into law. What if the governor and the attorney general disagree about the proper legal position of the state?

Some complications arise whether the executive stands alone or with many. Who checks the president or governor or other elected state executive branch official if an abuse of power occurs? Does the legislature have a role to play? Or is the next election or the formidable costs of impeachment the only recourse? And how often do in-state political rivalries or cases of competing ambition, whether within or across parties, affect these and other intra-branch and inter-branch disputes affecting executive power? These federal and state stories take on these issues.

Federal Story

What to do with presidents or cabinet members who allegedly broke the law has been with us from the outset. The near impeachment conviction of President Andrew Johnson, the resignation of President

Nixon, and the impeachment efforts directed at Presidents Clinton and Trump all confirm that the unitary executive makes the president a useful target, if sometimes an invited target, of challenges to the conduct of these individuals, whether driven by partisanship or not. In a country with an independently elected attorney general or independently appointed attorney general, one could well imagine challenges to executive-branch mischief running through that office. One might even think of such attorneys general as independent counsels. But that is not the federal model. How, then, to handle the problem short of waiting for the next election or resorting to impeachment?

Morrison v. Olson offers one take on how to handle this sticky problem. In 1978, a few years after Watergate, Congress enacted the "Ethics in Government Act." Title VI of the act provided for the appointment of an independent counsel to investigate and prosecute high-ranking government officials. Under the act, the attorney general could apply to a Special Division of the DC Circuit to appoint an independent counsel on the basis that there were "reasonable grounds to believe that further investigation or prosecution [was] warranted."[31] The act gave the independent counsel "full power and independent authority to exercise all investigative and prosecutorial functions and powers of the Department of Justice."[32] The act permitted the attorney general to remove the counsel "only for good cause, physical disability, mental incapacity, or any other condition that substantially impairs the performance of such independent counsel's duties."[33] An attorney general wishing to remove the counsel had to submit a report to the House and Senate Judiciary Committees spelling out the grounds for removal.

In 1982, the Environmental Protection Agency (EPA) and the Department of Justice were sorting out how to enforce the recently enacted "Superfund Law." Two subcommittees of the House asked the agencies to produce documents about their decision making. The president ordered the administrator of the EPA to invoke executive privilege and to withhold some documents on the ground that they contained "sensitive information." In response, the House Judiciary Committee investigated the Department of Justice's role in the controversy and eventually asked the attorney general to seek appointment of an independent counsel to investigate allegations against three Department of

Justice officials. An independent counsel was appointed and subpoenas served. The three officials objected that the counsel violated the Constitution's division of powers.

A divided panel of the DC Circuit agreed on the ground that the act denied the president the power to remove the independent counsel, who exercised a core executive function. The Supreme Court reversed by an 8–1 vote.

Through an opinion by Chief Justice Rehnquist, the Court acknowledged that the independent counsel performed an executive function. But it reasoned that the counsel's duties were so small-bore in scope that a "good cause" standard for removal did not interfere with the functioning of the executive branch. Thus: "we simply do not see how the President's need to control the exercise of [the independent counsel's] discretion is so central to the functioning of the Executive Branch as to require as a matter of constitutional law that the counsel be terminable at will by the President."[34]

Justice Scalia, nearing the end of his second year on the Court, saw it differently. For him, criminal prosecutions and the president's authority to remove the independent counsel were central to executive power. Under Article II, he reasoned, all executive power—"The executive Power"—is vested in the president. The scope of the independent counsel's executive duties had nothing to do with it. All that mattered was whether the independent counsel performs an executive function. If so, the exercise of that function was subject to exclusive control by the president, no matter how significant or not the job. The "Founders conspicuously and very consciously declined," he observed, "to sap the Executive's strength in the same way they had weakened the Legislature: by dividing the Executive power."[35]

Protecting the independent counsel from removal, he insisted, also protected the counsel from accountability to the executive's only elected officer. Drawing on Hamilton, he reasoned that one of the benefits of the unitary executive is that it focuses the accountability for executive failures on one, punishable officer.[36] An executive officer whom the president cannot remove escapes any such blame. While the president may discharge other officers in order to manage political consequences, the president is comparatively helpless to manage the political consequences of the counsel's actions.[37]

The singular focus of the independent counsel, Justice Scalia added, ran the risk of becoming an obsessive focus. The independent counsel would not benefit from the internal checks and balances that the executive branch normally provides, leaving the prospect of Javert-like characters compulsively searching for crimes by one person. A benefit of the unitary executive, Scalia explained, is that it brings multiple perspectives together to achieve unified goals. While this multiplicity of perspectives did not always lead to a more uniform application of the law, the unitary executive provided "the mechanism" to achieve that end.[38] In the prosecutorial context, isolating a prosecuting officer from these competing considerations would lead to blinkered zeal. In an amicus brief, several former attorneys general warned that an independent prosecutor could suffer from "too narrow a focus, the loss of perspective, [and] preoccupation with the pursuit of one alleged suspect to the exclusion of other interests."[39] Acknowledging that Congress often dressed up violations of the Constitution's separation of powers "in sheep's clothing," Scalia insisted that nothing of the sort was going on here: "this wolf comes as a wolf."[40]

Justice Scalia's lone dissent in *Morrison* did not lack company for long. History has vindicated his perspective. A decade after the decision, one scholar sized up the situation in this way: "In the decade since *Morrison v. Olson* was decided, nearly every float in the parade of horribles predicted by Justice Scalia has come to pass."[41] In 1999, the independent counsel mechanism of the Ethics in Government Act was allowed to lapse without re-enactment. A *Washington Examiner* article recounts the Clinton administration's approach to the law at the time:

> When the statute came up for renewal in 1999, the Clinton administration, through the Justice Department, changed its position. "Having worked with the act," attorney general Janet Reno told the Senate Committee on Governmental Affairs, "I have come to believe—after much reflection and with great reluctance—that [it] is structurally flawed and that those flaws cannot be corrected within our constitutional framework." Reno went on to discuss the separation of powers and the lack of accountability on the part of

independent counsels for exercises of power that are plainly executive. "Here," she said, "I am paraphrasing Justice Scalia's dissent in
Morrison."[42]

Even if both political parties today show no appetite for creating
authority for new independent counsels, the problems prompting such
laws remain. There's an understandable instinct to prevent any branch
from exercising exclusive powers in unfair ways and a natural inclina-
tion to distrust investigators controlled by the subject. Justice Scalia
anticipated the point in this way. "Is it unthinkable," he asked, "that the
President should have such exclusive power, even when alleged crimes
by him or his close associates are at issue?" "No more so," he answered,
"than that Congress should have the exclusive power of legislation, even
when what is at issue is its own exemption from the burdens of certain
laws," even criminal laws.[43]

Inspectors general housed in the executive and legislative branches
work to curb these kinds of problems. But they still report to these
branches and are not independent from them. In some ways, the idea of
independent counsels is reminiscent of the problem the Missouri Plan
tried to address in selecting independent judges. How to design a selection system that takes the politics out of choosing judges and preserves
independence from their selectors? One approach—the 1978 Ethics
in Government approach—inserts an independent official appointed
from another branch to fix the problem. Another approach—the
Missouri Plan—uses unelected, if well-connected, private individuals
to select a slate of potential judges for the governor to select. How
does either approach promote independence? And independence from
whom, it must be considered? If the goal is independence from the
electorate, that starts to create more accountability and representation
problems than it solves. It's hard to squeeze the politics out of the selection and removal process for any job, whether an independent counsel
or a judge, that exercises considerable power and, with it, holds the potential to comfort some citizens and frustrate others.

Either way, all of this comes back to "Power," as Justice Scalia
declared.[44] Compare what the states have done with similar and dis-
similar exercises of power.

The State Stories

If the plural executive removes one problem, it creates others. Is an independently elected attorney general in effect an independent counsel? Is there room for independent counsel laws at the state level? How does a state determine its legal position in pending litigation when it has separately elected executive branch officials, each with a stake in the matter? Who decides whether to defend the constitutionality of a law enacted by the legislature? And who decides whether the state joins an amicus curiae brief in its high court or the US Supreme Court?

These questions have led to plenty of cases and debates. In most states, the attorney general, as the constitutional legal officer of the state, has the final say about the legal position of the state.[45] But that does not fix everything. The governor still may have authority to obtain her own legal counsel to present her perspective in the case. The same can happen with other separately selected state officers.

The complications sometimes go beyond the executive branch. The legislature may ask to intervene in a case or file an amicus brief in a case, sometimes after obtaining permission from the attorney general to do so. In some states, the legislature may direct the attorney general to take particular legal action. A legislature may even direct the attorney general to sue the governor.[46] Many states do not follow the federal constitution's distinctions between "principal" and "inferior" executive officers.[47] And many governors have little authority over state court appointments, except to fill judicial posts left open when judges retire before the end of their terms. At the same time, however, the legislative role in judicial selections also has been diminished, as the legislature often has little say when a governor fills an empty seat or uses the Missouri Plan to fill a seat.[48]

It takes little imagination to see how the division of executive power could create artery-clogging problems and accountability benefits. In an effort to show the array of issues that can arise, this section addresses a state's effort to use an independent counsel law, a dispute over use of the appointment power between a governor and lieutenant governor, and several states' efforts to address a conspicuous problem over the last few decades: the role of state attorneys general in handling local and national legal disputes.

Pennsylvania

Pennsylvania has experimented with its own independent counsel law.[49] Much like the federal Ethics in Government Act of 1978, the Pennsylvania legislature adopted an independent counsel statute after allegations of corruption. In 1995, Pennsylvania attorney general Ernest D. Preate Jr. was charged with federal mail fraud. The charges stemmed from unreported campaign donations from video poker operators, which allegedly influenced his non-enforcement of the gambling laws against them. Preate pled guilty to the charges and spent twelve months in a federal prison.

The legislature responded to the scandal with a targeted fix. Fearful that the attorney general, as chief law officer of the state,[50] would be able to evade prosecution under state law, and fearful that this independently elected official[51] could prosecute the governor and other executive branch officials without oversight from anyone but the voters, the legislature enacted an independent counsel law.[52] The law permitted the independent counsel to prosecute only the attorney general, employees of his office, and individuals on his campaign committee.[53] Aside from its narrow scope, it was modeled after the federal provision. Upon suspicion of a conflict of interest, either the general counsel of the governor or the attorney general had to appoint a special investigative counsel. If the investigative counsel identified grounds to proceed, he could apply to a three-judge panel for the appointment of an independent counsel. As with the federal law, the judicial panel appointed the independent counsel and defined the limits of the counsel's jurisdiction. Within that jurisdiction, the counsel exercised the authority of a prosecutor and could be removed only for "good cause" by the governor's general counsel.[54]

Unlike the federal law, the Pennsylvania law remains on the books.[55] As a matter of policy and law, it has avoided the fate of the federal model. One explanation, as John Coles points out, may be the limited scope of the law and the lower political stakes that come with that focus. With a plural executive, Pennsylvania could center the law on one executive branch office and one corruption concern: law enforcement. At the same time, Pennsylvania could avoid the partisan risks that come with permitting an independent counsel to remove the leader of the executive branch, the governor, or for that matter the other elected executive branch officials. It also made a difference that the attorney general rarely plays a role in legislative matters, a topic of considerable partisan concern and thus considerable independent counsel risk.[56]

California

Having a multi-headed executive sometimes leads to opportunistic (and amusing) behavior.[57] Under the California Constitution, the people separately elect a governor and a lieutenant governor, and the two officials thus may come from different political parties.[58] The constitution vests the lieutenant governor with various powers, one being the authority to act as the governor when the governor leaves the state or is otherwise incapable of performing his duties. Here's the relevant language:

> The Lieutenant Governor shall act as Governor during the impeachment, absence from the State, or other temporary disability of the Governor or of a Governor-elect who fails to take office.[59]

What does it mean for a governor to be absent from the state? In 1979, California governor Jerry Brown, in a quest to become the next Democratic candidate for president, traveled to Washington, DC.[60] While there, Lieutenant Governor Mike Curb, a Republican, nominated a superior court judge for an appellate court vacancy.[61] Although the California Constitution gave this appointment power to the governor,[62] Curb defended the appointment on the ground that the governor's absence gave him the authority to nominate judges in his stead.[63] Governor Brown protested that the term "absence" required a governor's incapacity to perform the duties of the office and that any other interpretation in a world of ready travel and easy communication would be unreasonable.[64]

The California Supreme Court sided with the lieutenant governor. It held that the constitution's reference to "absence" merely required a governor to be outside the state. The history of the provision, the court explained, undermined Brown's interpretation, as the Constitution Revision Committee had considered modern communications technology before making the change. "The Governor could be some-place outside the state and be very capable of performing his duties by a long distance telephone,"[65] but it nonetheless insisted that he "would be legally disabled from doing so."[66] The court also feared that Brown's interpretation created an unworkable standard. Given modern communications technology, it would be difficult to know what duties a governor could perform outside the state, leaving the lieutenant governor with no reliable way of knowing when he was in charge. The court opted for an "all-inclusive" physical-presence test for determining when gubernatorial duties and powers transferred to the lieutenant governor.[67]

Brown prevailed anyway. The powers the lieutenant governor obtained when the governor left the state, as it happens, could be undone. Such nominations could "be changed at the will of the executive until title to the office is vested."[68] Brown returned to California before any vesting, and he successfully rescinded the judge's nomination. The pawn in this fight was future California supreme court justice Armand Arabian, who had to wait five more years for a seat on the appellate bench.

Georgia

The caption of *Perdue v. Baker* foreshadows a classic conflict that arises between governors and attorneys general.[69] Georgia's governor, Sonny Perdue, sued Georgia's attorney general, Thurbert Baker. The governor wanted the attorney general to end an appeal filed on behalf of the state over the validity of a legislative reapportionment plan under the federal Voting Rights Act. At stake was whether the attorney general "has the authority under state law to appeal a court decision invalidating a state redistricting statute despite the Governor's order to dismiss the appeal."[70] If fights over independent counsels amount to skirmishes about power, fights over redistricting amount to wars over power.

In the aftermath of the 2000 census and in compliance with the federal Equal Protection Clause,[71] the Georgia legislature reapportioned its senate districts, and the governor, then Roy Barnes, signed the bill into law. As required by section 5 of the Voting Rights Act at the time,[72] the state filed a preclearance action in the United States District Court for the District of Columbia to permit this redistricting plan to go into effect and to show that the plan did not have the goal or effect of "denying or abridging the right to vote on account of race or color or membership in a language minority group."[73] The district court denied preclearance because the state had failed to show that the redistricting plan would not have "a retrogressive effect on the voting strength of African-American voters in Georgia."[74]

In July 2002, the attorney general appealed the decision to the United States Supreme Court, as permitted in such actions. In January 2003, the Supreme Court agreed to review the case.

Ten days later, soon after being sworn in, Governor Perdue asked the attorney general to dismiss the appeal. The lines were drawn. On one side, the governor claimed that the Georgia Constitution vested the top executive official in the state to oversee a case when the state of Georgia is a party. On the other side, the attorney general claimed that the Georgia Constitution gave his office "exclusive authority in all legal matters related to the executive branch in state government."[75]

Writing for the majority, Chief Justice Fletcher laid out each officer's constitutionally delegated powers. Both were "elected constitutional officers in the executive branch of state government, which is responsible for enforcing state statutes."[76] As for the governor, he is "vested with the chief executive powers,"[77] including "the responsibility to see that the laws are faithfully executed."[78] In the words of the relevant constitutional provision: "The chief executive powers shall be vested in the Governor."[79] As for the attorney general, the constitution says that "the other executive officers shall have such powers as may be prescribed by this Constitution and by law."[80] The constitution provides that the attorney general "shall act as the legal advisor of the executive department, shall represent the state in the Supreme Court in all capital felonies and in all civil and criminal cases in any court when required by the governor, and shall perform such other duties as shall be required by law."[81]

State statutes authorized the governor *and* attorney general to participate in litigation for the state. Under a state law creating the Department of Law, the governor "shall have power to direct the Department of Law, through the Attorney General as head thereof, to institute and prosecute in the name of the State such matters, proceedings, and litigations as he shall deem to be in the best interest of the people of the State."[82] At the same time, state statutes provided for the attorney general's "constitutional duties to serve as the executive branch's legal adviser, represent the State in all capital felony appeals, and represent the State in all civil and criminal actions when required by the Governor."[83] On top of that, the statute gave the attorney general "independent authority to represent the state in any civil action without the governor's request: 'It is the duty of the Attorney General to represent the state in all civil actions tried in any court.'"[84]

According to the court, the pertinent constitutional provisions and statutes deny either officer "exclusive power to control legal proceedings involving the State of Georgia."[85] They instead show that the governor and attorney general have "concurrent powers over litigation in which the State is a party."[86] All of this allows both of them "to make certain that state laws are faithfully enforced," "both may decide to initiate legal proceedings to protect the State's interests," "both may ensure that the State's interests are defended in legal actions," and "both may institute investigations of wrongdoing by state agencies and officials."[87]

In one sense, the outcome of the case defied convention: Both sides lost. The court "reject[ed] the broader claim by each officer that he has the ultimate authority to decide what is in the best interest of the people of the State in every lawsuit involving the State of Georgia."[88] Calls for one and puts for the other won out. This approach, the court reasoned, "provides a system of checks and balances within the executive branch so that no single official has unrestrained power to decide what laws to enforce and when to enforce them."[89] The state of Georgia after all "is not one branch of government, one office, or one officer. The State's authority resides with the people who elect many officers with different responsibilities under valid law."[90]

It's worth pointing out how the state court construed one constitutional provision on which the governor had relied. The 1983 constitution, like all of the state's constitutions since 1868,[91] said that the attorney general "shall represent the state in all civil and criminal cases in any court when required by the governor."[92] But the court "decline[d] to address the Governor's contention, adopted by the dissent, that his express right to initiate litigation includes the implicit right to end any lawsuit."[93]

How, then, did the court resolve the dispute? Ultimately, on grounds specific to Georgia law and in some ways laws enacted with respect to this dispute. Not just the governor and attorney general had interests in the case; so too did the legislature, the author of the redistricting law. "The dispositive issue," the court said, "is whether any laws of this State grant the Attorney General independent authority to continue the litigation in this case."[94] As to that, the court noted that the legislature had enacted laws to that precise end.

A general and specific statute prompted the court to allow the attorney general to continue to litigate the appeal in the US Supreme Court. "In 1975, [the legislature] made explicit what had previously been only implicit: the Attorney General has the power to represent the State in civil actions independently of the Governor's direction."[95] "The amended code section provides authority for the Attorney General to represent legislators and other state officials 'on his own motion' without any request, requirement, or direction from the Governor."[96] At the same time, the court declined to determine "the full extent of the Attorney General's power to represent the State under this statute or the circumstances, if any, under which the Governor may compel the Attorney General to end his representation."[97] That was because "a more narrowly drawn statute provides authority for the Attorney General to continue the voting rights litigation despite the Governor's order to dismiss the appeal"[98] and conveyed a desire that the attorney general continue this precise dispute. All of this counseled in favor of allowing the attorney general to continue the appeal.

As one might anticipate, this last statute implicated another division-of-powers dispute. To what extent could the legislature affect whether the governor or attorney general controlled litigation over the constitutionality of *its* law? The legislature enacted the law after the district court "denied preclearance to the original Senate redistricting plan, but before the State filed an appeal of that decision to the U.S. Supreme Court," and it conveyed a desire to "obtain a final determination on the legality of the original plan under the federal Voting Rights Act."[99] One could imagine a state court saying that the legislature's preference has nothing to do with it. Sure, it might have a general desire to see its laws defended. But is that its prerogative? And isn't it worse to express a view about how to handle litigation over just one of its own laws?

Here's how the court framed the question: "We next consider whether Act 444 violates the doctrine of separation of powers by directing that it takes effect only after a final determination is made regarding the enforceability of the provisions of [the earlier redistricting plan] under the Voting Rights Act."[100] Here's how the court answered it: "Because Act 444 does not impermissibly encroach on the power of the executive branch to control litigation, but instead is a proper assertion of legislative power to determine reapportionment, we conclude that it does not violate separation of powers."[101] In more detail, it reasoned, a law "violates separation of powers when it increases legislative powers at the expense of the executive branch, or when the enactment 'prevents the Executive Branch from accomplishing its constitutionally assigned functions,' even if it does not increase legislative powers."[102] "The core legislative function," it explained, "is the establishment of public policy through the enactment of laws," and "the expressed intent of the legislative body to prefer one reapportionment scheme over another is plainly proper and within the sphere of legislative power."[103] All that happened, in other words, is that the legislature decided that, as between two potential reapportionment schemes, it was allowed to prefer the policy of one over the other. That was a legislative choice, not an executive choice.

What of the executive's authority to decline to enforce a law? That branch "generally has the power and authority to control litigation as part of its power to execute the laws, and a law that removes from the executive branch sufficient control of litigation may well violate separation of powers."[104] But that does not mean the executive may "decline to execute a law under the guise of executing the laws."[105] "The power to forbid the execution of the laws would enable the executive branch to nullify validly enacted statutes. In that situation, the executive branch would encroach upon the legislative power to repeal statutes or upon the judicial branch's power of judicial review. What the executive branch cannot do directly, it cannot do indirectly. Thus, even though the executive branch generally has the power and authority to control litigation, it cannot exercise this power in order to prevent the execution of a law."[106]

The court ultimately resolved this nettlesome issue on narrow grounds. In this instance, the "intrusion by the legislature into the executive branch function of control of litigation is justified by the limited nature of the encroachment—pursuit of one case—and by the subject matter of the litigation—legislative reapportionment."[107] "Because the legislative encroachment into the executive power of controlling litigation is limited to carrying out the legislature's chosen reapportionment plan, it does not impermissibly intrude into executive branch functions and does not constitute a separation of powers violation."[108]

This same question—does the attorney general or governor control litigation of the state?—has emerged in many settings: litigation over tobacco regulation, same-sex marriage, immigration; and general disputes about whether an attorney general (or governor) should, or must, defend the constitutionality of a state law. One recent dispute turned not on the validity of a state law but on a dispute over a national one: the Patient Protection and Affordable Care Act.

The States and National Health Care

In 2010, President Obama signed into law the Patient Protection and Affordable Care Act, frequently called the ACA. There are a lot of ways to look at the law. That it tried to increase the number of people in the country with health insurance by requiring them to buy it. That it tried to account for the reality that those without health insurance still needed healthcare, and it was unfair to impose those costs on hospitals and the medical profession. And that it tried to increase healthcare for low-income individuals by expanding Medicaid eligibility. No matter how you look at it, the central idea was to nationalize healthcare in this country.

When historians look back on this era, there will be plenty to say about the Affordable Care Act. Was it an emblem of a temporary phase of intense partisanship or what became a more permanent form of partisanship? In either event, one feature of the ACA story seems likely to stay, an increased role of the state attorneys general in public litigation.

While state attorneys general have long had authority to join forces in initiating litigation against the national government or in enforcing regulatory programs against shared targets, the prominence of these efforts has hit new marks in recent decades. In the 1990s, a group of state attorneys general banded together in launching lawsuits against the tobacco companies. The lawsuits succeeded, prompting a multi-state settlement that required the tobacco companies to change the way they marketed their products and that required them to pay $206 billion to the states.[109] By the time the litigation ended, all four of the major tobacco companies and all of the states had participated in it.[110] Since then, in what Margaret Lemos and Ernie Young call "entrepreneurial litigation," the state attorneys general have become lawsuit leaders. They now rival the American Civil Liberties Union (ACLU), the National Association for the Advancement of Colored People (NAACP), and the Chamber of Commerce in spurring change through litigation.[111] Whether in lawsuits against paint companies or car companies or drug companies or gun manufacturers, they have become influential players.[112] In the words of one frustrated lobbyist, the state attorneys general are "more powerful than governors" in some ways because they rarely "need a legislature to approve what they do." "Their legislature is a jury," which is "what makes them frightening."[113]

By 2010, state attorneys general had become accustomed to playing significant roles in all manner of federal and state court litigation. It thus should not have caught anyone by surprise when, on the day President Obama signed the Affordable Care Act into law, a group of states sued the national government in a federal district court in Florida, claiming the law violated the US Constitution. Led by Florida, thirteen states filed the initial lawsuit, and eventually twenty-six states joined it.[114] As with passage of the ACA, litigation over it largely was a partisan matter. The list of governors and attorneys general who joined the lawsuit was almost entirely composed of Republicans, with one exception being Louisiana attorney general Buddy Caldwell, who switched from Democrat to Republican shortly after joining the lawsuit.[115]

The states targeted two features of the program. One was the individual mandate, the requirement that all individuals obtain insurance or pay a fine. Congress, they argued, had the power only to regulate commerce. It could not compel a class of individuals to enter the insurance market on pain of a penalty, then regulate them once they were in it. Nor, they added, could Congress sustain the law on the ground that the penalty was merely a tax.

The other target was the law's expansion of Medicaid, a program of cooperative federalism that all states had participated in for decades.

The ACA increased the number of Americans who qualified for this government insurance program and required states to accept the expansion or be removed from the Medicaid program—and give up the substantial federal funding they had grown accustomed to receiving under it. This feature of the program, the states argued, exceeded Congress's powers under the "Spending Clause." Because Congress lacks direct authority to commandeer the states to implement a federal program, the states argued, it could not indirectly do the same thing by coercing them to join it.

The litigation generated intra–executive branch disputes over what states would join the litigation and who was in charge of it—and eventually over whether the same state and its public officials could appear on opposite sides of the case.

Washington

In 2010, Democrat Christine Gregoire sat in the governor's seat, and Republican Rob McKenna served as attorney general. On the same day the ACA became law, McKenna added Washington to Florida's lawsuit challenging the act.[116] Governor Gregoire threatened to sue General McKenna to prevent any state money from being used to support the litigation.[117]

She didn't need to file a case because the city of Seattle sued the attorney general, and Governor Gregoire eventually joined the case as an amicus curiae.[118] The city sought a writ of mandamus directing McKenna to withdraw the state of Washington from the litigation.

In her brief, Gregoire asked the court to hold that the attorney general could not litigate on behalf of the state when the attorney general and the governor disagree about whether to proceed. In such a case, Gregoire argued, the attorney general may sue only in his individual capacity, not on behalf of the state. The Washington Supreme Court acknowledged that the Washington Constitution vests the governor with "the supreme executive power of the state."[119] But the court refused to resolve the point, explaining that Gregoire would have to file her own lawsuit to challenge the funding point.

The court denied the city's mandamus request. Under existing precedent, the attorney general had "general discretionary authority" to represent the state in any court on a matter of public concern in the context of a cognizable cause of action.[120] That did not end the matter. While McKenna was able to place the state of Washington on the side of the plaintiffs throughout this constitutional challenge to the ACA, Governor Gregoire ultimately appeared as amicus curiae on the other side of the case, though in her capacity as governor, not as the legal representative of the state.

Arizona

Something similar happened in Arizona. By the time the ACA became law, Governor Jan Brewer (a Republican) and Attorney General Terry Goddard (a Democrat) already were locked in a feud over who had the right to control litigation on behalf of Arizona. The first spark came in *Horne v. Flores*, a case in which Arizona was sued on the ground that it provided inadequate English language instruction under federal law.[121] Unwilling to have his office defend this practice, General Goddard appointed outside counsel to handle the defense. Members of the legislature were skeptical of outside counsel's efforts, and the Speaker of the Arizona House of Representatives and the president of the Arizona Senate intervened to defend the law.[122]

Soon after the US Supreme Court granted review of the case, Jan Brewer became the governor. A few months later, she directed General Goddard to change the state's position and join the position taken by the Arizona legislators. Goddard refused, invoking an Arizona statute that treated the attorney general as the "chief legal officer" of the state.[123] According to Goddard, his position as chief legal officer included the discretion to determine the appropriate legal positions to take for the state.

Governor Brewer apparently let it go.[124] But the experience stiffened her resolve when the challenge to the ACA arose. Brewer asked Goddard to join the lawsuit on behalf of Arizona, and Goddard refused. Governor Brewer turned to the legislature rather than the courts to resolve the standoff. The Arizona legislature enacted special session legislation allowing the governor, for a short period of time, to direct counsel other than the attorney general to initiate litigation on behalf of the state.[125] With this authorization in hand, Brewer appointed counsel to represent the state in the case, and Arizona joined the lawsuit.

Arizona shows the limits of an attorney general's authority to direct the litigation of the state. Even in a state that recognized the attorney general as the top legal officer in the state, as is true in most states, that authority allowed a temporary victory for General Goddard in the *Flores* case but one that did not last long in the ACA case. Had the Arizona legislature been controlled by Democrats, it surely would have been a different story. In the end, Goddard refused to join the positions taken by the respective leaders of the Arizona State House and Senate. And they returned the favor in the ACA litigation, pushing him to the sidelines and allowing Governor Brewer to take over the litigation on behalf of the state.

Iowa

Iowa shows another path. In early 2011, Republican governor Terry Branstad joined the ACA lawsuit. Although Iowa separately elects its governor and attorney general, Governor Branstad claimed to represent Iowa in the lawsuit. Not long after, Democrat attorney general Tom Miller issued a response. General Miller, by then one of the longest-serving attorneys general in the country, maintained that the official capacity to represent Iowa rested with the attorney general, not the governor.[126] At the same time, Miller noted that "in this unusual set of circumstances, given what is at stake for the public, Governor Branstad should have the ability to express his viewpoint as Governor."[127] When all was said and done, General Miller added his name to briefs in defense of the act and did so as the lawyer for the state of Iowa.[128] The result? The state of Iowa appeared on both sides of the litigation, on one side as a party plaintiff represented by the governor's office, on the other side as an amicus represented by the attorney general and siding with the national government. All of this allowed the same state (Iowa) to declare victory (and defeat).[129]

Whether it's these states or others, the ACA litigation revealed a miniature version of a larger challenge of the plural executive. It's not clear who's in charge of litigation on behalf of the state. And that's just one challenge of serial executive branch officials separately elected by the people. From state independent counsel laws to appointment disputes between lieutenant governors and peripatetic governors to control over litigation, divided executive power at the state level raises all kinds of practical, political, and legal questions. These disputes do not remotely stand alone, and they are certainly not on the wane. There seem to be more and more such cases, as the attorneys general take an increasingly prominent role in litigating national questions. The work also is taking on an increasingly partisan cast. Just as Republican attorneys general pushed back against the Obama administration in the ACA litigation and later in litigation over DACA (Deferred Action for Childhood Arrivals),[130] so Democratic attorneys general have pushed back against the Trump administration. They have filed lawsuits challenging the president's travel ban, withdrawal of funding for sanctuary cities, and rescission of DACA—and indeed won an initial victory in the US Supreme Court on the rescission question.[131] The last section of the chapter returns to these issues.

The Line-Item Veto

The division of executive power across a range of separately elected offices weakens the power of governors relative to presidents. But the opposite is true when it comes to how the veto power works with respect to our fifty-one constitutions. Most state constitutions give governors the power to veto parts of appropriation bills and, in two states, other bills as well. In power-diminishing contrast, the US Constitution confines the veto power to an all-or-nothing-at-all proposition with respect to the bills presented to the president.

The Federal Story

The federal story is straightforward and involves one case, *Clinton v. City of New York*.[132] In 1996, Congress enacted the Line Item Veto Act. The law purported to give the president an authority the office had not had before, "line item" veto power to strike or cancel individual items within a bill presented for his signature. While the US Constitution does not expressly authorize this power, it does not expressly deny it either. That left the federal courts to draw the best inferences from what the Constitution does say. The Presentment Clause of Article I, § 7 of the US Constitution provides in relevant part: "Every Bill which shall have passed the House of Representatives and the Senate, shall, before it become a Law, be presented to the President of the United States; If he approve he shall sign it, but if not he shall return it, with his Objections."

Based on the detailed requirements of the clause and general structural inferences, the Court refused to allow Congress to give this power to the president. In his opinion for the Court, Justice Stevens was persuaded that "constitutional silence on this profoundly important issue" was "equivalent to an express prohibition."[133] The power to enact statutes under the Constitution could only "be exercised in accord with a single, finely wrought and exhaustively considered, procedure."[134] Because this "finely wrought" procedure did not mention such a vital qualification to the Presentment Clause, the Constitution prohibited it.[135]

In Justice Breyer's dissenting view, the Presentment Clause should be understood in the context of the smaller republic for which it was written. "At that time," Breyer suggested, the typical appropriations bill was so small that Congress "could simply have embodied each appropriation in a separate bill, each bill subject to a separate presidential veto."[136] But Congress does not have that option in a larger republic, where "a typical budget appropriations bill may have a dozen titles, hundreds of sections, and spread across more than 500 pages of the Statutes at Large."[137] To Justice Breyer, the new law amounted to a practical way for Congress to allow the president to veto individual sections without needing to pass each section as a separate bill. It came to nothing more than this, that "the Constitution permits Congress to choose a particular novel *means* to achieve this same, constitutionally legitimate, *end*."[138]

The State Stories

In contrast to many provisions in America's state constitutions, the line-item veto does not make an appearance at the constitutional founding—the 1776 founding, that is. Instead of appearing in the post-colonial charters, it arose during the Civil War, in the star-crossed

Constitution of the Confederacy. While the source of this innovation did not last long, the innovation did. It spread like kudzu, usually without harmful effect. State governors no doubt appreciated the flexibility provided by a line-item veto, and widespread adoption of the measure continued the trend begun in the early nineteenth century of adding constitutional restrictions on legislative power. More than forty states now give their governors the power to delete provisions of a bill.[139] In most of these states, the veto power applies only to appropriations bills, Washington and Oregon being notable exceptions that permit its use more broadly.[140]

An executive veto power operates as a conventional division-of-powers check on legislative overreach. But it does not amount to a pure exercise of executive power. In many ways, it is an exercise of legislative power. When a governor removes or changes part of a bill proposed by the legislature, she exercises a legislative power by altering, invariably re-creating, the law as opposed to rejecting it. Because the state constitutions not only create three branches of power but by some accounts deny the intermingling of them, this feature of state constitutions looks like an anomaly or at least a serious exception. Perhaps for this reason, line-item veto provisions have been a fruitful source of litigation in state courts. They often pit governors against their legislatures and implicate ever-rich debates over state policy and the money to fund it.[141]

California

Soon after the 2008 recession, Governor Schwarzenegger declared a fiscal emergency in California to account for a sudden drop in tax revenues. Responding to this cue, the legislature adopted midyear decreases to the budget. When the legislature presented the corrected budget bill to the governor, he reduced the reductions by almost $500 million, invoking the state constitution's line-item veto power for appropriation bills. A lawsuit followed.[142] It's one thing, the plaintiff claimed, for the governor to nix a new appropriation. But it's quite another to reduce an existing *reduction*. How, they asked, could that count as a veto of an *appropriation*?

Chief Justice George wrote the opinion for a unanimous court. When it comes to appropriation bills, he explained, the state constitution gives the governor "three options: (1) to sign the bill, (2) to veto the measure in its entirety, or (3) to *reduce or eliminate one or more items of appropriation.*'"[143] The issue at hand was "whether the Governor exceeded his limited powers" by using the line-item veto "to further reduce funding levels set forth in midyear reductions," what amounted to "imposing a reduction of appropriated sums greater than the reduction made by the Legislature."[144]

The court explained that, by the terms of the California Constitution, the governor generally "may not exercise legislative powers."[145] One exception is the governor's "more extensive" veto power with regard to appropriations. The governor has no authority to veto part of a bill that is not an "item of appropriation."[146] "Case law, commentators, and historians," the court explicated, "have long recognized that in exercising the veto the Governor acts in a legislative capacity."[147] Because the California Constitution generally prohibits one branch from exercising the power of another, it "follows that in exercising the power of the veto the Governor may act only as permitted by the Constitution. That authority is to veto a bill or to reduce or eliminate one or more items of appropriation."[148]

The court nonetheless rejected the plaintiffs' argument that the line-item veto applied only to increases in state funds, not reductions. "Whether spending authority is increased or decreased, it still fundamentally remains spending authority."[149] "There is no substantive difference between a Governor's reduction of an item of appropriation in the original 2009 Budget Act, to which interveners and petitioners raise no objection, and a Governor's reduction of that same item in a subsequent amendment to the 2009 Budget Act."[150] "Both actions involve changes in authorized spending."[151] "We discern no reason why the Governor should have the power to reduce items of appropriation when first enacted, and yet not retain that same power when the Legislature, in response to changed circumstances, sees fit to amend those same appropriations."[152] In sum: "Treating the exercise of line-item authority as an *increase in the reduction*, rather than as a *decrease in the appropriation* is as arbitrary as differentiating between the description of a glass of water as half full and a description of the same vessel as half empty."[153]

South Carolina

South Carolina faced a similar budget shortfall problem after the 2008 recession. There, too, an issue arose over the scope of the governor's line-item veto, but this time the South Carolina Supreme Court rejected the governor's position.[154] At issue was the annual appropriations bill. The legislature sought to fund some of an agency's expenditures from a general fund and some from other sources. Governor Sanford tried to veto the entire amount of general funds appropriated to the agency. In his veto message, Governor Sanford said the agency had "over $1 billion in carry-forward funds" and could use "available funds and cost-cutting measures" to "sustain the agency over the next fiscal year."[155]

Here's how the South Carolina Constitution describes the veto power:

> Every bill or joint resolution which shall have passed the General Assembly shall, before it becomes a law, be presented to the Governor, and if he approves he shall sign it; if not, he shall return it, with his objections, to the house in which it originated, which shall enter the objections at large on its Journal and proceed to reconsider it.
>
> Bills appropriating money out of the Treasury shall specify the objects and purposes for which the same are made, and appropriate to them respectively their several amounts in distinct items and sections. If the Governor shall not approve any one or more of the items or sections contained in any bill appropriating money, but shall approve of the residue thereof, it shall become a law as to the residue in like manner as if he had signed it. The Governor shall then return the bill with his objections to the items or sections of the same not approved by him to the house in which the bill originated, which house shall enter the objections at large upon its Journal and proceed to reconsider so much of the bill as is not approved by the Governor.[156]

Writing for the court, Justice Kittredge framed the issue as whether the veto amounted to "a nullification of legislation or a modification of legislation." A "veto of an item in its entirety is a nullification" and permissible, "while a veto of only part of an item is a modification" and impermissible.[157] The case turned on the meaning of "item." As to that, the court explained, "item" "embrace[s] a specified sum of money together with the 'object and purpose' for which the appropriation is made."[158] The problem was that the governor tried "to veto funds arising from a particular source, but he did not veto the purpose to which those funds were allocated. The net result, then, was that the total appropriation for each of the board's programs, positions, and expenses was reduced by the amount the General Assembly had designated to be drawn from the general fund, but the programs, positions, and expenses themselves were not eliminated."[159] The court barred the veto as a modification, not a permissible nullification, of the provision.

Wisconsin

Until recently, the Wisconsin Constitution has given the governor remarkably broad authority to veto appropriation bills. In adopting a line-item veto provision in 1930, the constitutional amendment gave the governor authority to veto appropriation bills "in part."[160] What that means was a perpetual source of litigation that over time gave the governor considerable latitude in making policy for the state. In the first case, a telephone company challenged the governor's veto of the "legislative intent" section of an appropriations bill.[161] The telephone company complained that the governor could veto parts of appropriations, not parts of appropriations bills that had nothing to do with money. The court responded that the amendment allowed the governor to veto anything that was a "part" of an appropriations bill, including sections that were not appropriations themselves. Invoking dictionary definitions, it reasoned that the governor could veto any "part" of an appropriations bill, which included any "piece, fragment, fraction or constituent," "whether actually separate or not."[162] It did not matter to the court that this interpretation gave the governor "quasi-legislative" power and permitted her to use the veto power to fundamentally alter the policy of a bill, as later cases concluded.[163] All that constrained the governor was that the post-veto bill must amount to a "complete, entire, and workable law."[164]

Governor Tommy Thompson tested the reach of this power in 1987. He vetoed 290 separate parts of the biennial state budget bill. No one before him had pushed the veto power this far or used it so creatively.[165]

In a provision allowing courts to detain juvenile offenders for "not more than 48 hours," the governor vetoed "48 hours" (a part of the bill) and substituted "ten days" by crossing out various words and letters (other parts of the bill) in the same section. In a provision appropriating $750,000 to the state Art Board, the governor crossed out an individual "o" (another part of the bill) to lower the appropriation to $75,000.

One might have thought that this approach reduced the veto power to a game of Scrabble. But the Wisconsin Supreme Court upheld the vetoes in a lawsuit filed by the state Senate.[166] As the court saw it, the broad definition of "part" applied to individual letters and numbers within a bill.[167] After the vetoes, the bill remained a workable, stand-alone law, and the post-veto language remained germane to the subject of the vetoed provisions even as it changed the substance.[168]

Governor Thompson's efforts likely represent the furthest incursion of gubernatorial power in rewriting legislation through well-spaced and well-placed vetoes. But as with Pickett's Charge at Gettysburg, Wisconsin governors did not occupy this legislative territory for long. By constitutional amendment, the people of Wisconsin reined in the governor's veto power. In 1990, Wisconsin voters ratified an amendment that prohibited the governor from creating a new word by nixing individual letters in a bill.[169] That apparently did not suffice. In 2008, they ratified an amendment that prohibited the creation of a new sentence by combining parts of two or more sentences.[170]

Are the Federal or State Models Superior?

How could the same people in the same country adopt such disparate approaches for their executive branches? Americans have spoken nearly as one in adopting a plural executive with line-item veto power in the states yet have retained the opposite approach for the federal executive throughout. Is one approach better than the other? Are the two approaches that different in practice? How does the rise of state attorneys general as litigation forces in this country reflect on the two approaches?

First, comparisons in design sometimes reveal preferences in design. Is this one of them? Most states, as Steven Calabresi confirms, "have diverged from the federal model by having other elected statewide officials, particularly an independently elected state attorney general. Which model is better: the federal or the state? Is a unitary executive optimal in a democracy like ours, or would an unbundled plural executive be better?"[171] Academics answer the question differently. Calabresi leans toward the unitary executive for both sets of sovereign, as the title of his piece suggests, "The Fatally Flawed Theory of the Unbundled Executive." William Marshall leans toward the plural executive for both of them, as the title of his piece suggests, "Break Up the Presidency— Governors, State Attorneys General, and Lessons from the Divided Executive,"[172] as do Christopher Berry and Jacob Gersen in their piece, "The Unbundled Executive."[173] These are top-shelf scholars, and two of them have considerable executive-branch experience to draw on.[174]

But is it possible that the plural executive and the unitary executive are each right for the governments that have them? Even the most vigorous defense of a unitary executive, supplied by Alexander Hamilton in *Federalist* 70, does not necessarily carry over to all governments. Emphasizing the benefits of "energy in the Executive," he speaks of the need for "unity," "duration," the "adequate provision for its support," and the "competent powers" that come with a unitary executive. For him, "unity is conducive to energy" because "decision, activity, secrecy, and dispatch will generally characterize the proceedings of one man in a much more eminent degree than the proceedings of any greater number," and "in proportion as the number is increased, these qualities will be diminished." "Whenever two or more persons are engaged in any common enterprise or pursuit, there is always danger of difference of opinion," a looming impediment when it comes to handling "the most critical emergencies of the state." Hamilton's advocacy for a unified executive not only carried the day in 1789, but the federal experience under it has tended to bolster his arguments. No meaningful effort has been made to break up the presidency by dividing it into constitutional offices, whether separately elected or not.

The most potent explanation for a unitary executive, however, does not apply to the states. Responsibility to defend a country's borders, the most existential threat a government faces, creates an imperative for concentrating power to be sure. But governors do not share that presidential responsibility. It's not even clear that Hamilton would have preferred a unitary executive for all fifty-one governments. Is it not likely that Hamilton's experiences during the Revolutionary War under the dysfunctional Articles of Confederation and the cash-starved Continental Congress—think of his service in the Continental Army at Valley Forge during the winter of 1778[175]—drove his view that the executive branch had to be energetic, unified, responsive to the task at hand? At least when it comes to national defense, unity in one place but not the others may work just fine.

While governors may not be responsible for protecting our borders, they face plenty of emergencies, as pandemics of the past and present confirm. But it's hard to think of too many instances, if any, in which the plural executive created decision-halting inefficiencies in handling these and other kinds of emergencies—emergencies in which they sometimes have a more immediate role to play than the president.

What of other potential problems created by breaking up the executive branch at the state level? Surely these divisions have created inefficiencies, as some of the state experiences illustrate. And surely Hamilton was right about the human-nature pitfalls of joint responsibility. In one direction, individuals "often oppose" something "merely because they had no agency in planning it" or because it was "planned by those whom they dislike." In the other, even when individuals "have been consulted, and have happened to disapprove, opposition then becomes, in their estimation, an indispensable duty of self-love."[176] That may argue too much. All branches of government, all divisions of power, face this problem. Even when it comes to the most prominent risks from a divided executive—separately elected or chosen attorneys general—"debilitating conflict has not materialized."[177] While forty-five of the state attorneys general are chosen by the people (or someone other than the governor) and while forty-eight of them cannot be fired by the governor, the fact remains that governors and attorneys general usually have learned to cooperate. Also deserving of mention, no state has turned back. Whatever the costs of separating the office of the attorney general from the office of the governor, no state has "reversed direction" and made its "Attorney General subservient to the Governor."[178]

How singular and efficient, moreover, is the presidency anyway? It's not always unitary. Think of independent agencies with leaders whom no president can discharge. Even in the federal agencies the president controls, the size and number of these agencies, together with the thousands of employees who work there, make singular control sometimes look like a mirage. And that's even assuming the employees support the president's mission, which is not always the case given career civil service protections. With or without independent counsels at the federal level, it's the rare month in any presidency when someone somewhere does not challenge the president publicly from the inside, whether openly or anonymously. Presidential power indeed seems to grow less unitary by the administration.

Second, in thinking about these different approaches to aggregating and disaggregating executive power, consider some practical realities at the state level that appear to ameliorate inefficiencies of a plural executive and often give governors control when they need it. Most executive branch officials at some point want to accomplish something. Why else hold office? It's difficult to run for re-election with nothing to say for a term in office. That creates incentives to cooperate. And that gives the executive branch official with the most authority, the governor, outsized influence, perhaps as much control in day-to-day government as the president. Only the governor may veto bills, not the other separately elected officials. Only the governor in most states may fill judgeships when someone retires before the end of their term. Only the governor in most states may nominate term-limited legislators to cabinet-level positions in charge of this or that agency, permitting the legislator to obtain more years of service in the state retirement system. Only the governor in most states may appoint individuals to state boards, which sometimes include pay, usually include status, and often include years-of-service pension credit. And only the governor in most states may weigh in on the budget allocation for the department run by each separately elected executive branch official with the threat of a line-item veto. Even as governors face the same electoral accountability as state attorneys general and even as they occupy a part of the same divided branch, they remain firsts among equals.

These practical considerations influence how many conflicts between governors and other elected executive-branch officials work themselves out. But that does not mean the governor always wins, as a story from Ohio, perhaps apocryphal, confirms. The state was involved in sensitive litigation, and the governor wanted to take one position, the attorney general another. Call it the *Perdue v. Baker* of Ohio. The two statewide officials met, and they could not resolve their differences. They met again, and they still could not resolve their differences. Losing hope that he could persuade the governor how to handle the case, the attorney general relented. "Okay, Mr. Governor," he said, "you win. I'll send a lawyer over later this afternoon to do what you want." The attorney general looked for the youngest, greenest, most innocent-looking attorney in the office he could find. He sent him to the governor's office with no explanation or background information about why the governor needed him. The hapless young lawyer did as asked. After he arrived, the governor took one look at him and told him to wait in the hall. He called the attorney general and said, "You win." Separation of powers can come to mean a lot of things in a lot of situations.

Third, do the state experiences with the line-item veto for appropriation bills suggest that the president should have that power too? After *Clinton v. New York*, any such change would require a federal constitutional amendment or a course correction by the Supreme Court. Would the effort be worth it? There's a lot to be said for this authority, at least as applied to appropriation bills. As a general matter, state constitutions require the states to balance their budgets every year or two, a requirement that the US Constitution does not impose on the national government. A governor's line-item veto power helps each state satisfy this requirement. One wonders whether the federal government could learn from this fiscal discipline and whether a line-item veto would help. The federal government, sure enough, may have a power the states do not—to print money—but that will not sustain itself forever. Governors have not misused this authority in the main, offering hope that it would be used responsibly at the federal level as well.

Fourth, a notable manifestation of the plural executive in recent decades has been the rise of state attorneys general as leading figures in national litigation. "In recent decades, state AGs have emerged as a uniquely powerful cadre of lawyers."[179] Has this development been good for the legal system? How has it impacted separation of powers? Has it furthered the local-innovation interests of federalism?

In defense of this development, the top legal officers of the states have the authority, often the duty, to challenge federal laws that exceed the enumerated powers of the national government under the US

Constitution. Who better to bring these claims? And why not join forces in bringing them, pulling together all of the affected states? Usually the largest law firms in their states, the offices of the attorneys general have the capacity, the authority, and the experience to explain why the federal government has crossed a federal constitutional line. This kind of vertical litigation is eminently appropriate in a federal system, with states led by their attorneys general "throwing off the federal yoke so that they can govern themselves."[180] When Congress enacts a law or the president signs an order that exceeds their power, the state attorneys general are ideally situated to challenge this use of authority. Facilitating these efforts in recent years has been the decision of state attorneys general across the country to create state solicitor general offices. The job has attracted top-flight lawyers and advanced state interests, whether at the trial or appellate level.[181]

State attorneys general also have worked as one to enforce state regulatory programs, sometimes even federal ones in conjunction with the US Department of Justice. This, too, furthers their mission and is sensible to boot. Each state attorney general has consumer, environmental, and other sections of their offices devoted to protecting their citizens, often citizens in no position to protect themselves. That creates a fiduciary duty to look after these interests, sometimes honored most formidably by collective action against a shared target. There is something to "the power of concerted multistate action."[182]

But there is an ambiguous middle when it comes to the rise of the state attorneys general. Proponents of multi-state lawsuits may applaud the reality that the tobacco industry had not lost a single case before the attorneys general joined forces in suing them to collect the costs of treating individuals with smoking-related health costs.[183] That suggests, to many, that more coordinated legal attacks against industries are for the good, whether to deal with environmental protection, consumer protection, healthcare protection, or some other concern the state attorneys general are supposed to look after. Not everyone sees it this way. Is national regulation by state prosecution necessarily a good thing? Multi-state lawsuits of this type can complicate national regulatory programs and blur the lines of accountability.[184] They also circumvent conventional limitations on the power of the federal courts. Many of the limitations on aggregate litigation—class action certification, standing requirements, arbitration clauses—do not apply in the same way to the attorneys general.[185] And the attorneys general have two sets of lawyers at their disposal, their own employees as well as privately retained counsel, sometimes eligible for significant attorney's fees. All of this creates pressure and temptation—pressure on the attorneys general to perform their customary functions and temptation to become tools for causes that are more private than public and more political than legal. State lawsuits that go beyond their parens patriae purpose give "entrepreneurial litigation" a bad name. Left unreformed, this kind of litigation may prompt responses by Congress or the courts if they become concerned that it merely circumvents existing limits on aggregate litigation.

Then there is this reality. While state attorneys general may have a fiduciary duty to file collective actions and while there may be uncertainty over when those actions serve the legal system and when they do not, there is no denying the increasingly partisan nature of these lawsuits. Group lawsuits have increasingly developed a partisan hue, the actions challenging the ACA, DACA, and DAPA (Deferred Action for Parents of Americans) being telling examples. One oddity is that we have many cases now in which large numbers of states litigate in favor of more federal power (by conceding that Congress has a given power) and less state power (by conceding that the state does not have a given power). In whose names, one has to wonder, are they bringing these lawsuits? Attorneys general may confess error, admitting a state law is unconstitutional or admitting that Congress or the president may regulate them in a given way. But when those decisions line up almost perfectly with the agenda preferences of the political company they keep, the state attorneys general look like politicians with ambitions, not lawyers with clients. In many of these situations, the attorneys general are ignoring the interests of large groups of their own citizens. At the bottom of this partisan slope is a situation in which the states no longer serve as sources of experimentation. More precisely, instead of fifty-one sources of experimentation, we will get just two. One virtue of federalism is to allow local experimentation. But when state politicians take their litigation cues from the national leaders of each political party, they destroy any impulse to try new approaches to deal with new problems. And they run the risk of creating a national and state "separation of parties, not powers," a separation of factions, not authorities—a development that would have caused our federal and state founders to cringe.[186]

The proper balance takes us back to another virtue of federalism. It not only permits local trial and error before the country adopts a nationwide rule. But it also contemplates the possibility that some differences will remain, that variation in circumstances will lead to variations in law and policy. In a functioning system of federalism, our state attorneys general should be the leading voices for identifying those areas suitable for local control and those suitable for nationwide rules, making them a leading voice in minimizing the polarizing tendencies that come with a national-only approach to problem solving. Our state attorneys general cannot perform that role, they in truth undermine that role, if they take their litigation prompts from the leadership of each national political party. A critical question for our time is whether a feature of the plural executive—the separate election of most state attorneys general—will "mitigate or exacerbate the polarization" that characterizes modern America.[187] The path of exacerbation proceeds down a trail in which the states' litigating positions flow from one perspective, not many. When one political party or the other sets the agenda for each state, that elevates the leader of the party in charge of the national government, the president of the United States, to authority no one would have foreseen in 1776. It would have the debate between the plural and unitary executives ending with the most unitary of executives, in which the current president sets two agendas—one for congenial attorneys general and governors of each state, another for their opponents.

6

Administrative Law

How to Write and Implement Our Laws

This chapter shifts from separation-of-powers features of the state constitutions that have no equivalent in the federal constitution (the plural executive and line-item vetoes) to a separation-of-powers topic that arises under both the state and federal constitutions (administrative law). Even though this topic has federal and state peers, that does not mean the lawyer has two opportunities to fix a state administrative law decision gone awry. Recall a difference between state structural limitations and state individual rights limitations. As to individual rights protected in the state constitutions and the federal Bill of Rights, such as free speech, free exercise, and so forth, a two-chance opportunity arises. If individuals object to a speech-restrictive state or local law, they usually may challenge the law under the First Amendment's Free Speech Clause and under the free-speech counterpart of that state's constitution. In the context of traditional individual rights, the lawyer customarily has two opportunities, not one, to defeat a law.

That is not what happens with most structural disputes and that is not what happens with administrative law. It will be the rare dispute covered in this chapter—over delegations of state legislative power and over deference to administrative agencies about the meaning of state laws—that a party may challenge on state *and* federal grounds. The key source of authority will arise from the state constitution. The US Constitution generally does not limit the structure of state governments established by their constitutions.[1] And the US Supreme Court to date has not treated the main candidate for such oversight—the republican form of government guarantee—as judicially enforceable.

That still leaves plenty of opportunity for state-federal dialogue, as the topic of administrative law confirms. While comparison may be the thief of happiness when it comes to personal matters, it is a rich source of insights when it comes to state and federal administrative law. Here, as elsewhere, state courts and federal courts may borrow historical, practical, and other useful insights from each other. The early state constitutions, particularly those drafted between 1775 and 1787, established the blueprints for our division of governmental power into legislative, executive, and judicial branches. Remember the 1780 Massachusetts Constitution, which (like many state constitutions) expressly separates legislative, executive, and judicial powers. That source of innovation gives state courts a special place in discussing the history and purpose of these guarantees and of separation of powers more generally. At the same time, any court—federal or state—may offer useful insights about how best to construe generally phrased, sometimes implied, limitations on the powers of each branch. That's why I treat this topic in much the same way as I treat the topics in most of the other chapters, as a comparative inquiry into representative examples of what the federal and state courts have done.

One last warm-up point. Administrative law is an area in which the state courts have not been reticent to act independently of federal precedent in construing the structural guarantees in their state constitutions. In contrast to individual rights, where state courts often start their analysis with an assumption that the state guarantee mimics the meaning of the federal guarantee, the federal precedents on delegation and administrative deference seem to have little pull and hardly the presumption of correctness often seen with individual rights. The state courts frequently have been innovative leaders in this area. Why is there so much lockstepping in the context of individual rights but not when it comes to administrative law? Some potential explanations, including the impact of the plural executive, appear at the end of the chapter.[2]

At the federal level, one could imagine calling the non-delegation doctrine the "delegation doctrine." Save for two cases decided in the fertile year of 1935, no other US Supreme Court cases impose a judicially enforceable non-delegation doctrine. But at the state level, a vibrant judicially enforceable non-delegation doctrine is on display. Forty-three state courts enforce the doctrine more vigorously than the US Supreme Court.[3] While the US Supreme Court "has been the beginning and the end of most legal inquiry into the non-delegation doctrine," there is plenty to learn from the rich experiences of the states.[4]

A similar story has unfolded in the context of state limitations on judicial deference to administrative agencies. In this area, too, state courts frequently have imposed limitations of their own, either by limiting the settings in which deference applies or by construing the separation-of-powers requirements in their state constitutions to bar judicial deference to agency interpretations of law. A lawyer in state court who tries to get clients what they want by framing arguments in *Chevron* terms—the federal doctrine that gives agencies considerable deference over the meaning of ambiguous federal laws—often will leave empty-handed. It's the rare state court that incorporates *Chevron* wholesale.

Delegation and Non-Delegation

The federal and state treatment of the non-delegation doctrine is a good place to start. The idea behind the doctrine is that the legislative branch may not empower the executive (or judicial) branch to exercise legislative authority. Until recently, the federal courts have been go-along-to-get-along enforcers of the doctrine, acquiescing in broader and broader delegations of power that might make even Professor Thayer blush. One explanation for this deference has been the difficulty of drawing a principled line between laws that legitimately permit executive branch agencies to exercise implementation authority and those that illegitimately exercise lawmaking authority. That practical problem, however, has not deterred the state courts, which have become frequent enforcers of their own non-delegation doctrines. Notice in considering these stories how often the courts seem most sensitive to delegation problems when criminal convictions and sentences are at stake.

The Federal Story

The terms of the US Constitution offer some grounds for skepticism about the growth of federal agencies and the power they wield. The

federal charter sets forth three distinct branches of government in language implying that each branch exercises a singular power. Article
I delegates "All legislative Powers herein granted" to Congress. Article
II delegates "The executive Power" to the president. And Article III
delegates "The judicial Power" to the federal courts. How, one might
wonder, could these three separate powers tolerate our current administrative state, in which federal agencies—housed in the executive
branch—regularly exercise all three powers: legislative authority (by
prescribing rules of conduct), executive authority (by enforcing those
rules), and judicial authority (by receiving deference over the meaning
of the statutes they implement). Something must have gone wrong between the founding and the present, it's easy to think, perhaps too easy
to think, when it comes to this president-centric development, which
has favored the growth of the executive branch and the vast agencies it
controls.

As with judicial review, the story is more complicated than a quick
look at the US Constitution might suggest. In *Federalist* No. 37 (and
again in No. 47), Madison acknowledged at the outset the difficulty of
"defin[ing]" "with sufficient certainty" the "three great provinces" of
government. Even while the checks and balances of the federal charter
require separation, they contemplate coordination of these difficult-to-
define branches. Think about the legislative power, which comes to
naught unless the president signs a bill into law or (as rarely happens)
Congress overrides the veto. Think about federal judges, who take their
seats only after the president nominates them and the Senate confirms
them. Think about the people who run the agencies. The president
nominates them, yes, but they take their jobs only after Senate approval.
On top of that, the courts and agencies can't get anywhere without
funds from the legislature and, in the case of agencies, statutes to implement from the legislature. The president can't get anywhere without
money either. Combination and coordination accompany nearly every
exercise of power. It's the rare instance in which any one of this trio of
powers is exercised reclusively. While each branch has blocking powers
(calling to mind separation), each branch inevitably needs the other
(calling to mind overlap and cooperation).

Matters grow more complicated from a strict separation-of-powers
perspective when one thinks about how the executive branch enforces

the many laws in the United States Code. No one contemplated a president exercising enforcement power alone. That's why the first federal cabinets included a secretary of state, a secretary of the treasury, an attorney general, a secretary of war, and other departments. Article II contemplated heads of departments, officers, and non-officer employees within each agency from the outset. Before long, lots of employees were needed to run these agencies and enforce the growing number of laws and policies associated with them. Even if one allowed the president only to administer the departments or agencies contemplated in 1789, that would still leave plenty of difficult-to-resolve questions about legislative delegation and administrative deference. Imagine something as basic as tariff legislation with respect to imported goods in 1789. Is it not likely that it would require some delegation of authority and discretion to the at-the-dock federal officials given the range of products affected and the range of circumstances when Congress might wish to impose a tariff? It's not easy to run a national government the size of the United States—then or now.

What's prohibited, what's allowed, by the US Constitution in terms of legislative delegation to the executive branch, as with so many things in law, turns on degree. For some time now, roughly the last eighty years, the degrees of authorized delegation have resembled a ratchet, favoring ever-growing, sometimes ever-more-casual, delegations of power to the executive branch and the agencies it oversees—and sometimes even to independent agencies that it does not oversee. Just as the policymaking imperatives created by the Great Depression, together with the changing nature of commerce, led the US Supreme Court to authorize Congress to enact more national laws in the name of regulating interstate commerce, so they seem to have led the US Supreme Court to authorize Congress to delegate more power to the president and executive-branch agencies.

Proof is the reality that the United States Supreme Court has not invalidated a law on non-delegation grounds since 1935, and apparently not before then either. That led Cass Sunstein to remark that the non-delegation doctrine has had "one good year" and "211 bad ones (and counting)."[5] Today, he would have to say, we are at 231 bad years (and counting). Hence Cynthia Farina's quip: "If Academy Awards were given in constitutional jurisprudence, nondelegation claims against regulatory statutes would win the prize for Most Sympathetic Judicial Rhetoric in a Hopeless Case."[6]

So what happened in 1935? The Court invalidated parts of the National Industrial Recovery Act as unconstitutional delegations of legislative power to the executive branch in two cases: *Panama Refining Co. v. Ryan*[7] and *A.L.A. Schechter Poultry Corp. v. United States*.[8] In *Panama Refining*, the Court invalidated § 9(c) of the act, which had given the president power to regulate oil producers. "Congress," the Court reasoned, "has declared no policy, has established no standard, has laid down no rule" to limit the president's authority to issue regulations.

In the second decision, *Schechter Poultry*, written by Chief Justice Hughes and worth exploring more fully, the Court invalidated § 3 of the act, known as the "Live Poultry Code."[9] At stake were criminal convictions premised on violations of it. The law allowed the president to promulgate "codes of fair competition" and gave him little direction beyond that. The main limitation was that the law could not be used "to promote monopolies or to eliminate or oppress small enterprises and will not operate to discriminate against them." President Roosevelt approved the law in 1934, and it prohibited an assortment of practices labeled "unfair methods of competition."[10] The government prosecuted the Schechters for "straight killing" chickens, the practice of allowing shoppers to select a live chicken for purchase and slaughter. Why the government went after the Schechters is not obvious.[11] One journalist suggests the government singled out the Schechters when they struggled over balancing the straight killing rule with accommodations for kosher customers. Either way, at the oral argument, the justices were not amused by the arbitrariness of the regulations and the target of enforcement.[12]

In a unanimous opinion for the court, Chief Justice Hughes explained that "Congress is not permitted to abdicate or to transfer to others the essential legislative functions with which it is thus vested." That does not hamstring Congress in dealing with intricate, dynamic, changing conditions, he acknowledged. "We have repeatedly recognized the necessity of adapting legislation to complex conditions involving a host of details with which the national legislature cannot deal directly." That's because the "Constitution has never been regarded as denying to Congress the necessary resources of flexibility and practicality, which will enable it to perform its function in laying down policies and establishing standards, while leaving to selected instrumentalities the making of subordinate rules within prescribed limits and the determination of facts to which the policy as declared by the legislature is to apply." But considerable flexibility does not mean horizonless flexibility. The "recognition of the necessity and validity of such provisions . . . cannot be allowed to obscure the limitations of the authority to delegate."[13]

That became a preamble to the essential question. Has "Congress in authorizing 'codes of fair competition'" ensured that it "established the standards of legal obligation, thus performing its essential legislative function, or, by the failure to enact such standards," tried "to transfer that function to others"? The Court answered that the law amounted to an unconstitutional transfer of legislative power. The act did not define "fair competition." The only limitation—the "Declaration of Policy" of the Recovery Act—provided little fencing around the president's or any agency's development of a code. It required only that the president find that it "will tend to effectuate the policy of this title," which encompassed a lot of nose-bleed-high general objectives—that it offer protection to "consumers, competitors, employees, and others," be "in furtherance of the public interest," and provide "exceptions to and exemptions from the provisions of such code as the president in his discretion deems necessary." Not even the phrase "unfair competition" limited the president. For "even if this clause were to be taken to relate to practices which fall under the ban of existing law," the Court reasoned, "it is still only one of the authorized aims" covered by the legislation.[14]

Such a broad delegation of policymaking power, the Court explained, was not consistent with a three-headed government. "Congress cannot delegate legislative power to the President to exercise an unfettered discretion to make whatever laws he thinks may be needed or advisable for the rehabilitation and expansion of trade or industry." The mere restriction that the code not "permit monopolies or monopolistic practices," the Court insisted, "leave[s] virtually untouched the field of policy" that the president "may roam at will."[15]

The Schechter family was understandably relieved. Mrs. Schechter celebrated the victory with a poem that included a refrain of relief that the cloud of prosecution hovering over her husband had ended. "I'm through with that experience, I hope for all my life, And proud again to be, Joseph Schechter's wife."[16]

Since 1935, the US Supreme Court has not invalidated a single congressional statute under the non-delegation doctrine. In 2001, in *Whitman v. American Trucking*,[17] the Court explained that, so long as Congress included an "intelligible principle" in the delegation, it would not create a constitutional problem. Section 109 of the Clean Air Act[18] gave the Environmental Protection Agency (EPA) discretion to make "such revisions . . . as may be appropriate" to the air quality standards and the underlying criteria at "five-year intervals."[19] While setting air quality standards includes considerable room for policy choice, the only guidance Congress gave was that they should be "based on [the] criteria" already set by the EPA, should be "requisite to protect the public health," and should "allow[] an adequate margin of safety."[20] Writing for the Court, Justice Scalia described the Clean Air Act's delegation as "well within the outer limits of our non-delegation doctrine precedents." "In the history of the Court," he emphasized, "we have found the requisite 'intelligible principle' lacking in only two statutes, one of which provided literally no guidance for the exercise of discretion, and the other of which conferred authority to regulate the entire economy on the basis of no more precise a standard than stimulating the economy by assuring 'fair competition.'"[21] This reaffirmation of a mere intelligible-principle constraint on delegation left room for doubt whether the non-delegation doctrine amounted to anything more than a precaution against 200-year floods.

But in 2019, the Court seemed poised to alter course. Some eighty-four years after 1935, and three years after Justice Gorsuch replaced Justice Scalia, the United States Supreme Court looked to be on the verge of accepting a non-delegation argument in *Gundy v. United States*.[22] At issue was another law with criminal ramifications, the Sex Offender Registration and Notification Act (SORNA). A divided Court rejected the claim, but no opinion captured five votes. Joining Justice Kagan's plurality opinion were Justices Ginsburg, Breyer, and Sotomayor. Justice Alito concurred in the judgment and wrote separately. And Justice Gorsuch dissented, joined by Chief Justice Roberts and Justice Thomas.

SORNA imposes registration requirements on convicted sex offenders. It delegates to the attorney general authority over how to apply the registration requirements to offenders convicted before the law's passage. "The Attorney General shall have the authority to specify the applicability of the requirements of this subchapter to sex offenders convicted before the enactment of this chapter . . . and to prescribe rules for the registration of any such sex offenders and for other categories of sex offenders who are unable to comply with subsection (b)."[23]

Justice Kagan opened by acknowledging in theory what few opinions had done in practice. The "nondelegation doctrine bars Congress from transferring its legislative power to another branch of Government." But the targeted provision, she reasoned, did not do what Gundy said. It did not grant the attorney general "plenary power" to apply the statute to prior offenders and "to require them to register, or not, as she sees fit, and to change her policy for any reason and at any time. If that were so, we would face a nondelegation question. But it is not." The law merely required "pre-Act offenders to register as soon as feasible," making the problem "administrative—and, more specifically, transitional—in nature." That kind of "statutory authority, as compared to the delegations we have upheld in the past, is distinctly small-bore."[24]

Concurring in the judgment, Justice Alito noted that the Constitution "confers on Congress certain 'legislative [p]owers'" and does not allow it "to delegate them to another branch of the government." But "since 1935," he said, "the Court has uniformly rejected nondelegation arguments and has upheld provisions that authorized agencies to adopt important rules pursuant to extraordinarily capacious standards. If a majority of this Court were willing to reconsider the approach we have taken for the past 84 years, I would support that effort. But because a majority is not willing to do that, it would be freakish to single out the provision at issue here for special treatment. Because I cannot say that the statute lacks a discernible standard that is adequate under the approach this Court has taken for many years, I vote to affirm."[25]

Justice Gorsuch penned the dissent, one unwilling to leave delegation matters to the political process alone and one sensitive to the subject of the delegation, a criminal law. "The Constitution promises that only the people's elected representatives may adopt new federal laws restricting liberty. Yet the statute before us scrambles that design. It purports to endow the nation's chief prosecutor with the power to write his own criminal code governing the lives of a half-million citizens." "The breadth of the authority Congress granted to the Attorney General," he worried, "can only be described as vast. As the Department of Justice itself has acknowledged, SORNA 'does not require the Attorney General' to impose registration requirements on pre-act offenders 'within a certain time frame or by a date certain; it does not require him to act at all.'" If the attorney general does choose to act, he can require all pre-act offenders to register, or he can "require some but not all to register." For those he requires to register, the attorney general may impose "some but not all of [SORNA's] registration requirements" as he pleases. And he is free to change his mind on any of these matters "at any given time or over the course of different [political] administrations," giving the attorney general "free rein" to write the country's sex-offender rules.[26]

If "we have an obligation to decide whether Congress has unconstitutionally divested itself of its legislative responsibilities, the question follows: What's the test?" Justice Gorsuch saw at least three guideposts. One, if "Congress makes the policy decisions" through standards "sufficiently definite" that the courts and public can tell whether they are being met, it may authorize another branch to "fill up the details." Two, "once Congress prescribes the rule governing private conduct, it may make the application of that rule depend on executive fact-finding." Three, Congress may assign the executive and judicial branches certain responsibilities if "the discretion is to be exercised over matters already within the scope of executive power."[27]

SORNA, the dissenters explained, failed this test. For "there isn't a single policy decision concerning pre-Act offenders on which Congress even tried to speak, and not a single other case where we have upheld executive authority over matters like these on the ground they constitute mere 'details.'" The dissenters feared that all of this was "deliberate." "Because members of Congress could not reach consensus on the treatment of pre-act offenders, it seems this was one of those situations where they found it expedient to hand off the job to the executive and direct there the blame for any later problems that might emerge." In sum, SORNA "sounds all the alarms the founders left for us. Because Congress could not achieve the consensus necessary to resolve the hard problems associated with SORNA's application to pre-act offenders, it passed the potato to the attorney general. And freed from the need to assemble a broad supermajority for his views, the attorney general did not hesitate to apply the statute retroactively to a politically unpopular minority."[28]

Gundy may not be the last word on the federal side of the story. Three justices, led by Justice Gorsuch, have now offered their reassessment of the doctrine. Justice Alito's concurrence suggests that he remains open to reconsidering the Court's long-standing resistance to non-delegation arguments. Justice Kavanaugh, who vigorously engaged separation-of-powers issues during his tenure as a court of appeals judge, took no part in the case. And neither did Justice Barrett, whose track record also suggests sensitivity to these issues.

One day, the federal non-delegation doctrine may have a second good year. If so, the state courts' experiences with similar issues may have a role to play.

The State Stories

In comparing federal and state delegation questions, it's useful to start by looking at the relevant provisions of the state charters. A quick overview of the state charters shows where the Framers got the idea for Articles I, II, and III of the US Constitution. The pre-1789 state constitutions all embrace separation of powers; usually divide power into legislative, executive, and judicial arms; and customarily present them in that order.[29] The post-1789 state constitutions stick to this path, a custom solidified by the US Constitution's adoption of the same structure.

But beneath the veneer of likeness is difference, some in state constitutions from the outset, some added to state constitutions later. At the founding, several state constitutions separated power implicitly *and* explicitly. Massachusetts, Georgia, Maryland, New Hampshire, North Carolina, and Virginia all had explicit "separation of powers" clauses.[30] And some of these clauses combined the belt of spelling out each power with the suspenders of denying the other branches the power to exercise it. As Massachusetts put it in 1780, "In the government of this commonwealth, the legislative department shall never exercise the executive and judicial powers, or either of them: the executive shall never exercise the legislative and judicial powers, or either of them; the judicial shall never exercise the legislative and executive powers, or either of them: to the end it may be a government of laws and not of men."[31] The Virginia Constitution of 1776 said that "the Legislative and Executive powers of the State should be separate and distinct from the Judicative."[32] This approach has become prolific. Forty state constitutions now have express separation-of-power provisions, and thirty-five of them take the belt-and-suspenders approach, spelling out each branch's power and denying that power to other branches.[33] As an example from a post-1789 state, the Texas Constitution says that "no person, or collection of persons, being of one of these departments, shall exercise any power properly attached to either of the others, except in the instances herein expressly permitted."[34] That or similar language counts as the norm. Only ten of the state constitutions parallel the federal constitution and lack an explicit separation-of-powers clause.

Do these differences in language create a difference in function between the state and federal models? It's not clear. As Gordon Wood suggests, the "separation of the executive, legislative, and judicial powers had a much more limited meaning in 1776 than it would later acquire in American constitutionalism."[35] The state clauses, and the federal one too, were designed to bar "all executive and judicial officeholders from simultaneously sitting in the legislatures." While "the British require their ministers to be members of Parliament—indeed it is the key to their system—we demand that the executive's cabinet officials be absolutely banned from sitting in the legislatures."[36] On this view, the federal and state clauses amount to separation-of-personnel, not separation-of-powers, provisions.

But the language of the federal and state clauses seems to go beyond this worthy, if confined, objective. Why give all legislative power to the legislative branch, for example, if other branches of the government could exercise the same power? No less importantly, a separation-of-personnel function of the provisions still speaks directly to something the state and federal Framers did not contemplate: the development of modern agencies. Even the most narrow reading of the state clauses would be in tension with the current administrative state. Legislators, true enough, do not run the agencies. But that is only because nothing of the sort is needed if the single head of the agency—especially an independent agency outside the control of the executive branch—exercises considerable legislative, executive, and judicial power. As for delegation, a narrow account of these clauses still would not allow the legislature to enact a law delegating all Article I "legislative" power to the president and to call it a day, whether a legislator became president or not.

A few states have accounted for the growth of agencies by updating their separation-of-powers clauses. Connecticut, a state with an explicit separation-of-powers clause, adds a modern exception to it for administrative delegation: "The legislative department may delegate regulatory authority to the executive department; except that any administrative regulation of any agency of the executive department may be disapproved by the general assembly or a committee thereof in such manner as shall by law be prescribed."[37] But that's an uncommon provision.

Whether due to differences in the architecture of the state and federal constitutions or to other features of state government, several state courts enforce a robust non-delegation doctrine. As Jason Iuliano and Keith Whittington note, "the nondelegation doctrine is alive and well" in this country, just "in a different location," the states.[38] The state courts use different approaches to the issue. Jim Rossi places the states into three categories of non-delegation approaches: weak, moderate, and strong. Only six states, he says, have weak approaches under which legislative delegations will survive so long as they adhere to the relevant procedural safeguards.[39] Twenty states have strong approaches, requiring delegations to agencies to contain specific standards for agency action. The remaining states have varying levels of in-between approaches, requiring more than just procedural safeguards but allowing for broad delegations.[40] The key lesson is that the state courts are "much more" vigorous than the federal courts in restricting legislative delegations.[41]

The following cases offer a sampling. They show the various ways in which state separation of powers can work, and they show that many state courts have not had a problem with line drawing, one of the perceived impediments to enforcing the non-delegation doctrine at the federal level. "The delegation doctrine," as these cases show, "has much greater practical significance at the state level than at the federal level."[42]

Nevada

The first state story involves a criminal law, and like *Gundy* it involves the regulation of a disfavored class of individuals, convicted sex offenders. At issue in *McNeill v. Nevada*[43] was whether the Nevada Board of Parole Commissioners could "impose conditions" not identified in a statute "on a sex offender subject to lifetime supervision." As a convicted sex offender, Steve McNeill left prison with a bevy of conditions imposed by the parole board: regular urinalysis, a curfew requiring him to be at home from 5 P.M. to 5 A.M., and employment. After McNeill failed to comply with some of these requirements, a parole officer insisted he submit to a urinalysis. McNeill did not appreciate the request. He "would not submit to urinalyses, had no plans to abide by a curfew, and would sleep where he chose," he answered. The state answered back with charges of violating the conditions of release. The trial court found McNeill guilty and ruled that the board had authority under the statute to add "conditions of lifetime supervision not enumerated in the statute."[44]

Reversing, the Nevada Supreme Court made short work of the state's added requirements. "Without a doubt," Justice Douglas wrote for a unanimous court, "the Legislature may not delegate its power to legislate." Because "a violation of a condition of lifetime supervision is a new crime," the state's position would mean that "the Board would effectively have authority to create law."[45] The court appreciated that the legislature could "delegate the power to determine the facts or state of things upon which the law makes its own operations depend." It thus could make a law "dependent upon the existence of certain facts or conditions" found by the agency. And that law would be upheld if "suitable standards are established by the legislature for the agency's use of its power."[46]

The problem, however, was that the Nevada Legislature did not grant "the Board the authority to create additional conditions." Even if the legislature had wished to make such a delegation, the court added, it "would fail because the Legislature has not provided guidelines informing the Board how, when, or under what circumstances[] it may create additional conditions." McNeil's conviction was reversed.[47]

Florida

Delegation problems arise under civil laws as well. A good example arose from a dispute about the "Florida Environmental Land and Water Management Act." It empowered an agency to identify areas of "critical state concern" that the agency could regulate when it comes to economic development. Here's the guidance the legislature provided:

> (2) An area of critical state concern may be designated only for:
> (a) An area containing, or having a significant impact upon, environmental, historical, natural, or archaeological resources of regional or statewide importance.
> (b) An area significantly affected by, or having a significant effect upon, an existing or proposed major public facility or other area of major public investment.
> (c) A proposed area of major development potential, which may include a proposed site of a new community, designated in a state land development plan.[48]

Once a tract of land became a "critical state concern," nearly every development of it became regulated. That included "all building, mining, and changes in the use or appearance of land, water and air and appurtenant structures; material increases in the density of its use; alteration of shores and banks; drilling; structural demolition; clearing adjunct to construction; and deposit of waste or fill."[49]

Property owners challenged the legislation after the agency designated a swamp and parts of the Florida Keys as areas of critical state concern. The Florida Supreme Court took on the controversy in *Askew v. Cross Key Waterways.*[50] Justice Sundberg introduced the case in this way. "At contest here are the competing philosophies that underlie two provisions of our fundamental document of government and the attempt by the legislature to accommodate those philosophies." On one side is a guarantee that "the policy of the State" is "to conserve and protect its natural resources and scenic beauty."[51] On the other side is a guarantee that the "powers of the state government shall be divided into legislative, executive and judicial branches. No person belonging to one branch shall exercise any powers appertaining to either of the other branches unless expressly provided herein."[52] A law violates Florida's separation-of-powers clause if it is "so lacking in guidelines that neither the agency nor the courts can determine whether the agency is carrying out the intent of the legislature," transforming the agency into 'the law-giver rather than the administrator of the law.'"

The defect in the law, the court reasoned, was that it gave the commission "the fundamental legislative task of determining which geographic areas and resources are in greatest need of protection." The court "emphasize[d]" that it is not the breadth of potentially covered areas that "faults the legislation." It is "the absence of legislative delineation of priorities among competing areas and resources."[53]

The court rejected the use of federal administrative law precedents in handling the case. As it saw things, the federal approach focused on procedural safeguards in the process of creating regulations and enforcement actions rather than on judicially enforceable limits on delegation. While this approach is "reasonable," as shown by "its adoption in the federal courts and a minority of state jurisdictions," it is not "the view in Florida." Under the Florida Constitution, "the legislature is not free to redelegate to an administrative body so much of its lawmaking power as it may deem expedient." The key problem in the court's eyes was that the "primary policy decision of the area of critical state concern" is "the sole province of an administrative body." "From that determination all else follows." Some flexibility "to administer a legislatively articulated policy" is one thing. But "reposing in an administrative body the power to establish fundamental policy" is another.[54]

In concurrence, Chief Justice England emphasized the gravity of resisting the temptation to abdicate enforcement of the non-delegation principle. In "revitaliz[ing] a vastly more important doctrine"—separation of powers—he "sincerely hope[d] that the significance of our decision today is not lost in a debate concerning its effect on the Environmental Land and Water Management Act." Separation of powers, he explained, "guarantees that Florida's government will continue to operate only by consent of the governed." "Whatever may be the governmental predilections elsewhere, in Florida no person in one branch of our government may by accident or by assignment act in a role assigned by the Constitution to persons in another branch." "Law giving," he emphasized, "is a responsibility assigned to the legislature, and that body is prohibited from relegating its responsibility wholesale to persons, whether elected or appointed, whose duties are simply to see that the laws are observed. The people of Florida placed that restraint on the legislature, as they had every right to do."[55]

Since 1978, the Florida Supreme Court has remained vigilant in enforcing the non-delegation doctrine. In *B.H. v. State*,[56] the court invalidated a criminal law, one that prohibited "escape from any secure detention facility" of a certain security level and that allowed the Florida Department of Health and Rehabilitative Services to define and establish up to eight security levels.[57] The power "to declare what the law shall be," it reasoned, remained with the legislature and could not be lateraled to an agency.[58] Ten years later, in *Bush v. Schiavo*,[59] the court invalidated a law that authorized the governor to stay the withholding of nutrition and hydration from a patient on life support. At fault was the law's failure to "limit the Governor from exercising completely unrestricted discretion."[60]

Michigan

As with many state constitutions, the Michigan Constitution explicitly "divide[s]" the branches of state government and warrants that "no person exercising powers of one branch shall exercise powers properly belonging to another branch."[61] A 2020 decision of the Michigan Supreme Court in *Midwest Institute of Health v. Governor of Michigan* shows how toothful this division-of-powers language can be. At stake was the Michigan governor's authority to issue statewide emergency orders in response to the COVID-19 pandemic.

The case did not take a traditional path to the Michigan Supreme Court. It started in federal court. Out of respect for the Michigan High Court's final say over the meaning of the Michigan Constitution, the federal district court judge deployed a little-used procedural device for certifying state law questions to the state supreme court.[62] The Michigan Supreme Court accepted the certification request.

In issuing her emergency orders, Governor Whitmer relied on the Emergency Powers of the Governor Act of 1945. The law grew out of race-related riots in Detroit in the summer of 1943, which had led the legislature to ensure that the Michigan governor would have authority to bring in federal troops without having to declare martial law in the future.

Here's when the law applies: "During times of great public crisis, disaster, rioting, catastrophe, or similar public emergency within the state, or reasonable apprehension of immediate danger of a public emergency of that kind, when public safety is imperiled," the "governor may proclaim a state of emergency."[63] Here's what the governor may do after declaring an emergency: She may "promulgate reasonable orders, rules, and regulations" as she thinks "necessary to protect life and property or to bring the emergency situation with the affected area under control."[64] Here's what the emergency orders did: They required residents "to stay home with limited exceptions," and "to wear face coverings in indoor public spaces and when outdoors if unable to consistently maintain a distance of six feet," including "requiring children to wear face coverings while playing sports." The orders closed all manner of businesses. And they prohibited "nonessential travel," recreational activities, and "private gatherings of persons not part of a single household."

A group of healthcare providers barred from offering elective surgeries, as well as a patient who needed a knee-replacement surgery, challenged the constitutionality of the underlying emergency powers law.[65] The Michigan Supreme Court, in a 4–3 decision, ruled that the law violated the Michigan Constitution "because it purports to delegate to the executive branch the legislative powers of state government—including its plenary police powers—and to allow the exercise of such powers indefinitely."[66]

Justice Markman wrote the majority opinion. While Justice Viviano wrote separately, he concurred in this aspect of the decision and this conclusion. Justice Markman's decision began with a frequent topic in non-delegation cases. Could the act be construed to avoid the non-delegation problem by limiting the governor's powers under it as a matter of statutory interpretation? No, the court explained. It was "not prepared to rewrite" the law or "construe it in an overly narrow or strained manner to avoid rendering it unconstitutional under the nondelegation doctrine or any other constitutional doctrine."[67] To do otherwise, to ignore the "genuine intentions of the statute's framers," it reasoned, "would be in ironic conflict with the fundamental premise of the non-delegation doctrine itself, which is that the laws of our state are to be determined by the Legislature."[68] No member of the court disagreed with the modest standard of review expressed in the majority opinion—that "statutes are presumed to be constitutional" and the court had "a duty to construe a statute as constitutional unless its unconstitutionality is clearly apparent."[69]

Unable to sidestep the constitutional question, Justice Markman proceeded to answer it. He started with the words of the Michigan Constitution, which prohibit anyone from "exercising powers of one branch" that "properly belong[] to another branch."[70] After that, he went to first principles undergirding this language. Quoting Thomas Cooley, as formidable an interpreter of the Michigan Constitution as there is, he explained that the Michigan Constitution's "legislative power" amounts to the authority "to regulate public concerns, and to make law for the benefit and welfare of the state," but it "cannot be delegated by that department to any other body or authority."[71] Quoting John Locke, he explained that the legislative power was "only to make *Laws*, and not to make *Legislators*," which meant that the "*Legislative* can have no power to transfer their Authority of making Laws, and place it in other hands."[72] The Michigan test, he explained, required "standards" for "guidance" that must be "as reasonably precise as the subject-matter requires or permits."[73] He invoked Michigan and US Supreme Court cases in discerning the meaning of the state constitution, perhaps because the Michigan Constitution came second, approved in 1835 before statehood in January 1837. Acknowledging the deferential "intelligible principle" that "has been subject to growing criticism," he noted limitations on it, more precisely areas in which it made sense to demand more guidance from the legislature—say, when the delegation went to a broad subject, as opposed to a "narrow" one; when it concerned "indefinite" measures, as opposed to temporary ones; when it concerned "criminal sanctions" as opposed to exclusively civil matters.[74] As a result, when "the scope of the powers conferred upon the Governor by the Legislature becomes increasingly broad, in regard to both the *subject matter* and their *duration*, the *standards* imposed upon the Governor's discretion by the Legislature must correspondingly become more detailed and precise."[75]

This was such a case. The emergency powers, in the court's words, were premised "on an assertion of power to reorder social life and to limit, if not altogether displace, the livelihoods of residents across the state and throughout wide-ranging industries."[76] In the context of this broad indefinite delegation of police-power authority, Justice Markman explained that words like "reasonable" and "necessary" did not suffice to meaningfully cabin or channel the delegation.[77] By the court's lights, "such illusory 'non-standard' standards" would give the governor "free rein to exercise a substantial part of our state and local legislative authority—including police powers—for an indefinite period of time."[78] Even as the court acknowledged the need for "singular assertions of governmental authority" in "response to a public emergency" and even as it acknowledged this pandemic as "one of the most threatening public-health crises of modern times,"[79] it concluded that this broad delegation of the legislature's police powers "lack[ed] any basis under Michigan law."[80]

That became the dividing line with the dissent. Writing for the three dissenters, Chief Justice McCormack acknowledged the breadth of the delegation. But she explained that the combination of the undoubted nature of the emergency (addressing a lethal pandemic), other judicial paths to holding the governor in check (challenging the governor's claim of an emergency and her claims that the orders are "reasonable" or "necessary"), and other legislative tools (revisiting the wisdom of the act) required the court to uphold the law.[81]

New Hampshire

As its caption suggests, *Guillou v. New Hampshire Div. of Motor Vehicles*[82] involved the validity of an allocation of power to implement a state licensing law. The law permitted the director of the agency to suspend a driver's license "for any cause which he may deem sufficient."[83] Writing for the New Hampshire Supreme Court, Justice Batchelder framed the issue as whether the law "prescribe[d] any policies or standards to guide the director" in deciding whether to suspend a license or instead was "vague and indefinite." The court acknowledged that a presumption of constitutionality applied to the law but saw no way to provide a limiting construction of the statute or otherwise to uphold it. It simply left too much discretion in the director, who "might determine that the commission of four offenses in a two-year period is cause for revocation" one day and that "five offenses in a two-year period" is cause for revocation on another, all without limits on the length of the suspension and all without "standards for administrative action."[84] "In the government of this state, the three essential powers" must "be kept as separate from, and independent of, each other, as the nature of a free government will admit."[85]

Texas

Suspect legislative delegations target all kinds of problems and rely on all kinds of agencies. The problem in a leading Texas case was an insect— formally called the *Anthonomus grandis Boheman*, informally called the boll weevil. The boll weevil presents a once-a-year risk to Texas's cotton farmers. To help deal with the problem, the legislature allowed cotton growers to create the Official Cotton Growers' Boll Weevil Eradication Foundation. The law permitted the foundation to hold elections over whether cotton growers in certain areas want to create a boll weevil eradication zone. Once a zone is created, the foundation determines what eradication programs to conduct and could impose penalties for failure to pay assessments on time. If a cotton grower fails to pay an assessment within ten days of the due date, he must "destroy his cotton crop." And if the grower does not do that, the crop became "a public nuisance." The Department of Agriculture then must "destroy it" and must do so "even if not infested with boll weevils," all at the owner's expense. Non-complying cotton growers are guilty of a misdemeanor.[86]

Several cotton growers challenged the program under Texas's non-delegation doctrine. In an opinion by Chief Justice Phillips, the Texas Supreme Court noted that the non-delegation rule is "rooted in the principle of separation of powers that underlies our tripartite system of Government."[87] Under the Texas Constitution, the court explained, "the power to pass laws rests with the Legislature, and that power cannot be delegated to some commission or other tribunal."[88]

But the court cautioned that "these blanket pronouncements" should not be construed too broadly. Legislative "power must almost always be exercised with a certain amount of discretion, and at times the line between making laws and enforcing them may blur." The test is whether the law establishes "reasonable standards to guide" the agency.[89]

Two questions loomed. Did this grant of power go to a private entity, which required greater scrutiny? And did the grant of power contain reasonable guardrails?

On the first point, delegations of power to private entities raise "even more troubling constitutional issues than their public counterparts." The entity may have "a personal or pecuniary interest which is inconsistent with or repugnant to the public interest," and "democratic rule under a republican form of government is compromised when public powers are abandoned to those who are neither elected by the people, appointed by a public official or entity, nor employed by the government." The foundation had mixed qualities—elections but with limited participation, assessments but with the funds not placed in the state treasury, criminal sanctions for violations of its standards but with a foundation run by non-state employees in charge of the standards. Even so, the court treated it as a private foundation "for purposes of applying the nondelegation doctrine."[90]

That conclusion eased the path to answering the second question. The Department of Agriculture did not oversee "the amount of assessments adopted by the growers, the total amount of funds expended on eradication, the amount of debt incurred by the Foundation, or the repayment terms for such debts." The foundation's authority also went beyond providing expertise for rulemaking. Instead of just "devising eradication guidelines," the foundation also "applied" them. At the same time, the foundation's board members were themselves "cotton growers who have a direct pecuniary interest in the eradication programs." Last, hardly least, the legislature did not circumscribe the foundation's discretion, offering "no guidance as to how assessments are to be set or the amount of debt that the Foundation may incur." That meant it "had free rein to incur over $9 million in debt in the Lower Rio Grande Valley Zone to be repaid by the growers there through several years of assessments, even though those growers voted within twenty-one months to discontinue their eradication program."[91]

The non-delegation doctrine, the court accepted, "should be used sparingly," solely "when there is, in Justice Cardozo's memorable phrase, 'delegation running riot.' "[92] That was this case, the court concluded.

In response, the Texas legislature gave the Texas Department of Agriculture more control over the operations of the foundation,[93] which apparently satisfied the objecting cotton growers. By 2015, the Texas Department of Agriculture could credit collaboration between the Texas Department of Agriculture and the Texas Boll Weevil Eradication Fund for nearly $3 billion in savings—and the near eradication of the boll weevil.[94]

Judicial Deference to Executive Branch Agencies

Separation-of-powers principles not only may limit delegations of legislative power to the executive branch and its agencies, but they also may limit delegations of judicial power—the power to say what the law means—to executive branch agencies. At stake is when, if ever, federal or state courts should defer to administrative interpretations of a law that the legislature has tasked the agency with implementing.

The federal side of the story, as too often happens, dominates the discussion. Fervent debates in recent decades focus on whether the US Supreme Court's *Chevron* decision—giving federal agencies implied authority to fill gaps in statutes with reasonable interpretations—should be revisited and indeed whether it violates the US Constitution's separation of powers or the Administrative Procedure Act (APA). For some time, little heed has been given to state court decisions about the topic. The remarks of Kenneth Davis, the author of the landmark "Administrative Law Treatise," may capture one explanation. Sometimes called the "father of administrative law,"[95] Davis observed that the "typical" state court opinion "strings together some misleading legal clichés and announces the conclusion."[96] Ouch. Maybe the "father of federal administrative law" would be a more appropriate moniker. At any rate, since 1958, when Davis dismissed the insights of fifty state courts, plenty of valuable (non-cliché) decisions with considerable insight have emerged. Typical or atypical, these state court decisions raise a provocative question. Which court system has resolved this vexing problem most insightfully?

The Federal Story

Start with the well-trodden federal story. One could be forgiven for thinking that before 1984, no one had thought about federal judicial deference to agency interpretations of federal laws. In that year, intentionally or not, a unanimous six-member decision of the United States Supreme Court[97] laid the groundwork for the modern rule of when federal courts would defer to an agency's interpretation of a statute that Congress charged it with administering.[98] The approach, now known as the *Chevron* doctrine, requires federal courts to defer to reasonable interpretations of statutes that Congress has directed the agency to administer. But before *Chevron*, there was an assortment of approaches to the issue. The Administrative Procedure Act seemed to take a stand. The "reviewing court," it said, "shall decide all relevant questions of law, interpret constitutional and statutory provisions, and determine the meaning or applicability of the terms of an agency action" and "hold unlawful and set aside agency action, findings, and conclusions found to be . . . in excess of statutory jurisdiction, authority, or limitations, or short of statutory right."[99] That seemed to support a nondeferential approach. The *Skidmore* doctrine gave deference to agency interpretations dependent on "the thoroughness evident in its consideration, the validity of its reasoning, its consistency with earlier and later pronouncements, and all those factors which give it power to persuade, if lacking the power to control."[100] The *Seminole Rock* doctrine gave deference to agency interpretations of their own rules, stating that an agency interpretation "becomes of controlling weight unless it is plainly erroneous or inconsistent with the regulation."[101] Professor Aditya Bamzai points out that nineteenth-century courts "'respected' long-standing and contemporaneous *executive* interpretations of law as part of a practice of deferring to long-standing and contemporaneous interpretation *generally*."[102] And there's plenty more.

Chevron, in fact, did not arise in a vacuum. It is not even clear that the Court realized how far-reaching the decision would be in 1984.[103] But the one thing worth remembering about *Chevron* is that it arose in an area, the highly reticulated provisions of the Clean Air Act, in which judges are most apt to be amenable to accepting guidance from those who wrestle with the meaning of a technical law day in and day out.

With the Clean Air Act Amendments of 1977, Congress created requirements for states that had not attained national air quality standards set by the Environmental Protection Agency. The law required "nonattainment" states to establish a program that oversaw new air pollution sources. Absent compliance with several conditions, a state could not issue a permit for the new source. What counted as a source? The relevant EPA regulation allowed a state to use "a plantwide definition" of "stationary source."[104] That meant a plant with many pollution-emitting devices could install a new piece of equipment "without meeting the permit conditions if the alteration will not increase the total emissions from the plant." At issue was whether the EPA's decision "to allow States to treat all of the pollution-emitting devices within the same industrial grouping as though they were encased within a single 'bubble' is based on a reasonable construction of the statutory term 'stationary source.' "[105]

In an opinion by Justice Stevens, the Court upheld the regulation. Two questions, he explained, emerge when courts review an agency's interpretation of a statute it administers. One is "whether Congress has directly spoken to the precise question at issue. If the intent of Congress is clear, that is the end of the matter; for the court, as well as the agency, must give effect to the unambiguously expressed intent of Congress." But "if the statute is silent or ambiguous with respect to the specific issue," the second question "is whether the agency's answer is based on a permissible construction of the statute."[106]

In justifying the Court's approach to the second question, the Court explained that an agency's implementation of a federal law "necessarily requires the formulation of policy and the making of rules to fill any gap left, implicitly or explicitly, by Congress." When it comes to an "express delegation of authority to the agency" to sort out the particulars of a federal program, the resulting regulations receive "controlling weight unless they are arbitrary, capricious, or manifestly contrary to the statute." When it comes to an "implicit" delegation of authority, the key issue in *Chevron* is this: "A court may not substitute its own construction of a statutory provision for a reasonable interpretation made by the administrator of an agency."[107]

In applying this framework to the Clean Air Act, the Court observed that the law did not contain any definition of the "bubble concept" and did not contain a definition of "stationary source." It then observed that a new president had taken office in 1981 and launched a "Government-wide reexamination of regulatory burdens and complexities." During that review by the EPA, led by Administrator Anne Gorsuch Burford, mother of then–future Supreme Court Justice Neil Gorsuch, the agency "reevaluated the various arguments that had been advanced in connection with the proper definition of the term 'source.'" In concluding that the plantwide definition made more sense, it explained that the old rule operated "as a disincentive to new investment and modernization by discouraging modifications to existing facilities" and "can actually retard progress in air pollution control by discouraging replacement of older, dirtier processes or pieces of equipment with new, cleaner ones."[108]

The Court concluded with these deferential thoughts:

> In these cases, the Administrator's interpretation represents a reasonable accommodation of manifestly competing interests and is entitled to deference: the regulatory scheme is technical and complex, the agency considered the matter in a detailed and reasoned fashion, and the decision involves reconciling conflicting policies. Congress intended to accommodate both interests, but did not do so itself on the level of specificity presented by these cases. Perhaps that body consciously desired the Administrator to strike the balance at this level, thinking that those with great expertise and charged with responsibility for administering the provision would be in a better position to do so; perhaps it simply did not consider the question at this level; and perhaps Congress was unable to forge a coalition on either side of the question, and those on each side decided to take their chances with the scheme devised by the agency. For judicial purposes, it matters not which of these things occurred. Judges are not experts in the field, and are not part of either political branch of the Government. Courts must, in some cases, reconcile competing political interests, but not on the basis of the judges' personal policy preferences. In contrast, an agency to which Congress has delegated policy-making responsibilities may, within the limits of that delegation, properly rely upon the incumbent administration's views of wise policy to inform its judgments. While agencies are not directly accountable to the people, the Chief Executive is, and it is entirely appropriate for this political branch of the Government to make such policy choices—resolving the competing interests which Congress itself either inadvertently did not resolve, or intentionally

left to be resolved by the agency charged with the administration of the statute in light of everyday realities.[109]

That left the Court, the parties, and the country with this rule. "When a challenge to an agency construction of a statutory provision, fairly conceptualized, really centers on the wisdom of the agency's policy, rather than whether it is a reasonable choice within a gap left open by Congress, the challenge must fail. In such a case, federal judges—who have no constituency—have a duty to respect legitimate policy choices made by those who do. The responsibilities for assessing the wisdom of such policy choices and resolving the struggle between competing views of the public interest are not judicial ones."[110] Professor Thayer would have approved.

While Justice Stevens wrote *Chevron* and stood by it throughout his tenure, Justice Scalia, a former professor of administrative law, was also a forceful defender of the *Chevron* doctrine, at least in the first twenty years of his tenure. In a 1989 lecture, he defended the doctrine. "An ambiguity in a statute committed to agency implementation," he explained, "can be attributed to either of two congressional desires: (1) Congress intended a particular result, but was not clear about it or (2) Congress had no particular intent on the subject, but meant to leave its resolution to the agency." The first category "is genuinely a question of law, properly to be resolved by the courts." But "the only question of law" raised by the second category "is whether the agency has acted within the scope of its discretion." *Chevron* replaced a "statute-by-statute evaluation" of which category applied "with an across-the-board presumption that, in the case of ambiguity, agency discretion is meant." Whether this is true or not, it "operates principally as a background rule of law against which Congress can legislate."[111] With Justice Stevens and Justice Scalia both lined up in support of *Chevron*, it would be easy to think the doctrine rose to the level of a biblical truth. Too easy, it turns out.

In the last ten to twenty years, the *Chevron* doctrine and judicial deference to agencies more generally have faced multi-front challenges. How, some wonder, could a Court simultaneously believe that it "was emphatically the duty of the judiciary to say what the law is" in *Marbury*'s words and yet permit federal agencies to exercise that power when it matters most, resolving the meaning of ambiguous statutes? Some, including Justice Scalia, began to have second thoughts when a central value of *Chevron*—clear accountability in the executive branch and a clear rule of decision—became less predictable after the Court's decision in *Mead*, which made deference turn on multiple factors, "tailor[ing] deference to variety" and making variety the only predictor of deference.[112] Another explanation for *Chevron* turned on complaints about the unpredictability of statutory construction in the 1970s and early 1980s, making it understandable for the Court to give politically accountable agencies the authority to fill gaps in statutes rather than politically unaccountable federal judges. But in the last three decades, considerable consensus has emerged about the shared principles undergirding statutory interpretation. If, as Justice Kagan acknowledges, "We are all textualists now," that makes deference to agencies less imperative, as judges more often will come to the same view about the meaning of a law and less often will need *Chevron* anyway.[113]

Philip Hamburger provoked more second thoughts with *Is Administrative Law Unlawful?*[114] In this history-laden and thought-filled book, he argued that current administrative law, including *Chevron*, could not be reconciled with separation-of-powers principles embraced at the federal founding. Justice Thomas has taken the lead at the Court on the point, explaining that "*Chevron* deference raises serious separation-of-powers questions" and "precludes judges from exercising [independent] judgment."[115] In 2020, he denounced *Chevron* in even stronger terms,[116] claiming that "*Chevron* compels judges to abdicate the judicial power without constitutional sanction," it "gives federal agencies unconstitutional power," it "undermines the ability of the Judiciary to perform its checking function on the other branches," it is "likely contrary" to the APA, and it "is inconsistent with accepted principles of statutory interpretation from the first century of the Republic."[117] No small matter, Justice Gorsuch, Justice Kavanaugh, and Justice Barrett took seats on the Court, and some of them had expressed skepticism of the modern administrative state in their court of appeals' decisions.[118]

Time will judge whether *Chevron* lives, shrinks, or dies. More on that at the end of the chapter.

The State Stories

The states' approaches to administrative deference, like their approaches to delegation, are all over the map and show little proclivity to follow the federal model reflexively. Daniel Ortner recently placed the states' approaches to administrative deference into six categories, what can be reduced to three rough categories.[119] Twelve states defer as much or more to state agencies as federal courts do to federal agencies. Ten states have expressly rejected any interpretive deference to agencies. And the other twenty-eight states defer to agencies in some cases but not others, akin to the variation that preceded *Chevron* and the growing variation since *Mead*. These last states vary wildly. Some defer to agencies' interpretations of their own regulations but not to their interpretations of the underlying statutes. Others defer to agencies that have a particularly high degree of expertise but not to other agencies. Still others don't have clear and consistent rules for when they do and do not defer.[120] All states considered, few of them expressly incorporate the *Chevron* model into state law.

Of the non-deferring states, some reject deference based on constitutional amendments or statutes that prohibit deference. Confirming the political resonance of the issue, 62% of Florida voters in 2018 supported an amendment to the Florida Constitution that banned judicial deference.[121] "In interpreting a state statute or rule, it says, state courts "may not defer to an administrative agency's interpretation" of the law and "must instead interpret such statute or rule de novo."[122] Two states, Arizona and Wisconsin, eliminated deference through state laws. In 2018, the Arizona legislature provided that in actions "brought by or against the regulated party, the court shall decide all questions of law, including the interpretation of . . . statutory provisions . . . without deference to any previous determination that may have been made on the question by the agency."[123] Wisconsin did something similar later that year. "No agency," the law says, "may seek deference in any proceeding based on the agency's interpretation of any law."[124] In enacting the law, the Wisconsin legislature relied on the following decision by its Supreme Court.[125]

Wisconsin

At issue in *Tetra Tech v. Wisconsin Department of Revenue* was a tax imposed by the Wisconsin Department of Revenue on "processing" river sediments into waste sludge, reusable sand, and water.[126] The challengers complained that "processing" did not apply to the separation of river sediment into its various parts. Before deciding the case, the court asked the parties to address a threshold question: "Does the practice of deferring to agency interpretations of statutes comport with Article VII, Section 2 of the Wisconsin Constitution, which vests the judicial power in the unified court system?"[127]

Writing the lead opinion, Justice Dan Kelly went back to ideas from the inception. The Wisconsin Constitution, he pointed out, puts the judicial power in one branch. "The judicial power of this state shall be vested in a unified court system consisting of one supreme court, a court of appeals, a circuit court, such trial courts of general uniform statewide jurisdiction as the legislature may create by law, and a municipal court if authorized by the legislature."[128] But permitting an "agency to authoritatively interpret the law raises the possibility that our deference doctrine has allowed some part of the state's judicial power to take up residence in the executive branch of government."[129]

Justice Kelly perceived a "duty" to "patrol[] the borders between the branches," not just as "a practical matter of efficient and effective government," but also because "it provides structural protection against depredations on our liberties." As a matter of constitutional design, the "powers of each branch of government fall into two categories: exclusive powers and shared powers." The shared powers "lie at the intersections of these exclusive core constitutional powers," and "these great borderlands of power are not exclusive to any one branch." "Core powers," however, "are not for sharing" and must "be jealously guarded by each branch of government."[130]

The judicial power, he explained, is "the ultimate adjudicative authority of courts to finally decide rights and responsibilities as between individuals." "Some would argue that the judiciary's law-declaring and law-applying power lies not at the core of what it means to be a court, but somewhere out on the periphery of our powers where we share it with the executive branch. Some of our older cases have spoken in terms that lend this proposition at least some superficial plausibility." But that approach refers to "interpretation and application *within the executive branch*. We are here concerned with the authoritative interpretation and application of the law as applied to a particular case *within the judicial branch*. 'Only the judicial interpretation as opposed to interpretations offered by the other branches would be considered authoritative in a judicial proceeding.' "[131]

These considerations brought Justice Kelly back "to the most central of our powers: 'No aspect of the judicial power is more fundamental than the judiciary's exclusive responsibility to exercise judgment in cases and controversies arising under the law.'" "Only the judiciary," he explained, "may authoritatively interpret and apply the law in cases before our courts. The executive may not intrude on this duty, and the judiciary may not cede it. If our deference doctrine allows either, we must reject it."[132]

The problem with giving "great weight" to an agency's interpretation is that it "cede[s] to the agency the power to authoritatively interpret the law." "Because that power belongs to the judiciary—and the judiciary alone—we may not allow an administrative agency to exercise it."[133]

The reasoning in Justice Kelly's opinion did not command a majority of the seven-member court. Justice Rebecca Bradley joined the separation-of-powers constitutional reasoning in full.[134] Justice Ziegler filed a concurring opinion, joined in part by Chief Justice Roggensack, to emphasize that, because the doctrine of deference was a judicially created administrative doctrine, the court could end Wisconsin's court-created deference practice without relying on the state constitution.[135] Justice Gableman, again joined by Chief Justice Roggensack, filed a concurring opinion, explaining that the court could use constitutional avoidance principles to eliminate judicial deference to agency interpretation of Wisconsin statutes.[136] Justice Ann Bradley, joined by Justice Abrahamson, defended Wisconsin's deference to agencies.[137] All perspectives accounted for, the court ended judicial deference to agencies by a vote of 5–2.[138] Later that year, as noted, the Wisconsin legislature enacted a statute that barred administrative deference to legal conclusions. "No agency," it commands, "may seek deference in any proceeding based on the agency's interpretation of any law."[139]

Mississippi

Mississippi recently traveled a similar path.[140] Justice Coleman wrote the opinion for the court, which re-examined its administrative deference decisions.

He described the existing judicial framework for reviewing an agency's construction of a statute as "'*de novo*, but with great deference to the agency's interpretation,'" an approach that conveyed more "contradiction" than reason. How can we "writ[e] on the one hand that we give great deference to agency interpretations of statutes and, then, with the next strike of the computer keyboard, writ[e] that no deference will be given if the agency's interpretation contradicts the best reading of the statute"?[141]

Not to be forgotten was "Mississippi's strict constitutional separation of powers." The Mississippi Constitution "divides the power of state government into three branches and assigns legislative powers to the legislative branch, judicial powers to the judicial branch, and executive power to the executive branch."[142] Beyond general allocations of power in the constitution was this doubt-removing provision, in the court's mind: "No person or collection of persons, being one or belonging to one of these departments, shall exercise any power properly belonging to either of the others."[143] The problem was not that agencies have no right to construe laws in performing their duties. They do, and the executive branch is free to give deference to those interpretations. The problem arises "when the interpretation of a statute comes before the courts, and when deference is given to an agency interpretation, we share the exercise of the power of statutory interpretation with another branch in violation of Article 1, Section 2."[144]

In "abandon[ing]" the old standard of "giving deference to agency interpretations of statutes," the Court saw itself as stepping "fully into the role the Constitution" provides "for the courts and the courts alone" to "interpret statutes." At the same time, in an example of cooperative federalism, it found "persuasive the reasoning of then-Judge Gorsuch," who wrote that courts should "'fulfill their duty to exercise their independent judgment about what the law *is*.'"[145]

Delaware

Not all state court decisions rejecting *Chevron* are of recent vintage. One of the more well-known state court decisions is nearly a quarter-century old and arose at a time when few people criticized federal administrative deference.[146]

The Delaware Supreme Court, through an opinion by Justice Walsh, rejected a "clearly erroneous test to an administrative agency's interpretation of statutory law" and instead required fresh review of the meaning of any state law. At issue was a request to the Department of Natural Resources and Environmental Control for two well permits. Opposing the application was the Public Water Supply Company, a public utility. The outcome of the appeal turned on whether the agency received deference over its reading of the law.[147]

Denying any such deference, the court made several points. One was that it would be "anomalous" for the "Court to accord a higher level of deference to the legal rulings of an administrative agency than that applied to trial courts subject to our appellate jurisdiction." Another was that interpretation of statutes is "ultimately the responsibility of the courts." It's one thing to give "due weight, but not defer, to an agency interpretation of a statute administered by it." But it's quite another to "defer to such an interpretation as correct merely because it is rational or not clearly erroneous." The court "expressly decline[d]" to adopt *Chevron* and stood by its "plenary standard of review." Last of all, the court left in place its deference decisions with respect to "an agency's construction of a regulation promulgated by it," what's called *Seminole Rock* or *Auer* deference at the federal level.[148]

Delegation and Administrative Deference for the Twenty-First Century

While I have separated the discussion of non-delegation and administrative deference up to now, the two topics overlap. They both deal with a similar problem. One involves an explicit delegation of power; the other involves an implicit delegation of power. In one setting, the legislature expressly gives an agency wide berth by granting capacious policymaking authority. In the other setting, the legislature by implication does something similar by leaving ambiguous terms in the law for an agency to resolve. The question is where, if at all, one preserves the lines of power: at the legislative stage (by invalidating the law then and there) or at the agency stage (by denying the agency a conclusive power of interpretation)? At either point, courts may pull back agencies perceived to have too much power and too little guidance over how to exercise it.

In considering how the states and the United States have handled these delegation issues in the past and could handle them in the future, there is a lot to consider. Why do state courts act more independently in construing state separation-of-powers guarantees than they do in construing individual-rights guarantees? How, if at all, have state or federal legislatures guarded their policymaking prerogatives? What insights do the state experiences provide when it comes to the federal approaches? Are there any subject-matter areas ripe for reconsideration when it comes to the future of state and federal administrative law? How do the roles of the courts and federalism fit into all of this?

Federal administrative law does not have the same pull on state judges that other areas of federal constitutional law often do. In contrast to the state courts' treatment of individual rights, where most state courts start with the presumption that the meaning of state guarantees mirrors the meaning of their federal counterparts, state courts do not use a similar presumption in handling administrative law disputes. The federal doctrine may influence state courts, it is true, but the state judges do not seem to orient their thinking around it in the same way that they do with individual rights. In the words of Aaron Saiger: "*Chevron* has been received spottily by the states," "few have endorsed it wholeheartedly," and "the majority of the states have deference doctrines meaningfully different from *Chevron*'s."[149] When one goes through the relevant state cases, it appears that only two states—Maine and Massachusetts—follow the two-step *Chevron* test and have expressly incorporated it into state law at some point.[150]

So too for non-delegation. Because "constitutional law is much too centered on the opinions of the Supreme Court of the United States," as Jack Balkin and Sandy Levinson point out, most lawyers and scholars overlook the possibility that the state courts might use different approaches in resolving non-delegation disputes and might have insights to offer in doing so.[151] Roughly forty-three states, it turns out, do not follow the hands-off federal approach.[152] As suggested by the title of their empirical study, "The Nondelegation Doctrine: Alive and Well," Keith Whittington and Jason Iuliano have shown that the non-delegation doctrine is indeed alive and well in the states. Relying on a data set of over 1,000 non-delegation challenges from the first one in 1799 to the last one through 2017, they show that about 15% of them invalidate the law and that this rate of invalidation did not change after 1937, when accepted wisdom holds that the non-delegation doctrine died.[153] All of this stands in sharp contrast with modern individual rights, where the debate so often starts with the federal doctrine and so often ends there. When it comes to administrative law, state court judges rarely act like territorial judges.[154]

Why? Several possibilities come to mind. One turns on the salience of federal individual rights. They are well known by most Americans and thus are difficult to ignore when considering the meaning of state individual rights. The same is not true of federal separation of powers in general and federal administrative law in particular. Both topics are taught in the law schools to be sure, far more, I should add, than state administrative law. But even in an era in which the federal non-delegation doctrine and *Chevron's* virtues and vices are suspensefully debated in the law journals, the language of federal administrative law has not become the sole, or even the dominant, language of debate.

Another possibility turns on the background of state court judges. They are more likely than their federal counterparts to have worked in state government at some point.[155] A stint in state government familiarizes the future judge with a state's separation of powers and administrative law. That background is bound to incline the judge facing a state administrative law case to think first about experiences navigating state administrative agencies, not a class on federal administrative law. State constitutions are local documents, state separation of powers even more so.

Still another explanation is that there are state-specific reasons for administrative law to operate differently at the local level. When it comes to explicit and implied delegations of power to agencies, one explanation for state courts to clamp down is the reality that positions in state legislatures often started out as part-time jobs and sometimes have remained that way—often in places where state term limits (non-existent for federal representatives)[156] impact how long a state legislator can stay in office.

Consider some examples. The Texas legislature sits once every two years for 120 days, and the Florida legislature sits once a year for sixty days.[157] The Montana legislature, like the Texas legislature, convenes for non-emergency sessions once every two years, for a maximum of ninety days. And Montana legislators are paid hourly and only when in session, at just over $11 an hour plus a per diem for travel.[158] The National Conference of State Legislatures identifies just ten states as having "full time" or "full time lite" state legislatures.[159] As for term limits, fifteen states have term limits, ranging from six to twelve years.[160] Short legislative sessions, together with experience and expertise gaps between career-service employees in the agencies and term-limited legislators, give legislatures ample reasons to make broad express or implied delegations to year-round agencies. If the temptation of legislating by delegating is greater in the states, the imperative of courts holding the line may be greater there, too.[161]

Still another reason for heightened skepticism of legislative delegation and administrative deference at the state level is that state legislatures have general jurisdiction. They have a general "police power" and thus may regulate (almost) anything within their state. That's less true for Congress, which may regulate only in connection with an enumerated power, whether it's a commerce, civil-rights enforcement, or spending power. "General jurisdiction," Aaron Saiger thinks, "is likely one reason for more rigorous nondelegation doctrine in the states."[162] Variations in design sometimes lead to variations in doctrine.

A last reason returns to a fresh topic, the plural executive at the state level. While all executive branch power in the national government flows from a single president, the same is not true in the states. That supplies an explanation of its own for local variation in administrative law. Many agency heads at the state level are separately elected. That could include a secretary of state responsible for elections in the state, an auditor, an insurance commissioner, or a head of the Department of Education. Others are appointed by the governor. Then there's the reality that the top legal official in the state, the attorney general, is usually separately elected, creating "a *Chevron*-confounding figure" who "constitutes a second source *within the politically accountable executive* that independently determines what the law is in the case of a legislative gap."[163]

Each office creates a risk of official differences of opinion about the meaning of a state law and about the deference appropriate to an agency in construing it. Which executive branch head receives deference under these circumstances? The attorney general? The separately elected agency head? Or the governor? When two separately elected officials disagree over the meaning of the same statute, administrative deference becomes useless.[164] Any "appeal of *Chevron* as a general principle, then, fades in the face of the widespread phenomenon of the plural state executive and intraexecutive conflict."[165]

In another sense, it's true, the separate election of executive branch officials at the state level mitigates some of the problems that come with little judicial oversight of delegations of legislative power. State executive branches offer plural layers of recourse for the people, who can punish the legislature, the governor, the attorney general, or the relevant agency head at the next election. Elected agency heads in particular may face direct consequences if they get too far ahead of the people in implementing a generally worded statute or a statute that delegates considerable policymaking discretion.[166]

Recall also that the judges who handle the dispute are likely to be elected or face retention elections. "Elections do more than make state judges *democratically* accountable; they also make them politically attuned and politically connected."[167] That takes away one of the central reasons for deference under *Chevron* and for refusing to enforce the non-delegation at the federal level—that the judge is unelected and unaccountable. That's less likely to be so at the state level. State judges are delegated far more policymaking authority than federal judges, whether it's to make common law, to issue advisory opinions, or to issue decisions in a court system that often will have diminished constraints—standing, ripeness, mootness, and justiciability—on judicial power.[168]

To put matters in comparative terms, there are many reasons to permit *more delegation* at the state level than at the federal level. The accountability problems are diminished at the state level. And the stakes are far lower if one state opts to allow sweeping express and implied delegations of power to an agency with authority over one topic in one state. That's simply not true for a federal agency. While it has authority over just one topic, that authority extends to an entire country. A striking feature of American administrative law is that the government that tends to be the most permissive when it comes to express and implied delegations of authority is the government with the broadest power.

Through it all, the plural executive, the election of judges at the state level, and other state-specific considerations offer ample explanations for the states to chart their own courses in this area. And indeed they have.

State and federal legislatures may take care of some of these issues on their own, and in some instances they already have. Why don't traditional turf-war considerations lead legislatures to avoid delegating power to agencies housed in another branch of government? Aren't legislatures reflexively jealous of giving power to a president or a governor or a separately elected agency head? Usually is the answer; not always is the qualification. Within a topic of legislation could linger a policy matter too controversial to handle, prompting legislators to let the cup pass to another branch under the cover of a sweeping delegation of legislative power to the agency. Justice Gorsuch acknowledged this problem in his *Gundy* dissent, noting that a general delegation allows the legislature to "pass[] the potato" to the executive branch and escape responsibility for determining how to handle a controversial matter.[169] State courts have tuned into the same concern. According to the Kentucky Supreme Court, the non-delegation doctrine prohibits lawmakers from enacting "vaguely worded special interest (or self-interested) legislation and acting surprised when the true nature of the legislation comes to light."[170] The other possibility is that the legislators cannot come to agreement on a point and paper over their differences with a pregnant ambiguity.

The first problem—an express delegation beyond legitimate bounds—is one for courts, and courts alone, to fix, either by invalidating the delegation or narrowing the law on constitutional-avoidance grounds. No other legislative answer appears. It is difficult to imagine a legislature passing a law that tells the courts not to respect express delegations of power that *it* enacted.

The second problem—an implied delegation and the potential agency deference that goes with it—is one that a legislature can fix. Some state legislatures recently have done just that. As shown, Wisconsin and Arizona recently enacted laws that expressly eliminate agency deference. Sixty-two percent of Florida voters, most striking of all, enacted an initiative to bar agency deference, confirming the resonance of the issue.

One might think Congress would propose something similar given the unrelenting criticism of *Chevron* by Justices Thomas and Gorsuch, Judges Ginsburg and Menashi, and Philip Hamburger as well as many other scholars and judges. Consider the force of just some of its perceived faults: that it creates "systematic bias in favor of the government and against the citizen," that its references to agency "expertise" ought to be acknowledged for what they are, a "euphemism for policy judgment," and that it overlooks the judiciary's time-honored duty to say what the law means.[171] These assessments would seem to demand legal *and* political responses.

Some members of Congress, as it happens, proposed such a law, one designed to curb judicial deference to agency interpretations of laws. They did so in 2016 and called it the "Separation of Powers Restoration Act."[172] The law has not yet been enacted and remains in search of majority support in both houses.

But is the proposed law needed? That is not obvious given the existing prescriptions of the Administrative Procedure Act. Enacted in 1946, the APA says that "the reviewing court shall decide all relevant questions of law, interpret constitutional and statutory provisions, and determine the meaning or applicability of the terms of an agency action" and "hold unlawful and set aside agency action, findings, and conclusions found to be . . . in excess of statutory jurisdiction, authority, or limitations, or short of statutory right."[173] A striking feature of the *Chevron* debate is that the federal courts have not wrestled with these features of the APA. *Chevron* itself does not answer the point. Making matters more unusual, the different approaches to agency deference in the states may turn on similar state laws. All fifty states have adopted their own state Administrative Procedure Acts.[174] Some attribute the prevalence of non-deference regimes to these state APAs.[175]

The state experiences defeat some of the federal explanations for declining to enforce the non-delegation doctrine and for continuing to embrace a broad deference model. One worry at the federal level is that judicial enforcement of the non-delegation doctrine will be difficult, if not impossible, to apply in a principled way. Justice Scalia often voiced this concern.[176] Justice Gorsuch acknowledged it when he sat on the Tenth Circuit, noting that the federal courts have "had a hard time devising a satisfying" way to apply the non-delegation doctrine.[177] The other worry is that if federal courts must answer every legal question generated by implementation of every federal enforcement scheme handled by every federal agency, they will face an unmanageable onslaught of cases.

The state experiences cast doubt on each consideration. Forty-three state courts enforce a non-delegation doctrine. Those decisions show that courts have been able to cabin impermissible delegations, a lesson the federal courts are free to embrace or reject. At a minimum, the state experiences suggest that the sky will not fall if the federal courts adopt a modest path for handling the line-drawing problems in the area, perhaps not unlike the approach the federal courts used to enforce limits on congressional power. Think of the US Supreme Court's decisions in *Lopez* and *Morrison*, which ended the myth created by *Wickard v. Filburn* in 1942 that Congress faced no limits on regulating interstate commerce. At the same time that these recent decisions limited congressional regulation of non-interstate or non-economic activities, they left room for some regulation or alternative paths for enacting comparable legislation. Or think of the US Supreme Court's decision in *City of Boerne*, which ended the myth created by *Katzenbach v. Morgan* in 1966 that there were no limits on Congress's power to enforce the Fourteenth Amendment against the states. After *Gundy*, the time may be ripe for something similar when it comes to horizontal separation of powers. Either way, the state experiences, together with these recent federal decisions, illuminate both sides of the debate for the federal courts: the degree of risk in imposing some judicially enforceable limits and the degree of risk in ceding responsibility.[178]

Six years before joining the Court, Justice Scalia, no distant observer of administrative law, offered these thoughts about the non-delegation doctrine:

So even with all its Frankenstein-like warts, knobs, and (concededly) dangers, the unconstitutional delegation doctrine is worth hewing from the ice. The alternative appears to be continuation of the widely felt trend toward government by bureaucracy or (what is no better) government by courts. In truth, of course, no one has ever thought that the unconstitutional delegation doctrine did not *exist* as a principle of our government. If it did not, the Congress could presumably vote all powers to the President and adjourn. The only issue has been whether adherence to this fundamental principle is properly enforceable by the courts, or rather should be left (except perhaps in extreme cases of the sort just mentioned) to the wisdom of the Congress. As an original matter, there is much to be said for the latter view. The sorts of judgments alluded to above—how great is the need for prompt action, how extensive is the social consensus on the vague legislated objective, and so forth—are much more appropriate for a representative assembly than for a hermetically sealed committee of nine lawyers. In earlier times heated constitutional debate did take place at the congressional level.

Recently, however, the notion seems to have taken root that if a constitutional prohibition is not enforceable through the courts it does not exist. Where that mind set obtains, the congressional barrier to unconstitutional action disappears unless reinforced by judicial affirmation. So even those who do not relish the prospect of regular judicial enforcement of the unconstitutional delegation doctrine might well support the Court's making an example of one—just one—of the many enactments that appear to violate the principle. The educational effect on Congress might well be substantial.[179]

During his thirty years on the Court, however, Justice Scalia never accepted his own invitation to enforce the non-delegation doctrine. Who knows what he would have done with *Gundy*? The Court's once-in-a-while enforcement of other structural principles—the Commerce Clause and the Fourteenth Amendment's Enforcement Clause—may offer a good reason for "making an example" of some extreme delegations. So also does the experience of the states.

Even as the state experiences offer room for optimism about experimenting with a judicially enforceable federal non-delegation doctrine, it's worth asking how exactly the state tests differ from the federal approach and what insights the state doctrines offer. The linguistic formulations in the states do not present a Eureka moment when it comes to articulating the distinction between permissible and impermissible delegations. The words used to explain the approaches seem to break down into little more than highly deferential and less deferential regimes.

On the highly deferential side, some state courts invoke an "intelligible principle" requirement or something equally rigor-free. A test that looks at whether a plausible principle guides the delegation looks a lot like rational basis review, which asks merely whether a conceivable justification supports the legislative classification.[180]

On the less deferential side, state courts offer a Thesaurus-rich set of verbal formulations. Consider the language of the Supreme Court of Oklahoma: requiring the legislature to establish the "policy of the law," a "rule of action," or a "framework" to guide the agency[181] or to "set out definite standards."[182] Or of Texas: "varying degrees of specific standards" that must provide "some criteria or safeguards."[183] Or of Nebraska: "adequate, sufficient, and definite standards."[184] Or of New Hampshire: "specific standards."[185] Or of Montana: "reasonable clarity" that is "sufficiently clear, definite, and certain."[186] Or of Massachusetts: "clear legislative standards."[187] Or of New Mexico: "specific legislative standards."[188] Or of West Virginia: "sufficient standards or policy for guidance."[189] Or of Vermont: "basic standard."[190] The key lesson comes not from one state linguistic approach over another; it comes from the reality that the state courts enforce the requirements by invalidating undue delegations to agencies from time to time.

The state stories offer similar lessons for agency deference. For anyone nervous about what awaits a federal court system that decides that the Administrative Procedure Act curbs agency deference, reconsiders what Congress means when it enacts agency-enforced statutes with ambiguous terms, or uses separation of powers to limit or overrule *Chevron*, the state court experiences have much to offer. One lesson is that administrative deference may not be an all-or-nothing-at-all proposition. The variation in the states shows plenty of ways to curb or eliminate agency deference for those so inclined. It also shows that a non-deference regime, whether inaugurated by a statute or a constitutional decision, does not bring government to a halt. It may be that there are many federal laws to enforce. But it does not follow that they all generate intractable litigation. Federal agencies accorded less deference, or no deference, in construing statutes may push their boundaries of authority less often, decreasing litigation over agency decisions, not generating it. At all events, if it were true that a non-*Chevron* regime would break the back of a court or regulatory system, we would have evidence of that fact in the states by now.

For state and federal courts that preserve substantial deference to agencies over legal interpretations, they may wish to consider curbing deference in some areas and eliminating exceptions to it in others. Several features of existing state and federal agency doctrine warrant renewed debate and perhaps re-consideration and modification.

* *The major question doctrine.* Attempting to take some of the sting out of *Chevron*, the US Supreme Court innovated a "major question" approach to the issue. The principle was first used in *FDA v. Brown & Williamson*, a case about the regulation of tobacco by the US Food and Drug Administration.[191] The idea is that the *Chevron* assumption—that when Congress leaves a gap in a statute it means for the relevant agency to fill it—does not apply to gaps in substantial statutes covering high-octane policy matters.[192] The Court has since deployed the doctrine in *King v. Burwell*, a case about the meaning of the health exchanges created by the Affordable Care Act.[193] It's easy to understand the impulse behind these cases—to rein in *Chevron* deference and to mitigate some of the dubious components of it. But does this exception have promise over the long haul? No state courts, best I can tell, have taken this approach. And while the major-question doctrine grapples with one problem—delegations of power over highly salient political issues—it seems tone deaf to another problem: the perspective of the regulated party. Ask how many regulated individuals would agree that the relevant delegation is "minor." This solution in the end seems to create more problems than it solves.[194]

* *Dual-application criminal and civil statutes.* Many of the state decisions that enforce the non-delegation doctrine or refuse administrative deference involve criminal law. If there is one area deserving the most attention on this topic, this would be it.

In one sense, this is an easy problem, one fixed in part already. Where it exists, administrative deference permits agencies to fill gaps in *civil* statutes that the legislature has delegated authority to the agency to interpret.[195] But administrative deference has no role to play in construing *criminal* statutes. The state and federal courts have never presumed that when an ambiguity arises in a criminal statute, silence signals that the legislature wants an executive-branch agency to fill the gap. That's because criminal statutes "are for courts, not for the Government, to construe."[196] Otherwise, that would leave this distasteful combination. The prosecutor would have the explicit (executive) power to enforce the criminal laws, an implied (legislative) power to fill policy gaps in ambiguous criminal statutes, and an implied (judicial) power to interpret ambiguous criminal laws.[197]

Use of administrative deference in enforcing criminal laws also would leave no room for the rule of lenity, a rule of construction "not much less old than construction itself,"[198] which resolves ambiguities in criminal statutes in favor of the individual. Because it falls to the executive branch to prosecute crimes, enforcement of the rule of lenity generally requires courts to *deny* deference to executive officials over the meaning of laws they enforce.[199] As the Supreme Court of Louisiana put it in overturning a driving-while-intoxicated conviction against an intoxicated man riding a bicycle, the rule "of lenity is premised on the idea that a person should not be punished unless the law provides a fair warning of what conduct will be considered criminal. The rule is based on principles of due process that no person should be forced to guess as to whether his conduct is permitted."[200]

But what happens when the same statute has criminal *and* civil applications? May the state or federal legislature sidestep these requirements by giving criminal statutes a civil application? The answer should be No. The courts must give dual-application statutes just one interpretation, and the criminal application controls. Because a single statute should have a single meaning and because a statute is not a "chameleon,"[201] the "lowest common denominator" governs all of its applications.[202]

A case in the federal system, more precisely one footnote, suggests a different rule. *Babbitt v. Sweet Home Chapter of Communities for a Great Oregon*[203] involved a facial challenge to a regulation interpreting a provision of the Endangered Species Act that imposed both civil and criminal liability.[204] The Supreme Court decided that it "owe[d] some degree of deference" to the Department of Labor's interpretation,[205] and cited *Chevron* in the process. Then it said that it "ha[d] never suggested that the rule of lenity should provide the standard for reviewing facial challenges to administrative regulations whenever the governing statute authorizes criminal enforcement."[206] What the statement means is hard to say. What it does not mean should be easier. It is doubtful that it (silently) overruled an entire line of cases that "hold that, if Congress wants to assign responsibility for crime definition to the executive, it must speak clearly."[207]

There may be some sticker shock with transforming a government-always-wins canon (*Chevron*) into a government-always-loses canon (rule of lenity), and it may be the case that many federal regulatory statutes have civil and criminal applications. But keep in mind that the Court's cases *require* just two things: that the one-statute/one-interpretation rule governs dual-role statutes, and that *Chevron* does not apply to that one interpretation. Those two requirements, however, may not dictate when the rule of lenity governs and when it does not. Statutory "ambiguity" may mean one thing under *Chevron* and something else under the rule of lenity. If American Inuits have more than one way to describe snow, American lawyers may have more than one way to describe ambiguity.[208] *Chevron*'s domain and the rule of lenity's domain may not necessarily overlap in some cases.[209]

What's not up for debate is this: A hands-off judicial approach to dual-role federal statutes has consequences for liberty. Consider these two numbers on the federal side. There are roughly 4,450 federal statutory crimes according to a 2008 estimate.[210] And there are over 300,000 regulatory crimes according to a 1990 estimate.[211] How could that be? The answer is dual-application statutes, in which Congress enacts a law saying that violations of the civil standard amount to criminal violations and, more consequentially, saying that violations of administrative rules promulgated under the civil rule amount to criminal violations. Putting the delegation issues raised by this approach to the side, think how it scrambles the conventional understandings of how we make criminal law and how we discern its meaning. Customarily, it hurts a criminal prosecution when the government must acknowledge that a law is ambiguous. That's because the rule of lenity may require a court to construe the statute against the government. But ambiguity *helps* the prosecution under the modern approach, as it facilitates the legitimacy of the regulation under *Chevron*. And it clears the way for a retroactive criminal prosecution of an unsuspecting individual who made the mistake of merely consulting the 4,450 federal statutory crimes without paying attention to the more than 300,000 federal regulatory crimes.[212]

If that does not generate sympathy, how about this? In 1982, the US Department of Justice asked Ronald Gainer to count the number of federal crimes. When he eventually gave up on the project, he gave this defense: "You will have died and been resurrected three times" before identifying each one.[213]

Courts should account for two competing considerations—the existing power of the state and federal courts and federalism—in navigating these issues. In thinking about administrative law, it's useful to keep track of the role of the courts, the capacity of the courts, to elevate their engagement in these areas. There is no judicially enforceable non-delegation doctrine, or very little of it, in a pure deference regime. And anyone who thinks that *Chevron* violates the US Constitution (or its equivalent violates a state's constitution) should account for how much that approach would increase the footprint of the state and federal courts. After all, "*Chevron* is fundamentally a judicially articulated restriction upon judicial power."[214] Others see judicial restraint in the area as abdication over a core area of constitutional law: separation of powers. Emblematic of that view are Judges Douglas Ginsburg and Steve Menashi, who are concerned that "our administrative law is marked not by fringe judicial zealotry but by judicial passivity in enforcing mainstream liberal norms."[215]

Who can deny the competing kernels of truth? For my part, during my first ten years or so on the bench, *Chevron* controlled many cases, and it served to bring diverse panels to a consensus because the range of discretion for the agency to exercise was broad. There's something valuable about that and lost without it. But in recent years, it's been the rare case that *Chevron* controlled. Far fewer judges are willing to rely on it today. In reality, disagreement over it tends to generate more disagreement than the meaning of the underlying federal statute. Today, as a result, most panels tend to resolve cases based on their own reading of the statute, not the agency's, in part due to increasingly shared first principles of statutory interpretation.[216] That change is probably here to stay, whether *Chevron* lasts or not, is modified or not. If that's true, it's worth assessing the value of sticking with a consensus-generating doctrine that over time has come to generate more disagreement than the meaning of the underlying statute itself. An exception to this trend may develop, or remain, for highly intricate statutes, perhaps because judges may trust seasoned agency experts about the meaning of technical laws. But that may be a practical (and hard to prove) development, not a doctrinal one.

In revisiting the dilemma between too much state and federal court review or too little, that leaves one other option. Delegations of legislative power to the executive branch, whether express or implied, often implicate separation-of-powers considerations or limits. One approach is for courts to handle above-the-surface or latent constitutional problems by construing the challenged law to avoid them. This has the virtue of preventing courts from looking the other way without emboldening them to do more than they need to. At the federal level, Dean John Manning claims, the non-delegation doctrine "operates exclusively through the interpretive canon requiring avoidance of serious constitutional questions."[217] The US Supreme Court's decisions in *Gundy* and *Kisor*, both written by Justice Kagan, offer examples of federal decisions that narrow the scope of the delegation problem through limiting constructions of the statutes. Both decisions illustrate the stakes. In each instance, these half measures generated delight in some quarters (for preserving some administrative deference) and deep frustration in others (for preserving perceived unconstitutional deference). Some state courts, as shown, have taken similar approaches. Nevada construed the statute narrowly to avoid the potential non-delegation problem in *McNeil*,[218] and Justice Gableman invoked constitutional avoidance in *Tetra Tech*.[219] Yes, a narrowing approach does not fix the constitutional problems underlying these deference doctrines. But it does lower the stakes. To like effect is the potential for state and federal courts to invoke, and rigorously enforce, the procedural guarantees of their respective APAs. A state, for example, might require an agency to adopt rules within eighteen months of passage of the statute, and require new authorization from the legislature for rulemaking after that.[220] Surely that is a more limited delegation than allowing an agency to exercise uncabined retroactive power decades after the original statute and without new input from the legislature. Similarly, limiting agencies to policymaking through rulemaking rather than through adjudication, along with enforcing other limits on rulemaking, lowers the representation-depriving aspects of horizonless legislative delegations.[221]

Whether the federal courts choose to borrow from the state courts' constitutional-avoidance approaches, their process approaches, or their constitutional-line-drawing approaches in the future, it's well to remember one last thing. In making that decision, the federal courts should account for a federalism-slighting consequence of the growth of federal agencies. In deciding that Congress could regulate the minimum wage and overtime requirements for the states' own employees in the *Garcia* decision in 1985, the US Supreme Court invoked a process principle—that it was better to use the "procedural safeguards inherent in the structure of the federal system" to protect the states' interests than to develop "judicially created limitations on federal power."[222] Six years later, in *Gregory v. Ashcroft*, the US Supreme Court indicated that when Congress chooses to regulate core state functions, it must provide a "clear statement" that it is doing so in order to permit the states to protect their interests in the federal legislative process.[223] But how does this work when a federal agency wields the power? How do states protect their policymaking prerogatives in a federal agency as opposed to the halls of Congress?

Recall what the current federal non-delegation approach and *Chevron* allow. The one permits Congress to ask an agency to sort out a policy dilemma however it wishes. The other permits ambiguities in statutes to be resolved however the agency wishes. What "procedural safeguards" exist in these settings? These realities show two ways in which federal administrative law circumvents state authority and two reasons why interest groups are incentivized to use federal rather than state law to advance their policy goals.

Here's a third. So long as federal administrative law allows Congress to delegate power to agencies and so long as ambiguous delegations of that power give agencies more rather than less power, they have provided still another incentive for interest groups to ignore the states. Why? Who would prefer to seek a state solution to a problem when state administrative law requires the legislature to spell out the solution rather than pass it off to an agency? The dilution of limits on federal administrative law—more particularly the dilution of the federal courts' role in construing laws and policing delegations of power—has facilitated the efforts of interest groups and other regulated entities to circumvent the strictures of state administrative law.

PART III

The Legislative Branch

If balance of power in American government could be reduced to a score card, it would show state legislatures in the pole position at the outset, whether you start in 1776 or 1789. When the colonies separated from Great Britain, the newly formed states assumed all sovereign power from the king and Parliament. Skeptical of executive power and little concerned about the potential uses of judicial power, the state framers staked their faith in representative government through elected state legislatures and lodged most of the power seized from Great Britain in that branch. There was no national government to compete with the states for power at the founding. And when a national government emerged, it had only what power the states delegated to it, first through the Articles of Confederation proposed in 1777 and ratified in 1781, and eventually through the US Constitution ratified in 1789. Even then, the Articles of Confederation gave the Continental Congress little power to interfere with state legislative authority, and the limited and enumerated grants of power to Congress in the 1789 Constitution established a modest rival to state legislative power at the beginning and for some time after that.

Much of American constitutional history can be described as the loss of state legislative power to the other state and federal branches. Two developments in particular helped to change the equation, each in different centuries, each from different directions. During the nineteenth century, the people curbed state legislative power in response to abuses of it and as part of an American skepticism of anyone with power, specially reserved for those with the most of it. Some limits on state legislative power came through state constitutional amendments that imposed process and substance restrictions on state legislation, some through state constitutional amendments that created individual rights beyond legislative control, and some through increases in gubernatorial power (through the creation of devices like the line-item veto) and in judicial power (through more frequent judicial review). Many of these changes took aim at documented legislative abuses, in which the representatives of the people showed a proclivity to represent some more than others. In response, the people sought to make it "harder to regulate" and harder "to make deals behind closed doors."[1]

If the nineteenth century saw the people weakening legislative power at the state level, the twentieth century saw limits on state legislative power coming from a different front: the national government. Decisions of the US Supreme Court in the 1930s and 1940s expanded Congress's authority to regulate interstate commerce—sometimes overlapping with state power, sometimes exclusive of state power—giving the federal legislature as much power as its fifty state counterparts, and often quite a bit more. In the middle of that century, the US Supreme Court shifted the balance of power in another way by making most of the Bill of Rights applicable to the states, creating another forceful and consequential national limit on state legislative power.

Many turns in the division of American power come down to new efforts to protect the people from the individuals *they* choose to represent them. Having put most of their trust in state legislatures at the start, the people came to appreciate Jefferson's observation that there is "no safe depository of the ultimate powers of society" other than the people themselves.[2] Before resorting to direct democracy—the initiative—as the answer to growing distrust of legislatures, the people tried other measures to ensure that legislatures were truly representative.

Before the United States hit the century mark, nearly every existing state placed procedural limits on legislation in their constitutions: single-subject rules, clear-title requirements, three-reading imperatives, uniformity clauses, and public-purpose clauses. Chapter 7 addresses these process-driven provisions, focusing on the clear-title, single-subject, and public-purpose requirements. While it is mainly a state story, it contains federal components and analogues. Chapter 8 looks at another way of ensuring that state legislatures fairly represent the people: efforts to rein in partisan gerrymandering. These are classic federal and state stories, each influencing the other, neither operating alone. Both chapters confirm the difficulty of making the legislature more responsive to the needs of the people and less responsive to the demands of interest groups, the elite, and the connected.

7

State Legislatures and Distrust

Clear-Title and Single-Subject Requirements

The Yazoo land fraud offers two for the price of one, a single scandal that inaugurated federal judicial power over state legislatures based on individual rights in the US Constitution and that prompted state efforts to curb legislative power through state constitutional amendments. In 1794, Georgia's western boundary extended to the Mississippi River, a swath of land occupied by Cherokees, Creeks, other Native Americans, and too few settlers for the tastes of the Georgia government. The state legislature sought to encourage more white settlers to move west and to find ways to pay its troops. Speculators enticed members of the Georgia legislature, in truth bribed them, to enact a law to further these and other aims. Here is the title of the innocent-sounding law:

> An Act supplementary to an Act for appropriating a part of the unlocated territory of this state for the payment of the late state troops, and for other purposes therein mentioned, and declaring the right of this State to the unappropriated territory thereof, for the protection and support of the frontiers of this State, and for other purposes.[1]

The law advertises lofty goals, to pay "the late state troops" and to "support" the "frontiers." But this was overstated. The most honest words in the title were the two "for other purposes" clauses. In reality, this 1795 law permitted several private companies, formed by land speculators, to buy 35 million acres of land at about two cents an acre from the government.[2] Some members of the Georgia legislature owned shares in these companies, a detail not known at the time of enactment.[3] When the details became known, backlash was swift. "It became a popular pastime," Jane Elsmere points out, "to burn Senator Gunn in effigy and excoriate members of the offending legislature."[4] Public embarrassment surrounding the Yazoo scandal prompted one of Georgia's US senators to leave his seat to return to Georgia and lead the anti-Yazoo faction.[5] In 1796, a new legislature repealed the law and publicly burned the old law for good measure.[6]

Before the old law could be burned and its remains repealed, several companies sold their land to others, presumably earning profits along the way. The resales continued even after the Georgia legislature rescinded the law, in some cases because news of the Rescinding Act of 1796 had not yet spread northward.[7] The result was several good faith purchasers who held title to land based on a sale that the Georgia legislature had declared invalid.

That generated two complications. Could the people of Georgia get their sovereign land back or would good-faith sales of it be upheld? And how could they prevent similar misdeeds from happening again? A federal story answers one question; some state stories answer the second one.

The Federal Story

Fletcher v. Peck arose from a title dispute between a seller and a purchaser of Yazoo land. "Peck, by his deed of bargain and sale dated the 14th of May, 1803, in consideration of 3,000 dollars, sold and conveyed to Fletcher, 15,000 acres of land."[8] This was not the first sale of the land. The tract had been sold and resold several times before that, from a Georgia company to James Greenleaf, from Greenleaf to Nathanial Prime, from Prime to Oliver Phelps, and from Phelps to John Peck.[9] The Peck-to-Fletcher transaction landed in the US Supreme Court in a fight over the promise of good title that Peck made to Fletcher. Claiming that the title was worthless, Fletcher sued Peck on the ground that he breached his promise.

What could have been a clash between lawyer titans at the US Supreme Court had become something of a mismatch by the time of argument. Fletcher was represented by Luther Martin, a leading anti-federalist, a leading lawyer, and once a skilled advocate.[10] But he had acquired a drinking problem by the time of argument and was no longer at the top of his game. Chief Justice Marshall had to postpone the proceedings at one point, it's been said, to allow Martin to sober up.[11] Representing Peck were two leading lawyers whose prominence would reach greater heights in the years ahead. One was Joseph Story, a future justice of the US Supreme Court,[12] and the other was John Quincy Adams, the future sixth president of the United States.[13]

Fletcher pressed two arguments that Peck's title was defective before the sale. He argued that the legislative act that originally authorized the sale of the land was invalid, noting "that some of the members of the legislature were induced to vote in favour of the law, which constituted the contract, by being promised an interest in it, and that therefore the act is a mere nullity."[14] But even if the original grant was valid, he added, it became invalid by a later act of the legislature, "annulling and rescinding the law under which the conveyance to the original grantees was made, declaring that conveyance void, and asserting the title of the state to the lands it contained."

Chief Justice Marshall, writing for the Court as was so often the case, met the first argument with skepticism. While he had no problem with the idea that corruption that "contaminate[s] the very source of legislation" must "be deplored,"[15] he questioned the competence of courts to judge the point. "It may well be doubted how far the validity of a law depends upon the motives of its framers, and how far the particular inducements, operating on members of the supreme sovereign power of a state, to the formation of a contract by that power, are examinable in a court of justice."[16] Marshall saw no principle to distinguish between laws that suffered from too much legislative self-interest and those that did not, between laws the courts would not recognize on this ground and those they would allow. Even if a court could declare a law null due to "the means" that created it, that would leave considerable "difficulty in saying to what extent those means must be applied to produce this effect." Consider the questions that would arise: "Must it be direct corruption, or would interest or undue influence of any kind be sufficient?

Must the vitiating cause operate on a majority, or on what number of the members? Would the act be null, whatever might be the wish of the nation, or would its obligation or nullity depend upon the public sentiment?"[17]

With so many questions and so few answers, Marshall refused to grant relief on this ground. In the end, he found it "indecent" in this setting "to enter into an inquiry respecting the corruption of the sovereign power of a state."[18] If the law covered a subject that "the legislature might constitutionally pass," and "if the act be clothed with all the requisite forms of a law," the judicial branch "cannot sustain a suit brought by one individual against another founded on the allegation that the act is a nullity, in consequence of the impure motives which influenced certain members of the legislature which passed the law."[19] That meant that legislative corruption could not defeat the original sale or later ones.

But could the Georgia legislature nonetheless rescind the sales? No, the Court answered again. While "one legislature is competent to repeal any act which a former legislature was competent to pass," Marshall explained, "[t]he past cannot be recalled by the most absolute power."[20] The legislature of Georgia thus could repeal the law; it just couldn't "recall[]" the "past" by invalidating a legal title permissibly created under the old title. When "a law is in its nature a contract, when absolute rights have vested under that contract, a repeal of the law cannot divest those rights." The "absolute rights" to which Marshall referred were the property rights of innocent third parties who purchased land unaware of any defects. The interests "of third persons, who are purchasers without notice, for a valuable consideration, cannot be disregarded," and "titles" that "are perfect" and "acquired with that confidence which is inspired by the opinion that the purchaser is safe" cannot be ignored.[21]

The Court also considered whether the Georgia legislature's rescinding act violated the US Constitution's command that no state shall pass a "law impairing the obligation of contracts."[22] A land grant by the legislature, the Court acknowledged, amounted to a contract. "A grant, in its own nature, amounts to an extinguishment of the right of the grantor, and implies a contract not to reassert that right."[23] A law that rescinded a land grant thus violated the Contract Clause. All told, "Georgia was restrained, either by general principles which are common to our free institutions, or by the particular provisions of the constitution of the United States, from passing a law whereby the estate of the plaintiff in the premises so purchased could be constitutionally and legally impaired."[24]

Fletcher v. Peck was the first case in which the United States Supreme Court refused to enforce a state law because it violated an individual right guaranteed by the US Constitution.[25] As justification, Chief Justice Marshall reasoned, "Georgia cannot be viewed as a single, un-connected, sovereign power, on whose legislature no other restrictions are imposed than may be found in its own constitution. She is a part of a large empire; she is a member of the American union; and that union has a constitution the supremacy of which all acknowledge, and which imposes limits to the legislatures of the several states, which none claim a right to pass."[26]

Fletcher became known as the first decision to review the validity of a state law under the US Constitution.[27] That ranking may come with minor qualifications. *Ware v. Hylton*[28] refused to enforce a state law that conflicted with a national treaty. And Justice Paterson, while riding circuit, hinted at the possibility of judicial review of state laws in *Vanhorne's Lessee v. Dorrance*.[29] But these cases do not detract from *Fletcher's* place as the first state law the US Supreme Court refused to enforce because it violated a guarantee of the US Constitution. That would not be the last legacy of the Yazoo land scandal in limiting the power of state legislatures.

The State Stories

If Georgians could not get their land back, at least they could make it more difficult for the next set of legislators to steal it. They were joined in that quest by citizens in other states, who also suffered from game playing by their representatives. Nationwide, state legislatures found other ways to earn the distrust of the people through comparable, if less costly, bargains between some motivated citizens and some open-for-business legislators.

Reforms in the states, usually through amendments to their constitutions, followed, most of them focused on process-driven safeguards. One was a clear-title rule, which required the subject of each bill to be expressed plainly in its title.[30] Another was a single-subject requirement, designed to ensure that each bill enacted by the legislature contained just one subject.[31] Still another was an original-purpose requirement, which required a final bill to line up with the stated purpose of the original bill.[32] These limitations grew naturally out of a preoccupation of the Jacksonian era, curbing special interests. "The distrust of the legislature, seen by Jacksonian democrats as an engine for churning out special privileges for interest groups, produced a wave of constitution-making in half of the states between 1844 and 1853."[33] Here's how Alan Tarr puts the point: "In 1835 Alexis de Tocqueville observed that 'the legislature of each state is faced by no power capable of resisting it.' But beginning in the 1830s, state constitution-makers sought to impose limits on these supreme legislatures. Initially, their restrictions focused on the process of legislation."[34]

Rather than regulate subjects of lawmaking, these restrictions "regulate[d] only the process by which legislation is enacted."[35] They are "designed to eradicate perceived abuses in the legislative process, such as hasty, corrupt, or private interest legislation," not to impose substantive limits on the legislation itself.[36] Each of them made it more difficult for legislators to engage in logrolling: adding unrelated provisions to a bill to obtain the votes to support the original provisions of the bill.[37] Or made it more difficult for legislatures to add riders to a bill: late-stage amendments to a bill assured of passage and likely to escape scrutiny or opposition blocking.[38]

These state constitutional provisions, never added to the US Constitution, took root throughout the United States. As of 2017, forty-three states have single-subject requirements.[39] Of those states, forty have clear-title requirements, usually expressed alongside the single-subject rule.[40] The current Georgia provision is a good example: "No bill shall pass which refers to more than one subject matter or contains matter different from what is expressed in the title thereof."[41]

Georgia

The sale of Yazoo lands in 1795 generated controversy for several reasons. It was the product of risible corruption, and it transferred public land to a few private entities for their benefit alone. The vehicle of abuse was a deceptive title, which allowed the proponents to "smuggle" the bill "through the Legislature."[42] Recall that the title referred to "an act for appropriating part of the unlocated territory of this state for the payment of the late state troops" and "for the protection and support of the frontiers of this state."[43] By marketing the sale of Yazoo land to private companies on these grounds, the public had little idea what the key parts of the bill did and little reason to be tipped off by the "for other purposes" clauses.

Once burned, the people of Georgia sought to prevent similar abuses when they wrote the Constitution of 1798. It included the first ever clear-title provision: "nor shall any law or ordinance pass, containing any matter different from what is expressed in the title thereof."[44] Joseph Henry Lumpkin, a nineteenth-century justice of the Georgia Supreme Court, confirmed the obvious. "I would observe," he wrote in an opinion for the state high court, that the "necessity" for this addition to the Georgia Constitution "was suggested by the Yazoo Act."[45]

New Jersey

While the clear-title requirements now found in most state constitutions arose from the Yazoo land fraud, the single-subject requirements came later. Not until 1844 did New Jersey become the first state to adopt a general single-subject rule. The inaugural language read as follows: "To avoid improper influences which may result from intermixing in one and the same act such things as have no proper relation to each other, every law shall embrace but one object, and that shall be expressed in its title."[46] It's unclear what motivated the drafters, but it's clear the provision did not generate controversy. In one scholar's recounting: "This 'title clause' became a part of the constitution of 1844, apparently without debate." While the local newspaper "kept a reporter regularly at the convention" and he "reported the debates with surprising fullness, the only reference to the adoption of this provision is the words, 'section 26 agreed to.' "[47]

As a side note, some scholars claim that other states launched this innovation. The landmark article on the topic, written by scholar Millard Ruud, claims that two states had single-subject provisions of a more limited nature before the New Jersey provision. According to Ruud, the Illinois Constitution of 1818 included a provision that "limited bills appropriating salaries for members of the legislature and for officers of the government to that subject."[48] But it is unclear whether that is so. A provision with this language, to be sure, shows up in the 1848 Illinois Constitution.[49] But it does not seem to appear in the 1818 constitution. Ruud also points to an 1843 amendment to the Michigan Constitution, which said that "every law authorizing the borrowing of money or the issuing of state stocks . . . shall embrace no more than one such object."[50] While that amendment was proposed in 1843, it was not ratified until November 1844,[51] a few months after the ratification of the New Jersey Constitution of 1844.[52]

First, second, or third, New Jersey's single-subject rule contains a prototypical requirement that now appears in most state constitutions. Few doubts accompanied its purpose. The rule was designed to "avoid improper influences which may result from intermixing in one and the same act such things as have no proper relation to each other."[53]

One reason that little doubt surrounded the targets of a single-subject rule was that the idea behind the rule was not new, even if it took until 1844 for an American constitution to add one. History had long recorded the "improper influences" to which the New Jersey constitution referred and long tried to prevent them as a matter of customary legislative procedure. According to Robert Luce's 1922 work, *Legislative Procedure*, the rule showed up as early as 98 B.C. in Rome, where the *Lex Caecilia Didia* prohibited laws with diverse topics.[54] The prohibition was not inconsequential. In 91 B.C., a Roman senator secured the franchise of Italian allies as part of an omnibus law, but the combination of provisions violated the prohibition and could not be enforced.[55] Not long after, there was an insurrection among the allies, leading to one of too many Roman civil wars.[56]

Evidence of a single-subject custom also existed in the American colonies. In 1695, the Committee of the Privy Council in Massachusetts complained of acts "joined together under ye same title."[57] Around the same time, the royal governor of New Jersey, Lord Cornbury, recommended to the assemblies of New Jersey "that each different matter may be enacted by a different law, to avoid confusion."[58] In 1760, the colonial Board of Trade objected to a Pennsylvania bill on the ground that one of its provisions "[had] not the least necessary relation" to the rest of the bill.[59] Sly mixing of subjects in one bill has plagued legislatures—and the people—for some time.

After New Jersey adopted a single-subject requirement in 1844, several states followed its example during the next decades, an era of frequent constitutional conventions and of frequent admissions of new states with new constitutions. Louisiana and Texas added single-subject rules to their constitutions in 1845, and New York and Iowa did so in 1846.[60] Now that forty-three states have placed a single-subject requirement in their constitutions,[61] that leaves just seven states without the rule: Connecticut, Maine, Massachusetts, New Hampshire, North Carolina, Rhode Island, and Vermont.[62] Notice that it is only eighteenth-century states that have not changed, just as another eighteenth-century government (the United States) has not changed in this respect either.

Placing a single-subject imperative in a constitution is one thing; enforcing it is another. Judicial enforcement of the guarantee raises elusive separation-of-powers problems. It asks courts to regulate *how* legislatures enact laws as opposed to *what* they may regulate. But legislative enforcement of the guarantee alone raises risks of its own. It requires faith in legislators to bar passage of laws that a majority of them otherwise want to enact. Perhaps because the provision trains its sights on the legislative process, most courts initially declined to enforce it.

In 1867, over two decades after New Jersey ratified its single-subject requirement, the New Jersey Supreme Court indicated that the state's single-subject and clear-title provisions were "only directory"— admonitions to be followed by the legislature, not mandates to be enforced by the courts.[63] The court pointed to a treatise by Theodore Sedgwick, published in 1857, that referenced the directory nature of the rule in other states, including California.[64] The treatise in turn invoked this language from an 1854 decision of the California Supreme Court: "We regard this section of the Constitution as merely directory, and if we were inclined to a different opinion, would be careful how we lent ourselves to a construction which must in effect obliterate almost every law from the statute book, unhinge the business, and destroy the labor of the last three years."[65] In the early years of the single-subject prohibitions in our state constitutions, well indeed into their first century, jurists were skeptical of providing this kind of oversight to a co-equal branch of government.

Over time, however, most state courts have come to believe that they may and should enforce the guarantee.[66] The norm today is for courts to say that single-subject requirements are judicially enforceable and mandatory, not directory and unenforceable in the courts, to use the language of nineteenth-century decisions. "Directory" indeed is a term that has fallen out of usage and perhaps favor in the last seventy-five years. Before a court these days, whether federal or state, decides not to enforce a constitutional command, it usually requires the dispute to implicate a political question. It says something about the modern balance of power between courts and legislatures that there are so few areas of constitutional debate today that the courts have ceded to legislative enforcement alone. Even as the state courts have almost uniformly agreed that they may enforce these constitutional directives, their enforcement has been riddled with exceptions.

Illinois

Illinois illustrates how unforgiving the single-subject rule can be when state courts enforce it. *People v. Cervantes*[67] addressed a revision to the Illinois criminal code through a law referred to as "the Safe Neighborhoods Law."[68] By the time the legislature passed it, the law covered 157 pages and expanded criminal laws in areas as diverse as "child pornography, juvenile pimping, prostitution, criminal use of firearms, and fraud in the Women, Infants and Children (WIC) program."[69] The law also "established privately operated juvenile secure residential facilities to house delinquent minors."[70] During debates over the bill, one representative said this: "The long and short of this Bill is that it has provisions which are attempting to go after the main problems we're having on our streets these days. It's going after gangs, drugs and guns, namely."[71]

In the view of the Supreme Court of Illinois, the bill stretched beyond the subject of "safe neighborhoods." The act violated the single-subject clause "no matter how liberally" it is interpreted.[72] Two provisions in particular did not fit with the rest of the bill. One amended the Women, Infants, and Children nutrition program to allow a state agency to govern its vendors. The other created licenses for privately owned youth detention centers. Nor did the umbrella subject of neighborhood safety suffice. As for the government's arguments that these provisions were designed to prevent fraud in the provision of these benefits, the court did not see the connection in the statute; none of the provisions mentioned abuse of benefits or fraud.[73] The court felt comfortable concluding that "the statute, on its face, clearly embraces more than one subject."[74] As to the private juvenile detention centers, "there is no natural and logical connection between the privatization of these facilities and the subject of neighborhood safety."[75]

To the court, this hodge-podge of regulations in the name of "neighborhood safety" epitomized the "evil the single subject rule is intended to prevent," and it refused to enforce the entire bill.[76] That prompted a debate, a recurring one in the area, about severability. Even if some provisions fell outside this subject, many other parts of the 157-page bill furthered neighborhood safety. That led Justice McMorrow, the author of the original opinion, to vote to rehear the case to consider severing the bill's unrelated provisions. As he explained: "On the basis of the severability argument raised in the amicus brief filed by Governor Ryan and on the basis of the severability argument raised in the amicus brief filed by the City of Chicago, I dissent from the Court's denial of rehearing. I express no opinion on the ultimate merits of the severability argument."[77] He would not be the last judge to pause over severability in this area.

Delaware

Turnbull v. Fink offers competing versions of how state courts should enforce single-subject clauses in a distinct, highly consequential context: spending bills.[78] Justice Hartnett offers one perspective, Justice Holland another, from the Delaware Supreme Court.

The Hartnett approach captured a majority in rejecting a single-subject challenge to an appropriation law. At issue was a bill that contained, among many expenditures, a limited waiver of sovereign immunity for claims against the government. The Delaware Constitution carves out a single-subject exception for appropriation bills: "No bill or joint resolution, except bills appropriating money for public purposes, shall embrace more than one subject, which shall be expressed in its title."[79]

Delaware is not the only state that excepts appropriation bills from its single-subject requirement. Justice Hartnett pointed out that "18 states had adopted constitutional provisions specifically dealing with the limitation of contents of bills making appropriations," whether general or specific expenditure bills. "The Constitutions of seven of those 18 states," he explained, "expressly excepted only general appropriation bills from the one subject restriction. There are only four States, including Delaware, in which a 'one subject' limitation provision in the State's Constitution is exempted as to all appropriation bills."[80]

For the majority, just two things mattered: This was an appropriation bill, and Delaware's single-subject requirement exempted all appropriation bills. Not just that, but the "provision relating to the waiver of sovereign immunity in Section 68 relates to the insurance authorized" to be bought by the law.[81] Nor was this exception an oversight. "The framers of the Delaware Constitution undoubtedly recognized, even in 1897, the difficulties in limiting an appropriation bill to one subject."[82]

Justice Holland completed the story in his dissent. "The potential problem caused by an omnibus bill" with "unrelated provisions on heterogeneous matters," he pointed out, "is an uninformed legislative vote," a concern going back to Roman law.[83] In establishing single-subject and clear-title requirements in the 1897 Constitution, the authors said: "Oftentimes bills have been introduced in the Legislature with very harmless titles, but amendments have been added to those bills and when they have passed both Houses, they are entirely different from what they were originally." Thus: "If a bill contains multiple subjects or the title of the bill is such that it would 'trap the unwary into inaction,' it must be struck down as a violation of this section of the Delaware Constitution."[84]

While "appropriation bills have traditionally been conditionally exempted" from "the single-subject and the title provisions," the exception is a "narrow" one, requiring that the relevant provision "relate only to appropriations."[85] That "does not mean that an appropriation bill must merely be a list of monetary appropriations and respective recipients." The bill may create conditions or incidental requirements that relate to "specific appropriations" and generally are not "permanent in nature, extending beyond the life of the appropriation act."[86] Any other approach, Justice Holland reasoned, would render the single-subject and title rules "meaningless" because they "could be circumvented simply by putting a substantive change into legislation otherwise primarily devoted to appropriations."[87]

Justice Holland offered a few other useful insights. He reminded readers of the connection between single-subject rules and line-item vetoes. "The narrow exemption for appropriation bills" parallels "the limited authorization for the gubernatorial line-item veto."[88] Just as the Delaware Supreme Court has limited the governor's line-item veto only to "appropriations," so the court should do the same for single-subject purposes. As to appropriations, "the Governor has line-item veto power, but as to the latter, the Governor may only approve or veto the bill in its entirety."[89] So too with the single-subject rule: "The exception for appropriation bills . . . was not intended to allow substantive provisions other than money appropriations to be included in appropriation bills."[90] It was only "to allow the legislature to make appropriations for many different purposes at once," not "to permit the passage of 'sleeper' legislation by including substantive non-monetary enactments in an appropriation bill."[91]

Public-Purpose Requirements

Many state constitutions require that public funds be spent only for public purposes, another prohibition that would have done the people of Georgia some good in the late eighteenth century. The Illinois Constitution, as one model, says that "Public funds, property or credit shall be used only for public purposes."[92] The Wisconsin Constitution, as another, implies a public-purpose requirement when it comes to state spending and lawmaking.[93] The requirement that a state legislature dedicate public funds just for public purposes is an omnipresent requirement of state constitutional law.[94]

North Carolina

The Tar Heel State offers a classic example of the kind of litigation that arises under public-purpose clauses and deals with economic development challenges every state faces today. At stake in *Maready v. City of Winston-Salem* was the extent to which a legislature could subsidize private entities to improve the economic fortunes of a community.[95] A state law allowed local governments to make "economic development incentive grants to private corporations."[96] With this authority, the city made twenty-four grants totaling $13,200,000. The money came from taxes imposed on property owners in the city of Winston-Salem and Forsyth County. Local officials supported the incentive grants on the ground that they would increase the local tax base by over $225 million and add 5,500 jobs. It would take three to seven years, they estimated, to recover the "investment." The grants went toward things like "on-the-job training, site preparation, facility upgrading, and parking."[97]

Through an opinion by Justice Whichard, the North Carolina Supreme Court rejected a challenge to the law. The North Carolina Constitution, he observed, mandates that "the power of taxation shall be exercised in a just and equitable manner, for public purposes only."[98] Under the guarantee, the North Carolina Supreme Court had previously determined that "tax revenues may not be used for private individuals or corporations, no matter how benevolent." At the same time, however, the court allowed only modest review of challenges under the guarantee. In ascertaining "whether legislation serves a public purpose, the presumption favors constitutionality. Reasonable doubt must be resolved in favor of the validity of the act." The General Assembly, it said, may "experiment with new modes of dealing with old evils," and "initial responsibility for determining what constitutes a public purpose rests with the legislature, and its determinations are entitled to great weight."[99]

In the past, the court had "not specifically defined 'public purpose,'" allowing "each case to be determined by its own peculiar circumstances as from time to time it arises" and acknowledging that there is no "slide-rule definition to determine public purpose for all time." The idea "expands with the population, economy, scientific knowledge, and changing conditions. As people are brought closer together in congested areas, the public welfare requires governmental operation of facilities which were once considered exclusively private enterprises, and necessitates the expenditure of tax funds for purposes which, in an earlier day, were not classified as public." One criterion, however, is that the "benefits must be in common and not for particular persons, interests, or estates," and the "net gain or advantage must be the public's," not "an individual or private entity."[100]

"Economic development," the court reasoned, "has long been recognized as a proper governmental function." The power "to acquire land for an industrial park, develop it for its intended use, and then convey it" parallels the authority under urban re-development legislation, which the court had "consistently upheld." Just as city "redevelopment commissions have power to acquire property, clear slums, and sell the property to private developers," so they have economic re-development authority. In both situations, "a private party ultimately acquires the property and conducts activities which, while providing incidental private benefit, serve a primary public goal." The key is whether the programs "primarily benefit the public and not a private party."[101]

The law met this test, the court concluded. Its goal is to "increase the population, taxable property, agricultural industries and business prospects of any city or county." The expenditures "should create a more stable local economy by providing displaced workers with continuing employment opportunities, attracting better paying and more highly skilled jobs, enlarging the tax base, and diversifying the economy." Nor were the "public advantages" "indirect, remote, or incidental." Each was "aimed at furthering the general economic welfare of the people of the communities affected. While private actors will necessarily benefit from the expenditures authorized, such benefit is merely incidental." In the end, "each community has a distinct ambience, unique assets, and special needs best ascertained at the local level," and the law permits each one "to formulate its own definition of economic success and to draft a developmental plan leading to that goal."[102]

In upholding the law and these local expenditures, the court acknowledged a report by the Legislative Research Commission about the imperative of economic development in the state. "The traditional foundations of North Carolina's economy—agriculture and manufacturing—are in decline. And the traditional economic development tool—industrial recruitment—has proven inadequate for many of North Carolina's communities. Low wages and low taxes are no longer sufficient incentives to entice new industry to our state, especially to our most remote, most distressed areas." Adding to that concern was competition from other states. In this "economic climate," the "pressure" to encourage "responsible corporate citizens to relocate to or expand in North Carolina is not internal only, but results from the actions of other states as well. To date, courts in forty-six states have upheld the constitutionality of governmental expenditures and related assistance for economic development incentives." The trial court's ruling to the contrary left North Carolina to "stand[] alone" in invalidating such laws.[103]

Justice Orr's dissent shows that this is not the only way to read a public-purpose clause. As he saw it, the question was whether the state's constitution allowed local "public funds" to be spent "directly . . . for the benefit of" "selected private businesses as an inducement to these businesses to either expand or locate in the community." If that's okay, he worried, "little remains" of this "constitutional restraint on governmental power to spend tax revenues collected from the public." The "fallacy" of the court's reasoning, he explained, "begins with the assumption that new jobs and a higher tax base automatically result in significant benefit to the public." But that was far from clear, as there was "no evidence" that these incentives would "improve[] the unemployment rate" or would "reduce[] the net cost of government" or lower "property taxes." To Justice Orr, it was "obvious" that "the $13.2 million" was for "the specific benefit of the companies in question," as it went to their expenses for "on-the-job training for employees, road construction, site improvements, financing of land purchases, upfitting of the facilities, and even spousal relocation assistance."[104]

The dissent wanted nothing to do with the court's "changing times" theory of interpretation. The theory that "constitutional interpretation" is "subject to the whims of 'everybody's doing it' cannot be sustained." Even accepting the economic re-development premises of the law, he could not understand why the constitution allowed "direct grants to specific, selected businesses," which amounts to "selected corporate welfare to some of the largest and most prosperous companies in our state and in the country." What "about the economic loss and devastation to smaller North Carolina communities that lose valued industry to larger, wealthier areas," such as the relocation of a bank's headquarters from a small North Carolina town to Winston-Salem? Also "troubling" was the lack of "limits" of "the majority's theory." "If it is an acceptable public purpose to spend tax dollars specifically for relocation expenses to benefit the spouses of corporate executives moving to the community in finding new jobs or for parking decks that benefit only the employees of the favored company, then what can a government not do if the end result will entice a company to produce new jobs and raise the tax base? If a potential corporate entity is considering a move to Winston-Salem but will come only if country club memberships are provided for its executives, do we sanction the use of tax revenue to facilitate the move?" So long as a "company promises to create new jobs" and the government projects new taxes from the grants, he saw no way to ban such expenditures under the majority's view.[105]

By 1996, North Carolina was not the first state to authorize such economic redevelopment grants, and it would not be the last. The difficulty of discerning an enforceable line between direct and indirect monetary assistance has made all the difference, facilitating many revitalization efforts, from new stadiums for private sports teams to tax breaks for relocated companies.

Wisconsin

Three cases from Wisconsin show the breadth of projects that governments can support and illustrate the latitude some state courts have given their legislatures in defining a permissible public purpose.

In the first one, *Hopper v. City of Madison*,[106] the Wisconsin Supreme Court, through an opinion by Justice Hanley, addressed an expenditure of local funds from a city to a union that oversaw tenant rights. Even though "not established by any specific clause in the state constitution," the court explained, "the public purpose doctrine is a well-established constitutional tenet."[107] The implied guarantee means that public monies may be spent just for "public purposes," and it applies to all governments, including cities. At the same time, the court recognized that the Wisconsin courts had not policed these expenditures in a skeptical way. What amounts to a public purpose starts as "a question for the legislature to determine and its opinion should be given great weight."[108] So long as "any public purpose can be conceived which might reasonably be deemed to justify or serve as a basis for the expenditure," it will be upheld.[109] That the appropriation goes to "a private agency" does not make it unconstitutional if it has "a reasonable probability" of advancing these public goals.[110]

At issue was a grant by the Madison City Council of public money to a private tenant union "in exchange for services," namely, "an information and grievance service for tenants, designed to inform tenants of their rights and assist them with problems in the landlord-tenant relationship." The problem, from the perspective of the challengers, was that only the "part of the city comprised of tenants could benefit" from the purchased services. On top of that, the challengers complained, the union favored one set of participants in landlord-tenant disputes; it was "not concerned with promoting peaceful and equitable landlord-tenant relations," and would favor "the promotion of rent strikes, picketing, boycotts, and blacklisting of selected landlords."[111]

The court was not moved. It noted that "the appropriated funds may be used only as provided in the contract"[112] between the city and the union, and the contract does not cover protest activities. Almost half of the "housing units in the city" were "occupied by tenants," it added, and a "community with such a significant tenant segment has an interest in equitable landlord-tenant relations," making them "a matter of public welfare."[113]

In the next case, *Libertarian Party of Wisconsin v. State*,[114] the court faced a vintage debate of our times. Should a government be able to use public monies to fund a sports stadium for a privately owned sports team? The Milwaukee Brewers were the team, Miller Park the stadium, the state the source of the funds. The libertarians, forgive me, struck out. The court upheld the expenditures on the ground that creating jobs and enhancing the tax base sufficed to justify this use of public dollars. "The purpose of the Stadium Act," the court reasoned, "is to promote the welfare and prosperity of this state by maintaining and increasing the career and job opportunities of its citizens and by protecting and enhancing the tax base on which state and local governments depend." The whole community "will benefit from the expenditures of these public funds. Creation of new jobs is of vital importance to the State of Wisconsin and economic development is a proper function of our government."[115]

In the third case, *Town of Beloit v. County of Rock*,[116] through an opinion by Justice Crooks, the court upheld a town's authority to use public money "to develop and sell property" in a subdivision.[117] A judicial decision that "no public purpose exists," the court explained, requires a court to conclude that it's "clear and palpable" that "no benefit to the public" exists.[118] Relying on prior decisions of the court, it noted that the "concept of public purpose is a fluid one and varies from time to time, from age to age, as the government and its people change. Essentially, public purpose depends on what the people expect and want their government to do for the society as a whole and in this growth of expectation, that which often starts as hope ends in entitlement."[119]

In upholding the expenditures under this fluid approach, the court noted that "the town was motivated to develop the land by its desire to create jobs, expand the tax base and create an orderly growth of single family housing for the benefit of members of the community."[120] "The town," it added, was "concerned with the environmental impact that a subdivision would have in this ecologically sensitive area."[121] Because "increasing the tax base and creation of new jobs" count as "legitimate public purposes" and because "preserving and conserving environmentally sensitive lands" counts too, the court upheld the expenditures.[122]

Chief Justice Abrahamson dissented. Accepting the deferential review of such claims, she drew the line at "rubber-stamp[ing]" public spending. She accepted that public funds "designed to create jobs, promote orderly growth, increase the tax base, and preserve an environmentally sensitive area" would satisfy the test. Her concern was that some of these "goals" were "merely assertions unsupported by the facts of this case while others are admittedly hoped for but distant outcomes, not justifications." The public-purpose requirement "becomes a charade if a town may justify expenditures by merely offering enough of the proper buzzwords—"job creation," "orderly growth," "increasing the tax base," and "environment[al] concerns"—without backing the claims up with facts. On the current record, the taxpayers of Beloit will pay taxes to further "the sale of lots for the future construction of private housing from which any benefit to the taxpayers is indirect, remote, and uncertain."[123]

As for job creation, "no evidence in the record" shows that the town ever planned to spend the money for this subdivision to create jobs. And she did not think that the creation of "one-time" jobs and the "conjecture" related to future jobs sufficed. Reliance on "the public purpose of preservation of an environmentally sensitive strip of land along the Rock River also amounts to reliance on buzzwords." Why in any event would the creation of this subdivision, as opposed to an environmental easement, help to protect the "land the town owns along the river"? Nor was there a showing or any evidence indicating how these public funds would contribute to "orderly growth." The court's position "thus boils down to this," she insisted: "the expenditure serves an acceptable public purpose because the town's tax base might be enhanced." But an increased "tax base from the sale of land and the construction of homes is an indirect, remote, and uncertain benefit of the expenditure in the present case and is not a sufficient public purpose to justify the town's running a for-profit real estate development business and engaging in the non-traditional enterprise of building residential home sites."[124]

Are There Ways to Improve Enforcement of the Clear-Title, Single-Subject, and Public-Purpose Limitations on State (and Some Federal) Legislation?

What is the value of these provisions today? How should they operate? Should state courts enforce them or are they for legislatures and the political process alone to police? If enforced, what is the remedy for a violation? In thinking about these questions, it's difficult to ignore the happenstance that the same Yazoo land scandal that led to the first of these process-driven state constitutional limitations on state legislatures also generated the first case in which the US Supreme Court invalidated a state law based on a federal individual-rights guarantee. Recall that the Georgia land scandal not only produced the first state clear-title rule, but it also led to *Fletcher v. Peck*, which thwarted Georgia's effort to undo the Yazoo land "sales." One fraud by one legislature set the stage for so much of what would come in checking state legislative power.

The Yazoo land grab also foreshadowed additional disillusionments with individual state legislators in periodic years to come. It raised the possibility that the people could not be counted on consistently to pick trustworthy legislators or that trustworthy people could not be counted on to stay that way once they entered office. It's exhibit A for the dictum of Montana legislator and copper baron William Clark—"I never bought a man who wasn't for sale"—an observation he made in the context of trying to sidestep a scandal of his own.[125] Claiming truth as a defense, he used the "for sale" argument to justify bribing state legislators to elect him to a seat in the United States Senate. The defense did not work, and the US Senate refused to seat him in 1899. But he ran again and, apparently bribe free, became a US senator from 1901 to 1907.[126]

That scandal had other consequences. It furthered then-existing efforts to diminish state legislative power in another way, ratification of the Seventeenth Amendment in 1913. The amendment allowed the people to elect their US senators directly instead of having their state legislatures select them. Whether it is state constitutional amendments placing process restrictions on legislation, US Supreme Court review of state legislation, or the removal of state legislatures from the selection process for US senators, local scandals drove much of this loss of power. Perhaps state legislatures, one could say, got what they earned, a point amplified when the federal courts and Congress were needed to bring Jim Crow to heel. All of this history, and much else besides, might suggest that clear-title and single-subject guarantees, like the impairment of contract guarantee and other individual rights, should be vigorously enforced in the courts. But the right approach to implementing these process guarantees has proved elusive. The question prompts a range of considerations, some of them competing, some complementary.

Not every constitutional limit that the people place on a branch of government is for the courts to enforce. Americans often casually assume, or at least presume, that every state and federal constitutional provision should be enforced in the courts in one way or another. That modern perspective turns in part on division-of-powers grounds. If the people care enough about a limit on a branch of government to put it in the constitution, the idea goes, why would they trust that same branch of government to enforce it? Think of the late citizens of Georgia. Having once been exploited by their legislators' corruption in the Yazoo land fiasco and having tried to stop the next act of self-service by placing the clear-title provision in the Georgia Constitution, wouldn't they want the courts to enforce it? What harm, they might add, could result from judicial enforcement of the guarantee anyway? The legislature has a simple remedy. With respect to single-subject and clear-title problems, all the legislature needs to do is to re-enact new laws, accent on the plural, just parceled into smaller subjects with honest titles. As for public-purpose problems, the legislature just needs to identify a more plausible public end.

It is easy to assume that in the absence of judicial review, enforcement of clear-title, single-subject, and public-purpose provisions becomes a responsibility for the legislature alone. But governors retain the veto power, and an unconstitutional bill offers a legally and politically sound reason for exercising it. All state officers in fact take oaths to uphold their respective constitutions, and a failure to honor that obligation can be a politically potent way to enforce and dignify some provisions.

It is also easy to assume that the authors of these guarantees would have wanted the courts to enforce them. But when one looks at the history of the clear-title, single-subject, public-purpose guarantees, that is not clear. Some state courts enforced them early on; others did not. The nature of the single-subject and clear-title guarantees does not demand judicial enforcement. Each provision is directed at the legislature's own process for enacting laws. Save for occasional gubernatorial vetoes, that process is something a state legislature might be expected to look after for itself to prevent judicial intrusion into the legislature's own manner of enacting laws.

History supports the point. When Georgia adopted its clear-title prohibition, the concept of state or judicial review was in its infancy. And its initial uses tended to focus on court enforcement of individual rights guarantees, like the impairment-of-contract guarantee enforced in *Fletcher*, not process-driven limits on the passage of legislation. By the time the states began to adopt single-subject and public-purpose limitations in the mid-nineteenth century, the prevalence of judicial review had increased to be sure. But the modern presumption that most constitutional terms would be enforced in the state and federal courts remained a distant one.

Historical grounds for skepticism about judicial enforcement of these guarantees do not end the conversation. The state and federal courts have altered the original meaning of their constitutions before; they may alter them again. But that still leaves this pragmatic question: Has judicial enforcement of these guarantees worked? A key problem has been a lack of judicially discernible principles to guide enforcement. Adding variable judicial enforcement of a guarantee to variable enforcement of it by legislators and governors may not advance the cause of good government.

The pragmatist also might consider whether a target of single-subject rules—logrolling—is problematic in the first place. One person's logrolling may be another person's compromise. Consider minority groups and discrete interest groups and the challenges they face in advancing their goals without trading support for one provision in favor of another. Sure, a minority interest group could arrange a deal to work through two bills rather than one. But what's wrong, as Michael Gilbert points out, with interest groups that "prefer to give and receive simultaneously by adding a measure they favor to the supporter's bill"?[127] It allows each group to "benefit[] from the other's backing, receiving its preferred provision and tolerating the other side's measure."[128] It's transparent. And all of it "looks suspiciously like a common and considerably less-maligned practice: legislative compromise."[129] If deliberation and compromise between parties in the legislature are a good thing, why should we complain when that compromise manifests itself in one multi-topic bill instead of two separate bills? Perhaps we shouldn't, or at least the state courts should account for these realities before flyspecking single-subject challenges and before doing anything more than knocking out the most egregious violations with the most clearly apt remedies.

Riders, it is fair to say, are harder to justify. While "logrolling consists of exchange,"[130] riding exploits the legislative process by adding a provision when "the information available to legislators and the transaction costs of haggling" make the provision practically irremovable.[131] The goal is to ensure that "the combined bill amounts to a take-it-or-leave-it offer" that will force opponents to enact it "despite not receiving compensation from the measure's supporters."[132] For courts inclined to apply constitutional guarantees in functional ways, it's easy to imagine more rigorous enforcement of the prohibition on riders. They are less likely to be part of a fair, bargained-for exchange, and they are less likely to appear in the title of the bill because they were added after the initial bill was proposed.

Before leaving this topic, one more perspective deserves consideration. How would state courts feel about putting the shoe on the other foot? How would they react if the legislative branch opted to second-guess enforcement of constitutional provisions directly related to *their* core functions and *their* processes for handling them? It's possible that keeping the accountability spotlight on the legislature when it comes to these process limits offers the greatest hope for dignifying them. Does anyone doubt that the people of Georgia in 1800 would have made quick work of unseating their representatives if they had launched another brazen act of corruption, this time in violation of the clear-title requirement? No one would have needed the courts, federal or state, to fix the problem.

If state courts have a role to play in enforcing process guarantees, such as single-subject rules and clear-title provisions, are there ways to improve their handling of these lawsuits? Having considered the pros and cons of judicial enforcement of these legislative-process requirements, let us consider ways to improve the courts' handling of them.

Several complications have hovered over state court enforcement of single-subject and clear-title requirements. Satisfactory definitions of what constitutes a "subject" often have eluded the courts. Remedies are not easy either. Even when the subject of a bill comes into view, should a court remedy the violation by refusing to enforce the offending provisions and agreeing to allow the remainder of the law to be accepted in court? Or should a court refuse to enforce the entire statute due to its process defect?

The definition of "subject" faces a soaring level of generality problem. How high up the ladder of abstraction should a court go in deciding what counts as a subject? We can all agree on one forbidden height. A state cannot defend a bill on the ground that its "subject" is "legislation" or "public policy" or "good government" or anything so vast. That type of approach was correctly rejected in an opinion by Judge Susan Graber, then a justice on the Oregon Supreme Court, now a judge on the Ninth Circuit.[133] If that problem is easy, the ones that follow are not, as one case after another confirms.

One possibility is for the state courts to adopt a halfway measure between enforcing the guarantees and leaving them alone: defer to the legislature in one respect but not in another. Allow the legislature to define the subject of the bill in its title however it wants, short of calling it "A Bill to Enact Legislation." Once the legislature settles on a title, the courts have a warrant to police the requirement that the rest of the bill confine itself to that subject alone. Most state constitutions with single-subject rules also have clear-title rules.[134] And almost all of the litigation in this area turns on alleged violations of the single-subject rules. So far as the cases show, it is the rare legislature that cannot bring itself to place a descriptive title on each bill.

That leaves the problem of appropriation or spending bills. Because the states, unlike the national government, must balance their budgets regularly, usually every one to two years, high-need spending bills are a common occurrence in state legislatures. Here a different reality complicates matters. It is politically legitimate and politically tempting to place substantive legislation in spending bills—legitimate because accountability tends to follow money, and legislatures deserve a say in how state agencies spend the people's money; tempting because balanced-budget requirements force legislatures and governors to enact these bills on time, making them easy vehicles in which to include riders or hide controversial legislation, especially since it is the rare law to which some funding cannot be added. The problem in this setting is not as simple as excising every non-monetary item, and the inevitable budgetary calendar milestones for mischief never go away. Resolution of the dilemma seems to come down to this: either create a carve-out for appropriation bills and thus a gaping hole in the rule as the Delaware case reveals or identify principled standards for prohibiting substantive legislation in spending bills. The principled standards goal has eluded the courts so far.

That leads to fluctuating state court applications of the rule in the context of appropriation bills, decisions that do not bring honor to the courts even when judges honorably try to enforce the rule. Non-controversial substantive provisions—take the sovereign immunity addition in the Delaware case—tend to get approved. Controversial substantive provisions—take the pilot school voucher program in Ohio—sometimes get nixed.[135] This approach imposes a non-sustainable tax on the state judiciary. Whether in the setting of appropriation bills or conventional bills, the most biting criticism of judicial enforcement of single-subject (and clear-title) rules is that they promote uneven decision making or, worse, policymaking masquerading as decision making. It is not a favorable trade-off to use one branch of government (the courts) to rein in another branch of government (the legislature) when the solution generates less confidence in *both* branches.

That leaves the last challenge: remedies. If the focus of these provisions is to prohibit logrolling, riders, and other process problems, one would think the only remedy is to refuse to enforce the whole bill. *Any* logrolling would seem to taint all parts of the compromised bill. So also for riders, especially when added to appropriations bills.

The states roam all over the map in addressing this last set of complications. Some state constitutional provisions provide an answer to the problem by choosing severability. The Iowa and Oregon Constitutions, for example, require severance and use the clear-title requirement to facilitate enforcement: "If any subject shall be embraced in an act which shall not be expressed in the title, such act shall be void only as to so much thereof as shall not be expressed in the title."[136]

For states with provisions that do not spell out a remedy, some courts as a matter of statutory interpretation have followed a general preference for severability rather than refusing to enforce the entire law. Consider the criteria used by the Missouri Supreme Court in *Hammerschmidt v. Boone County* to sort this out.[137] It started with the assumption that if a bill has more than one subject, "the entire bill is unconstitutional." But if the court determines "beyond reasonable doubt" that one of the subjects was the "original, controlling purpose" of the bill, it will enforce only that one. Through it all, the court asks whether the "additional subject is essential to the efficacy of the bill, whether it is a provision without which the bill would be incomplete and unworkable, and whether the provision is one without which the legislators would not have adopted the bill."[138] The effort is commendable, but the target is hard to catch if the single-subject imperative is a *process* guarantee. Maybe that's the best the courts can do. But it's hardly a model of clarity, and do-it-yourself reckoning rarely bodes well for courts. One thing is for sure, though. Most state courts as a matter of practice, if not theory, view the remedy of invalidating an entire bill, particularly an appropriation bill, as stronger medicine than they are willing to impose.

One last point concerns a benign feature of these cases. A critique of the potential value of re-invigorating state constitutions is that, too often, it will not make a difference. Because many states are politically homogenous, it is said, there is little likelihood that the state courts will cut against the political grain of their state.[139] That may be true in some settings. But just because a state is thought to be politically of one stripe, that does not mean the state's courts will not enforce these prohibitions. Enforcement of these guarantees in the forty-three states that have them has not only been unpredictable politically, but it also has involved high-stakes matters. They have been used to invalidate Oklahoma's regulation of abortions,[140] Ohio's creation of a pilot voucher program,[141] and many other significant laws in other states.[142]

Judicial enforcement of public-purpose clauses raises a different set of considerations, some of which may favor more frequent enforcement of the guarantees. The states' public-purpose provisions reflect a procedural *and* substantive limit on state legislation, in partial contrast to the purely procedural clear-title and single-subject provisions. Given this substantive component, one could imagine the state courts enforcing these provisions rigorously. But that has not happened.

As the examples from North Carolina and Wisconsin illustrate, the state courts have been hands off in the main in limiting their legislatures' assessment of what counts as a public purpose.[143] If state courts uphold allocations of public money to private entities for a business's relocation expenses or for a sports team to build a stadium, it shows that the concept of public purpose can be stretched far and wide. I don't mean to suggest there is no legislative spending or lawmaking the courts would stop. A state court, I have little doubt, would halt a twenty-first-century equivalent of the Yazoo land scandal on absence-of-public-purpose grounds. But that's probably due to its audacity, not to the principle—a transfer from the public fisc to a money-making entity.

This lack of enforcement of state public-purpose clauses shines a light on a paradox in state and federal constitutional law. In reading about the public-purpose clause cases, the alert reader may wonder how the lack of judicial enforcement of these "public purpose" clauses interfaces with judicial enforcement of the federal Takings Clauses and the state takings clauses. These fifty-one clauses all say that when a government exercises the power of eminent domain, taking private property for governmental uses, it must compensate the property owner. A key limitation is that the clauses permit these governmental seizures of property only for a "public purpose" or "public use" or words to that effect.[144]

The federal "public use" story in the takings context looks a lot like the state story in the "public purpose" context. The federal courts have been exceedingly deferential in allowing local governments to determine what a public use is. The high-water mark of that hands-off approach is captured by *Kelo v. City of New London*, in which the US Supreme Court upheld a city's decision to take over a neighborhood in order to facilitate the relocation of a Pfizer plant there. The Connecticut Supreme Court upheld the seizure of land, and the US Supreme Court did so too in a 5–4 decision. The determinative question in the case was whether such an exercise of eminent domain counted as a "public use," given that the fruits of the seizure would go most directly to a private entity, in truth a large profit-making business.

The decision to uphold this transfer of land from middle-class homeowners who had lived in the community for generations caused a national stir. It may be one of the more unpopular decisions in recent decades, perhaps because it was easy for everyday Americans to wonder whether they would be next in losing their homes to public efforts to lure businesses to the community.

What's interesting for present purposes is that the states, almost across the board, registered disapproval of *Kelo* and did so in myriad ways. They construed their own "public use" restrictions to prohibit such transfers in several state supreme court cases, two of them within a year of *Kelo*, both rejecting *Kelo* as the way to construe their similarly worded state takings clauses.[145] The other branches joined in as well. State legislatures amended their eminent domain laws, imposing stiffer requirements for identifying a public use. And local governments became less aggressive in using eminent domain, fearful they would generate the next *Kelo*-like outcry.

Kelo is nearly twenty years old, and it is the rare state court that embraces its understanding of a "public use" for takings-clause purposes.[146] That creates a dissonant feature of state constitutional law. Why is it that state courts in the last two decades have not also sharpened their "public purpose" clauses, limiting their legislatures' copious definitions of public ends? The reaction to the one experience would seem to cry out for something similar in the other. A skeptic might say there is a difference between taking a home and building a stadium. That's true; there is. But the difference cuts the other way. At least the homeowners get paid for the seizure. The private sports team gives nothing in return, just high-priced tickets when citizens choose to visit the stadium. At some point, one might expect this same modifier—"public" purpose or use—to develop more consistent interpretations within and among the state courts, and perhaps after that within the federal courts.

8

Trying to Make Legislatures More Representative

IN TRYING TO MAKE state legislatures responsive to their needs, the people have not only experimented with state constitutional amendments that impose process-driven limitations on how, and to what ends, each legislature enacts a law. They also have tried to make legislatures more representative. Most familiar are extensions of the suffrage, eventually guaranteeing to all men and women eighteen and over the right to vote. Many of these efforts eventually ended in federal laws: federal constitutional amendments and the 1965 Voting Rights Act. The states had a prominent role in kick-starting many of these changes. The admission of Vermont and Kentucky to the Union paved the way for eliminating property requirements for voting, with Georgia and Delaware soon following their newcomers' leads.[1] New York and New England set the example of extending the franchise to African Americans and other racial minorities.[2] The early nineteenth century saw Jacksonian sentiments take root in many states, spreading some of these electoral reforms and others also. With one passing caveat, states in the West and Midwest that entered the Union in the last half of the nineteenth century led the effort to extend the right to vote to women, an effort that culminated in the Nineteenth Amendment in 1920.[3] New Jersey, the caveat, allowed women to vote from 1776 to roughly 1807.[4]

It is tempting to think of these developments as part of a single federal-centric story. That's understandable given how many of these provisions eventually made their way into US constitutional amendments: the Fourteenth Amendment (apportionment and race), the Fifteenth (race), the Seventeenth (popular election of US senators), the Nineteenth (gender), the Twenty-Fourth (no poll tax), and the Twenty-Sixth (18 and over). That is a federal story to be certain. But even then, these federal constitutional amendments still amount to a form of representation-enhancing federalism. No amendment becomes part of the US Constitution without the approval of three-quarters of the states. Efforts to change the US Constitution always start as local stories and sometimes end as federal ones. But the state-federal story about extending the right to vote, worth a book all its own, is not the focus of this chapter.

The focus instead is a different representation problem—efforts to curb extreme gerrymandering, the time-honored, if usually scorned, practice of drawing legislative districts to favor incumbents and the prevailing political party. It's a knotty division-of-powers problem for American governments that has been with us for as long as politicians have drawn legislative districts. Remember that Eldridge Gerry, a signer of the Declaration of Independence, is the source of the eponym. Whether in efforts to thwart it or to put lipstick on it, gerrymandering implicates unique features of American federalism, most notably the reality that state legislatures draw state *and* federal electoral districts and that attempts to curb it involve state and federal law and state and federal actors.

The Federal Story

Once the American people chose a government that featured representative legislatures and once they opted not to select all representatives based on statewide elections, there was no escaping the need to draw district lines for some elections. That imperative came with this reality: There is no inherently fixed and geographically fair way to draw district lines. When the Ice Age receded from what became the mainland United States, it left behind ample geographic markers, like mountains and rivers, but no fairly etched legislative districts for each state legislature to adopt—or any state or federal court to impose. Even the creation of counties and townships, another potential source for drawing election districts, did not establish forever ideal legislative maps. Shifts in population can transform a representative district into an unrepresentative one, making the dynamic demographics of this restless country a constant challenge. These realities come with a federalism component of the national constitution. It not only delegates to the states the power to set the terms and rules for elections to state legislatures, but it also does the same for the members of Congress, whether the House of Representatives or the Senate. In the words of Article I, § 4, "The Times, Places and Manner of holding Elections for Senators and Representatives, shall be prescribed in each State by the Legislature thereof," though Congress "may at any time by Law make or alter such Regulations." The US Constitution also allocates representatives to the states based on population, and the states generally elect those representatives based on geographical lines within each state.[5] Whether legislatures draw district lines in incumbent-leaning ways, party-leaning ways, or largely neutral ways, the decisions have rippling stakes for control of all houses of the state legislatures and the House of Representatives.

Those stakes no doubt influence the map-making decisions of state legislatures and the individuals who challenge them. Both motives were in play in Tennessee in the early 1960s. Claiming that outdated reapportionments in Tennessee had come to favor voters from rural communities over voters from urban communities, citizens of the Volunteer State filed a lawsuit in federal court under the Fourteenth Amendment, seeking to require state legislatures to draw districts along more representative lines after each decennial census. The lawsuit became *Baker v. Carr*, decided in 1962, and one of the landmark cases in American constitutional law.[6]

After the Civil War, Tennessee had reapportioned the seats in their state legislature every ten years between 1871 and 1901. But after 1901, each attempt to reapportion the seats failed. Over the next three score years, Tennessee's demographics progressively changed in one direction. The cities grew at a faster rate than the rural communities. One house of the Tennessee General Assembly, the House of Representatives, had ninety-nine members, and from 1901 forward the state map allocated one representative to combinations of low-population counties and more than one representative to larger counties.[7] But the recalibration, fair in 1901 and fair in the abstract, did not keep up with population growth, prompting increasing disparities in voting power. By the time of the complaint, one vote in rural Moore County was worth nineteen votes in Hamilton County (Chattanooga), and one vote in Stewart County was "worth nearly eight times a single vote" in Shelby County (Memphis) or Knox County (Knoxville).[8]

An impediment to the lawsuit was precedent. In 1946, the Court had rejected a similar challenge.[9] *Colegrove v. Green* dealt with a challenge to the Illinois state legislative boundaries, which also had stayed the same since 1901. With no one opinion commanding a majority of the Court, *Colegrove* deemed the claim a non-justiciable political question, meaning that this kind of claim exceeded the power of the federal courts to correct.

But the Court changed course in *Baker*. Writing for a six-justice majority, Justice Brennan ruled that the equal protection claim was not a political question beyond the capacity or ken of the federal courts to resolve. The Court acknowledged that the lawsuit sought to protect a political right. But labeling claims about political rights non-justiciable under the political question doctrine, he wrote, is "little more than a play on words"; the relevant doctrine turns on "political questions," not on "political cases." "The courts cannot reject as 'no lawsuit' a bona fide controversy as to whether some action denominated 'political' exceeds constitutional authority." Nor did it matter that the Court had treated claims under the "Guarantee Clause" (guaranteeing the states a Republican form of government) as non-justiciable due to "the lack of criteria by which a court could determine which form of government was republican."[10] Even if the plaintiffs' claim implicated the Guarantee Clause, that did not change the reality that it implicated the Equal Protection Clause, too. The "non-justiciability of claims resting on the Guarant[ee] Clause which arises from their embodiment of questions that were thought 'political,'" he explained, "can have no bearing upon the justiciability of the equal protection claim presented in this case." The Court finished by saying that the plaintiffs' "allegations of a denial of equal protection present a justiciable constitutional cause of action upon which appellants are entitled to a trial and a decision" and remanded to the three-judge panel to hold a trial.[11]

Baker produced three concurrences, each acknowledging room for discretion at the state level when it came to remedying the problem.

Justice Douglas acknowledged that "universal equality is not the test; there is room for weighting" to protect the influence of different regions.[12] Justice Clark emphasized that "37% of the voters of Tennessee elect 20 of the 33 Senators while 40% of the voters elect 63 of the 99 members of the House," and denied that "mathematical equality among voters is required by the Equal Protection Clause."[13] He lamented that the people of Tennessee seemed to have had no recourse in correcting the problem locally. "Tennessee has no initiative and referendum," and calls to amend the state constitution have been "fruitless" because they must obtain the blessing of the same misapportioned legislature.[14] The Tennessee courts, he added, have not been helpful either, criticizing "state judges" who "often rest" their *state law* decisions on the "ground that this Court has precluded adjudication of the federal claim."[15] Justice Stewart also concurred, observing that, in holding that a complaint alleging an "utterly arbitrary" method of apportionment is justiciable, the Court had not required the states to structure their legislatures to "reflect with approximate equality the voice of every voter."[16]

Baker also produced two dissents and behind-the-scenes drama that took a lasting toll on two justices. Unsure how to handle the case after the first argument, the Court reargued it. Then, according to some, various justices placed so much pressure on Justice Whittaker to join one side or the other that he suffered a nervous breakdown, prompting him to recuse from *Baker* (making it a decision with an imperfectly apportioned eight votes) and eventually to retire from the Court.[17] Just two weeks after the Court decided *Baker*, Justice Frankfurter suffered a stroke from which he never recovered and for which he reputedly blamed *Baker*.[18]

Justice Frankfurter channeled that angst into his dissent, insisting the majority had "reverse[d] a uniform course of decision established by a dozen cases," "catapult[ed] the lower courts of the country" into a "mathematical quagmire," and "inject[ed] itself into the clash of political forces in political sentiments." He deeply lamented that the Court was abandoning its recognition of "a class of controversies which do not lend themselves to judicial standards and judicial remedies." And he pointed out that the practice of starkly uneven political districts was and had always been common in all regions of the country.[19] That was by way of warming up.

Returning to first principles and recalling the modest "role of this Court in our constitutional scheme," Justice Frankfurter cautioned that the Court's "authority" "rests on sustained public confidence"— a "feeling" that "must be nourished by the Court's complete detachment, in fact and in appearance, from political entanglements and by abstention from injecting itself into the clash of political forces in political settlements."[20] In such riven debates, the answer in "a democratic society like ours" must turn on "an aroused popular conscience that sears the conscience of the people's representatives," not on judicial pocket parts to the Constitution.[21] Justice Frankfurter was not persuaded by the majority's effort to distinguish precedent, noting that this was a "Guarantee Clause claim masquerading under a different label." "Where judicial competence is wanting, it cannot be created by invoking one clause of the Constitution rather than another."[22] "To divorce 'equal protection' from 'Republican Form' is to talk about half a question."[23] The heart of the matter remained that there was no discernible test for ascertaining a violation. "Talk of 'debasement' or 'dilution' is circular talk. One cannot speak" of either one "until there is first defined a standard of reference as to what a vote should be worth. What is actually asked of the Court in this case is to choose among competing bases of representation—ultimately, really, among competing theories of political philosophy—in order to establish an appropriate frame of government for the State of Tennessee and thereby for all the States of the Union."[24] Even after sorting out "what is to be represented in a representative legislature"—what, in short, is the meaning of a democratic republic—there are many considerations and "extraordinary complexity" in each district-drawing exercise: "geography, demography, electoral convenience, economic and social cohesion or divergencies among particular local groups, communications, the practical effects of political institutions like the lobby and city machine, ancient traditions and ties of settled usage, respect for proven incumbents of long experience and senior status, mathematical mechanics, censuses compiling relevant data, and a host of others." This was not something judges were equipped to do, whether by training or "native wit," especially "because in every strand of this complicated, intricate web of values meet the contending forces of partisan politics."[25]

In his dissent, Justice Harlan noted that the case did not present a question of law but of "competing political philosophies [that the] federal courts [had] not been empowered by the Equal Protection Clause to judge." "Nothing in the Equal Protection Clause or elsewhere in the Federal Constitution," he reasoned, "expressly or impliedly supports the view that state legislatures must be so structured as to reflect with approximate equality the voice of every voter," and "those who consider that continuing national respect for the Court's authority depends in large measure upon its wise exercise of self-restraint and discipline in constitutional adjudication[] will view the decision with deep concern."[26] Harlan wondered why a legislature could not create or preserve "electoral imbalance between its rural and urban population" in order "to protect the State's agricultural interests from the sheer weight of numbers of those residing in its cities."[27] Especially hard for the dissenters to accept was the idea that the general language of the Equal Protection Clause gave the Court a warrant to invalidate a type of electoral district that was never as non-representative as the makeup of the US Senate—with its guarantee of two senators for every state, no matter how sparsely or heavily populated, to say nothing of Article V's guarantee that this "equal suffrage" provision could not be changed without the "consent" of every state.[28] Justice Harlan finished with a word of caution about the growing practice of relying on the Court to fix social problems: "Those observers of the Court who see it primarily as the last refuge for the correction of all inequality or injustice, no matter what its nature or source, will no doubt applaud this decision and its break with the past. Those who consider that continuing national respect for the Court's authority depends in large measure upon its wise exercise of self-restraint and discipline in constitutional adjudication, will view the decision with deep concern."[29]

That was not the end—it really was just the beginning—of this political-question ruling. In 1964, the Court applied *Baker* to federal House districts in *Wesberry v. Sanders*.[30] As in *Baker*, the Court found a lack-of-proportionality challenge to the congressional districts in Georgia to be justiciable.[31] And as in *Baker*, it held that the requirement "that Representatives be chosen 'by the People of the several States' means that as nearly as is practicable one man's vote in a congressional election is to be worth as much as another's."[32]

That set the stage for *Reynolds v. Sims*, just four months later, to establish a national rule for drawing all legislative districts in the country, whether for the House of Representatives or for the one or two houses of each state legislature.[33] Seven members of the Court agreed that the Alabama legislative reapportionment violated the Equal Protection Clause and ordered a new reapportionment. While the decision happened to address Alabama's districting plan, it invalidated the apportionment decisions of at least six other states then facing apportionment challenges: Alabama, Colorado, Delaware, Maryland, New York, and Virginia.[34] "As a basic constitutional standard," Chief Justice Warren wrote, "the Equal Protection Clause requires that the seats in both houses of a bicameral state legislature must be apportioned on a population basis" and that states must "make an honest and good faith effort to construct districts, in both houses of its legislature, as nearly of equal population as is practicable." "Legislators represent people," he observed, "not trees or acres."[35] Because "legislators are elected by voters, not farms or cities or economic interests," and because "ours is a representative form of government, and our legislatures are those instruments of government elected directly by and directly representative of the people, the right to elect legislators in a free and unimpaired fashion is a bedrock of our political system."[36] "If a State should provide that the votes of citizens in one part of the State should be given two times, or five times, or 10 times the weight of votes of citizens in another part of the State," the Court worried, "it could hardly be contended that the right to vote of those residing in the disfavored areas had not been effectively diluted." Any reapportionment of state legislative seats less often than every ten years would be "constitutionally suspect," the Court announced.[37] Even as it declined to determine appropriate remedies when states fail to reapportion every ten years, it accepted the district court's remedy of ordering a provisional map based on portions of the invalid plans as not "usurp[ing] the primary responsibility for reapportionment which rests with the legislature" and found it was an "appropriate and well-considered exercise of judicial power."[38]

Justice Clark concurred in the judgment. He agreed that the map violated the Equal Protection Clause but found it unnecessary to require mathematical equality among voters in a district.[39] "If one house of the State legislature meets the population standard," he noted, "representation in the other house might include some departure from it so as to take into account, on a rational basis, other factors in order to afford some representation to the various elements of the States."[40] Justice Stewart also concurred separately, explaining that the Alabama plan violated the Equal Protection Clause on the ground that it was "completely lacking in rationality."[41]

Justice Harlan was the lone dissenter, as Justice Frankfurter had retired by then due to complications from his stroke. Harlan objected to "placing basic aspects of state political systems under the pervasive overlordship of the federal judiciary" and found it "remarkable" that the Court refused to account for "the language of the Fourteenth Amendment," "the understanding of those who proposed and ratified it," and "the political practices of the States at the time the Amendment was adopted."[42] "'Developing' constitutionalism" could not justify the ruling, he explained, "when both the language and history of the controlling provisions of the Constitution are wholly ignored," confirming that the decision "amounts to nothing less than an exercise of the amending power by this Court."[43] Before and shortly after the Fourteenth Amendment in 1868, he explained, most states did not apportion voters solely based on population, and the same was true in 1964, when just fifteen States "apportioned solely according to population."[44] Neither original norms nor "developing" ones thus could support the decision. As for the Court's reasoning that "legislators represent people, not trees or acres," he "conceded" the point. "But it is surely equally obvious" and "more meaningful to note," he responded, "that people are not ciphers and that legislators can represent their electors only by speaking for their interests—economic, social, political— many of which do not reflect the place where the electors live."[45] He concluded by expressing concern that the judiciary's entry into state legislative re-districting "cut deeply into the fabric of our federalism" and was "profoundly ill-advised and constitutionally impermissible," remarked that "the vitality of our political system" becomes "weakened by reliance on the judiciary for political reform," and worried that "in time a complacent body politic may result."[46]

Correctly decided or not, *Baker v. Carr* and *Reynolds v. Sims* seemed to create a fair and relatively easy set of national rules to implement. Every ten years after the decennial census, all each state legislature had to do was to ensure that it redrew state and federal district lines in order to honor the "one person, one vote" mandate. How hard could that be? It looked like a math problem, no longer a political problem, one objectively easy to follow and one not susceptible to political machinations by incorrigible legislators. But a higher law, the law of unintended consequences, intervened. At least two problems made what looked easy in fact hard and replaced old difficulties with new ones.

Problem one arose from the *requirement* to redraw re-districting lines—for state legislative branches and for the House of Representatives—every ten years.[47] A compelling case can be made that the Tennessee state legislative lines at issue in *Baker v. Carr* had become unjustifiably slanted in favor of rural votes—or at least irrational after sixty years of inaction—and that a federal response was in order, whether by Congress or the federal courts. It's fair to add that the facts in *Baker v. Carr* establish the high ground for John Hart Ely's *Democracy and Distrust*—a representation re-enforcing theory of federal judicial review that urges federal courts to focus their constitutional-interpretation capital on correcting voting and franchise irregularities, not on entering the fray over substantive due process fights about social issues. But a "mandate" of "periodic redistricting" every ten years creates considerable room for mischief, permitting "partisan political exploitation of the procedural strand of one-person, one-vote."[48] It means the same legislators distrusted for manipulating district lines in the past have an excuse—no, a mandate—to return to the scene and draw new lines with all of the individual-capacity self-interest and official-capacity self-interest that go with it. Keep in mind that ensuring that each legislative district within a state has the same number of voters does not prevent gerrymandering. And requiring the legislature to redraw districts every ten years creates decennial opportunities for partisan gerrymandering—and perhaps more covert gerrymandering because the legislators can say the US Supreme Court made them do it.

Problem two arose from an unexpected consequence of another well-intended source of change: the Voting Rights Act of 1965. Section 2 of the Voting Rights Act provides that "no voting qualification or prerequisite to voting or standard, practice, or procedure shall be imposed or applied by any State or political subdivision in a manner which results in a denial or abridgement of the right of any citizen of the United

States to vote on account of race or color."[49] It is not hard to implement a law that prohibits facial or intentional restrictions on voting based on race. And it is usually not hard to implement a law that limits ostensibly neutral voting procedures and requirements that have a disparate impact—disparate "results"—based on race. What gets complicated is applying the law in the context of district line drawing and in the context of political decisions about the number of representatives from each district every ten years.

Take states with large multi-member districts. In these districts, a cohesive and large racial minority group normally would have enough political power to elect a representative from a smaller single-member district but could be outweighed by the political power of a majority group and receive no representation of their interests in the larger multi-member district. To ensure that multi-member districts do not result in a "denial or abridgement of the right of any citizen of the United States to vote on account of race," the court announced a three-part test to prove vote dilution in *Thornburg v. Gingles*.[50] A minority community must be (1) "sufficiently large and geographically compact to constitute a majority in a single-member district"; (2) the group must be "politically cohesive"; and (3) the "white majority" must vote "sufficiently as a bloc to enable it . . . usually to defeat the minority's preferred candidate."[51] While this test applied only to multi-member districts at the start, the Supreme Court proceeded to apply it to single-member districts in *Growe v. Emison*.[52]

In practice, all of this required areas with large minority groups and racially polarized voting to be drawn with majority-minority districts or at least some districts where the minority did not "usually lose." At the same time, and here's the rub, the Supreme Court has stood by its aversion to racial classifications in the re-districting process, holding in *Shaw v. Reno* that a districting plan that "rationally cannot be understood as anything other than an effort to separate voters into different districts on the basis of race" is subject to strict scrutiny.[53] All of this makes it simultaneously unlawful to dilute minority voting power based on the impact of new districting lines *and* to re-district with the goal of creating separate districts on the basis of race.[54] What looked fair and relatively easy to implement has revealed severe complications over time. It also gave some legislators an explanation for packing politically cohesive minority voters in one district, which diluted their force elsewhere. That is partisan gerrymandering by another name, and state legislators could accurately (if disingenuously) say the 1965 Voting Rights Act made them do it.

The Court's mixed success in handling claims of racial gerrymandering foreshadowed the difficulties posed by partisan gerrymandering challenges. The Court initially addressed the question of whether political gerrymandering—drawing district lines to favor one political party over the other—presented a cognizable constitutional claim in 1986 in *Davis v. Bandemer*.[55] Competing intuitions underscored the claim. In one direction, an equal protection challenge to a "political gerrymander" sounded odd given that gerrymandering had always had a political component to it. In the other direction, the one-person-one-vote mandate at some point could become a silent guarantee if a political party, while superficially honoring the rule, nonetheless made it very difficult to elect candidates from one party or the other. Taking its cue from *Baker*, the Court gave half a loaf. It agreed that a political gerrymandering challenge under the Equal Protection Clause raised a justiciable question—one the federal courts could resolve—but declined to say more.

Three decades of political gerrymandering claims followed.

Vieth v. Jubelirer[56] revealed the vexing complexities of the litigation. At issue was whether Pennsylvania's congressional districts, drawn to favor Republican candidates, violated equal protection. The three-judge district court dismissed the claim, and the Supreme Court affirmed the decision without any single opinion speaking for all five of them. A four-vote plurality, written by Justice Scalia, took the position that the federal courts had no business, and no basis for, assessing political gerrymandering claims and that *Bandemer* should be overruled.[57] Justice Frankfurter would have smiled that an FDR appointee and a Reagan appointee saw the problem similarly. Three separate dissents, joined by four justices, suggested three distinct standards for resolving political gerrymandering claims.[58] Justice Kennedy concurred in the judgment. "A decision ordering the correction of all election district lines drawn for partisan reasons," he worried, "would commit federal and state courts to unprecedented intervention in the American political process." At the same time, he "would not foreclose all possibility of judicial relief if some limited and precise rationale were found to correct an established violation of the Constitution in some redistricting cases." But the "determination that a gerrymander violates the law must rest on something more than the conclusion that political classifications were applied." Rather, "the classifications, though generally permissible," must be "applied in an invidious manner or in a way unrelated to any legitimate legislative objective." "The failings of the many proposed standards for measuring the burden a gerrymander imposes on representational rights," he believed, "make our intervention improper." But "if workable standards do emerge to measure these burdens" in the future, courts should be prepared to grant relief.[59] From *Vieth* until Justice Kennedy's retirement in June 2018, the Court's gerrymandering jurisprudence clung to this fine line, creating considerable suspense over whether a political gerrymander would ever be sufficiently extreme to justify federal judicial involvement and, if so, how the Court would define the line between permissible and impermissible partisan gerrymanders.[60]

In the first year after Justice Kennedy's retirement, the Court gave an answer. In their final opinion of the Term, the Court decided *Rucho v. Common Cause*,[61] which involved two partisan gerrymanders, not one. Republicans led the district-redrawing effort in North Carolina, and Democrats led the effort in Maryland. In each case, the state legislature acknowledged with refreshing, if disturbing, candor what it had done. A Republican co-chair of the North Carolina re-districting committee said, "I think electing Republicans is better [for the country] than electing Democrats" and the North Carolina map was designed with the goal of electing ten Republicans and three Democrats because he did "not believe it [would be] possible to draw a map with 11 Republicans and 2 Democrats." In Maryland, the Democratic governor appointed a self-described "serial gerrymanderer" to lead the process, insisting that the goal of re-districting was to "change the overall composition of Maryland's congressional delegation to 7 Democrats and 1 Republican by flipping [Maryland's Sixth Congressional District]."[62]

Writing for a unified five-justice majority, Chief Justice Roberts wrote that the political question doctrine deprived federal courts of jurisdiction to handle partisan-gerrymandering claims. He acknowledged what everyone accepted: these congressional districting maps were "highly partisan, by any measure."[63] But the highly partisan underpinnings of a constitutional claim did not prove that it was " 'of a Judiciary Nature' " in the words of James Madison.[64] "Sometimes," he wrote, " 'the judicial department has no business entertaining the claim of unlawfulness— because the question is entrusted to one of the political branches or involves no judicially enforceable rights' " that are discernible.[65] "Aware of electoral districting problems," he observed, the Framers "settled on a characteristic approach, assigning the issue to the state legislatures, expressly checked and balanced by the Federal Congress."[66] While that reality has not prohibited the Court from resolving refusal-to-reapportion claims or race-based claims, it has "proved far more difficult" to identify enforceable standards for political gerrymandering claims. "To hold that legislators cannot take partisan interests into account when drawing district lines would essentially countermand the Framers' decision to entrust districting to political entities."[67] Once it's accepted that some politics will go into reapportionment, it becomes difficult to identify how much is "too much."[68] And the most likely measure of "too much"—reversions to proportional representation—is not the measure the Constitution imposes. Such claims are based on the mistaken "conviction that the greater the departure from proportionality, the more suspect an apportionment plan becomes."[69]

In the absence of a request for proportional representation, "plaintiffs inevitably ask the courts to make their own political judgment about how much representation particular political parties *deserve*—based on the votes of their supporters—and to rearrange the challenged districts to achieve that end."[70] That requires federal courts "to apportion political power as a matter of fairness," something they are not "equipped" to do,[71] in part because "it is not even clear what fairness looks like in this context."[72] Should the focus be on creating more competitive races, more safe seats, or greater use of traditional criteria, such as "maintaining political subdivisions, keeping communities of interest together, and protecting incumbents"?[73] The trade-offs between these and other values turn on "political" value judgments, not "legal" determinations.[74] It is only *after* determining an acceptable measure of fairness that a court can determine "How much is too much?" and "At what point does permissible partisanship become unconstitutional?"[75] No judicial test can make these decisions any less driven by value judgments—and political value judgments at that. That does not mean that excessive partisan gerrymandering is just or consistent with democratic values. It only means that such injustices must be remedied by the states, whether through traditional democratic processes, state constitutions and state courts, or state commissions.[76] Nor did the Court's one-person-one-vote cases require a different conclusion. "It hardly follows from the principle that each person must have an equal say in the election of representatives that a person is entitled to have his political party achieve representation in some way commensurate to its share of statewide support."[77] Given "all the justiciability conundrums" that come with identifying a "fair share of political power and influence," a "partisan gerrymandering claim cannot ask for the elimination of partisanship."[78] It may be that "excessive partisanship in districting leads to results that reasonably seem unjust," but that reality "does not mean that the solution lies with the federal judiciary."[79] He then explained that the states had adopted many reforms to address extreme gerrymandering, and Congress eventually could do the same.[80]

Justice Kagan's dissent blew the whistle on the "politics of polarization and dysfunction" left in place by the Court's decision.[81] *Baker* in her view charted the path for turning aside any political question concerns raised by entering this fray and, if followed, would have allowed the Court to correct a despairing problem in American democracy—that too often gerrymandering allows politicians and interest groups to "cherry pick" their voters. Even as more sophisticated computer technology allowed political parties to gerrymander with more precision than at any time in the past, she thought technology could help the federal courts sort out what gerrymanders went "too far" based on a state's own acknowledged reapportionment priorities.[82] Accepting the difficulty of refining some constitutional principles in this area, she thought it easy enough to decide *these* cases given the egregiousness of the gerrymanders. And she found the majority's belief that state courts could help solve partisan gerrymandering while federal courts could not "perplexing." "If [state courts] can develop and apply neutral and manageable standards to identify unconstitutional gerrymanders," she asked, "why couldn't we?"[83]

Unlike many landmark US Supreme Court cases in modern times, just two opinions came out of the case. Both reveal two justices at the top of their game. Anyone trying to understand the pitfalls and promise of federal court engagement with partisan gerrymander claims would do well to read both opinions. As for their dueling positions about the role of the states in addressing the partisan dysfunction caused by partisan gerrymandering, there's no better way to gauge the situation than to look at two state court opinions: one from Pennsylvania before *Rucho* and one from North Carolina after it. What's complex in federal court is no less complex in state court.

The State Stories

Pennsylvania

The Pennsylvania Supreme Court entertained a gerrymandering challenge to the congressional districts under its constitution in 2017—after *Vieth* rejected a similar challenge to the Commonwealth's apportionment plan and before *Rucho* foreclosed the federal option. According to a metric developed by the Brennan Center, the Pennsylvania map was the second-most gerrymandered in the country and thus the second-least representative in the country based on proportionality.[84] Democrats challenged the new map, culminating in a series of far-reaching rulings by the Pennsylvania Supreme Court in *League of Women Voters of Pennsylvania v. Pennsylvania*.[85]

Many features of the case stand out. The Pennsylvania Supreme Court heard the case as an exercise of its "extraordinary jurisdiction," a practice allowing the court to assume plenary jurisdiction over any pending state court case in the Commonwealth.[86] In November 2017, the court took jurisdiction of the case, giving the trial court a deadline of December 31 to complete its findings of fact and conclusions of law, all with the aim of resolving the dispute before the 2018 election.[87]

In a short per curiam order on January 22, 2018, the Pennsylvania Supreme Court ruled that the map violated the Commonwealth's Constitution.[88] It determined that the map "clearly, plainly and palpably violates the Constitution of the Commonwealth of Pennsylvania" and could not be enforced. The order directed the legislature to submit a new map to the governor by February 9 and gave the governor until February 15 to accept the plan and submit it to the Supreme Court.

One way or another, the court announced, the court would put a new re-districting plan in place by February 19, 2018, and the May congressional primaries would take place under the new map.[89]

Pennsylvania selects its supreme court justices based on partisan elections. At the time, the court had five Democrats and two Republicans. Joining the court's order were four justices, all Democrats. The court's fifth Democrat, Justice Baer, concurred in part and dissented in part, agreeing that the map violated the state constitution but declining to apply the ruling to the 2018 election given the absence of time to draw a new map.[90]

The two Republican justices dissented. Chief Justice Saylor wrote that he opposed the court's exercise of extraordinary jurisdiction, that he was skeptical that a judicially manageable standard for resolving gerrymandering could be identified, and that he thought the court should wait for guidance from the United States Supreme Court in related lawsuits (including *Rucho*) before wading into this arena.[91] Justice Mundy joined Chief Justice Saylor's opinion. He added that the court's order failed to identify what part of the constitution the map violated, did not give the legislature guidance on what was required for a map to comply with the constitution, and warned that it might violate Article I, Section 4 of the US Constitution (providing that the "Manner of holding Elections for Senators and Representatives, shall be prescribed in each State by the Legislature thereof") if the court, rather than the "Legislature," drew the map.[92]

Four days later, the court issued another per curiam order. It appointed Stanford Law professor Nathaniel Persily as "an advisor to assist the Court in adopting, if necessary, a remedial congressional redistricting plan" and directing the legislature to submit political data to the court to assist them in drawing a new map if that became necessary.[93]

The Republican-led legislature was not amused. The president pro tempore of the Senate, a named defendant, informed the court that because it was usurping legislative authority, the legislature would not comply with the court's order to submit data.[94] One representative called for the impeachment of the five Democratic members of the court.[95]

Undeterred, the court released a full opinion on February 7, explaining their initial order and announcing that the original map violated the Commonwealth Constitution's Free and Equal Elections Clause.[96] "Elections," the clause says, "shall be free and equal; and no power, civil or military, shall at any time interfere to prevent the free exercise of the right of suffrage."[97] The court explained that the clause's "language, its history, the occasion for the provision and the circumstances in which it was adopted, the case law interpreting this clause, and consideration of the consequences of our interpretation" all support the conclusion that "the Clause should be given the broadest interpretation, one which governs all aspects of the electoral process, and which provides the people of this Commonwealth an equally effective power to select the representative of his or her choice, and bars the dilution of the people's power to do so."[98]

To gauge the constitutionality of the apportionment plan, the court looked to the factors contained in Pennsylvania's requirements for state legislative boundaries: "compactness, contiguity, and the maintenance of the integrity of the boundaries of political subdivisions."[99] Measured by these standards, the court reasoned, the map failed. Based on expert testimony presenting a simulation of a range of possible congressional districts at trial, it was statistically impossible for the plan to have been drawn with the goals of compactness and minimized breaks in political subdivisions—and that was consistent with lay examination of the "tortured" congressional districts.[100] Further evidence of a violation, the court noted, arose from the reality that the map systematically favored Republicans more than one would expect from a district drawn in keeping with traditional criteria. The court finished by defending its role in the process, stating that "it is beyond peradventure that it is the legislature, in the first instance, that is primarily charged with the task of reapportionment. However, the Pennsylvania Constitution, statutory law, our Court's decisions, federal precedent, and case law from our sister states, all serve as a bedrock foundation on which stands the authority of the state judiciary to formulate a valid redistricting plan when necessary."[101]

Justice Baer agreed that the map was unconstitutional under the Free and Equal Election Clause. But he dissented from the remedy of forcing the creation of a new map before the 2018 elections and from the imposition of the compactness, contiguity, and political sub-division test. He also emphasized that it was unclear how the court would draw a remedial map, whether they would rely on the trial record or on Professor Persily.[102] Chief Justice Saylor emphasized that re-districting is an inherently political exercise and that the court's decision raised serious separation-of-powers problems.[103] Justice Mundy emphasized his disagreement with the creation of a three-part test for assessing gerrymanders under the general language of the Free and Equal Elections Clause.[104]

The court's more detailed explanation for its decision did not placate the General Assembly's Republicans, and they did not meet the Supreme Court's deadline for a new map. In response, the Supreme Court issued a new map on February 19 and instructed the executive to implement the map in the upcoming elections according to new filing deadlines created by the court.[105] The same three justices dissented, emphasizing that they did not believe the legislature had sufficient time to adopt a new map and noting the oddity of "the adoption of a judicially created redistricting plan apparently upon advice from a political scientist who has not submitted a report as of record nor appeared as a witness in any court proceeding in this case."[106]

Political observers from all sides called the new map an unambiguous victory for Democrats. To the *New York Times'* Nate Cohn, "The new map is better for Democrats—by nearly every measure—than the maps that the Democrats themselves proposed." Cohn said that the map appeared to make a series of subtle choices that consistently favored Democrats when, "in all of these cases, there were Republican-leaning alternatives of seemingly comparable merit." He stopped short of calling the map a Democratic gerrymander, but he noted that the map counteracted Pennsylvania's political geography, which naturally favors Republicans and achieved something closer to proportional representation.[107] The Republican legislature went further, though more to bury than to praise. A joint statement by the Speaker of the House and the Senate president pro tempore lambasted the new map and the process of drawing it: "This entire exercise, while cloaked in 'litigation,' is and has been nothing more than the ultimate partisan gerrymander—one brought about by the Democrat governor acting in concert with liberal politically connected litigants."[108] The *Wall Street Journal* Editorial

Board was no less sparing. It labeled the new map "a judicial coup d'etat" and warned that, if the US Supreme Court allowed this practice to continue, "judges [would become] redistricting kings."[109]

Whatever the intent, no matter the method, the map benefited Democrats in the 2018 election. While Republicans had won thirteen congressional seats and the Democrats five in the 2016 election,[110] the parties split the congressional delegation 9–9 in the 2018 election.[111] Control of the House of Representatives changed from the Republican Party to the Democratic Party in the 2018 election, though not based on the Pennsylvania elections alone.

North Carolina

The next state case of note came after the US Supreme Court's 2019 decision in *Rucho* and involved the *same* North Carolina map that the US Supreme Court upheld in *Rucho*. As in Pennsylvania, congressional districts in North Carolina featured intense political redistricting efforts. After the 2010 census, North Carolina undertook its mandated decennial re-districting process, which spurred years of litigation over whether the map sank to a prohibited racial gerrymander. That culminated in a US Supreme Court decision invalidating North Carolina's First and Twelfth Congressional Districts as impermissible racial gerrymanders under the Fourteenth Amendment and the Voting Rights Act.[112] The North Carolina legislature drew a new map, which soon became the subject of gerrymandering litigation. The Brennan Center rated the old and new North Carolina maps as having the largest proportional-representation gap.[113] That federal court challenge led to *Rucho* and the Supreme Court's decision that the political question doctrine prohibited the federal courts from resolving these federal claims.

But that decision did not end the effort to challenge the gerrymander. Four months after *Rucho*, a three-judge state court panel in Wake County Superior Court granted a preliminary injunction against the same map on the grounds that it likely violated North Carolina's Constitution.[114] The court rejected the argument that North Carolina's political question doctrine barred the lawsuit, noting that the complaint fell within the "broad" "category of constitutional cases our courts are empowered and obliged to decide on the merits" and invoking *Rucho*'s recognition that "state constitutions can provide standards and guidance for state courts to apply."[115]

On the merits, the court identified a constitutional prohibition against excessive partisan gerrymandering from four provisions in the state constitution. The Free Elections Clause mandates that "all elections shall be free," and the legislature violates the provision when partisan gerrymandering skews elections from the true will of the people.[116] The Equal Protection Clause says that "no person shall be denied the equal protection of the laws," and the legislature violates the provision when gerrymandering treats members of one party less favorably than members of another party.[117] The Freedom of Speech Clause says that "freedom of speech and of the press are two of the great bulwarks of liberty and therefore shall never be restrained," and the legislature violates the provision when gerrymandering heightens the impact of some political speech relative to other political speech.[118] The Freedom of Assembly Clause mandates that "the people have a right to assemble together to consult for their common good, to instruct their representatives, and to apply to the General Assembly for the redress of grievances," and the legislature violates the provision when gerrymandering undermines the ability of some voters to influence their representatives.[119] Relying on the factual record compiled in the federal court litigation, the state court found that the North Carolina map likely violated the North Carolina Constitution and enjoined use of the map in future elections.[120] The court urged the legislature to fix the problem by enacting a new reapportionment law, noting that the state legislature had recently done the same thing on an expedited timeline after a three-judge panel found the map for the *state legislature's* elections unconstitutional.[121]

The state legislature drew a new map. Unlike the prior 10–3 split, it projected eight Republican seats and five Democratic seats. In creating the new map, the legislature relied on a template drawn by judges at a live-streamed re-districting conference, and an expert computer simulation showed that an 8–5 split was the most likely outcome given North Carolina demographics. Democrats protested that the process still unfairly favored Republicans and would lead to lopsided results (and wasted Democratic votes) in many districts. The litigation continued.[122]

Citing the approaching 2020 election, the three-judge panel allowed the election to proceed under the new maps passed by the state legislature.[123] Progressive election commentators called the process "a win for gerrymandering" and complained that "justice delayed is justice denied when it comes to re-districting. Rulings like this one allow legislators to get away with illegal gerrymanders for an election or two simply because litigation takes so long."[124]

As these complaints suggest, the claimants did not get everything they wanted. But their invocation of the state constitution still benefited them. *Rucho* placed a red light in front of these claims. And the state court gave the green light on similar claims and provided some relief to the claimants, independently interpreting its constitution to forbid extreme partisan gerrymandering even after the US Supreme Court rejected a challenge to the *same map*.

Extreme Partisan Gerrymandering and the Paths Available for Curbing It

It is hard to think of a higher-stakes division-of-powers question confronting the people of a state than the one covered by this chapter: Do the members of the legislature fairly represent the people they serve? The more uncomfortable the answer to that question becomes, the more one would expect the people to demand change. But change is not easy. If the members of the legislature—the branch delegated power to draw new districts every ten years—chafe at removing incumbency protections or the political party in control wants to keep it that way, it is fair to worry about the promise of representation-enhancing measures created by these same legislatures. What are the options?

The federal courts. One might have thought that the US Supreme Court would follow the path marked by *Baker* and *Reynolds* in using the Equal Protection Clause to address incorrigible gerrymandering. The Court took the first step down that path when, in *Davis v. Bandemer* in 1986, it held that partisan gerrymandering claims raised non-political questions. What *Davis* meant for gerrymandering challenges seemed to foreshadow what *Baker* meant for reapportionment challenges. It was not for lack of trying. *Davis* led to *Vieth* in 2004, a case about Pennsylvania's 2000 re-districting lines. Note by the way how the same two states, politically balanced Pennsylvania and North Carolina, figure prominently in the federal and state cases. Whether in *Vieth* or in cases after it, the Court could not settle on a judicially enforceable solution. Not until *Rucho* in 2019 did a majority of the Court agree on the same approach. Through an opinion by Chief Justice Roberts, the Court determined that the claims defied judicially discernible standards.

How is it that the federal courts may decide reapportionment challenges but not partisan gerrymandering challenges? Why didn't the US Supreme Court take the *Reynolds* step in *Rucho*? In some ways, the problems with extreme gerrymandering have grown worse over time. The use of computers and prior voting data to draw legislative districts has become highly refined, prompting the most sophisticated gerrymandering in American history and further polarizing public debates as more districts grow safe from general election threats each year.[125] Three potential explanations come to mind.

First, the Court faced a problem in *Rucho* that returns to a core explanation for the political question/non-justiciability doctrine: the unsuccessful quest for a discernible standard. A claimant does not advance the cause of individual rights or the credibility of the federal courts by inviting them into tangled thickets that offer no principled rules for decision and no strategy for departure. One advantage of the *Reynolds* "one person, one vote" test was its ease of implementation. Right or wrong, historically justified or not, the standard was one that legislatures and courts could readily enforce. All the legislatures had to do was to redraw the maps every ten years to ensure each district contained the right number of voters. That is not a difficult standard for legislatures to meet or for courts to enforce.

In revealing contrast, the *Rucho* claimants proposed elastic and complex tests for ensuring compliance with equal protection. Under the proposed test, the plaintiff first had to demonstrate that "the legislative mapdrawer's predominant purpose in drawing the lines of a particular district was to subordinate adherents of one political party and entrench a rival party in power." After that, the plaintiff had to show "that the dilution of the votes of supporters of a disfavored party in a particular district"—whether by "cracking" (dispersing disfavored voters) or by "packing" (aggregating disfavored voters)—was "likely to persist in subsequent elections such that an elected representative from the favored party in the district will not feel a need to be responsive to constituents who support the disfavored party." If the plaintiff met these two prongs of the test, the burden shifted to the state to prove that these discriminatory effects were "attributable to a legitimate state interest or other neutral explanation."[126] That is not a straight-line rule, and it left considerable room, perhaps too much room, for the perception that the test would invite political judging—gerrymandering the gerrymanders.

Justice Kagan favored a different methodology for determining whether a map crossed the line, one presented in an amicus curiae brief in the case. In her words, the proposal began "by using advanced computing technology to randomly generate a large collection of districting plans that incorporate the State's physical and political geography and meet its declared districting criteria, *except for* partisan gain." "For each of those maps, the method then uses actual precinct-level votes from past elections to determine a partisan outcome (i.e., the number of Democratic and Republican seats that map produces)." The court could then "line up those maps on a continuum—the most favorable to Republicans on one end, the most favorable to Democrats on the other." That would leave a "median outcome—that is, the outcome smack dab in the center—in a world with no partisan manipulation." Armed with this information, the court could "see where the state's actual plan falls on the spectrum—at or near the median or way out on one of the tails? The further out on the tail, the more extreme the partisan distortion and the more significant the vote dilution"—and the more likely it counted as unequal representation.[127]

But this test raised complications of its own. Was it any easier to describe? Was its use of computer technology and sophisticated algorithms likely to give the citizenry confidence that courts could deploy it in neutral, apolitical ways? In the Court's words, does it "make sense to use criteria that will vary from State to State and year to year as the baseline for determining whether a gerrymander violates the Federal Constitution"?[128] Even that test left, as every test seemed to leave, "the original unanswerable question": "How much political motivation and effect is too much? Would twenty percent away from the median map be okay? Forty percent? Sixty percent? Why or why not?"[129] Whatever the reader thinks of these tests, no matter who you think won this debate, this much is clear: The proposed tests are not as easy to describe or to enforce as one person, one vote. That's one explanation why *Rucho* did not become *Reynolds*.

Second, the one-person-one-vote requirement, even if easy to implement, had generated other questions and had created other problems. Was it necessarily a good idea to *compel* legislatures to redraw new districts every ten years, even when a state does not gain or lose a House seat, even when population changes do not create significant variations between and among state and federal districts, and even when the only time a legislature is not gerrymandering, as some fear, is when it is *not* redrawing districts? The *Reynolds* requirement had the unexpected consequence of generating more partisan gerrymandering by requiring self-interested legislators to do it every ten years, often in states that would have been content to leave things as they were.

Efforts to judicially refine prohibitions on racial gerrymandering had generated complications of their own. How do courts ensure that legislators draw majority-minority districts that are consistent with the 1965 Voting Rights Act but do not overly pack such districts for partisan ends every ten years? Both experiences confirmed that constitutional innovation designed to fix one problem sometimes creates another. The Court could understandably pause about taking on another source of re-districting litigation given that "one person, one vote" and racial gerrymandering claims had generated several unexpected consequences, some of them leading to less rather than more representative districts.

Third, one other explanation for the difference between the *Baker/Reynolds* story and the *Davis/Vieth/Rucho* story occupies a different plane of comparison. When it came to reapportionment, the state courts had offered little reason for hope as an engaged forum for adjudicating such claims under state constitutions. By the time of *Baker*, the Tennessee legislature had already defied the Tennessee Constitution's requirement that the legislature redraw district lines every ten years.[130] Things were no better in the Alabama state courts at the time of *Reynolds* or for that matter the northern courts that declined to correct apportionment lapses by their legislatures. The state courts had not shown themselves to be paragons of independent judicial review in dealing with politically dysfunctional issues, whether related to Jim Crow in general or political representation in particular. In his concurrence, Justice Clark observed that "it is interesting to note," a passive-aggressive formulation if ever there was one, "that state judges often rest their decisions on the ground that this Court has precluded adjudication of the federal claim," citing a Michigan Supreme Court case along those lines to make the point.[131]

The same was not true with partisan gerrymandering claims. The same states that had won the two most recent US Supreme Court gerrymandering cases—Pennsylvania (*Vieth*) and North Carolina (*Rucho*)—later lost state court cases under their state constitutions. The second shot prevailed in both cases. The Pennsylvania Supreme Court decision also came before *Rucho*, making it easier for the Court to say something it could not say in *Baker* and *Reynolds*: that state court and other local solutions remained a legitimate way for handling these issues. During oral argument and in the *Rucho* opinion itself, the Court mentioned the prospect of local solutions to these issues.[132] Recent experiences show that state courts can be as promising as federal courts in enforcing constitutional guarantees, sometimes more so.

State-federal sequencing. In the face of little textual or historical support for partisan-gerrymandering claims, in the face of difficulty identifying a workable constitutional test, and in the face of state court openness to such claims, there is room for skepticism about the strategy behind the *Rucho* litigation. Why ask the US Supreme Court to embrace a test that no state had yet implemented? When litigation tries to break new ground, as this litigation assuredly did, federalism and the possibility of state court experimentation that goes with it offer a promising way for federal courts to assess such claims without abdicating their duty to enforce discernible constitutional requirements. Sometimes the US Supreme Court should hesitate when it is asked to operate as one national laboratory to try out never-before-implemented solutions.

At a minimum, this is the kind of litigation in which claimants would have done well to test run innovative claims and innovative solutions in the state courts at the outset. Why not require trial and error in the state courts under state constitutions? Let the claimants prove the courage of their legal position by convincing state courts to adopt and implement this theory or that one, particularly in an area with considerable overlap between the state and federal claims.

The 2020s are not the 1950s. State courts today have not shut the door on such claims and have been just as willing as the federal courts, sometimes more willing, to consider the claims—and even to grant relief from time to time. It is not as if the claimants and other supporters of this institutional litigation did not have time to try out one approach or another. *Davis v. Bendemer* was decided in *1986.* That left plenty of time to develop the right method, the perfect algorithm, or some other insight suitable for national resolution of these claims. By 2019, however, just one court, the Pennsylvania Supreme Court, had attempted to articulate a general standard for assessing such claims—and it developed an approach better suited for one state than for the whole country. No one in *Rucho,* best I can tell, proposed that the US Supreme Court adopt the Pennsylvania approach as the national solution for these claims. That is fine of course. But it may suggest that gerrymandering claims were not ready for nationwide acceptance.

It is no criticism of the Pennsylvania and North Carolina courts to say that, in this area of civic-minded grasps for solutions, the state courts have yet to identify a workable approach suitable for export— and national implementation by the US Constitution. No state, notably, has yet tried the approach suggested in *Rucho,* whether by the challenger or the amicus groups, for identifying outlier and unconstitutional re-districting plans. The claimants still seem stuck on identifying a meaningful line between (1) the kind of partisan gerrymandering that has been with us since the beginning and (2) the kind of extreme partisan gerrymandering American constitutions should prohibit.

That is the regrettable news for proponents of a national gerrymandering solution. *Rucho* is a glaring stop sign when it comes to federal claims of this sort, and the states have yet to identify any approach suitable for the US Constitution.

The silver lining is that claimants not only have an extant shot under the state constitution, but they also have the chance to identify a workable solution for federal claims over time. If challengers manage to identify an approach that works in state courts because it can be enforced in principled ways, nothing prohibits a return to federal court. Just ask Georgians who were the subject of *Bowers v. Hardwick.*[133] They later convinced the Georgia Supreme Court to adopt a state constitutional prohibition against barring sodomy[134] and paved the way for others to return to the US Supreme Court to convince it to overrule *Bowers* in *Lawrence v. Texas.*[135] Or ask the losing side in *Baker v. Nelson.*[136] It followed a similar path in convincing the Massachusetts High Court to recognize a right to same-sex marriage and eventually convinced the US Supreme Court to overrule *Baker* in *Obergefell*.[137]

No doubt, the approaching 2020 elections placed the *Rucho* North Carolina and Maryland litigants on the clock. No doubt, they thought their best hope lay in the federal courts at that point, though the North Carolina litigants need not have thought so in retrospect. And perhaps they worried about getting the case to the US Supreme Court before Justice Kennedy retired. But all of this confirms the worst fears of such litigation: that it suffers from its own efforts at cherry picking votes. When litigants wish to change existing constitutional norms and when they have no clear textual and historical hook in the US Constitution to do so, is it asking too much to expect them to develop the theory in the states and obtain support for it there first? Otherwise, it looks like a supreme form of gerrymandering of its own.

Other state options. The states not only offer a venue for auditioning potential national solutions to this problem, but they also offer a rich source of state-customized approaches to fix, or at least ameliorate, the problem at the local level. That's why *Rucho* did not "condemn complaints about districting to echo into a void."[138] The people have heard the cry and begun to take notice of the pernicious effects of extreme partisan gerrymandering. Start with state constitutional amendments targeted at limiting partisan gerrymandering. Florida added a "Fair Districts Amendment" to its constitution, prohibiting a districting plan from being "drawn with the intent to favor or disfavor a political party."[139] The amendment was not window dressing. The Florida Supreme Court invoked the provision in invalidating a congressional re-districting plan in 2015, making it the third state court to use state law to correct a partisan gerrymander in recent years.[140]

Other states have enacted statutes to similar effect. Since 2016, the Iowa Code has mandated that "no district shall be drawn for the purpose of favoring a political party, incumbent legislator or member of Congress, or other person or group."[141] Following suit, the Delaware Code says that no districts shall "be created so as to unduly favor any person or political party."[142]

Another local option is to delegate reapportionment decisions to independent commissions. Nine states—Alaska, Arizona, California, Colorado, Idaho, Michigan, Montana, Utah, and Washington—have taken this path, some through constitutional amendments.[143] The commissions seek to avoid partisan considerations in drawing maps and often operate under mandates to hew to traditional re-districting criteria or even proportionality. Different states have made different choices about what their commissions' criteria should be, aptly charting courses of their own in addressing this complex problem. In Colorado, the commission members must strive to maximize the number of competitive districts.[144] In states like New Jersey, they use politician commissioners who, instead of striving for neutrality, strive to balance openly partisan actors.[145] That approach respects a pointed question by Alexander Bickel: "Is it irrational and does it represent *no* policy to wish to maintain two-party balance in a State of predominantly Democratic registration by ensuring Republican control of one house of the legislature?"[146] A two-party system does not work well if a state has just one party with power.

The use of commissions to draw legislative maps calls to mind the use of commissions to select state court judges, suggesting a warning sign of its own. In both types of delegations, the commission purports to distance political actors from decision making *and* tends to undermine accountability for those decisions. Just as it is difficult to squeeze the politics out of judicial selection, it may prove difficult to squeeze the politics out of legislative map drawing. Time will inform how independent the commissions are and how neutral and acceptable the people find their choices.

Another potential solution is for states to require bipartisan majorities in re-districting legislation. Ohio took this route. With a wide spectrum of support in the state legislature, it amended the Ohio Constitution to require a baseline threshold of 50% of each of the major parties in the legislature to vote in favor of a new map. If the legislature fails to adopt a map in this way, a commission of the governor, auditor, secretary of state, and four legislators will suggest a map. If that plan doesn't pass the legislature, the voting requirement becomes lower for the legislature, but it has to follow stricter rules for what the map may and may not include.[147]

Whether the future lies with imposing strict requirements on legislatures to follow in creating maps or with creating independent commissions that draw the maps, these kinds of proposals have considerable popular support. In 2018, five states—Ohio, Colorado, Michigan, Utah, and Missouri—put constitutional changes to re-districting processes on the ballot.[148] All of them passed. Ohio's new requirements won 75% of the vote.[149] Colorado's independent re-districting commissions for state and federal re-districting both won 71%.[150] Only in Utah, where the Speaker of the House opposed the initiative, was the vote close.[151] The public does not seem to be looking the other way on this issue. State legislators in the future may opt to favor more neutral maps either out of a sense of duty to the electorate or out of a healthy fear of losing their jobs. At some point, there may be no higher law or better branch of government to sort this out than the people through the constitutional initiative process, traditional consti-tutional amendments, or the election of new representatives to their legislatures.

The role of Congress. As each of these approaches potentially works out local solutions, Congress also has a partial role to play. The Elections Clause of the US Constitution, recall, provides that "the Times, Places and Manner of holding Elections for Senators and Representatives, shall be prescribed in each state by the Legislature thereof; but the Congress may at any time by Law make or alter such Regulations, except as to the Places of chusing Senators."[152] In various reapportionment acts between 1842 and 1928, Congress used this power to impose conditions on how states may draw their districts, including requirements that districts be single member, that they be composed of "compact territory," even that they contain "as nearly as practicable an equal number of inhabitants."[153] Congress lifted these requirements in the Reapportionment Act of 1929, which capped the size of the House of Representatives and auto-mated future congressional reapportionment processes.[154] But nothing prevents Congress from reimposing some of the earlier requirements, something Chief Justice Roberts and Justice Frankfurter pointed out in justifying their positions that the courts should not enter the re-districting briar patch.[155]

The Elections Clause does not give Congress the same plenary au-thority to regulate state legislative elections. That general power starts with the states and sometimes ends there. Congress's supplementary power in the area exists for federal regulations of state elections to pro-hibit voting discrimination based on race (the Fifteenth Amendment), sex (the Nineteenth Amendment), and age (the Twenty-Sixth Amendment). Given the increasing political valence of gerrymandering, a future Congress could well use this authority to try to affect the re-districting decisions of the states.[156] Then there's the possibility that if it opts to exercise its paramount authority to regulate congressional re-districting, it will use that example to encourage the states to follow the course it lays out. At a minimum, Congress has authority to do what it has done before: use its constitutional power to try to bring more reason and less self-interest to congressional maps.

Future role of the state courts. The state and federal legislative options on the table, together with the realistic possibility of state constitu-tional amendments, take us back to an initial point: the role of the state courts and the question of whether they remain a useful means of reform. Not every state, it is true, has improved matters through direct or indirect democracy. And plenty of extreme gerrymanders, it is also true, likely remain. These gaps explain why many people still advocate an active role for state courts in fighting extreme gerrymandering.[157] Given the success of the Pennsylvania, North Carolina, and Florida lawsuits, many state courts, it takes little imagination to anticipate, will face challenges over the new maps once they become law in 2021.

In thinking about this litigation, two competing questions come to mind. Facing one way: How could anyone be critical of litiga-tion that seeks to enforce specific or fairly specific constitutional or statutory guarantees? The Florida Supreme Court's 2015 decision en-forced the people's recent amendment to their constitution on this precise issue. Other state constitutional guarantees, like the election-specific constitutional guarantee of "free and equal" elections found in thirteen state constitutions, also offer election-specific guarantees, if highly generalized guarantees, to enforce.[158] Even when these kinds of decisions err, they affect just one state, not the country. And they allow the people of that one state to take matters into their own hands.

Facing the other way: Have the state courts come to grips with the challenge of deriving judicially manageable tests from the more general of these constitutional guarantees and have they come to ap-preciate the costs to the courts of decisions that look as political as the gerrymandered districts? As the Pennsylvania and North Carolina experiences show, those decisions require more judicial policymaking than most people would accept, at least with a veil of ignorance about which political party won. As with all constitutional questions, state-level trial and error lowers the risks. But that doesn't mean state-level attempts to create neutral, judicially manageable standards to evaluate gerrymandering claims will work or are cost free.

Keep in mind why a simple solution—pure proportionality—has not generated widespread acceptance at the state or federal level. So many accepted features of American government do not have it. Take the popular election of two US senators from every state no matter how few voters live in the state. Did the Fourteenth Amendment on reflection compel the later Seventeenth Amendment, which required the direct election of senators rather than allowing state legislatures to select them? Or is the Fourteenth Amendment incompatible with the Senate, a body in which California has as much representation as Wyoming? Or consider the electoral college, which permits the election of a president who did not win the popular vote. Or the three-quarters threshold for changing the US Constitution, which allows just thirteen states, no matter how sparsely populated, to block any proposed amendments to it. And never forget judicial review, which allows unrepresentative courts to strike down popular laws, surely a feature of American government at odds with a view that majority rule and proportionality are the ultimate benchmarks of republican government. The US Constitution and most state constitutions have one feature after another that does not turn on pure majority rule or proportional representation.

All of this makes re-districting look like parenting. Trying is often the most a legislature can do. And humility is the watchword for courts assessing their work. Identifying judicially enforceable standards inevitably seems to come back to identifying hard-to-pin-down theories about the best form of representative government. Absent state constitutional or statutory clauses that impose direct and discernible limits on gerrymandering, it's hard to know where to begin. In Alexander Bickel's (and Louis Jaffe's) framing, it is either the case that "legislative apportionment is a matter of the sort for which we have no rules" or the problem is one "to which rules are applicable, though they 'should be only among the numerous relevant considerations.' "[159] Under either option, judicial efforts to address the point should not pretend they have access to information and insights that legislators do not. That makes it "a task of pragmatic trial and error to construct representative, deliberative institutions that are responsive to the views, the interests and the aspirations of heterogenous total constituencies."[160] Sound apportionment, seconds Herbert Wechsler, requires a "government responsive to the will of the full national constituency, without loss of responsiveness to lesser voices, reflecting smaller bodies of opinion, in areas that constitute their own legitimate concern."[161] In the end, back to Bickel, "apportionment is a very high percentage of politics with a very small admixture of definable principle."[162] Unless the constitutional guarantees are reserved merely for negating occasional state "temper tantrums"[163] or "an orgy of inactivity,"[164] judicial line drawing about the starting and stopping place of the constitution remains a perplexing task, one that even the best judges may not be equipped to handle.

If state court judges opt to enter the fray, they may wish to think about judicial involvement from another perspective. The people in a state, a court may opt to assume, trust judges more than legislatures to fix new societal problems such as extreme gerrymandering. But that does not alter what the judges are doing. It just means the people want the judges to do it. When push comes to shove and societal (or political) pressures prompt a state court to act in what amount to legislative ways, the court should accept the tools and limits of legislators even as they act as judges. That means borrowing from other state experiences, whether legislative or judicial. It means using compromise on the court. It may support the election of judges. It surely supports term limits for judges. And it may support more representative high courts, bigger and more broadly representative state courts with some positions reserved for some segments of the state. It also should mean that stare decisis has little role to play with the decisions that come out of this judicial process. How can judges engage in trial-and-error experimentation if the errors are locked in place for future generations? Stability in constitutional law must give way when judges perform policymaking tasks. Else, to borrow from Lincoln, the only law left standing will be stare decisis. Any other approach is gerrymandering by another name: locking in one view of apportionment that favors one party with no possibility of change or compromise between competing views.

One last consideration, in truth one last question: Is the flexibility of state courts unlimited when it comes to enforcing state constitutional guarantees in this area? Recall that the Pennsylvania Supreme Court eventually created *its own* re-districting map for the 2018 election. That may be entirely permissible for state legislative races and a matter for Pennsylvanians alone to control. But it is not clear whether it is permissible for federal congressional races. Article I of the US Constitution gives "the Legislature" of each state authority to make the rules for such elections. Query whether a state map drawn by a state court counts as the legislature. A similar issue arises when state courts, as opposed to state legislatures, revise the time, place, and manner of federal elections, whether for representatives or senators under Article I or presidential electors under Article II. The 2000 presidential election implicated this issue, and the 2020 elections led to all manner of disputes about it.[165]

PART IV

Federalism Within Federalism

9

Local Governments

WHEN THE AMERICAN COLONIES broke from Great Britain, the issue was not just "home rule"; it was "who should rule at home," as Robert Williams and Carl Becker remind us.[1] What counts as "home" and who should "rule" there have meant different things to different people. In 1776, home rule meant the transfer of power from Parliament to the newly created state legislatures or the fledgling Continental Congress. But few Americans today think of state or federal legislatures as the objective of home rule. Greater control over the destiny of local communities is what many proponents of change want today, and in some ways this parallels the complaints of 1776.

Think of it as federalism within federalism or, depending on taste, cities' rights within states' rights. Like federalism, local power allows smaller groups of citizens to audition innovative fixes to policy challenges and to customize solutions to a discrete group of people and place. But like federalism, it also creates friction over when to keep things local and when to keep things more general for the larger government. Just as federalism offers a path for ameliorating friction between polarized views and an option short of winner take all, so the same is true of municipal governments. But just as federalism generates debates about who decides (the national government or a state?), so does local government law (the state or a local government?). Local government offers gears-within-gears benefits and challenges, both a new source of solutions for today's problems and a new source for dividing opinion about how best to govern. What the US Supreme Court has said in lauding the virtues of federalism applies with equal measure to state and municipal powers. It permits "local policies more sensitive to the diverse needs of a heterogeneous society, permits innovation and experimentation, enables greater citizen involvement in democratic processes, and makes government more responsive by putting the states in competition for a mobile citizenry."[2]

The Federal Story

In one sense, there is little to say about the US Constitution and local governments. The national charter, as Richard Briffault observes, "treats state-local relations as almost entirely a matter for the states."[3] So far as the federal charter is concerned, the operative political bodies in American government are the United States, the fifty states, and the tribal governments. The US Constitution never mentions "city," "county," or "township," not even "local" or "municipal" governments.[4] It concerns itself only with sovereign entities: the national government, the states, Native American tribes, and foreign countries. The implication is that the federal charter governs only the relationship between states and these other entities, not the relationship of local governments within each state. The US Supreme Court has made express what's implied. "A municipal corporation, created by a state for the better ordering of government, has no privileges or immunities under the federal Constitution which it may invoke in opposition to the will of its creator."[5] Because local governments "cannot claim to be sovereigns"[6] and because whatever power a local government has tends to flow from delegations by its state, that sounds like the end of the matter.

But local governments still exercise sovereign powers, including law enforcement, eminent domain, taxing, public education, zoning, and other indispensable "attributes of sovereignty."[7] Even if the US Constitution does not mention cities by name and even if cities cannot claim sovereign status, the federal charter still has ample consequences for municipal governments. The national government interacts with local governments every day, and the US Constitution offers ways to safeguard individuals from municipalities and to block national initiatives taken against municipalities. As agents of the states, they can be restricted by the US Constitution *and* they can invoke its protections. Federal individual rights guarantees limit the authority of cities and city officials. Much of federal individual rights law indeed grows out of cases involving individuals who invoked the Fourteenth Amendment and comparable guarantees against cities, counties, and townships as well as the people who lead them. At the same time, federal structural guarantees and federal individual rights safeguard local governments from "state attempts to control the political discretion of towns and cities,"[8] as in *Romer v. Evans*[9] and *Washington v. Seattle School District No. 1*,[10] and sometimes even to prevent encroachment by the national government.

Pull *Printz v. United States* off the shelf for a good example of a case in which federal structural protections affected local governments.[11] Jay Printz was the sheriff of Ravalli County, Montana, and Richard Mack was the sheriff for Graham County, Arizona. In 1993, they sued the national government, challenging the constitutionality of a provision of the Brady Act that required the "chief law enforcement officer" of each local government to perform background checks of handgun purchasers. The act required the sheriffs, after learning of a proposed sale, to "make a reasonable effort to ascertain within 5 business days whether receipt or possession would be in violation of [federal] law, including research in whatever State and local recordkeeping systems are available and in a national system designated by the Attorney General."[12] In a 5–4 decision written by Justice Scalia, the Court ruled that the provision violated the Tenth Amendment and core principles of sovereignty and protected the sheriffs from "being pressed into federal service."[13] In doing so, it built on an earlier decision, *New York v. United States*,[14] that prohibited Congress from requiring state legislatures to enact laws as part of a federal program, one to dispose of nuclear waste in that instance.

Justice Scalia started his opinion by noting that earlier Congresses never used "this highly attractive power."[15] Neither was there any public understanding that the US Constitution would give Congress such authority.[16] In establishing a system of "dual sovereignty," the states may have "surrendered" many powers to the national government but they still retained "a residuary and inviolable sovereignty," leaving "a Constitution that confers upon Congress the power to regulate individuals, not states" and not local officials.[17] What made this approach a "great innovation," he explained, "was that our citizens would have two political capacities, one state and one federal, each protected from incursion by the other—a legal system unprecedented in form and design, establishing two orders of government, each with its own direct relationship, its own privity, its own set of mutual rights and obligations to the people who sustain it and are governed by it."[18] Quoting Madison, he added: "The local or municipal authorities form distinct and independent portions of the supremacy, no more subject, within their respective spheres, to the general authority than the general authority is subject to them, within its own sphere."[19] "This separation of the two spheres," he emphasized, "is one of the Constitution's structural protections of liberty." But the authority of the national government "would be augmented immeasurably if it were able to impress into its service—and at no cost to itself—the police officers of the 50 States."[20] Echoing his dissent in *Morrison v. Olson*, Justice Scalia insisted that this is the administrative responsibility of the president, not congressionally deputized sheriffs throughout the country.[21]

Just as "Congress cannot compel the States to enact or enforce a federal regulatory program," he concluded, so it "cannot circumvent that prohibition by conscripting the State's officers directly." The national government "may neither issue directives requiring the states to address particular problems, nor command the states' officers, or those of their political subdivisions, to administer or enforce a federal regulatory program."[22]

Any doubt about the durability of this anti-commandeering principle was put to bed in *Murphy v. National Collegiate Athletic Association*.[23] By a 7–2 vote, the Court invalidated the Professional and Amateur Sports Protection Act of 1992, which required state legislatures to adopt laws banning sports gambling. The lopsided nature of the vote confirmed the vitality of the anti-commandeering principle, whether applied to state legislatures or local sheriffs.

That has not gone unnoticed. Many cities have invoked the doctrine as a defense to recent presidential orders requiring local assistance in enforcing the country's immigration laws, whether by requiring them to obtain and share information about illegal immigrants within their jurisdictions or by threatening to withhold federal funds from cities that do not support the federal efforts.[24] Expect to see more of this sort of litigation between the national government and cities over time. All that's needed to trigger it is disagreement between the national government and American cities over a politically fraught policy—and aggressive assertions of power in one direction or the other.

The no-commandeering bar of the Tenth Amendment is not the only way local governments can push back against regulation by the national government. It's one of many. Some of the US Supreme Court's most important division-of-power cases arose from challenges by cities to federal laws. Think of *City of Boerne v. Flores*, in which a city successfully challenged the application of the Religious Freedom Restoration Act of 1993 to it on the ground that it exceeded Congress's authority under section 5 of the Fourteenth Amendment.[25] So too for *National League of Cities v. Usery*, in which a city (for a time) successfully established that Congress could not regulate the working conditions of local employees.[26]

The State (and Local) Stories

If any sovereign should appreciate the virtues of local government, it should be the states. The key premise of federalism is localism, the principle of subsidiarity—that some problems are best resolved by a smaller government, one closest to, hence most educated about, the problem at hand. Everything useful about federalism—that it "promotes choice, competition, participation, experimentation, and the diffusion of power," in the helpful words of Heather Gerken[27]—is just as true at the municipal level. Probably more so, as "most of the subnational governance that federalism protects," Richard Briffault adds, "actually occurs at the local level."[28] The push and pull between states and the national government often turns on answering the same questions about larger geographical units. Which government is best equipped to solve the problem? Is there one best answer to the underlying policy problem? Would experimentation be beneficial? The US Constitution has little to say about how states organize their governments, including whether states delegate power over certain matters to their local governments. Cities in truth generally do not have federal "constitutional rights against their states,"[29] save for the occasional types of equal protection claims mentioned above. That leaves the policy considerations of who's best equipped to solve a problem and how best to try out new approaches to it with state constitutions and state legislation.

With a century-deep culture of town meeting government in New England by 1776, one might have expected the new state constitutions to place considerable constitutional authority in local governments. As a matter of state constitutional structure, that did not happen with the small towns or large cities, even if local communities largely continued to govern themselves. America, unlike Europe or for that matter ancient Rome or Greece, has no tradition of city-states. The pertinent unit of power relative to Great Britain was the colonial government, and when the colonies became states, that unit of government for the most part and with some variations along the way remained the key one relative to the new national government.

But even if influential cities did not become city-states and even if the key units of sovereignty became the federal and state governments, that did not mean the local governments lacked the customary features of a sovereign power. They not only acted like sovereigns in many ways, but they also looked like them. Local governments in most ways mirror the structure of the national and state governments. They have charters, mayors, unicameral city councils, courts, and agency-like commissions. Separation of powers sometimes applies there too, as we will see.

States began adding provisions to their constitutions that regulated the relationship between the state and municipal governments in the mid-nineteenth century, as the local governments grew frustrated with twin evils: arbitrary, sometimes petty, oversight of local governments, and negligent, sometimes intentional, neglect of local conditions. In the 1850s, as John Dinan has shown, states began adding constitutional provisions that barred their legislatures from enacting "local or special laws."[30] Michigan wrote the first one at a convention that led to its 1850 Constitution. It dealt just with roads and prohibited the legislature from eliminating "any road laid out by commissioners of highways or any street in any city or village."[31] The Indiana 1851 Constitution created the first general prohibition, which banned the passage of "local or special laws" on a variety of subjects, including "county and township business."[32] It became de rigueur for states to include such prohibitions, and most have them now.[33] The idea behind them was easy to see. They were designed to "protect[]" "cities of the state against legislative encroachment."[34] The no-special-law principle forced state legislatures to enact general laws, say for cities with more than 50,000 residents, as opposed to parochial legislation designed to tinker with one local charter or overrule one local policy.[35]

Some states added "ripper" laws later in the nineteenth century to similar effect. They prohibited the state from enacting laws that "remove"—rip—"certain tasks from cities and transfer them to state-appointed officials or commissions."[36] By 1900, at least eight states had adopted them: Pennsylvania, New Jersey, Colorado, California, Montana, South Dakota, Wyoming, and Utah.[37] They took aim not just at improving government but also at curbing corrupt government. Pennsylvania's prohibition, the first in the country according to Dinan, grew out of a state law that created a "self-perpetuating commission" in Philadelphia that "could require the city council to provide an unlimited sum of money for the construction of public buildings," money spent neither wisely nor honestly too much of the time.[38]

These laws became a preamble for the key state constitutional innovation in this area: home rule guarantees. Instead of restricting how state legislatures regulated local governments, they licensed local governments to regulate. Instead of "placing restraints" on state legislatures, they "empower[ed] local citizens with the ability to articulate their preferences over institutional forms and functional powers within their local communities."[39]

Ohio (and Linndale)

Before we turn to the state and city stories that prompted many of these innovations, it is useful to look at these issues through the lens of a most pedestrian of local disputes: speed traps.

It usually takes a village of more than 200 residents to catch the attention of state legislators. Not so for Linndale, Ohio.[40] Located just outside of Cleveland, Linndale has 179 residents and thirty-five residential homes,[41] and occupies less than a square mile. Running through Linndale is about 450 yards of Interstate Highway 71, a section of the highway that connects downtown Cleveland to Columbus and many towns in between. For most people, Linndale is a drive-by city, not a destination or home. Interstate 71 does not even offer an exit for Linndale.

That did not stop the powers that be of this municipal government from establishing their relevance. With one eye focused on prohibiting speeding and one eye focused on filling the local fisc, Linndale began stationing officers in the 1960s on their stretch of Interstate 71. The officers were vigilant—and profitable. Before long, Linndale gained a reputation for an unforgiving speed trap. In some years, Linndale generated nearly $1 million from traffic violations alone.

Not everyone appreciated this laboratory of home rule. Linndale's policing of the highway rubbed many people the wrong way. Word of the speed trap made its way to Ed Kasputis, then a representative in the Ohio state legislature, who heard about Linndale's revenue-raising efforts from an employee of a nearby company. Kasputis went to Linndale's municipal court to see for himself. He discovered several disgruntled drivers being told to pay up or face consequences. Although Linndale officials did not take ticketed individuals to the county jail for their offenses, Kasputis observed, they threatened to do so and extracted their pound of fines in the process.

Kasputis did something about it. He introduced a bill in the Ohio legislature that would prohibit local police from handing out speeding tickets on this highway if fewer than 880 yards of highway cross through their town, a generally written rule but hardly an ignorantly written rule. Because Linndale fell under the 880-yard mark, the bill would shut down Linndale's speed trap. The bill became law in 1994.

Now it became Linndale's turn to challenge an oppressive government. It sued the state based on the home rule provision of the Ohio Constitution.[42] The amendment grants Ohio municipalities "authority to exercise all powers of local self-government and to adopt and enforce within their limits such local police, sanitary and other similar regulations, as are not in conflict with general laws."[43] Many of the things that the first part of the guarantee gives to municipalities are potentially taken away by the last words, that local laws may not "conflict with general laws." If a state law regulating local self-government is not "general," however, that makes it unconstitutional.

According to the Supreme Court of Ohio, "general" laws tend to be "statutes setting forth police, sanitary, or other similar regulations and not statutes which purport only to grant or to limit the legislative powers of a municipal corporation."[44] Another measure of a general law, it said, is one that "operat[es] uniformly throughout the state" and "prescrib[es] a rule of conduct on citizens generally."[45] The Ohio Supreme Court agreed with Linndale that the law was not general, reasoning that the law was "simply a limit on the legislative powers of municipal corporations to adopt and enforce specified police regulations."[46] Because the law was "not a part of a system of uniform statewide regulation on the subject of traffic law enforcement,"[47] it was unconstitutional. Linndale had a constitutional right to create a speed trap.

The victory had a ten-year shelf life. About a decade later, another bill passed, this one also prompted by Linndale's law-enforcement and revenue-raising efforts. The legislature took a safer path. The new bill stipulated that villages falling under a certain population would be required to dissolve their mayor's courts. The bill originally set the threshold at 150 residents but increased the threshold to 200 after the 2010 census revealed Linndale's population, 179 residents. Without a mayor's court, Linndale still could issue tickets, but the tickets would be processed outside of the municipality. Linndale's ticket revenue went into free fall.

Linndale sued again. This time it lost.[48] To this day, Ohio law prohibits municipal corporations with under 200 residents from holding mayor's courts.[49] So ended one speed trap.

But it did not end the town's creativity when it comes to raising revenue. Undaunted, Linndale placed speeding cameras near the town's busiest street. Located close to Cleveland, Linndale had plenty of traffic, which meant plenty of opportunities for the cameras to catch unsuspecting speeders. After being caught speeding on camera, a motorist would receive a ticket directly in the mail. What made this work is that each ticket amounted to a civil infraction, not a criminal one, and thus did not require a court for processing. All ticket proceeds went to the village. Linndale ended up making *more* money with the cameras than it did with the speed trap.

Ohio legislators did not like that either. After Linndale set up the cameras, the legislature passed a bill that prohibited the use of traffic cameras unless an officer was "present at the location of the device."[50] In response, the village stationed an unmarked police cruiser near the cameras to ensure they were always in sight of an officer. Long shifts in a cruiser became uncomfortable for the officers, however, prompting Linndale to try something else. Within sight of the cameras, the village built a small hut for officers, complete with a TV, microwave, and refrigerator.

Back to court the two sides went. In 2017, the Ohio Supreme Court invalidated this state law as unconstitutional under Ohio's Home Rule Amendment in *City of Dayton v. State*.[51] Again, the case turned on whether the law was a "general" law. The court used a four-factor test to gauge the point. To be a general law, it "must (1) be part of a statewide and comprehensive legislative enactment, (2) apply to all parts of the state alike and operate uniformly throughout the state, (3) set forth police, sanitary, or similar regulations, rather than purport only to grant or limit legislative power of a municipal corporation to set forth police, sanitary, or similar regulations, and (4) prescribe a rule of conduct upon citizens generally."[52]

Because the state's traffic camera law did not pass this test, the court invalidated it. The court maintained that "requiring an officer's presence at a traffic camera directly contradicts the purpose of a traffic camera" and "tells municipalities how to use their law-enforcement resources when enforcing their traffic laws, thereby limiting municipalities' legislative power."[53] The court held that the regulation "infringe[d] on municipalities' home-rule authority without serving an overriding state interest."[54]

After the decision, the Ohio legislature passed a nearly identical regulation, but this time in the context of additional requirements.[55] Presumably, the new regulation is designed to appear more "general" and, hope springs eternal, withstand the court's scrutiny. Whether it can do so remains to be seen. If local history is any guide, one thing seems certain. Linndale will keep looking for ways to work around the new law. Constitutional protections for local authority can go a long way, even for the smallest of cities.

Iowa (and Clinton)

Additional perspective on the tale of Linndale comes from two competing approaches to municipal power. One is skeptical of any local power not expressly granted by the state. The other is open to inherent local power to regulate some matters.

The dominant approach in the area owes its origin to a leading scholar and state court judge of the era, John Dillon. He served on the Iowa Supreme Court from 1862 to 1868 (and as chief justice for the last two years) and wrote *Municipal Corporations*, the leading treatise on local government of its time. President Grant eventually nominated him to be a federal judge. Perhaps seeing life tenure as a life sentence, he resigned from the bench in 1879 and spent the rest of his life back in the state of his birth, New York, where he taught at Columbia and Yale Law Schools and practiced law.

Before leaving the Midwest, Dillon wrote several opinions for the Iowa Supreme Court that became the cornerstone of what's now called Dillon's Rule and elaborated on all of it in his influential treatise. At issue in *City of Clinton v. The Cedar Rapids & Missouri River R.R. Co.*[56] was another transportation dispute, a classic conflict of the era between a municipal corporation (the city of Clinton) and a private railroad (the Cedar Rapids & Missouri River Railroad Company). In 1859, the Clinton City Council passed an ordinance that barred any "railroad company from constructing its track through or upon any streets within the limits of the city." A railroad company wished to lay tracks between Cedar Rapids and Council Bluffs. And in 1867, over the objection of the city, it entered the streets to begin its construction project, relying in part on authority from the state to do so.

What counted: permission of the city to use the land for its railroad tracks? Permission of the state? Or both? In his opinion for the Iowa Supreme Court, Chief Justice Dillon explained that the state grant of permission was all that the railroad needed. He framed the debate this way: "Has the legislature given to the municipality of Clinton such power that it can defeat the construction of a railroad required by public law and demanded by public utility?"

His answer created a *presumption against local power* and turned on the thinking that any power of the city came from the state, whether through its constitution or legislation. He expressed the point in this way:

> Municipal corporations owe their origin to, and derive their powers and rights wholly from, the legislature. It breathes into them the breath of life, without which they cannot exist. As it creates, so it may destroy. If it may destroy, it may abridge and control. Unless there is some constitutional limitation . . . the legislature might, by a single act, if we can suppose it capable of so great a folly and so great a wrong, sweep from existence all of the municipal corporations in the State, and the corporation could not prevent it. We know of no limitation on this right so far as the corporations themselves are concerned. They are, so to phrase it, the mere tenants at will of the legislature.[57]

This approach created a predisposition against local power. [58] As he put it in his treatise: "Any fair, reasonable, doubt concerning the existence of power is resolved by the courts against the [municipal] corporation, and the power is denied."[59] Unless the state legislature clearly gave the city power over the matter, Dillon's Rule said it had none.[60] As then-professor, now-judge David Barron puts it, Dillon's Rule means "that state law alone defines the scope of local governmental independence."[61]

Thirty-one states currently follow Dillon's Rule and its presumption against local autonomy and authority.[62] Iowa is not one of them.[63] While it became a home rule state, it does not follow the approach of its own John Dillon.

Michigan (and Detroit)

Self-government at the local level generated similar debates in other midwestern states in the nineteenth century. Count Michigan as one of them. It has the honor of calling home one of the leading state and federal constitutional scholars of the era, maybe *the* leading scholar. Like Dillon, Thomas Cooley served as a chief justice, in his case as the leader of the Michigan Supreme Court. And like Dillon, Cooley was a professor. He was the dean of the University of Michigan Law School and wrote many influential books and treatises, including *A Treatise on the Constitutional Limitations Which Rest Upon the Legislative Power of the States of the American Union*, perhaps the most widely read treatise of its day. Cooley understood state constitutional law and helped to shape it.

That makes his concurring thoughts in *People v. Hurlbut*,[64] a case about the power of local governments to rule themselves, worth examining. Just three years after Chief Justice Dillon's *City of Clinton* decision, Cooley offered another way to look at it. At issue was the authority of the Michigan legislature to select the members of local boards of water commissions in Detroit. The court held that the state legislature could not select the local commissioners.

In his concurring opinion, then-Justice Cooley went above and beyond the question at hand. Those were "matters of secondary importance," he thought, which should not obscure "a question of the highest interest and concern," one that cannot "be answered without a careful scrutiny of the structure of our government and an examination of the principles which underlie free institutions in America."[65] He proceeded to do just that. The essential "question, broadly and nakedly stated, can be nothing short of this: Whether local self-government in this state is or is not a mere privilege, conceded by the legislature in its discretion, and which may be withdrawn at any time at pleasure?"[66]

In undertaking this examination of the extent of the right of self-representation at the local level, Cooley, ever the scholar, invoked all manner of historical precedents and references. He acknowledged the prevailing assumptions: that "the state creates the municipal bodies," that these "corporate entities are mere agencies which the state employs for the convenience of government, clothing them for the time being with a portion of its sovereignty, but recalling the whole or any part thereof whenever the necessity or usefulness of the delegation is no longer apparent."[67] But "such maxims" had limits. The state constitutions "have taken great pains to surround life, liberty, and property of the individual with guarantees, but we have not, as a general thing, guarded local government with similar protections."[68] But that did not deny the possibility that such limits could be implied. The Michigan Constitution, like other state constitutions, was adopted in the immediate context of local rule—"a system of local government, well understood and tolerably uniform in character, existing from the very earliest settlement of the country, never for a moment suspended or displaced, and the continued existence of which is assumed" and "the liberties of the people have generally been supposed to spring from, and be dependent upon that system."[69]

He then looked to history and de Tocqueville, who spoke "of our system of local government as *the American system*," one contrasted "forcibly with the French idea of centralization, under the influence of which constitutional freedom has hitherto proved impossible."[70] A few pages of history later, with invocations of Jefferson, Story, and the New England town meeting form of government, he reached for his central message: Local governments have inherent power to rule themselves. For the people who "framed our institutions," "it has been an axiom" that "our system was one of checks and balances"—that "each department of the government was a check upon the others, and each grade of government upon the rest." These municipalities, he thought, arose "under the protection of certain fundamental principles which no power in the state could override or disregard."[71] Even if the state legislature "may [mold] local institutions according to its views of policy or expediency," "local government" remains a "matter of absolute right," and "the state cannot take it away."[72] All in all, "when the state reaches out and draws to itself" those "powers" that "from time immemorial have been locally possessed and exercised, and introduces into its legislation the centralizing ideas of continental Europe, under which despotism, whether of monarch or commune, alone has flourished, we seem forced back upon and compelled to take up and defend the plainest and most primary axioms of free government, as if even in Anglican liberty, which has been gained step by step, through extorted charters and bills of rights, the punishment of kings and the overthrow of dynasties, nothing was settled and nothing established."[73] The "right" of "the state is a right, not to run and operate the machinery of local government, but to provide for and put it in motion."[74]

Powerful though it is, this was not the language of a purist. As Cooley acknowledged, the conventional approaches to municipal power all were grounded in the text of the federal and state constitutions. But "some things," he added before making his key pitch, were "too plain to be written" and turned on traditions and common law norm shifting— "usages," "customs," things that "have sprung from the habits of life, modes of thoughts, methods of trying facts by the neighborhood, and mutual responsibility in neighborhood interests."[75]

What drove Cooley, says Judge Barron, was the goal that "every one has a right to . . . be governed by general rules."[76] Legislative interference with local government, Cooley feared, did the opposite. That orientation "led him to distrust public attempts to empower the private realm."[77] In these ways, "the judicial protection of the local community from state interference served as a means by which the individual right to equal administration of the laws could be protected."[78]

Cooley's approach was consistent with other developments. As shown in earlier chapters and as will be shown in Chapter 10, the people became more skeptical of state legislatures over time. Hence the many restrictions placed on them in the nineteenth and early twentieth centuries through constitutional amendments together with countless devolutions of power away from state legislatures. Treating municipal governments as another bulwark—another "check" on state legislatures—made sense in this context. It avoided the problem of "class legislation" and other state legislative efforts to favor some over others.[79]

For all of Thomas Cooley's remarkable influence on the path of state (and federal) constitutional law as a Michigan Supreme Court chief justice and as a leading constitutional scholar, this was not destined to be one of those areas. The Cooley approach "has been applied by the courts of very few states" and "even in these states its application has been limited."[80] Perhaps that owes to the difficulty of identifying a rule of decision, of identifying a judicially enforceable line between explicit and inherent municipal power. The influence of the Cooley approach does not even extend to Michigan, as it turns out. By 2006, after intervening constitutional conventions and amendments, the Michigan Supreme Court had little good to say about this form of local control. "Local governments have no inherent jurisdiction to make laws or adopt regulations of government; they are governments of enumerated powers, acting by a delegated authority; so that while the State legislature may exercise such powers of government [that] are not expressly or impliedly prohibited, the local authorities can exercise those only which are expressly or impliedly conferred."[81] All has not been forgotten in Michigan, however, when it comes to Cooley. Even as the state leaves ultimate control with its legislature, it still says that the broad "powers" of "Michigan's cities and villages" under the Michigan Constitution of 1963 "over municipal concerns, property and government are to be liberally construed."[82]

Cooley's approach and Dillon's Rule have come to define the poles of local governmental power. While these two scholars and state court judges came to dominate the national debate during their lives and after them, they had little success in the one place in which home rule should have been easiest: their own communities. Prophets they no doubt were, just not in their own towns and states.

Missouri (and St. Louis)

Against the backdrop of the Dillon/Cooley debate, states eventually took matters into their own hands. They added home rule provisions to their state constitutions, provisions that honor Cooley's emphasis on local control and Dillon's perspective that the state should oversee the authority of local government. Missouri gets credit for creating the first of these guarantees. In its Constitution of 1875, it added this provision: "Any city having a population of more than one hundred thousand inhabitants may frame a charter for its own government consistent with and subject to the Constitution and laws of this State."[83] St. Louis prompted the change. The new provision made the city an "imperium in imperio," a government within a government, under the state's home rule amendment.[84]

One explanation for the amendment had little to do with whether Dillon or Cooley was right. It had to do with time and knowledge. The home rule amendment allowed the Missouri legislature to focus on statewide matters and to leave the nitty gritty of local politics to the people of St. Louis. As one speaker at Missouri's 1875 convention put it: "If there is any one thing I would wish to keep out of the Legislature, it is legislation upon St. Louis affairs. It has created more confusion & trouble in the Legislature & has done more to prolong the session than anything else & I am in favor of giving as far as possible to the people of St. Louis the regulation of their whole internal affairs."[85]

Missouri paved a path that others soon followed. Three more states—California, Washington, and Minnesota—added home rule provisions to their constitutions before the end of the century.[86] Nine more states approved them in the first two decades of the twentieth century.[87] Many more were added in the decades that followed, and Dinan tells us that more than half the states have strong home-rule protections in their constitutions today.[88] "All but three states make some provision for home rule," Briffault says, with home rule "grounded in the state constitution" in "forty-one states."[89] Six more states provide for home rule through statutes.[90]

Why have these guarantees? Start with American preferences for "self governance," as Cooley pointed out and as John Dinan reminds us today.[91] To obtain "real self-government," "all those, and only those, who are appreciably affected by governmental activities," Dinan relays, "should have a voice as to what that government should be."[92] Absent home rule, "the people of the cities are left in a position where they have absolutely no control over their own destinies," leaving no mechanism "to stir up civic pride and political activity" and local "responsibility" for their wherewithal.[93] The people closest to a city charter were apt to be the most informed about what it should say and the most responsive to problems that arose under it.

New York (and New York City)

The governing challenges of today's cities sometimes create separation-of-powers problems that mirror those that arise in the states and the national government. One example turns on delegation of policymaking power and its cousin—administrative deference—under municipal charters of government. As Nestor Davidson helpfully has shown, a substantial body of administrative law operates in our cities and towns under these charters,[94] an observation confirmed by this example.

A decade or so ago, New York City sought to curb consumption of soft drinks—"soda" to some, "pop" to others, "sugary drinks" to New Yorkers. To that end, the New York City Board of Health adopted a "Sugary Drinks Portion Cap Rule" that prohibited the sale of soft drinks in containers that exceeded sixteen ounces. Claimants challenged the rule on the ground that the board overstepped its power.[95] As they saw it, the city's charter allocated this lawmaking power to the city council or the state legislature, not to agencies of the city.

Any "food service establishment," the rule said, "may not sell, offer, or provide a sugary drink in a cup or container that is able to contain more than 16 fluid ounces." The rule thus did not ban soft drinks; it just made it difficult to get super-sized containers of them.

In an opinion by Judge Eugene Pigott, the New York Court of Appeals invalidated the rule on local separation-of-powers grounds.[96] Under the New York City Charter, he explained, the city council is "the sole legislative branch of City government; it is '*the* legislative body of the city vested with the legislative power of the city.'" Consistent with the New York Constitution, he added, "'every local government shall have a legislative body elected by the people thereof,'" and "that elective body in New York City is the City Council." He rejected the argument that "the Board of Health is a unique body that has inherent legislative authority." To the contrary, the "Charter contains no suggestion that the Board of Health has the authority to create laws." Not just New York Constitution's and the city charter's division of powers undermined the rule's validity. So too did "practical" considerations, such as "the difficulties that would arise from treating the Board and the City Council as coequal legislative bodies." How, the court wanted to know, would anyone understand "what the law in New York City" is "were the Board to pass a health 'law' that directly conflicted with a local law of the City Council"? In the end, "the Board's authority, like that of any other administrative agency, is restricted to promulgating 'rules necessary to carry out the powers and duties delegated to it' by 'state or local law.'"

Having determined that the board had authority only to regulate, not legislate, the court proceeded to consider whether the sugary drinks rule amounted to a permissible regulation. No is the short answer. Even if the board had authority to "balance" some health "costs and benefits" in the area, the court explained, it still had to be able to point to guidelines established by the city council that it was implementing. Instead of "balancing costs and benefits according to preexisting guidelines," the rule embraced "value judgments" that entailed complex choices "reserved to the legislative branch." Because the board adopted the rule "without benefit of legislative guidance," because it "did not simply fill in details guided by independent legislation," and because in the last analysis "there was no legislative articulation of health policy goals associated with consumption of sugary beverages upon which to ground the Portion Cap Rule," the court invalidated the rule as "policymaking" that exceeded its authority.

Home rule ultimately permits more governments within governments. That combines the sweet of local control with the bitter of local separation-of-power imperatives, as the New York City Board of Health now knows. But these three-dimensional division-of-power debates don't change anything in one respect. They take us back to the same question, just on a different plane: Who gets to decide?

Local Governments: Gears Within Gears Within Gears

What do so many cross-cutting layers of American government say about us? That we as a country believe in the capacity of government to do good, and that's why we have so much of it? Or that we distrust government so much that we insist on checking and dividing it in as many ways as possible? A qualified Yes to both questions hits the mark and is consistent with deep, if conflicting, strands of American history. What is the state of municipal power today? How, if at all, should it be changed?

First, an oddity of modern political discourse is its obsession with national power and relative ignorance of local power. Short of an attack on our borders, a deep recession, or some other existential threat to the country, most government policy that affects us directly occurs at the local level. Take a few seconds to think about it. How do we get water, electricity, and natural gas into our homes? How do we get rid of our waste? Where do we go for food? Where are our children educated? What streets do we use to commute to work? Where are our parks and other communal spaces? Where do we worship? Whom do we call if someone breaks into our house or threatens our security? Where do we own property? Where indeed do we live? Local at every turn.

What is closest to home is also usually the best place to think about reform. What is the best place to try out a new policy initiative? Where is it easiest to obtain acceptance of an innovative idea? Where is it least costly if the innovation goes awry? Whether it is the rhythms of daily life or efforts to change them, it is hard to deny the import of place, each local community.

But what should matter to us greatly—how local government works—is more often accompanied by a deep reservoir of apathy or a happy-go-lucky attitude. It would be one thing if that is how we also reacted to national or even state politics. But that is assuredly not the case. A few decades ago, a national poll showed that more than half of Americans, 52%, did not know their state had a constitution.[97] Confirming the plight of local government law, the poll did not even ask about cities. The poll thus did not add these questions: Did you know your city has its own constitution, a charter? Or do you know how power is allocated in your city? Yes, the typical American knows when their property taxes increase, when the sanitation department alters the rules for collecting trash, or when the city council changes the speed limit. But ask who does what at the local level and be prepared to meet an awkward gaze. Think about that. We tend to understand the electoral college, the Senate's filibuster rules, the president's veto power, and the tenure and health of US Supreme Court justices. But we have little idea how the levers of power and policy work in our backyards. For reasons all our own, Americans "do not think of local governments, such as towns and cities, as important components of the federal constitutional structure."[98] Perhaps that's what made Robert Caro's *The Power Broker* so remarkable. He convinced us to read a book about a man most of us had never heard of, Robert Moses, the New York City Parks commissioner, and a man who understood these levers of power and knew how to make them work to his and others' advantage.

But that's an exception to a prevailing truth. We care least about what affects us most. Judge Barron has come to a similar conclusion. "Too much of our daily experience with self-government occurs at the local level for us to dismiss localism as an embarrassing feature of constitutional democracy. Local governments are too central to the lives of too many people to serve as passive administrative agents of state majorities without an independent interest in enforcing constitutional norms."[99] The question on the table is whether that lack of engagement has undermined local government law and whether it needs renewed attention, particularly in its interrelation with state and federal constitutional law.

Second, in thinking about the future, it's helpful to recall the Cooley/ Dillon debate about the nature of local government and its source(s) of authority. Was the power of a local government merely derivative of a state's delegation of power to the municipality, as Dillon claimed? Were cities, then, merely like other state agencies, able to act only when the state delegated power to them and elsewise engaged in *ultra vires* lawmaking? Or was there a part of local government authority that was inherent, as Cooley claimed? A part of local government protected by our state and federal constitutions' implied reflection of an American tradition of self-government—"too plain to be written"?[100]

Framed by two of the most distinguished state court judges and scholars of the nineteenth century, the debate might have been expected to end with a prominent role for judges. It did not. The people by and large sorted out the key rules by themselves, mainly through amendments to state constitutions, in some instances by state lawmaking. With Missouri's passage of a home rule constitutional amendment in 1875, the state lit the way for other states, now almost all states, to resolve the debate in a manner that tipped its hat to Dillon *and* Cooley: Dillon because he thought that state constitutions and legislation were the only legitimate sources of local power, and Cooley because the placement of home rule provisions in state constitutions embraced the virtues of self-government that he exalted in his *Hurlbut* opinion as a treasured component of the American political tradition.

Sky-high consequences surrounded the debate at the start. It would have changed the division of powers equation significantly if, in the last 150 years, the state and federal courts had used the American tradition of local self-government to innovate judicially enforceable safeguards about when cities may act only with the permission of their state and when they have inherent rights to govern themselves. For those unhappy with the position of local power today, "Cooley's City," in Judge Barron's welcoming phrase, is not a bad place to start.[101] With fifty state constitutions to pick from and fifty traditions to consider, it is well within the plausible to think that a state in the future might embrace some of Cooley's insights to sort out a state/municipal conflict. No matter what happens, those insights remain relevant to states that alter this constitutional protection in the future.

Third, even if the people ended up making the key choices about the balance between state and local power through home rule amendments of various sorts to their constitutions, that did not sideline judges from state/local conflicts. Judge Dillon made another contribution in the area—Dillon's Rule—a lasting feature of local government law. Consistent with his view that local power is delegated power, Dillon's Rule creates a presumption against local power. In a case in which it is unclear whether the state has delegated power to a city, the city loses. Here we have a debate that lingers and may be intensifying. Owing to the growing divide between some Republican-controlled state legislatures and some Democrat-controlled cities, there has been an increase in tension between the two forms of government. Some of it is fueled by the growing economic power of cities. As of 2017, ten cities in the country generated "$6.8 trillion in economic value," "more than the collective output of thirty-seven states."[102] Some of it is fueled by state efforts to preempt local lawmaking on controversial topics: gun regulation; environmental initiatives; taxation; plastic bag restrictions.[103] Pick a public policy topic with any political resonance to it, and the odds are high it has generated local preemption debates. Anything that divides the country nationally tends to divide states and cities.

While these divisions have led to more fights over "states' delegations and preemptions of local legal authority,"[104] the controversies rarely turn on structural questions, such as: May the State delegate power to the local level? May the State preempt this local power? Yes and Yes, at least until someone creates Cooley's City. Those are today's givens. The debate instead has shifted to what policy disputes the state legislature should preempt, a fight customarily (though not invariably) between the priorities of blue city councils and red state legislatures. And that debate resembles some trends in the use of the constitutional initiative at the state level. Instead of using the initiative to restructure state government, the initiative has come to be used most frequently to take a stand on policy issues of the day, especially ones the voters have developed convictions over.

Today's conflicts between cities and legislatures call to mind the gerrymandering complaints of the 1950s and 1960s. Then, cities claimed they lacked the power in state government they deserved because the legislatures had not changed the voting districts since 1900. Now cities claim they lack the power in state government they deserve in part due to lingering gerrymandering complaints and in part due to frustrations over lack of authority to adopt local policies of their own.

Presumptions often make a difference when turf wars go to the courts. That raises the question of whether we should accommodate local variations by flipping the presumption. Many scholars think so. Eight of the top local government scholars in the country recently wrote a paper for the National League of Cities, "Principles of Home Rule for the Twenty-First Century," that features the point.[105] It proposes a model home rule provision for state constitutions (or state legislation) that reinforces home rule and places significant restrictions on states before they may preempt local lawmaking. It converts Dillon's Rule into Cooley's Rule: "The state shall not be held to have denied a home rule government any power or function unless it does so expressly."[106] And it limits state efforts to restrict home rule: "The state may expressly deny a home rule government a power or function . . . only if necessary to serve a substantial state interest, only if narrowly tailored to that interest, and only by general law."[107]

Not all states will embrace this approach. And for now, the long-term neutrality of the approach and its local-customs virtues are apt to get caught up in motivated thinking about what these changes would mean for substantive policy choices. While it's understandably difficult for elected officials facing the ballot box to ignore the current preferences of their constituents on the policy debates that drive them, whether gun regulation, speeding tickets, limits on sugary drinks, or plastic bag bans, it is useful to remember that the same experimental benefits of federalism for a country can work for a state.

Just because a state follows Dillon's Rule, moreover, that does not mean little local power exists. "As the data shows, there is no substantial link between the Dillon Rule and less local authority."[108] That may be because home rule and Dillon's Rule complement each other, and the people either make suitable amendments to their constitutions in response to it or add legislation that clarifies local lawmaking power. But this sword has another edge. The less likely it is that Dillon's Rule will make a difference in creating the right balance of power between states and cities, the more debatable it is that states should transform it into Cooley's Rule.

Fourth, whatever states choose to do in amending home rule constitutional provisions or that their courts potentially do in identifying presumptive limits on state authority over localities, there seems to be little room for federal constitutional innovation. For some time, the US Supreme Court has accepted the agency theory of local government. In 1907, it observed that "municipal corporations are political subdivisions of the state, created as convenient agencies for exercising such of the governmental powers of the state as may be entrusted to them," and that the state "at its pleasure may modify or withdraw all such powers."[109] Other than state-imposed limitations on local government that violate federal individual rights guarantees, as in *Romer v. Evans* under the Fourteenth Amendment, it is hard to see room for more federal court involvement in the area, at least based on the ideas proposed thus far. Plus, few complain that the US Supreme Court's largely hands-off approach to the relationship of the states to their municipal governments has created long-term damage anyway.

The Tenth Amendment, even so, seems to distinguish the people's powers from the states' powers. It says: "The powers not delegated to the United States by the Constitution, nor prohibited by it to the states, are reserved to the states respectively, or to the people." We may know what reserving powers to the "states" means. But what does reserving those same powers to the "people" mean? Is it a doublet, a shorthand for emphasizing the powers of the states? Does it refer to their power to ratify new constitutions or to other powers of the states as authorized or circumscribed by their citizenries? Or does it refer to their power over local governments? There are many questions there, but no one to my knowledge has shown how the answers to any of them lead to significant federal constitutional limitations on state regulation of local governments.

Fifth, local government law is one of the few areas in which the people largely have taken control of their own fate, leaving little room for significant state and federal court involvement over local structure. Whatever stand one takes on current and past debates in the area, they have tended to be worked out in democratic ways, not through the courts for the most part. That raises a paradox in American constitutional law. The state and federal courts have innovated least in the area most likely to affect local government and innovated most in the areas least likely to affect our day-to-day affairs. How unusual that we have so much constitutional litigation over general phrases that have all kinds of impact on policy and government today. But through it all, we have declined to innovate inherent limitations on state regulation of local power—of perhaps the right that matters most to us, the right of self-government at home. It's not as if this is an obscure area of experience. It happens to be the one form of local help and local limits that people see every day.

Hamilton's observations in *Federalist* 17 hint at the beginning of an explanation. "It is a known fact in human nature, that its affections are commonly weak in proportion to the distance or diffusiveness of the object. Upon the same principle that a man is more attached to his family than to his neighborhood, to his neighborhood than to the community at large, the people of each State are apt to feel a stronger bias towards their local governments than towards the government of the Union." Even if Americans may not know they have city charters and may not be able to describe the finer points of their local governments, they instinctively seem to be best suited to impact the direction of those governments closest to home. Local knowledge and local understanding lead to greater efficiency and fairness in deciding what local regulations should be. Democracy indeed may work most effectively at the local level today.

PART V

The Amendment Process

10

Amending Constitutions to Meet Changing Circumstances

JUST AS LITTLE DISTANCE (twenty-one miles) separates Monticello and Montpelier, few ideas separated the worldviews of Thomas Jefferson and James Madison. They agreed on most of the key debates at the founding, they became political partners, they became sequential presidents of the United States, and they were two of the most pivotal authors of change at the founding, one given credit for the Declaration of Independence, the other credit for the Bill of Rights. But they did not agree about a signal feature of a constitution: How often should it be amended? If these two Virginians could not agree about the answer, be prepared for a vexing topic.

Jefferson insisted that all constitutions should provide each generation with an opportunity to choose its own form of government. Fearful of dead hand control, in which the living had little influence over the rules of power created by a long-gone generation, he wrote:

Let us provide in our Constitution for its revision at stated periods. What these periods should be, nature herself indicates. By the European tables of mortality, of the adults living at any one moment of time, a majority will be dead in about nineteen years. At the end of that period then, a new majority is come into place; or, in other words, a new generation. Each generation is as independent as the one preceding, as that was of all which had gone before. It has then, like them, a right to choose for itself the form of government it believes most promotive of its own happiness; and it is for the peace and good of mankind, that a solemn opportunity of doing this every nineteen or twenty years, should be provided by the constitution.[1]

Madison staked out a different view. As he explained in *Federalist* No. 49, a readily amendable constitution would undermine stability.[2] The longevity of a constitution would promote veneration for it, making it critical that charters be altered sparingly.[3] His ever-present fear of government by factions also made him skeptical of changeable constitutions.[4] For him and for many in the founding generation, legislatures were the place to look for accommodating change. The people's representatives would come from their own communities and thus would be receptive to their evolving needs, meaning that the legislature, as he put it in *Federalist* No. 51, rightfully "predominates" in a republic. "It seemed preposterous to worry that a legislative assembly composed of one's friends and neighbors," usually "subject to annual popular election, "would impinge on the other branches of government or endanger liberty."[5] There would be little need to change constitutions with legislatures exercising most of the power and freshly elected legislators replenishing their ranks—at least, that was, "until the states" and the people lived through "the experience of an untrammeled legislature."[6]

Who won? The national government has followed Madison, while the states have followed Jefferson. The United States has had just one Constitution, and the states have had 144 constitutions since the founding, an average of just under three apiece.[7] The US Constitution has been amended twenty-seven times, and the state constitutions have been amended 7,586 times (as of the beginning of 2017), an average of 150 amendments apiece.[8] John Dinan, the author of a highly accessible resource on this topic, *State Constitutional Politics*, confirms what one would expect: "Every state constitution is amended more frequently than the US Constitution."[9]

Who was right? That takes more development and a few more considerations to answer.

Whether it is the creation of a new constitution or the amendment of an old one, both actions are designed to correct a short-sighted provision or to deal with altered circumstances. It is revealing to contrast how the US Constitution and the state constitutions have adapted to new understandings and shifting conditions—and to see how the competing visions of Jefferson and Madison have played out roughly halfway into America's third century.

Constitutions say who is in charge. Amendments remind politicians that it is not them. The capacity to change a constitution respects a truth in any democracy, that the people hold the ultimate reins on power. When, and how often, the people should be able to grasp that power is harder to sort out. The ready amendability of state constitutions over time has placed the people more directly in charge at the state level than at the federal level in many ways. Consider these state-only increases in the people's control over their governments through constitutional amendments: direct democracy in the form of initiatives and referenda, direct election of judges, term limits on legislators, direct election of various members of the executive branch.[10] What does it say about American government that where the people can readily change their constitutions, they have constantly done so to obtain more control over their leaders, all the while deepening the chasm between the same people's disparate control of their state and federal leaders? Does it raise a red flag to have two increasingly different forms of government at the national and state levels? Or do the differences reflect what is appropriate for two distinct types of government?

The Federal Story

The United States of America has held just one constitutional convention, the Philadelphia Convention of 1787. Since then, our national constitution has undergone twenty-seven amendments. The key impediment to change is Article V, which has always required ratification by three-quarters of the states, a most Madisonian of provisions when it comes to perpetuating longevity and generating venerability.

Obtaining such a super-majority vote is a back-breaking lift, accomplished seventeen times since the people ratified the Bill of Rights in 1791, just fifteen times after netting out the addition and subtraction of the Prohibition amendments. This rate of amendment does not reflect a lack of effort. More than 10,000 amendments to it have been proposed.[11] Hard as the US Constitution is to amend, the Articles of

Confederation were harder still. They required 100% support by the states, and starting in 1781 operated more like a treaty in determining the power of the Continental Congress until 1789, once the drafters of the US Constitution agreed to permit it to go into effect if three-quarters of the states ratified it.

The federal charter's amendment rate, as John Dinan computes it, comes to 0.12 amendments per year since 1789 and to a 0.07 rate since 1791.[12] With 144 state constitutions since the founding, no state constitution is harder to amend or has been amended less frequently than the US Constitution.[13] The state with the most glacial rate of change is Vermont, whose current constitution has been amended 0.24 times per year, still a pace leaving the United States far in the distance.[14] Widening the lens, the US Constitution, says Donald Lutz, is the most difficult constitution in the world to amend among countries with shared political traditions, and only the Australian Constitution has a less frequent amendment rate among its cohorts.[15]

The difficulty of amending the US Constitution stands out in other ways. It betrays a salient premise of the charter or at least is in tension with it. A key reason for separating power in every direction was the conviction that men and women, even if capable of growth through education and religion, remained fallible. That explains the Framers' singular obsession with forbidding concentrations of power. No leader could be trusted to keep the people's interests ever at heart. But if perfection, even consistent virtue, would elude citizens and the representatives they elect, that would suggest that the US Constitution itself would have flaws—that the authors of it would not anticipate every future contingency, that the charter would have unintended consequences, that *it* would need to be amended. Did the Framers appreciate everyone else's imperfection but their own? All constitutions eventually become monuments to humility.

One unintended consequence of making the Constitution nearly impervious to amendment, when combined with its provision for life tenure of US Supreme Court justices and its implied license to the federal courts to review the constitutionality of state and federal laws, was to dilute another defining premise of the charter: the checks-and-balances imperative. If the US Constitution gave just one branch of government the final say over interpretation of the charter in the cases before it and if those interpretations could rarely be corrected by the people through an amendment, that left the federal courts doing a lot of checking and rarely being checked in return.

One reason for allowing amendments to a constitution that permits judicial review is to correct decisions that misapprehend it. But how often have the people overruled decisions of the final federal decision maker, the US Supreme Court? At the outset, it looked like that might become commonplace. In 1793, just four years after ratification, the US Supreme Court decided *Chisholm v. Georgia*, permitting a citizen of South Carolina to sue the state of Georgia in federal court to recover a Revolutionary War debt from the state.[16] The Court rejected Georgia's claim that, as a sovereign state, it could not be sued without its consent. Just two years later, the people offered their opinion on the matter. They overruled *Chisholm* by ratifying the Eleventh Amendment, which returned to the states their immunity from suit, save with their consent or save with the use of a congressional power that permissibly overrode it. Twelve of the then-fifteen states ratified the amendment by February 1795. South Carolina did so in 1797, and New Jersey and Pennsylvania never took a position on it.[17]

What could have been a traditional way of responding to uncongenial US Supreme Court decisions never took root. It has only happened a few more times. Most famously, the people responded in similar fashion to *Dred Scott*,[18] an 1857 decision whose list of sins is hard to top: a refusal to treat African Americans as citizens, an endorsement of treating African Americans as property, an invalidation of Congress's most recent effort to placate the competing sides (the Missouri Compromise), and a trigger for the Civil War. Through the Thirteenth, Fourteenth, and Fifteenth Amendments, the people overruled this decision and offered affirmative protections against future acts of race discrimination along with other protections.

Just four more overrulings followed these two—four more times in which the people rejected US Supreme Court constitutional decisions. The people overruled *Pollock v. Farmers' Loan & Trust Co.*—that the federal government could not impose an income tax—with the Sixteenth Amendment.[19] They effectively overruled *Minor v. Happersett*—upholding a Missouri law that prohibited women like Virginia Minor from voting—with the Nineteenth Amendment.[20] They effectively overruled *Breedlove v. Suttles*—permitting a Georgia poll tax—with the Twenty-Fourth Amendment, which barred such taxes in the context of federal elections.[21] And they overruled *Oregon v. Mitchell*—prohibiting Congress from extending the right to vote to eighteen-year-olds—with the Twenty-Sixth Amendment.[22] That's just six cases through eight amendments. Is it really the case that the US Supreme Court has made just six mistakes that it did not correct itself over two centuries?[23] One price of the Madisonian three-quarters requirement is a dearth of corrective amendments, and the near impossibility of dialogue between the people and the Court over the correct meaning of our constitution.

What areas have the people prioritized in using this difficult-to-deploy power? How often have they used amendments to create new individual rights (due to new social norms) or to change the structure of government (due to new balance-of-power concerns)? Of the twenty-seven federal amendments, we need not worry about two because launching Prohibition and returning it to harbor became a wash. That leaves twenty-five amendments. Mindful that the line between individual rights and structure sometimes blurs, the breakdown reveals these priorities.

Fifteen of the amendments address individual rights. That's the first nine amendments plus the three Civil War Amendments (prohibiting slavery; applying the Due Process, Equal Protection, and Privileges and Immunities Clauses to the states; and prohibiting race-based denials of the right to vote), the Nineteenth Amendment (giving women the right to vote), the Twenty-Fourth Amendment (outlawing poll taxes), and the Twenty-Sixth Amendment (extending the right to vote to those eighteen and over). While all of these provisions promote individual rights, it is well to remember that they also rebalance power because they give the state *and* federal courts a role in enforcing these federal constitutional guarantees. The Fourteenth Amendment in particular has given the federal courts considerable power over state legislatures and the state executive branches.

The other ten amendments deal directly with structure. For those keeping score, two of the structural provisions promote state authority. The Tenth Amendment underscores that powers not delegated to the United States through the US Constitution are "reserved to the States." And the Eleventh Amendment limits the federal judicial power when it comes to lawsuits filed by individuals against states. Two of these amendments enhance federal power and federal prestige. The Sixteenth Amendment permits Congress to enact a federal income tax. And the Seventeenth Amendment permits the popular election of US senators, making them directly accountable to the people rather than to the state legislatures that once selected them and enhancing their station as independent federal officials. One of the amendments, the Twenty-Second, places a limit on executive power by limiting presidents to two terms. Another amendment, the Twenty-Seventh, modestly limits legislative power by requiring a new election to take place before an increase in congressional pay becomes effective.

The rest of the amendments have less to do with rebalancing power and more to do with filling gaps in existing structural guarantees. The Twelfth Amendment refines the rules for presidential elections, all under the umbrella of the state-heavy electoral college. The Twentieth Amendment establishes rules for presidential vacancies and terms. The Twenty-Third Amendment creates rules for presidential electors from the District of Columbia. And the Twenty-Fifth Amendment adds more rules to handle the contingency of a presidential vacancy or disability.

Whether it's federal changes to constitutional structure or individual rights, or recalibrating power throughout, the key tool for handling shifting national norms and the live-and-learn lessons of experience *has not been* amendments to the US Constitution. Instead, congressional lawmaking, executive branch orders, administrative agencies, and US Supreme Court decisions have been the leading agents of change at the federal level. Most conspicuous has been the US Supreme Court's interpretations of constitutional guarantees, either because they facilitated broader exercises of national power by the elected branches and agencies or because they innovated new individual rights over which the federal courts took custody.

Whether it counts as a legitimate justification or not, necessity has been the proverbial parent of invention.[24] Article V's three-quarters ratification requirement stymied realistic hopes of amending the constitution to deal with urgent matters—say, presidential power during a war, congressional power to enact the New Deal in the midst of a depression, or judicial power to curb the indignities of Jim Crow.

Maybe it is not worth worrying about these end runs around the amendment process given that the people over time have come to accept many of these decisions. Scholars note that the national high court usually is more of a follower than a leader when it comes to constitutional innovation, issuing decisions that reflect the world they live in and thus amending the constitution by interpretation in ways that Jefferson might have approved: decisions that simply dignify the preferences of the living over those of the dead.[25] That may be right in the main.

But whether this approach will work throughout our third century remains to be seen. It is one thing to say that an inventive US Supreme Court decision reflects the preferences of a majority of Americans. It is quite another to show that it reflects a super-majority preference or for that matter a three-quarters preference. The stakes of these decisions and the potential resentment generated by them drop considerably if they reflect societal norms demonstrated in the states through state court decisions or legislation—and reflect the kind of super-majority sentiments required to amend the charter. If not, it is hard to understand why this approach is consistent with another national norm, our collective distaste for gerrymandering.

There is another risk with amendment by interpretation. The stakes are highest at the federal level, giving citizens and interest groups every incentive to keep returning to this well until it goes dry. So far, that has meant that a constitutional amendment through Article V on anything remotely controversial has become a tool of the distant past, one few people take seriously today, one most people would insist is naïve.

Take stock of this transformation through the lens of how we as Americans handled our ancestors' views of gender. When women sought to obtain the right to vote, they first tried to include it in the Fourteenth Amendment.[26] That did not work, whether because the country was not open to it or the federal courts were not ready for it. Then they shifted their efforts to the states. That did work. One state after another, particularly states in the West, added the protection to their constitutions or legislation.[27] With the groundwork laid in the states, it became easier to ratify the Nineteenth Amendment—and meet the three-quarters requirement—in 1920.

Shift to gender equality beyond the right to vote. In 1923, three years after the Nineteenth Amendment became law, Crystal Eastman and Alice Paul introduced in Congress an amendment to guarantee equal treatment regardless of sex. That effort took roughly as long as the extension of the right to vote, but it ended up taking a different route. In 1972, Congress finally approved an Equal Rights Amendment through the leadership of Michigan representative Martha Griffiths and submitted it to the state legislatures for ratification before March 22, 1979. In the first two years, thirty states supported it.[28] By 1977, thirty-five states had approved the ERA. In a country with fifty states, that meant the proponents needed just three more states to get to the thirty-eight-state finish line. Put another way, thirteen is the blocking number, the modest number of states needed to stop an amendment.[29] The momentum slowed, and the amendment fell short, as no other state supported it by that deadline or by the extension of the deadline to 1982.[30]

That did not end the story. A Supreme Court decision did. In 1996, *United States v. Virginia* presented the question whether the Fourteenth Amendment's Equal Protection Clause prohibited the Virginia Military Institute, a state military school, from denying admission to women.[31] The Court said it did and prohibited VMI from enforcing its admissions policy. In an opinion by Justice Ginsburg, the Court applied "heightened" and "skeptical" scrutiny to the policy.[32]

After the VMI decision, it is fair to ask what the ERA could have accomplished that *United States v. Virginia* did not. More than that, it is fair to wonder what the Nineteenth Amendment does that *United States v. Virginia* does not. Does anyone think that a state could deny women the right to vote under the Fourteenth Amendment after this decision? It gave the proponents of the ERA and the Nineteenth Amendment everything they wanted, except a constitutional amendment in the case of the ERA.

Reflect on how far we have come. One of the US Supreme Court's inaugural decisions, *Chisholm v. Georgia*, was reversed two years later by a constitutional amendment in 1795. From the Seneca Falls Convention to ratification of the Nineteenth Amendment, it took roughly three-quarters of a century to give women the constitutional right to vote. From the first iteration of the Equal Rights Amendment in 1923 to

United States v. Virginia in 1996, it took roughly another three-quarters of a century to give women the constitutional right to equal protection. But this time, it took a Court decision, one that effectively overruled prior Court decisions like *Minor* and *Bradwell v. Illinois*.[33]

Does anyone think that citizens and interest groups have missed the point? Who can deny that obtaining five votes in the US Supreme Court is easier than obtaining majorities in two houses of thirty-eight state legislatures (or one-house Nebraska)? People are rational actors, often self-interested actors, and they will continue to pursue amendment by interpretation as long as it works. Among the many questions prompted by this trend in American government and by the 201-year journey from *Chisholm v. Georgia*/the Eleventh Amendment to the Equal Rights Amendment/*United States v. Virginia* is this one: Why are the state approaches to constitutional change so different?

The State Stories

If the key gauge of federal constitutional history comes through interpretation of the US Constitution by the US Supreme Court, not amendments by the people, the same cannot be said about state constitutional history and state courts. Almost everything you need to know about state constitutional guarantees, whether about structure or individual rights, comes from amendments to our fifty state constitutions. Generally speaking, it's all there in one place, the constitutions themselves. What's "indisputable," confirms Alan Tarr, "is that today's state constitutions were established at various points in the nation's history, reflecting the political ideas reigning at those particular points in time, and that this in turn has affected the institutions that were created and the relationships established among them. Even within specific states, one can trace how the constitutional text has changed over time to reflect shifting political ideas."[34] So it is that "virtually every state's constitution reflects similar changes in orientation. As a result, those interpreting state constitutions must be prepared to act as constitutional geologists, examining the textual layers from various eras in order to arrive at their interpretation."[35]

In juxtaposition to the federal approach, the Jeffersonian view has taken hold in the states. They have handled changed circumstances by changing their constitutions frequently and copiously through many conventions and many amendments. In responding to debates about the frequency of amendments that the Virginia Constitution should allow, Jefferson put it this way:

> Some men look at constitutions with sanctimonious reverence, and deem them like the ark of the covenant, too sacred to be touched. They ascribe to the men of the preceding age a wisdom more than human, and suppose what they did to be beyond amendment. I knew that age well; I belonged to it, and labored with it. . . . But I know also that laws and institutions must go hand in hand with the progress of the human mind. Let us, as our sister states have done, avail ourselves of our reason and experience, to correct the crude essays of our first and unexperienced, although wise, virtuous, and well-meaning councils. And lastly, let us provide in our constitution for its revision at stated periods. Each generation is as independent as the one preceding, as that was of all which had gone before. It has then, like them, a right to choose for itself the form of government it believes most promotive of its own happiness.[36]

All states have embraced the Jeffersonian view in one way or another. Whether in changes to the organization of state governments, the balance of power among the branches, or above all the people's persistent efforts to obtain more direct power over the policy levers of government, the vehicles for bringing our state constitutions up to date invariably have been constitutional amendments. The relative ease of amending state constitutions makes them a wandering showcase of American history over what we prefer our governments to do in various epochs and at various places. When the people have the option of amending their constitution with a 51% vote, as nearly every state constitution provides, they are apt to use that option frequently to deal with changing values and priorities in society (especially when it comes to individual rights) and to deal with changing levels of confidence in this branch or that one (especially when it comes to governmental structure). If a 75% requirement at the federal level incentivized citizens to use the courts to account for changed circumstances, a 51% requirement at the state level incentivized citizens to use the amendment process to do the same.

Earlier chapters illustrate the theme; the whole book in truth illustrates the theme. The creation of the line-item veto, designed to give the governor more power and the legislature less, shows a changing assessment in the states of the power of the legislature and a way to curb it through gubernatorial line-item vetoes of appropriation bills. The creation of judicial elections reveals a comparable change, one designed to uplift the prestige and accountability of the judicial branch and to empower it to check legislative over-reach more aggressively. The direct election of many members of the executive branch is still another. The creation of process-based limitations on state legislation adds another, making it more difficult for the agents of the people to disregard the preferences of the people by bundling distinct subjects into one bill. On the individual rights side, one could identify all manner of new state constitutional rights created over the last two-and-a-half centuries, some consistent with, indeed the source of, national trends, others deeply local.

These state-level trends, all giving the people a firmer grasp on the levers of power, culminated in a natural place, the initiative. The adoption of the initiative by Oregon in 1902 became the most direct way, and eventually the way of eighteen states, for the people to influence directly the policies of the state by removing the middlemen: the legislature, the leaders of the executive branch, the agencies, the courts. Direct democracy eventually became the way of twenty-four states if one accounts for state constitutions that permit the people directly to amend their constitutions through initiatives or directly amend statutes through referenda.[37]

If that is where these trends culminated, how did they start? Initial designs of a formal amendment process originated in the state constitutions. The 1776 Pennsylvania Constitution authorized a convention to create a new constitution.[38] "By 1780," Donald Lutz tells us, "almost half the states had an amendment procedure, and the principle that the fundamental law could be altered piecemeal by popular will was firmly in place."[39] The first state constitutions to authorize amendments proposed by the legislature through super-majority votes and repeated approval by different legislatures, often after an election, came from Delaware and Maryland.[40]

Not until 1818 did a state establish that the people should ratify a legislatively approved amendment. That year, Connecticut required legislative support by a majority of the lower house, then reapproval by a two-thirds majority of both houses after an intervening election, then approval by a majority of the people.[41] Maine's 1820 constitution simplified matters by requiring two-thirds approval in both houses of the legislature once and ratification by a majority of the electorate after that.[42] As John Dinan points out, most states shifted to variations on this model through the rest of the nineteenth century, with states "generally follow[ing] Connecticut's approach" before 1850 and largely following Maine's approach after 1850.[43] All fifty states today permit their legislatures to write and propose amendments.[44] Beyond that, forty-one states require a majority vote of the people to ratify it, eight states require ratification by a super-majority vote, and only Delaware does not require the people to ratify a legislatively proposed amendment.[45]

Of the eight states requiring more than a simple majority for approval of an amendment, most do not raise the bar high. It borders on overstatement to say that four states (Hawaii, Minnesota, Tennessee, and Wyoming) require super-majority votes. They just demand that the amendment "obtain support of a majority of voters participating in the *election*," as opposed to the amendment vote. Illinois demands approval by "a majority of voters in the election or by three-fifths of votes cast on the amendment."

True super-majority requirements appear in just three states. Colorado requires "most amendments" to receive 55% approval of the "votes cast on the amendment," while Florida demands 60% approval of votes cast on it, and New Hampshire requires two-thirds support of the people voting on the amendment.[46] The key state norm, the key difference between the US Constitution and the states, is the prevailing requirement of a 51% vote by the people to approve nearly all state amendments, as opposed to majority votes in each house of each legislature in three-quarters of the states to approve a federal amendment. It is difficult to think of a greater difference between the two modes of change than this one—or a better explanation for the ease of obtaining traction in amending state constitutions and the difficulty of obtaining it in amending the federal charter.

Just over a third of the states, nineteen of them, still have their original constitutions, though with plenty of amendments to them.[47] The other thirty-one states have had at least two constitutional conventions, most of them more than that.[48] The total of 7,586 amendments to state constitutions in reality undercounts the number of state amendments, as it counts only amendments to the states' *current* constitutions.[49] The states with just one constitution, and those with the least frequently amended and most succinct constitutions, tend to be the early states, the ones that wrote constitutions when the federal Framers wrote the national charter and the ones that approved the federal charter. Massachusetts has kept its 1780 Constitution (the eldest here and abroad) and Vermont has kept its 1793 Constitution.[50] So too of the 1784 New Hampshire Constitution. More often, however, the state constitutions reveal a "layering" of the shifting norms throughout American history, remarks Robert Williams,[51] sometimes setting negative examples for national lawmaking, sometimes positive ones. The newest constitutions as it happens come from two of the oldest states: Rhode Island in 1986 and Georgia in 1983.[52] For every state constitutional provision that history has not favored, there are many that it has, including extension of the right to vote, women's rights, minority rights, and balanced-budget amendments, along with many others.[53]

Time and place have revealed five ways to update state constitutions: conventions, proposals by legislatures, initiatives, commissions, and "judicial interpretation."[54] State constitutions of course refer by name only to the first four of these approaches.

The convention route is the oldest and holds the potential to involve the people substantially in its formation and development. Forty-two states provide for conventions in their constitutions, and fourteen state constitutions, with Jefferson-colored eyes, require the people to be given a regular option to vote for a convention.[55] New York inaugurated this general referendum with its 1846 constitution. The Empire State and seven other states (Connecticut, Illinois, Maryland, Missouri, Nebraska, Ohio, and Oregon) now require a convention vote every twenty years, Michigan every sixteen years, four states (Alaska, Iowa, New Hampshire, and Rhode Island) every ten years, and Hawaii every nine years.[56] For all of the options to hold a new constitutional convention provided by these regular ballot opportunities, none of these states has voted for a convention in decades.

Eighteen states permit initiatives as a way for the people to directly amend their constitutions. Eight of them come from the West and Mountain West: Arizona, California, Colorado, Montana, Nevada, North Dakota, Oregon, and South Dakota. Six come from the Midwest: Illinois, Michigan, Missouri, Nebraska, Ohio, and Oklahoma. Three come from the South: Arkansas, Florida, and Mississippi. Just one comes from the East Coast or for that matter the original thirteen states: Massachusetts.[57]

Why have initiatives in over a third of our states? One explanation is that the other amendment sources (legislatures, conventions, commissions) come with the risk that the same problem that led to the need for an amendment—a political class "captured by interests seeking to preserve the status quo"—will stand in the way of any quest for change.[58] Another is the basic desire to remove the agent, to allow the people directly to vote for policies they prefer.

Direct democracy is not as direct or free-wheeling as it sounds. For the most part, initiatives may cover just one topic, and plenty of single-subject litigation has arisen over ballot proposals.[59] States with the initiative option all require a minimum number of petition signatures before the initiative goes on the ballot, mainly 3% to 15% of the votes cast in the last election for governor.[60] Usually the secretary of state, sometimes the governor or attorney general, must approve the language to ensure that it meets the requisite requirements, including clarity and accuracy in the title and summary, a set of duties that often leads to pre-voting litigation and sometimes to removing the initiative from the ballot.[61] Several state constitutions restrict topics subject to change by initiative. Two states, Massachusetts and Mississippi, prohibit initiatives from altering individual rights and other core guarantees in their constitutions.[62]

There is also a frequently litigated debate over whether the amendment amounts to a "general revision" suitable only for a convention or a single topic suitable for an initiative. A recent decision by the Michigan Supreme Court illustrates how such a controversy can arise and proves it can implicate impassioned policy debates. At issue was whether a voter-initiated amendment—to create a commission to oversee legislative redistricting—could be placed on the ballot.[63] The test was whether the initiative proposed "changes that do not significantly alter or abolish the form or structure of the government in a manner equivalent to creating a new constitution." Noting that the Michigan Constitution says that "all political power is inherent in the people," that the people adopted the initiative based on "popular distrust of the Legislative branch of our state government," and that this proposal was not akin to a "new constitution," it allowed the initiative to go forward. That approach is largely par for the course in other states.

While the initiative brings us direct democracy in its most full-flowering form, Alan Tarr shows the ways in which it shares populist tendencies with the convention approach to constitutional change: (1) "the membership of state constitutional conventions tended to mirror the populace of the states" and "did not tend to be professional politicians"; (2) "the people exercised control over the calling of conventions," giving them "a ready-made agenda of popular concerns to guide their deliberations"; and (3) "ratification by referendum afforded the people an opportunity to approve or reject the measures proposed by constitutional conventions—not an approximation of direct democracy but the real thing."[64]

The legislation referendum, the people's right to overrule a statute duly enacted by the legislature and signed by the governor, offers a direct-democracy variant on initiatives. A significant plurality of states, fourteen, permit direct democracy with respect to legislation. Here, too, we see a lot of western and midwestern states, often the same states with initiatives: Arizona, Arkansas, California, Colorado, Idaho, Missouri, Montana, Nebraska, North Dakota, Oklahoma, Oregon, South Dakota, Utah, and Washington.[65] Seven more states give state legislatures an opportunity to act on a petition before it goes to a statewide vote: Alaska, Maine, Massachusetts, Michigan, Nevada, Ohio, and Wyoming.[66]

To date, constitutional commissions have offered the least effective route to constitutional change, but in view of the dearth of constitutional conventions over the last fifty years or so, they may have a more promising future. The idea behind commissions is to pull a representative group of people together to propose changes to the legislature or the people, whether for singular amendments or the kinds of revisions that a convention could address. Commissions may be authorized by law or state constitutions. Most often, they are put together on a periodic basis, in some states just before the constitutionally required popular vote over whether to have a constitutional convention. That has the virtue of giving the people an idea of the kinds of things a convention might address. The weakness of commissions is that they have only the power of recommendation, the power to suggest that the legislature or the people place an amendment proposal on the ballot. But that may be their strength too, as they do not pose a threat of runaway conventions yet still allow the people input about what should stay and what should go in a constitution. Florida is a conspicuous exception to all of this. Its constitution allows such commissions to place amendments directly on the ballot.

The verdict on the use of commissions in the years leading up to a statewide convention remains under deliberation. Yes, they let the people know what might be on the table in a convention if they vote for one. But commissions also may have the effect of discouraging conventions, as suggested by the refusal of any state to vote for a convention in several generations of statewide votes. A more jaundiced view is that state leaders use these commissions to create the impression that the state has the people covered, making it unnecessary to call a convention on matters the commission is already addressing and to avoid the peril to those already in office that comes with conventions.[67] Some support for this perspective comes from the reality that legislative funding for the commissions often dries up after the people vote not to have a convention.[68] That raises the dispiriting possibility that commissions today have come to block constitutional change more often than they have facilitated it. The Florida experience offers another way to think about it.

Florida

Florida uses constitutional commissions in a novel way. Before 1968, the Sunshine State used temporary commissions for occasional amendments just like the other states.[69] In the 1960s, the commission proposed several major revisions that eventually became the 1968 Florida Constitution. The new constitution included two changes to the rules for altering it: a constitutional initiative and an independent commission to review the constitution.[70] Called the Florida Constitutional Review Commission, it is the only commission among the states with the power to recommend amendments and revisions directly to the people for a vote.[71] It was required to meet in 1977–78 and every twenty years after that. Florida has two commissions in truth. The state also has a Tax and Budget Reform Commission, which may "propose revisions only to parts of the constitution 'dealing with taxation or the state budgetary process,'" and which meets in alternative decades from meetings of the general commission.[72] In creating these independent commissions, freed from many restrictions imposed on temporary commissions by legislatures and governors, and in giving them the power to submit proposals directly to the voters, Florida is "unique" in its use of constitutional commissions.[73]

The background for the 1968 Constitutional Convention explains its focus on future amendments. Throughout American history, conventions have been prompted by local crises or sea changes in the national political landscape. The 1968 Convention was initiated "by the first legislature to take office after reapportionment on a one-person, one-vote basis."[74] One distortion created by reapportionment dysfunction was friction "between North Florida and South Florida" caused by differences in politics, economics, and "North Florida's domination of the state legislature due to the several decades long failure of the legislature to reapportion itself as the population base grew in South Florida."[75] Something similar happened in other states affected by the US Supreme Court's *Reynolds* and *Baker* reapportionment decisions. These developments helped to make "the 1960s the last major decade for state constitutional conventions and total rewriting of state constitutions. The last constitutional convention which was successful in winning voter approval of its recommendations was held in Louisiana in 1974."[76]

Participants in the 1968 Florida Convention had every reason to correct prior political distortions and to avoid future distortions by facilitating amendments that would allow the constitution to stay current with the times. Hence the creation of the initiative and commission.

Florida's Constitutional Review Commission has thirty-seven members and represents in one way or another every branch of government. The members are the attorney general, fifteen gubernatorial appointees, nine appointees selected by the leader of each of the two legislative houses (eighteen total), and three appointees selected by the chief justice. The governor picks the commission's chairman. Any amendment proposal must be filed 180 days before the election with the secretary of state, and no legislative approval is needed before the proposal goes on the statewide ballot.[77]

The Constitution Revision Commission has met three times so far: 1977–78, 1997–98, and 2017–18. None of the eight proposals from the first meeting was approved, though several were approved later by initiatives and legislative proposals, and some became statutes. The second commission proposed nine amendments, and eight passed. The most recent one proposed eight amendments for voter approval, and seven eventually passed.[78]

The work of the 2017–18 Commission led to its first lawsuits. While the commission "was created to be independent from interference from the legislative and executive branches," it "encountered interference from the judicial branch" in 2018.[79] Since 1986, the Florida Constitution has required its supreme court to review all citizen-initiated ballots,[80] a form of review that triggers rejection if the title and summary of the proposal are "clearly . . . defective."[81] The Florida Supreme Court does not apply the single-subject rule to proposals by the commission in view of its broad revision authority. That feature of the process permits the bundling of proposals and has led to take-it-or-leave-it conundrums for voters.[82] That is what happened in 2018, generating considerable public consternation, including calls to end the authority of the commission to place proposals on the ballot.[83] The court ultimately allowed most of the proposals to go on the ballot in 2018. The exception was an amendment to allow the legislature to establish charter schools, invalidated on a 4–3 vote *after* the amendment passed.[84] The power of judicial review, it is fair to say, hits a pinnacle when a court invalidates a constitutional amendment that the electorate just passed.[85] The seven remaining proposals all passed, including a Marcy's Law victim's rights provision.[86]

In gauging Florida's use of commissions, remember that it is the rare state that has a super-majority requirement for amending the constitution by any method. As of 2006, the Florida Constitution requires at least 60% support to approve an amendment. Even so, some Floridians have raised skepticism about the commission. In particular, the bundling of some provisions—banning offshore drilling and prohibiting indoor vaping in workplaces in 2018 is one example—led to confusion and resentment. In 2020, Floridians had a chance to revise the amendment process by requiring *consecutive* statewide 60% votes in succeeding general elections to amend the constitution.[87] Only 47.5% of voters supported the measure, and it failed. While commissions have considerable potential for prompting measured answers to change, they have an uncertain future as a meaningful author of change.[88]

Nebraska

If, as a young lawyer, George Norris set out to have one chamber of the Nebraska legislature named after him, he decreased those chances by half during his career. Alone among our fifty-one federal and state governments, the Nebraska legislature has one chamber, one house of the legislative branch of government. The other forty-nine state legislatures and one federal legislature have a lower and upper house. Much of the credit for that distinction goes to Norris.

Born and raised in Ohio, the eleventh child of farmers, Norris moved west to Indiana to obtain a law degree and moved farther west to practice law in Nebraska. He was a prominent United States politician, serving in the House of Representatives from 1903 to 1913 and in the Senate from 1913 to 1943. One of eight senators profiled by future-president John F. Kennedy in *Profiles in Courage*, he had many other accomplishments during his forty-year tenure in elective office, including sponsorship of the Tennessee Valley Authority in 1933. While serving as a US senator, he also brought a unicameral, non-partisan legislature to Nebraska.

Nebraska did not start with this approach. Welcomed to the Union in 1867, the state used a bicameral, party-based legislature for the next seventy years. Nor did the Cornhusker State innovate the one-house legislature. A trio of the first states, Georgia, Pennsylvania, and Vermont, used one-house legislatures in their first constitutions.[89] But the practice had ended in all states by 1836.[90] During the Progressive Era, several midwestern and western states, including Nebraska, tried to rehabilitate the idea. Three states put the issue to a constitutional amendment vote, Arizona, Oklahoma, and Oregon, but the proposal lost each time.[91]

As a Republican with an independent streak, Norris had convictions about the virtues of a state unicameral legislature that grew out of his federal experiences. He came to see "blind partisanship" as a "way of life in Congress."[92] "To get along," he came to appreciate, "you had to go along" with party leadership, particularly when it came to committee assignments, and as a result he rarely received such assignments or for that matter "pork" for his constituents.[93]

Norris had supported this legislative reform for a while.[94] In 1923, he published a widely circulated article in the *New York Times* advocating a non-partisan unicameral legislature.[95] In 1934, supporters finally obtained enough signatures to place a constitutional initiative— Nebraska is an initiative state—on the ballot in favor of this reform. In advocating the reform, Norris reminded voters that the two-house system originated in Britain and was rooted in a class system, a lower house for commoners and an upper house for aristocrats.[96] Even if "two such classes exist" in England and even if the "conflict" in their "interests" justified a two-house system, as he put it, "we have no such classes and the constitutions of our various States are built upon the idea that there is but one class."[97] He criticized the work of the conference committee, which was needed to reconcile competing bills enacted by each house in a bicameral legislature. He thought a partisan legislature, whether one or two houses, furthered "special interests" as opposed to the needs of the people.[98] In this respect, Norris was alone. Other state efforts to create a unicameral legislature up to then had not proposed eliminating partisan elections for the legislative branch.[99] These and other arguments, including the significant cost savings of reducing the number of legislators by nearly 100,[100] carried the day.

Opponents by the way emphasized the risk of eliminating the "checks and balances" of a two-house system.[101] Perhaps some of them appreciated John Roche's addendum to Lord Acton's dictum about power and corruption: "Power corrupts, and the prospect of losing power corrupts absolutely."[102]

Voters approved the constitutional amendment in 1934 with roughly 60% of the electorate favoring it.[103] The first unicameral legislature under the new system went into effect in 1937. Norris spoke at the initial session, noting that "every professional lobbyist, every professional politician, and every representative of greed and monopoly is hoping" that this "work will be a failure."[104] In the same session, state senator John Norton remarked that "the faults of the unicameral are the faults which marked the bicameral, but the virtues of the unicameral are the virtues of the one-house system alone."[105]

While Nebraska's experiment with a one-house system continues to distinguish it from the other state legislatures and Congress, that does not leave it alone. Most city, county, and other local governments use a one-house system. While some well-populated cities in the country had a two-house council for a while, "most large cities" recognized by 1911 that this system was "unwieldy and unnecessary."[106]

In 1984, the people of Nebraska used this one-house system to honor Norris by naming the legislative chamber in the state capitol after him.

Oregon

Oregon launched America's experiment with direct democracy in 1902.[107] Weary of elected representatives unwilling to check their own excesses, the people seized the power to second-guess for themselves. The state established the right of the people to alter amendments and statutes through direct statewide votes without the blessing of any of the three branches of the government. The objective, as some colorfully saw it, was to bypass a legislature consisting of "briefless lawyers, farmless farmers, business failures, bar-room loafers, Fourth of July orators, [and] political thugs,"[108] and a legislature where "fraud and force and cunning were for so many years features of Oregon politics that they came to be accepted, not only as part of the game, but by many as the attractive features of the game."[109] The change did not happen overnight, and Oregon had company in seeking it.

If one-time Oregon Supreme Court Justice Hans Linde deserves national acclaim for launching Oregon's first-things-first approach to state constitutional interpretation,[110] William Simon U'Ren deserves credit as one of many national parents of the initiative and referendum. Born in Wisconsin, U'Ren moved to Oregon in 1889. He had more than one skill, as one suspects many people did then. He was a blacksmith, a lawyer, and a newspaper editor. And a committed reformer, too. Faced with poor health, he left Wisconsin for more hospitable climates, expecting only a few more years of life. He settled in Portland in 1889 and went to live with a family who gave him a copy of *Direct Legislation through the Initiative and Referendum*, an 1893 book by James Sullivan.

Inspired by the book, "he didn't find time" to die,[111] and started lobbying for the initiative in 1894. He took on leadership positions in the Direct Legislation League,[112] an offshoot of a national organization that grew out of the aptly named People's Power League.[113] The initiative eventually became part of the platform for the State's Populist Party, of which he became chairman. Once elected to the legislature, he worked to bring the initiative and referendum through the legislature. Success came in 1901, when the legislature approved it for the ballot with just one dissenting vote, and the people approved it by an eleven-to-one margin a year later.[114]

Before the amendment, Article IV of the Oregon Constitution vested the exclusive legislative power in the two houses of its General Assembly. After the amendment, the clause came with this precaution: "But the people reserve to themselves power to propose laws and amendments to the Constitution, and to enact or reject the same at the polls, independent of the legislative assembly."[115] The change thus allowed the people directly to amend the constitution through an initiative and overturn laws enacted by the legislature through a referendum.

U'Ren later described what became his life's work and the unbargained-for change in his career prompted by early-in-life injuries. "Blacksmithing," he said, "was my trade and it has always given color to my view of things. I wanted to fix the evils in the conditions of life. I couldn't. There were no tools. We had tools to do almost anything within the blacksmith shop; wonderful tools. So in other trades, arts and professions . . . in everything but government. In government, the common trade of all men and the basis of social life, men worked still with old tools, with old laws, with institutions and charters which hindered progress more than they helped it. Men suffered from this. There were enough lawyers. . . . Why didn't some of them invent legislative implements to help people govern themselves: Why had we no tool makers for democracy?"[116]

Oregon used the initiative 384 times between 1904 and 2014, making it the state with the highest average use. It also has placed the most initiatives up for a vote in one year, twenty-seven of them in 1912.[117] Use of the initiative has been consequential in the state, often for progressive causes but not exclusively for them. Through direct democracy, Oregon has changed its constitution in the following ways: extended the initiative and referendum to local governments (1906); made Oregon the first state to allow the electorate to vote directly for US senators (1908); established the first presidential primary system (1910); gave women the right to vote (1912); established an eight-hour workday on public works projects (1912); established Prohibition (1914); abolished the death penalty (1914); required children to attend public schools (1922), later invalidated in *Pierce v. Society of Sisters* in 1925; allowed physician assisted suicide (1994); required vote by mail for biennial primary and general elections (1998); and legalized marijuana (2014). One unsuccessful amendment worth mentioning occurred in 1912, when Oregon tried but failed to adopt a unicameral legislature.[118]

Oregon not only receives credit for using the initiative and referendum before anyone else, it also generated the litigation that has inoculated initiatives from federal constitutional challenge. In 1906, the people of Oregon used the initiative to impose new taxes on various classes of corporations, including a 2% tax on the gross receipts of telephone and telegraph companies earned in the state. One of the newly taxed companies objected. It challenged the tax on the ground that initiatives violate the US Constitution's republican form of government guarantee. How, the company complained, could direct democracy be compatible with the kind of representative democracy that characterizes republican government?

The US Supreme Court, like the Oregon Supreme Court before it, rejected the claim. The "political character" of the federal guarantee, Chief Justice White explained for the Court, made it one for the First Branch, not the Third Branch, the last of which had authority only to review cases and controversies that were "judicial in character."[119] It is "a singular misconception of the nature and character of our constitutional system of government," he reasoned, to maintain that the distinction "between judicial authority over justiciable controversies and legislative power as to purely political questions tends to destroy the duty of the judiciary in proper cases to enforce the Constitution."[120] Only by "failing to distinguish between things" that "are widely different" can the mistake be made.[121] The challenge is "not on the tax as a tax, but on the State as a State"—on "the framework and political character of the government" by which "the tax was passed."[122] With that, the case came to rest. And with it came to rest any realistic possibility of successful across-the-board challenges to government by initiative for over a century and counting.

Since then, to be sure, the US Supreme Court has heard challenges to initiatives on other grounds. Prominent examples include *Romer v. Evans*, which held that the substance of a state initiative violated the federal Equal Protection Clause,[123] and *Arizona State Legislature v. Arizona Indep. Redistricting Comm'n*, which held that a state initiative did not violate the federal Election Clause's requirement that only a state "Legislature" could regulate elections.[124] Through these cases and others, the Court has left in place the division-of-powers point that only Congress, not the US Supreme Court, has authority to second-guess direct democracy as a method of amending constitutions or enacting statutes. The Oregon experiment has borne considerable fruit since 1902, often in favor of progressive causes, sometimes in favor of conservative ones, and it has been used more often in some eras (the early 1900s, the Depression, the 1970s) than in others.[125]

U'Ren's political fortunes rose and fell, too. At the peak of his influence in 1906, Portland's leading newspaper, with some exaggeration and apparent contempt, said this about him:

In Oregon the state government is divided into four departments— the executive, judicial, legislative and Mr. U'Ren—and it is still an open question which exerts the most power. One fact must be considered in making comparisons: That the legislature does not dare to repeal the acts of Mr. U'Ren, the executive has no power to veto them, and thus far the judiciary has upheld all his laws and constitutional amendments. On the contrary, Mr. U'Ren has boldly clipped the wings of the executive and legislative departments, and when he gets time will doubtless put some shackles on the supreme court. To date, the indications are that Mr. U'Ren outweighs any one, and perhaps all three, of the other departments.[126]

That was an overstatement, time showed. In 1912, U'Ren lost the race for governor, and the legislature by then had no trouble rejecting his proposals. With glee and some overstatement in the other direction, *The Oregonian* wrote: "It is Oregon's message to the world that the disastrous U'Ren epoch has passed."[127]

In honor of U'Ren, a plaque in Oregon City describes him as "the author" of the Oregon initiative and referendum, "giving the people control of law making and lawmakers."[128] That's a suitable epitaph for him and a suitable birth announcement for initiatives.[129]

California

While Oregon gave birth to the initiative and has used it most often, California has used it most prominently. No less a source than Ronald George, the former chief justice of the California Supreme Court, says that "in no other state is the practice as extreme as in California."[130] California allows a citizen petition to be placed on the ballot with the signature of at least 8% of the voters in the last gubernatorial election. If a majority of those voting in the next election approves the measure, it promptly goes into effect.[131] The legislature also may place proposed constitutional amendments on the ballot with a two-thirds vote of each house. The state is "unique" in America "in prohibiting its legislature, without express voter approval, from amending or repealing even a statutory measure enacted by the voters, unless the Initiative measure itself specifically confers such authority upon the legislature."[132]

California adopted the initiative in 1912. According to the California secretary of state's office, 376 initiatives have qualified for the ballot through 2017. Of those, the people approved 132 of them, with forty amending the constitution, seventy-eight revising statutes, and fourteen doing both in parts. Of the initiatives that qualified for the ballot, the voters approved roughly 35% of them.[133]

Through the initiative, Californians have embraced the following changes: abolition of poll taxes (1914); suspension of Prohibition amendment (1914); legislative reapportionment (1926); selection of judges (1934); property tax limits (1978); state lottery (1984); English-only voting material (1984); campaign funding contribution limits (1988); state legislative term limits (1990); criminal law sentencing increases for repeat offenders (1994); minimum wage increase (1996); medical use of marijuana (1996); ban on affirmative action in public universities (1996); English-only as language of instruction (1998); definition of marriage (2000); stem cell research (2004); increased regulation and sentences for sex offenders (2006); limits on use of eminent domain (2008); elimination of right of same-sex couples to marry (2008); victims' rights (2008); three-strikes law for repeat felony offenders (2012); legalization of marijuana (2016).[134]

One could fairly profile many eras of American history based on what the people of California have chosen to prioritize through their gamut-running initiative process over the last century. Through the process, Californians have weighed in on many of the hot-button issues of the times, often at the forefront of national debates over them.

The approval of Proposition 13 in 1978 by a 65% vote is the best known initiative in the Golden State, perhaps in the country. When it comes to the strengths and weaknesses of government by initiative, Proposition 13 has a bit of everything. At one level, it was a pocketbook issue, a revolt against the tax policies of the legislature. The initiative allowed the people to retain control of property taxes, by capping rates at 1% of market value and imposing a 2% ceiling on market valuation increases per year. No one doubted that property values were increasing as more people moved to the state. But that did not mean the homeowners had new sources of revenue to pay for the tax increases, save for the face-spiting remedy of selling their homes.

Proposition 13 also equalized property taxes among cities as well as between homeowners and businesses,[135] and it served to shrink government, both state and local. Going forward, the initiative required a two-thirds majority in both houses to increase state taxes and required a two-thirds majority in local elections for local tax increases.[136]

At still another level, Proposition 13 amounted to an indirect response to the California Supreme Court's *Serrano* decision in 1971, which invalidated the state's system for financing public schools on inequality grounds under the California Constitution.[137] With a mandate from the California Supreme Court to increase funding for public schools, the legislature understandably needed to find new revenue sources, making property taxes, the traditional source for funding public schools, an attractive option. In this sense, the people chose not to overrule the *Serrano* decision, as they might have; they chose instead to limit, in truth monetarily cap, its effectiveness, and thus limit at the same time the redistributive tendencies of the school-funding decision. The people of California ultimately responded to the court's mandate with a mandate of their own. A "constituency that would have opposed Prop 13 *prior to Serrano*," William Fishel notes, "would have found it rational to vote for Prop 13 *after* the court decision."[138]

Whatever the causes or effects of Proposition 13, it has changed California government. It has limited the legislature's efforts to fund policy initiatives. It has led to more initiatives that increase spending for popular items or that reduce other types of taxes, creating hard-to-resist "something for nothing" ballot options. From 1988 to 2008, 127 of 259 ballot measures increased spending or reduced taxes without offsetting funds, and 80 of them passed.[139] Nor has "the two-thirds vote requirement" done what one would expect: "limit higher levels of spending. In practice, it encourages it."[140] The minority party in the legislature often uses the supermajority requirement to hold budget negotiations hostage, conditioning votes on cutting taxes or boosting spending for their own districts.[141] Twice, the legislature was so paralyzed that California paid government bills with IOUs.[142]

One undoubted feature of the initiative, after more than a century of experience, is that it has exacerbated a tendency to amend state constitutions to cover topics normally covered by legislation. Bloated constitutions create the long-term concern that if you try to constitutionalize everything, you run the risk of constitutionalizing nothing.[143] Neither Jefferson nor Madison would have approved of that. As one-time chief justice of the California Supreme Court Ronald George points out, "United States Supreme Court Justice Hugo Black was known to pride himself on carrying in his pocket a slender pamphlet containing the federal Constitution in its entirety. I certainly could not emulate that practice with California's constitutional counterpart."[144] Initiatives, he adds, "have enshrined a myriad of provisions into California's constitutional charter, including a prohibition on the use of gill nets and a measure regulating the confinement of barnyard fowl in coops." As if that was not bad enough, he thought, "this last constitutional amendment was enacted on the same 2008 ballot that amended the state Constitution to override the California Supreme

Court's decision recognizing the right of same-sex couples to marry. Chickens gained valuable rights in California on the same day that gay men and lesbians lost them."[145]

The larger problem from a governance perspective, he writes, is the "fiscal straitjacket" created by a two-thirds-vote requirement "for raising taxes." "A similar super-majoritarian requirement governs passage of the state budget." The issue "is compounded by voter Initiative measures that have imposed severe restrictions upon increases in the assessed value of real property that is subject to property tax, coupled with constitutional requirements of specified levels of financial support for public transportation and public schools."[146]

At the same time, it is hard to deny that some measures are well suited for initiatives. Think of term limits on state elected officials. Is it not asking a lot of public officials to impose tenure restrictions on themselves? Before California enacted term limits by initiative, the legislature rejected a bill to impose them, a bill in which the opponents outspent supporters by a 2–1 margin. Of the twenty states that have adopted term limits for their legislators, just one occurred through a vote of the legislature.[147]

George also rightfully worries that well-funded special interests have an outsized role in getting initiatives on the ballot and in getting them approved. When a proposal is "sufficiently funded by its backers, it most likely will obtain the requisite number of signatures to qualify for the ballot, and—if it does qualify—there is a good chance the measure will pass."[148] All kinds of ploys are used, some vaguely amusing, to convince citizens to sign the proposals.[149] And the opposite is true, as "poorly funded efforts, without sufficient backing to mount an expensive television campaign," fail if they cannot get on the ballot in the first place.[150] "A student of government might reasonably ask," as George damningly asks: "Does the voter Initiative, a product of the Populist Movement that reached its high point in the early 20th century in the mid-west and western states, remain a positive contribution in the form in which it now exists in 21st century California? Or, despite its original objective—to curtail special interests, such as the railroads, that controlled the legislature of California and of some other states—has the voter Initiative now become the tool of the very types of special interests it was intended to control, and an impediment to the effective functioning of a true democratic process?"[151]

That leaves this lingering problem, which George to his credit acknowledges. "Approximately 60% are of the view that decisions made by Californians through the Initiative process are better than those made by the legislature and the governor."[152] Logic and experience have been no match for that so far.

How Should Our Fifty-One Constitutions Handle Change?

Nothing is more basic to a democracy than the rules for change. A country does not have much of a democracy if a swirling fad suddenly can shift the balance of power in a systemic or despotic way. And a country does not have much of a democracy if tomorrow's citizens have little say over how their government meets the challenges of the day. While it's been said that "the institutions" created by the state and federal constitutions have a "surface similarity," those comparable forms of government "quickly evaporate" when "one proceeds below the surface."[153] None more so than the methods for amending the state and federal charters.

Different though their views were, Madison and Jefferson both were right in the main. Time has confirmed the virtues of having a Madisonian federal charter that's difficult to amend and fifty Jeffersonian state charters that are easier for each generation to amend. A variable national constitution presents serious risks to the fortunes of a democracy. That is why there is something to the imposing demands of Article V of the US Constitution. A three-quarters ratification requirement stands sentinel against the threat of a fickle constitution, one that cannot be counted on when it is tested most. A stable national constitution, as well, provides a foundation for states to experiment with different forms of government and different rights protections—and to give each generation a chance to offer its input on the best form of free and secure democratic government. In this way, as Mark Graber says, "state constitutionalism provides" yet another fruitful "laboratory," this one "for testing the vices and virtues of frequent constitutional alterations."[154]

While the changeability of state constitutions facilitates modern experiments in how best to design a government, the existence of a sturdy national backstop diminishes the risks to democracy and to liberty and to property of each state-based audition of new ideas.[155] Those experiments have value not just for citizens of that state and that era. They also offer examples for other states to follow or to avoid.

So too for the United States. As some ideas generate consensus and others fall by the wayside, the state experiences carve a potential roadmap for the national government to follow. When the states show that new ways of balancing power work well or that new rights deserve protection, they mark a path for Americans to follow in amending the US Constitution. For all the maddening inefficiencies and complications of American federalism, the imperative of fifty-one constitutions, with fifty-one approaches to change, creates complementary and bet-hedging methods for handling new challenges and adopting new insights.

As state experiments go, the initiative has had the most far-reaching consequences. Even before Oregon became the first state to embrace direct democracy, the possibility of many states adopting initiatives looks inevitable in retrospect. The path from 1776 to 1902 is littered with efforts by the people to regain control over governments that they did not perceive to be acting in their interests. Whether it's the early transformation from complete trust in legislatures to growing restrictions on them, the election of judges, or the independent election of several officials in the executive branch, all of these historical paths led naturally to the most fundamental experiment in a republic: do-it-yourself lawmaking.

Has direct democracy been good for the states that have adopted it? On the affirmative side, federalism allows and embraces innovations of this sort. It would have been irresponsible to try this out at the national level first. And it would have been perilous to try this out on all states at once. As it turned out, the spread of the initiative to eighteen states occurred in two stages, in two times of turbulent change: the Progressive Era and the 1960s.

Who can blame the people of some states, moreover, for experimenting with direct democracy? As some citizens saw representative government at the time, corporate interests had captured their legislatures, blocking Progressive-Era proposals designed to improve working conditions and to prohibit public support for private entities, among other reforms. So it was that Oklahoma adopted the initiative "to thwart the power that the railroads held over the state legislature," what became "a form of direct grassroots democracy."[156] Malapportionment in some state legislatures became another reason for adopting the initiative, namely, to ensure that legislatures didn't preserve out-of-touch district lines or brazenly gerrymander them in the future.

Alan Tarr defends "the initiative and direct democracy" as "generally fit[ting] comfortably within the state constitutional tradition." That "compatibility," he adds, comes "from the belief, basic to the state constitutional tradition, that the primary danger facing republican government is minority faction—power wielded by the wealthy or well-connected few—rather than majority faction." Because many states shared "skepticism about the 'republican remedies' proposed in *The Federalist Papers*," it is understandable that "the state constitutional tradition" became "characterized by a distrust of government by elected representatives." For citizens imbued with this perspective, "representation not only fails to solve the problems afflicting republican government, but it may even aggravate those problems by empowering minority factions." In that context "direct democracy—or mechanisms designed to approximate it—become much more attractive."[157]

On the negative side, initiatives have become vulnerable to the same moneyed interests that created them. It has become a readily accessible, some fear readily exploited, vehicle to change a state constitution. The key expense is gathering the requisite number of signatures to place the proposal on the ballot, a requirement that favors endowed interest groups, often headquartered outside the state and often driven by a country-wide agenda, not a local one.[158] In the face of these considerations, one may wonder who checks the people (or interest groups) when they use the initiative. While state courts have enforced single-subject rules, clear title, and ballot-accuracy requirements, they have rarely interfered with the substance of such proposals under state constitutions. It is after all an effort by the people to amend the same constitution, suggesting that the amendment supersedes what came before it. Recall, too, that the United States Supreme Court has been hands-off when it comes to state initiatives as a structural choice free to the people ever since the Court's 1912 decision in *Pacific States Telephone & Telegraph v. Oregon.*

To minimize the initiative's warts, states might do well to separate more clearly the requirements for constitutional initiatives from legislative referenda. One reason many interest groups gravitate toward initiatives is that the requirements often are just as easy to meet as they are for referenda. Why not, they ask, put a policy in the state constitution rather than a state code if they are equally easy to enact? A similar comparison applies to state legislation. If an initiative requires just a 51% vote, as most do, that makes it tempting to pursue the initiative route over the conventional lawmaking route. Otherwise, we will continue down the calf's path: loading state constitutions to the brim and doing so based on support by the kinds of interest groups that initiatives were designed to thwart.

What is the modern role of constitutional conventions? One might expect conventions and initiatives to grow in popularity together. They both are quite democratic, even populist. And conventions were a frequent vehicle for constitutional change for much of American history. Conventions remained commonplace after the introduction of the initiative. But in recent decades, conventions have fallen out of favor. The same thing that prompts conventions has made many citizens skeptical of them: "public suspicion and distrust of politicians and the political process" together with the concern that they will degenerate into clashes between powerful interest groups on social and economic issues.[159] "Some groups," it's said, "will seek to preserve the protected position they have in the current constitution; they will be competing with those who have a vested interest in seeking special treatment for themselves."[160] That assessment is hard to counter. It is easy to imagine—it is hard not to imagine—a modern constitutional convention that became dominated by interest groups eager to hold the line on captured gains and to set out for new conquests.

True or not, there is no denying the ebb of constitutional conventions. Recent decades, as Galie and Bopst observe, have watched the "decline of the constitutional convention as a mechanism for achieving constitutional change." While "twenty-six state constitutional conventions were held between 1960 and 1995," they say, "thirteen of these were held during the 1960s. Only one state constitutional convention was held between 1988 and 1993." The "trend" is likely to "continue" because they are "viewed as 'Pandora's boxes,'" they raise the specter of

"dangerous additions to the constitution," "they threaten to upset established relationships between the governing institutions and organized interests," and "they are viewed as cumbersome, unwieldy and
expensive mechanisms."[161]

All of this may provide a basis for commissions to play an invigorated
role. Many of these problems go away if conventions are limited to a
range of proposals pulled together by a well-represented and ideolog-
ically diverse commission. If the people, interest groups, and officials
in power fear that the commission's agenda is too broad, they can reject it. But if the commission targets its proposals on removing dated
provisions and unconstitutional provisions, and adding one or two
provisions that take on glaring gaps in the current constitution, it is
reasonable to anticipate more support for them and to see commissions
and conventions used more often in the future—even one day perhaps
to see another national convention.[162] The commission "has the potential to break this constitutional logjam,"[163] and even to return us to an
essential requirement of the conventions of the past: the need to compromise from time to time.

*Even if the approval requirements of the federal and state constitutions
err in the right direction—with the 75% requirement in the federal constitution properly harder to meet than the 51% requirement in most states—
they still seem to err.* It is no doubt difficult to pin down the precise
balance between constitutions that are too easy and too hard to amend.
Who can deny Robert Williams's assessment: "If state-constitutional
revision is too difficult, constitutionalism overwhelms democracy; if
it is too easy, democracy overwhelms constitutionalism. It is difficult
to achieve exactly the right balance, and the optimum balance might
change over time."[164]

But there are costs to both models, to the federal and predominant
state approaches of today. Start with the states' side of things, the one
most in need of change and the one easiest to change. Here "democracy overwhelms constitutionalism." Too many state constitutions
have become too amenable to change, making them quasi-legislative
documents in the process. Serial constitution-amending at the state
level has converted our to-the-point, principle-driven charters of the
founding into "super-legislative" documents.[165] Consider this contrast: The first state constitutions on average contained 7,150 words,

and by 1985 they averaged 26,150 words.[166] No one calls that progress to my knowledge. A straightforward remedy is available, a super-majority approval requirement worthy of a *constitution*. Whether it's as little as 55% or as much as 67%, any change along these lines would fix a central problem with state constitutions. They are not taken seriously because they do not expect to be taken seriously when a fleeting 51% majority can change them. All of this would sand some of the edges off the initiative, increase the venerability of state constitutions, and still ward off dead-hand control.

Change at the federal level is more tangled because the risks are greater. Yes, the federal amendment process is glacial. Witness the mere fifteen meaningful amendments since 1791 to the national charter, three of them prompted by a civil war. Article V's three-quarters requirement has long seemed to be the central defect in the US Constitution, the one provision over every other that we should fix, say, by reducing it to a two-thirds requirement.[167] Because most advocates of change have balked at scaling Article V's heights, they have resorted to other approaches. Congress and the president have seized powers the federal Framers would have found remarkable, and the federal courts have amended the charter through interpretation.

But it is not that simple. There is no getting around a super-majority requirement of *some sort* for the US Constitution. Not many people advocate a 51% threshold for amending the US Constitution, for allowing just twenty-six states to alter it.[168] The American people, quite correctly, seem to embrace the benefits of a super-majority requirement to avoid the pitfalls of a variable constitution in which everything is up for grabs at any time or in which one segment of the country can impose controversial measures on another. I doubt many people would accept anything less than a two-thirds requirement for changing the US Constitution, and I know of no one who wants it to be *harder* to amend the US Constitution. That means the debate turns on whether it should take thirty-four states or thirty-eight states to approve an amendment or some number in between. It would be a significant super-majority threshold either way, one that demands the hard work of developing a meaningful consensus in the country. For my part, a two-thirds requirement would be a beneficial change, one apt to decrease, if not eliminate, pressure to use the federal branches of government to change the constitution on their own.

But the broader concern, the missed opportunity, is finding ways to engage the state experiences as a way to promote federal constitutional change, whether it is a two-thirds or three-quarters threshold. That is how we used to do it. Once one takes national security out of the mix, nearly every federal constitutional question about structure and rights has a parallel in the state constitutions. Should that not be the way we identify consensus? Is it not a way we can use more fruitfully in the future?

Epilogue

IF A CONSTITUTION'S RULES for change remind us who is in charge, our fifty-one constitutions offer the best evidence of what Americans want. Yet those American preferences seem to occupy two distinct registers today. When it comes to the who-decides questions at the local level, the states have been versatile over time, developing more and more democratic answers. At the national level, the country remains largely fixed in an eighteenth-century republican form of government, one that remains non-democratic in many ways.

How could the same people adopt such disparate approaches to government? Is there not a risk of swift and sudden change in response to pent-up demand at the federal level? That is one way of looking at it.

Another way of looking at it is more optimistic and pragmatic. Are there ways in which these two different approaches to government can complement each other? The conviction of this book is that American constitutional structure cannot be understood without appreciating how the national *and* state governments handle it. The hope of this book is that a greater appreciation of American federalism offers ways to improve the functioning of each side. To that end, let me conclude with a few observations.

First, one should not separate the rules for changing constitutions from the rules for interpreting them. If Cass Sunstein is right that judicial restraint can be "democracy-forcing,"[1] the same is true for judicial engagement. When the people of California thought that their Supreme Court was over-enforcing the state's search-and-seizure guarantee, they amended the state constitution to prohibit the state courts from interpreting it beyond the federal baseline. Both restrained interpretations of constitutions and engaged interpretations of them can be democracy-forcing.

The rules for interpreting a constitution should respect the rules for amending it. That suggests that the constitution most difficult to change by amendment—the US Constitution—should be the least susceptible to change by judicial interpretation. Else, interpretation circumvents the preference of the people at the federal level for stability and veneration. How Madisonian, it is fair to ask, are the federal rules for changing the Constitution given the many alterations to it over the decades by judicial interpretation? But now consider why that transformation happened. A constitution that facilitates change places less pressure on judges to do the work of handling shifting norms, while a constitution that insists on continuity places considerable pressure on judges to adapt the document over time.[2] Then there is still another perspective on stability versus adaptability, one focused on constitutional precedents. When judicial precedents alter a constitution through interpretation, particularly a constitution difficult to change by amendment, legitimacy and political pressure clash. Precedents altering a difficult-to-amend constitution ought to be the easiest to overrule, but they often face the greatest political pressure to let them be.

Difficult though it may be to navigate these cross-currents, this much can be said. If we must have federal constitutional rights ungrounded in the words and history of the federal charter, should we not insist that the federal and state courts work together in identifying what they should be? The state courts (and state legislatures) ought to be in the vanguard in identifying new norms. A useful gauge for the legitimacy of what the federal courts do as they reach the outer edges of their interpretive authority is to ask whether their opinion has the kind of super-majority support that would be needed to take the conventional route to change: amendment. The same is true regardless of whether a federal court thinks about creating a new interpretation or preserving an old one. If the new right, unanchored in a clear textual principle, does not have a clear consensus—whether shown through state court decisions, state legislation, or state executive-branch refusal to enforce laws on the books—discretion beats valor each time. So too in debating whether to preserve a decision of the past. Give it due time of course. But after that, if the federal courts' approach defies consensus and if it cannot be shown to be legitimate to begin with, it is hard to see any reason to keep it other than the political reality that someone got what they do not deserve and wants to keep it.

It is easy to doubt this approach and to think of favored decisions of the past that might not work under it. But it is harder to second-guess it as a fair-minded design for a system going forward. In the absence of certainty about the composition of the US Supreme Court of the future, it is the rare citizen willing to commit to accepting whatever a future majority of the US Supreme Court is willing to give them *or* their political opponents tomorrow, through 5–4 decisions of a document meant to require three-quarters of the states to change. Citizens of today and tomorrow might ask what is the better gauge for assessing change: The input of passing majorities of the next 115 justices to serve on the US Supreme Court? Or the input of the American people through their next 7,500 amendments?

Second, just as state constitutions and state courts offer evidence of shifting American norms, so do other features of state and local government. At the founding, the people unleashed a theory of divided government and representation with few stopping points. If the country could be divided into state and national governments, why not into municipal governments as well? And if democratic votes were the test for government by consent, how far could that go? "By assuming that the electoral process was the criterion of representation," Gordon Wood shows us, "Americans prepared the way for an extraordinary expansion of the idea of representation. If governors elected by the people were thereby representative of the people, then all elected officials could be viewed as representatives of the people."[3] Once each state senate became representative and no longer aristocratic, it had "momentous implications. If the people could be represented twice, why not three, four, or more times?"[4] Four or more times indeed.

While the states and the national government thought about representation and democracy in comparable ways at the founding, with elections for executive branch leaders and both houses of the legislature, their paths diverged. Once unleashed, this theory of representation, easily accommodated by amendable state constitutions, led to a thoroughgoing revamping of state and local governments. The election of judges offered a new way in which the people could be represented. The plural executive took a founding form of representation, the election of a chief executive, and spread the concept to more officials, giving the people still more democratic choices over who represented them. These same choices spread to local governments, our most humdrum, least understood, and arguably most essential reservoirs of power.

The initiative culminates these developments, the absolute power of the people to control their own governments. In some ways, the initiative takes us back to an insight at the outset. Just as initiatives today represent a general way to control the meaning of a constitution, so our early jury trials in the states offered the people a specific way to control the meaning of a constitution.

One lesson throughout is the capacity of the American people to keep a halter on those in power, eventually making the states far more democratic than the United States. It is "clear beyond reasonable doubt," observes Sanford Levinson, "that each and every one of the 50 state constitutions is considerably more democratic than is the United States Constitution, even as amended, albeit infrequently and insufficiently, over the past 225 years."[5] Our national government, he adds, "is committed to the exclusivity of *representative democracy* and therefore excludes the slightest scintilla of *direct democracy*, with significant consequences for the national polity."[6] If the states offer the most contemporaneous insights into what the people want, that makes them the best judges of what kinds of *implied* individual constitutional rights, if any such rights, the federal courts should adopt.

While evidence of shifting American norms in the states may affect the adoption of implied individual rights in the US Constitution through the federal courts, that evidence rarely offers a handhold for the federal courts to modify *express* structural features of the US Constitution. Here we run into a different form of dialogue. The states' new ways of doing things sometimes reflect ideas that work only in states and cities, and for that reason the innovations ought to remain there. The initiative and referendum, for example, likely would not work well at the national level. But other local innovations, such as term limits on federal legislators or judges, might make considerable sense for the national government. In the end, because "state constitutions are more solicitous of the majority, while the federal Constitution is more skeptical of majoritarianism," as Jessica Bulman-Pozen and Miriam Seifter point out, "state and federal constitutions help to address distinct shortcomings of the other."[7]

Third, can there be too much democracy? Yes, no doubt. State and federal majorities of the past have much to account for, confirming that no one structure of government is beyond reproach. Whether through representative government majorities or direct democracy majorities, the people have offered one proof after another of the perils of self-government. Hence the needs for checks and balances, state and federal governments.

But when it comes to state and federal constitutions, these risks often are used to justify support for counter-majoritarian judicial decisions. That impulse does not create a counter-majoritarian problem; it creates a counter-majoritarian myth. In an important sense, too often forgotten, counter-majoritarian court rulings are never apt. At issue in federal constitutional cases is a debate between whether a super-majority policy (in the federal constitution) or a majority policy (in a statute) should prevail. That is a choice between a 75% measure of popular support and a 51% measure of support. In most state constitutional cases, the debate is between two simple majority policies, as most state constitutions required 51% approval at the outset and have required 51% approval ever since. In both systems, that creates a choice between democratic laws and super-democratic laws, not an invitation to invent non-majoritarian policies under the guise of judicial decision.

The point of placing a liberty or property guarantee in a constitution is to guard against future majorities that, for reasons all their own, opt to ignore the protection. But that does not breed and should not encourage non-democratic decisions. If the courts identify a clearly discernible rule from the words and history of the constitution, that assures us, or at least improves the odds, that a group of Americans at some point ratified that protection. Remember the practices of the early state courts. They invoked popularly supported constitutional guarantees to invalidate democratically enacted laws only if a clear rule emerged from the court's interpretation of the constitutional guarantee. It is a lesson worth heeding. If the courts cannot identify a clear rule from the constitutional provision, the odds increase that the innovation does not honor what the people chose to place in the constitution. And the odds increase that judicial review becomes something it was never designed to be: gerrymandering.

Fourth, some approaches to change may require a difference in attitude and a renewed appreciation for the virtues of localism. Americans tend to be congenitally impatient, eager to fix things sooner rather than later and inclined toward national solutions over local ones. That is fine in some instances. Some problems, some crises, require action: national solutions, nothing less. But a rush to nationalize as a conventional practice comes with risks—circumventing the normal requirements for adopting national rules and, when it comes to amendment by interpretation, generating distrust in the US Supreme Court as a politically neutral body, particularly as more Americans become tempted to follow that path.

If I had to put a finger on a way of illustrating our collective impatience, it would go something like this. My neighbor in Bexley, Ohio, wakes up one day and decides that the country needs to adopt this or that idea. Say it is an impassioned view about a new individual right, a policy concern that demands attention, or a new way to organize a government. What bothers me is not the state of mind; it is his approach to change. My neighbor's first answer, too often, is to seek a national solution to the problem and to support national interest groups along the way. Sometimes that means pressing Congress to enact a national law. Sometimes that means urging the president to push the limits of his or her authority in issuing an executive order or an agency to push its limits in promulgating a new national regulation. Quite often in the last seventy years, it means making a federal case out of it, using the federal courts to create a new national right.

Who can blame my neighbor? These paths have worked before. When he prevails at the US Supreme Court, he not only has obtained a decision that requires Ohio to protect this right, but it also requires every other state in the country to protect it, too. It's not enough that he has required other Ohioans to follow this approach. He can now take satisfaction in requiring the people of Arkansas and California and Colorado to follow it also.

Short-sighted though the American people may be in the short term, they are not short-sighted in the long term. Having witnessed the success of my neighbor, other Americans and other interest groups opt for the same approach. People in Arkansas or California or Colorado will return the favor by convincing the US Supreme Court or Congress or the President to adopt a measure that requires Ohioans and my neighbor to adopt a policy they dislike or look the other way when it comes to a policy problem they want to fix. Suddenly resentment consumes my neighbor: What right do these people have to tell me what to do?

Instead of drawing the lesson from these kinds of experiences that perhaps some matters should not be nationalized or that some matters deserve more percolation before they become nationalized, my neighbor and other Americans tend to dig in their heels. Who can blame them? Having seen citizens obtain national victories in this way to protect some rights, how can they fairly be criticized for trying to do the same thing? The lesson is not to fight for fewer winner-take-all solutions but to fight for more of them, channeling escalated political energies onto the national stage, where most of us eventually will win about half the time and lose about half the time. That may be fair and sustainable in its own way. But it is not cost free. Besides the polarization and distrust it engenders, it misses out on the opportunity to customize resolution of some issues to local circumstances and it shortchanges the possibility of building a greater consensus on the rights and policies that should be nationalized.

Perhaps my neighbor should start local. Begin with his city and county and identify a path for protecting his preferred right or under-protected cause. Once that works, use the state legislature or state court to convert this local solution into a statewide solution. After that, after ensuring that his state has come to grips with this new problem, why not have the courage of his convictions that like-minded individuals in other states will take up the cause and follow his state's example? Instead of impatiently forcing something on people they do not want, will resent if they have no say in the matter, and will come to think of as gerrymandering by another name, it is much better to enlist all fifty-one approaches to change and create the best possibility of all: lasting and effective change.

Appendix

Gubernatorial Selection. Nine states, all in the Northeast, allow the governor to appoint judges to all courts: Connecticut, Delaware, Maine, Massachusetts, New Hampshire, New Jersey, New York, Rhode Island, and Vermont.[1] In New Jersey, the governor appoints justices of the state supreme court and trial judges subject to confirmation by the state senate. The state supreme court chooses judges for the intermediate appellate courts from among the state's trial judges. New York, the state that accelerated the trend toward judicial elections, elects its trial judges, who run in partisan elections. The governor appoints judges to the New York Court of Appeals (the state's highest court) and the intermediate appellate courts, all of whom the senate must confirm. New York also uses binding nominating committees, which produce a list of nominees from which the governor must choose the state's appellate judges.

Legislative Selection. Only two states, Virginia and South Carolina, still use the legislature to select judges to all courts. The General Assembly of Virginia takes nominations from legislators, who may consult bar groups or commissions. Legislative committees then hold hearings to evaluate the qualifications of candidates and report nominees to their respective houses of the state legislature. "The candidate receiving the most votes in each house is elected."[2] In South Carolina, the legislature votes on a list of candidates provided by an independent nominating commission. The state legislature then meets in joint session and may choose one of the candidates to fill the vacancy or reject all of the commission's recommendations.[3] A successful candidate must receive a majority of the vote.[4]

Vermont combines gubernatorial and legislative selection. The governor appoints judges to all courts for their initial term. The state is thus included in the "Gubernatorial Selection" tally above. But once a judge's term is up, he may apply to the General Assembly for reappointment. Vermont's legislature then approves each additional term with an up-or-down vote of both houses.

"Life" Appointments. Three New England states allow judges to serve for "life": Massachusetts, New Hampshire, and Rhode Island. Massachusetts and New Hampshire, however, require judges to retire at age seventy. Rhode Island has no mandatory retirement age.

Terms and Term Limits. Other states appoint judges to fixed terms. Judges on the New York Court of Appeals serve longest: fourteen years. All judges in the state of Delaware serve twelve-year terms upon appointment, as do the justices of the supreme court of Virginia. The Commonwealth's lower-court judges serve shorter terms, typically eight years. Justices of South Carolina's supreme court serve ten-year terms, while lower-court judges in the Palmetto State serve shorter terms of six years. All judges serve for eight years in Connecticut, for seven years in Maine and New Jersey, and for six years in Vermont. None of the states that allows the governor or legislature to appoint judges imposes term limits on them, but a few have a mandatory retirement ages: 90 in Vermont, 72 in South Carolina, 70 in Connecticut, New Jersey, New York, and Virginia.

Partisan Elections. Four states elect state supreme court justices and the judges of intermediate appellate courts in partisan elections: Texas, Louisiana, Alabama, and North Carolina. Another three, Tennessee, Indiana, and (as we have seen) New York, elect trial court judges in partisan elections. Two states, Illinois and Pennsylvania, elect all judges to their first term in partisan elections but allow judges to seek additional terms in unopposed retention elections.

New Mexico defies categorization. The governor appoints judges to their first term on the binding recommendation of an independent commission. After one year in office, they stand in a retention election that is partisan in nature. If elected, they complete the eight-year term. They are then eligible to stand in *non-partisan* retention elections for subsequent terms. But retention requires at least 57 percent of the vote.

Non-Partisan Elections. Fifteen states elect their supreme court justices in non-partisan elections: Washington, Oregon, Nevada, Idaho, Montana, North Dakota, Minnesota, Wisconsin, Michigan, Ohio, West Virginia, Kentucky, Arkansas, Mississippi, and Georgia. Another five elect lower court judges in non-partisan elections: California, South Dakota, Oklahoma, Florida, and Maryland.

Terms and Term Limits. As in most states that appoint their judges, all the judges in states that hold judicial elections serve fixed terms. And as in the states with appointed judiciaries, elected high-court judges often serve longer terms than their lower-court colleagues. But elected judges as a rule tend to serve shorter terms than their appointed counterparts in other states. Popularly elected trial-court judges in New York serve the longest. Like the appointed judges of the Empire State's highest court, its elected judges hold office for fourteen years. In West Virginia, high-court judges serve twelve years, while lower-court judges serve eight years. Judges in four states serve up to ten years: Illinois, Louisiana, North Dakota, and Pennsylvania. Judges in six states serve up to eight years: Arkansas, Kentucky, Michigan, Mississippi, Montana, and North Carolina. New Mexico re-elects its judges to eight-year terms as well. Nine states elect their judges to terms of six years or less: Alabama, Georgia, Idaho, Minnesota, Nevada, Ohio, Oregon, Texas, and Washington. No state, to my knowledge, currently imposes term limits (other than through age limits), though over the past few decades proponents of term limits have unsuccessfully pressed this issue in a number of states.

Retention Elections. Sixteen states use retention elections for supreme court justices (not counting Illinois and Pennsylvania); all allow the governor to appoint judges to their first term, with or without a binding recommendation from an independent commission. Only six do so uniformly for trial courts. California uses an unusual nomination process for its supreme court justices' first term: "The governor's nominee must be confirmed by a majority vote of the Commission on Judicial Appointments, which consists of the Chief Justice, Attorney General of California, and the senior presiding justice of the state's courts of appeal."[5] Successful nominees run in an up-or-down retention election after at least one year on the bench and every twelve years thereafter.

Missouri Plan. Fourteen states use the Missouri Plan's combination of gubernatorial appointment based on a binding recommendation from an independent commission and unopposed retention elections for state supreme courts. While these commissions are outside the political branches, they rarely are independent of various influential forces. These states are included in the "Retention Election" tally above. Eleven use the "Missouri Plan" for intermediate appellate courts, and eight for trial courts. Ironically, not all courts in Missouri follow the "Missouri Plan." Some Missouri judicial circuits elect judges through partisan elections instead.[6]

Hawaii also defies categorization. Like "Missouri Plan" jurisdictions, the Aloha State allows the governor to choose judges from a list of binding recommendations developed by an independent commission. But unlike the fourteen states that follow the "Missouri Plan," it does not let voters decide whether to retain judges for additional terms. That decision falls to the independent commission that initially recommended the judge to the governor.

Terms and Term Limits. The length of a judge's initial term varies in states that use retention elections. Take California. When a justice is appointed to the California Supreme Court, she serves no less than one year before standing for retention in the next general election, and serves twelve-year terms after that. In Utah, Nebraska, and South Dakota, an appointed justice serves at least three years before facing the voters. But in Tennessee, a supreme court justice might stand in a retention election as little as thirty days after appointment. Judicial terms after retention vary as well. Supreme court justices in California and Missouri serve the longest: twelve years. Five states retain their justices for ten-year terms: Alaska, Colorado, Indiana, Maryland, and Utah. Four states retain their justices for eight-year terms: Iowa, South Dakota, Tennessee, and Wyoming. And five states retain their judges for six-year terms: Arizona, Florida, Kansas, Nebraska, and Oklahoma. As in states that elect their judges, none of these states has term limits to my knowledge, though some states permit recall elections.[7]

NOTES

Preface

1. The opening of this foreword borrows from Jeffrey S. Sutton, *Response to the University of Illinois Law Review Symposium on 51 Imperfect Solutions*, 2020 U. ILL. L. REV. 1393 (2020).

2. *See* ELWYN B. ROBINSON, HISTORY OF NORTH DAKOTA 207–08 (2017); JOURNAL OF THE CONSTITUTIONAL CONVENTION FOR NORTH DAKOTA 52 (1889).

3. *See* THE OREGON CONSTITUTION AND PROCEEDINGS AND DEBATES OF THE CONSTITUTIONAL CONVENTION OF 1857, 471 (Charles Henry Carey, ed., 1926); W. C. Palmer, *The Sources of the Oregon Constitution*, 5 OR. L. REV. 200, 204 (1926); McIntire v. Forbes, 909 P.2d 846 (Or. 1996) (relying on interpretations of the Indiana Constitution's single subject requirement as of 1857 to determine the meaning of Oregon's "verbatim" adoption of the same guarantee in the Oregon Constitution); *Crafting the Oregon Constitution, State Archives*, OREGON SECRETARY OF STATE (Sep. 17, 2020, 3:32 P.M.), https://sos.oregon.gov/archives/exhibits/constitution/Pages/after-compare.aspx (explaining that the framers of the Oregon Constitution were primarily from Indiana).

Introduction

1. KONSTITUTSIIA SSSR [USSR Const.] [CONSTITUTION] 1977, art. 50 (U.S.S.R.); SOCIALIST CONSTITUTION OF THE DEMOCRATIC PEOPLE'S REPUBLIC OF KOREA [DPRK Const.] 2016, art. 67 ("Citizens are

guaranteed freedom of speech, the press, assembly, demonstration and association.").

2. USSR Const. art. 49; *cf.* DPRK Const. art. 69 ("The State shall investigate and deal with complaints and petitions impartially as stipulated by law.").

3. USSR Const. art. 51; DPRK Const. art. 67 ("The State shall guarantee the conditions for the free activities of democratic political parties and social organizations.").

4. USSR Const. art. 52; DPRK Const. art. 68 ("Citizens have the freedom of religious belief."). The rest of Article 68, however, is less protective on this front: "This right is granted through the approval of the construction of religious buildings and the holding of religious ceremonies. Religion must not be used as a pretext for drawing in foreign forces or for harming the State or social order."

5. USSR Const. arts. 54–55; DPRK Const. art. 79.

6. Antonin Scalia, *The Importance of Structure in Constitutional Interpretation*, 83 Notre Dame L. Rev. 1417, 1418 (2008).

7. *See* Constitución de la República de Cuba 2019, arts. 46–80; Xianfa [Constitution] 2018, arts. 34–37, 39–41, 47, 51 (China).

8. Scalia, *supra* note 6, at 1418.

9. Antonin Scalia, Scalia Speaks: Reflections on Law, Faith, and Life Well Lived 163 (Christopher J. Scalia & Edward Whelan eds., 2017).

10. New State Ice Co. v. Liebmann, 285 U.S. 262, 311 (1932) (Brandeis, J., dissenting).

11. *Court Statistics Project Publishes 2019 State Court Caseload Digest, State Court Caseload Digest 2017* 2, State Just. Inst.: (2019), http://www.courtstatistics.org/~/media/Microsites/Files/CSP/Overview/CSP%20 2017%20Data%20-%20Spreads%20for%20viewing.ashx; *Federal Judicial Caseload Statistics 2018*, U.S. Cts., https://www.uscourts.gov/statistics-reports/federal-judicial-caseload-statistics-2018 (filings for year ending March 31, 2018).

12. By the way, the same is true for all cases. In 2017, there were 83 million cases filed in the state courts and 359,000 cases filed in the federal courts. *See* State Just. Inst., *supra* note 11, at 2; U.S. Cts., *supra* note 11.

13. *See, e.g.*, United States v. Lopez, 514 U.S. 549 (1995) (holding that the Gun-Free School Zones Act exceeded Congress's power under the Commerce Clause).

14. *See* Cal. Const. art. VI, § 16 (requires a retention election for supreme court justices after an initial gubernatorial appointment); Colo. Const. art. VI, § 25 (requires a retention election for supreme court justices after an initial gubernatorial appointment); Colo. Const. art. VI, § 23 (age limit of seventy-two); Ohio Const. art. IV, § 6 (requires election for supreme court justices) (age limit of seventy); Fla. Const. art. V, § 10 (requires a retention election for supreme court justices); *id.* § 8 (age limit

of seventy-five); ILL. CONST. art. VI, § 12 (requires election for supreme court justices); MISS. CONST. art. VI, § 145 (requires election for supreme court justices); MONT. CONST. art. VII, § 8 (requires election for supreme court justices); OKLA. CONST. art. VII, § 3 (requires election for supreme court justices). *But see* U.S. CONST. art. II, § 2 (president appoints all supreme court justices with advice and consent of the Senate for life tenure). *See generally Judicial Selection in the States*, BALLOTPEDIA, https://ballotpedia.org/Judicial_selection_in_the_states.

15. *See* CAL. CONST. art. V, § 11; COLO. CONST. art. IV, § 1; OHIO CONST. art. III, § 1; FLA. CONST. art. IV, § 5; ILL. CONST. art. V, § 2; MISS. CONST. art. V, § 143; MONT. CONST. art. VI, § 2; OKLA. CONST. art. VI, § 4. *But see* U.S. CONST. art. II, § 1. *See generally State Executive Offices*, BALLOTPEDIA, https://ballotpedia.org/State_executive_offices.

16. *See* People v. Wright, 639 P.2d 267, 271 (Cal. 1982) (requiring "suitable safeguards" for a constitutional delegation of policymaking powers); *cf.* CAL. CONST. art. III, § 3 (prohibiting any branch from exercising the powers of another); *see also* Ass'n of California Ins. Cos. v. Jones, 2 Cal. 5th 376, 397 (Cal. 2017) (giving less deference to state agencies than federal courts give to federal agencies); *cf.* CAL. CONST. art. III, § 3.5 (declaring that a state agency has no power to interpret a statute as unenforceable); Cottrell v. City of Denver, 636 P.2d 703, 709 (Colo. 1981) (requiring a "combination" of statutory and administrative standards and safeguards in place before the state legislature can delegate policymaking power to the executive branch); *cf.* COLO. CONST. art. III (prohibiting any branch from exercising the powers of another branch beyond what the Colorado Constitution allows); *see also* BP Am. Prod. Co. v. Colo. Dep't of Revenue, 369 P.3d 281, 285 (Colo. 2016) (listing several caveats to Chevron-like deference); Blue Cross v. Ratchford, 416 N.E.2d 614, 618 (Ohio 1980) (requiring a statute to provide a "practical standard" or an "intelligible principle" as well as procedures to constrain agency discretion). Some justices have dissented from Chevron-like deference to agency interpretations. *See, e.g.,* In re 6011 Greenwich Windpark, L.L.C., 134 N.E.3d 1157, 1172-73 (Ohio 2019) (Kennedy, J., dissenting); *see also* R. Patrick DeWine, *A Few Thoughts on Administrative Deference in Ohio*, YALE J. ON REG. NOTICE & COMMENT BLOG (Oct. 26, 2020), https://www.yalejreg.com/nc/a-few-thoughts-on-administrative-deference-in-ohio-by-justice-r-patrick-dewine/ (expressing skepticism of Chevron-like administrative deference: "Prior to the United States Supreme Court's 1984 decision in Chevron, our Court seemed to see little need for agency deference[]" and "the Court has never explicitly adopted the Chevron framework"). *See also* FLA. CONST. art. V, § 21 (prohibiting courts and officers from deferring to agency interpretations in cases and hearings); Thygesen v. Callahan, 385 N.E.2d 699, 701–02 (Ill. 1979) (striking down a statute under a strong non-delegation test); *cf.* ILL.

CONST. art. II, § 1 (prohibiting any branch from exercising the powers of another branch); King v. Miss. Mil. Dep't, 245 So. 3d 404, 407 (Miss. 2018) (rejecting the use of Chevron deference); Gold Creek Cellular of Mont. Ltd. P'ship v. State, 310 P.3d 533, 535 (Mont. 2013) (explaining that Montana courts defer less to agency interpretations than federal courts do); Democratic Party v. Estep, 652 P.2d 271, 277–78 (Okla. 1982) (requiring definite standards for any delegation of policymaking power to an agency); *cf.* OKL. CONST. art. IV, § 1 (prohibiting any branch from exercising the powers belonging to any other branch). On state nondelegation doctrines in general, see Jim Rossi, *Institutional Design and the Lingering Legacy of Antifederalist Separation of Powers Ideals in the States*, 52 VAND. L. REV. 1167 (1999) (analyzing the strengths and differences of the states' nondelegation doctrines). On state deference doctrines in general, see Daniel M. Ortner, *The End of Deference: The States That Cannot Make Up Their Mind*, YALE J. ON REG. NOTICE AND COMMENT BLOG (Apr. 2, 2020), https://www.yalejreg.com/nc/the-end-of-deference-the-states-that-cannot-make-up-their-mind-by-daniel-m-ortner/.

17.   All eight states, for example, have single-subject rules. See CAL. CONST. art. IV, § 9; COLO. CONST. art. V, § 21; OHIO CONST. art. II, 15 (D); FLA. CONST. art. III, § 6; ILL. CONST. art. IV, § 8(d); MISS. CONST. art. IV, § 69 (single-subject rule applies only to specific appropriations bills); *id.* § 71 (clear-title provision); MONT. CONST. art. V, § 11; OKLA. CONST. art. V, § 57.

18.   *See* CAL. CONST. art. II, § 10; COLO. CONST. art. V, § 1 (requiring initiatives to obtain 55% support); OHIO CONST. art. II, § 1; FLA. CONST. art. XI, §§ 3, 5 (requiring initiatives to obtain 60% support); ILL. CONST. art. XIV, § 3 (direct initiative limited to Article IV of the Illinois Constitution, which addresses the state legislative branch); MISS. CONST. art. XV, § 273; MONT. CONST. art. XIV, § 9; OKLA. CONST. art. V, § 3. *See generally Forms of Direct Democracy in the American States*, BALLOTPEDIA, https://ballotpedia.org/Forms_of_direct_democracy_in_the_American_states.

19.   Jessica Bulman-Pozen & Miriam Seifter, *The Democracy Principle in State Constitutions*, 119 MICH. L. REV. 859, 862 (2021).

Part 1

1.   Two exceptions are neighbors Colorado and New Mexico. Both states devote Article I of their constitutions to describing their boundaries in considerable detail, noting the longitudinal and latitudinal markings of each. On a first look, I wondered whether the people of both states were justifiably proud of their land. Or perhaps had some finicky lawyers: Why not first identify the area covered by a constitution before describing it? On reflection, a surveyor or two made a mistake, prompting each state's

preoccupation with the place covered by their constitutions and generating a US Supreme Court decision that resolved the location of their common boundary. *See* New Mexico v. Colorado, 267 U.S. 30 (1925).

Chapter 1

1. ALEXIS DE TOCQUEVILLE, DEMOCRACY IN AMERICA 93 (Harvey C. Mansfield & Delba Winthrop eds., 2002).

2. In truth, de Tocqueville could not have been referring to constitutional rulings by courts because, by 1835, there still were relatively few cases in which state or federal courts invalidated laws or executive branch orders. *See* Mark A. Graber, *Resolving Political Questions into Judicial Questions: Tocqueville's Thesis Revisited*, 21 CONST. COMMENT. 485 (2004). But that does not mean state and federal courts of that era had little say in developing the common law and in resolving disputes between citizens.

3. *A Symposium on the 40th Anniversary of the Joint Econ. Comm.: Hearing Before the Joint Econ. Comm.*, 99th Cong. 262 (1986) (statement of Herb Stein, Senior Fellow, American Enterprise Institute) ("[I]f something cannot go on forever it will stop.").

4. *Confirmation Hearing on the Nomination of John G. Roberts, Jr. to Be Chief Justice of the United States Before the S. Comm. on the Judiciary*, 109th Cong. 56 (2005) (statement of John G. Roberts, Jr., Judge, U.S. Court of Appeals for the DC Circuit).

5. *Id.* at 55.

6. In case the reader wonders, Gerry supported judicial review: "When we have established the courts as they propose . . . [w]ill they not attend to the Constitution as well as your laws? The Constitution will undoubtedly be their first rule; and so far as your laws conform to that, they will attend to them, but no further." KEITH E. WHITTINGTON, REPUGNANT LAWS: JUDICIAL REVIEW OF ACTS OF CONGRESS FROM THE FOUNDING TO THE PRESENT 57 (2019) (quoting Gerry in speech before House of Representatives, 1 ANNALS OF CONGRESS 861 (1789)).

7. Ariz. State Legislature v. Ariz. Indep. Redistricting Comm'n, 567 U.S. 787, 824 (2015) (quoting Mitchell N. Berman, *Managing Gerrymandering*, 83 TEX. L. REV. 781, 781 (2005)). *See* T. Alexander Aleinikoff & Samuel Issacharoff, *Race and Redistricting: Drawing Constitutional Lines after Shaw v. Reno*, 92 MICH. L. REV. 588, 588 (1993) ("In a democratic society, the purpose of voting is to allow the electors to select their governors. Once a decade, however, that process is inverted, and the governors and their political agents are permitted to select their electors.").

8. Keith E. Whittington, *The Least Activist Supreme Court in History?*, 89 NOTRE DAME L. REV. 2219, 2245–46 (2014) (observing that Justice Kennedy was the most likely member of the Roberts court to vote to invalidate a statute on constitutional grounds through 2012 and the most likely to vote with the majority to do so); *see also* Lee Epstein & Andrew

D. Martin, *Is the Roberts Court Especially Activist: A Study of Invalidating (and Upholding) Federal, State, and Local Laws*, 61 EMORY L.J. 737, 757 & n.61 (2012) (noting that Justice Kennedy is the "most aggressive" member of the Court in striking down legislative actions).

9. *See, e.g.*, Robert H. Bork, *The Constitution, Original Intent, and Economic Rights*, 23 SAN DIEGO L. REV. 823, 824 (1986) (observing that the United States "appear[s] to be at a tipping point in the relationship of judicial power to democracy"); Robert H. Bork, *Styles in Constitutional Theory*, 26 S. TEX. L.J. 53, 54–55 (1985) (criticizing "non-interpretive" methods in constitutional law).

10. *See, e.g.*, Finzer v. Barry, 798 F.2d 1450 (1986) (deferring to Congress's judgment about what restrictions on public protests near embassies in Washington, DC, are appropriate); Dronenburg v. Zech, 746 F.2d 1579, 1583 (1984) (statement of Bork, J., regarding denial of rehearing en banc) (explaining that "'[j]udicial restraint' is shorthand for the philosophy that courts ought not to invade the domain the Constitution marks out for democratic rather than judicial governance").

11. *Finzer*, 798 F.2d at 1459.

12. *See* Boos v. Barry, 485 U.S. 312 (1988).

13. *Dronenburg*, 746 F.2d at 1583.

14. *See, e.g.*, *id.* at 1391–97 (declining to extend the doctrine of substantive due process to protect homosexual conduct in the military and noting the Constitution does not specify, or give inferior court judges any guidance over how to discern, penumbral privacy rights in the Due Process Clause); ROBERT H. BORK, THE TEMPTING OF AMERICA: THE POLITICAL SEDUCTION OF THE LAW 31–32 (Simon & Schuster 2009) (1991) (discussing *Dred Scott v. Sanford* as the birth of substantive due process); *id.* at 110–25 (criticizing the right to privacy invoked in *Griswold* and *Roe* as "not to be found in the Constitution," and criticizing the extension of that logic to homosexual conduct narrowly defeated by a 5–4 vote in *Bowers v. Hardwick*).

15. *See* ROBERT H. BORK, SLOUCHING TOWARDS GOMORRAH: MODERN LIBERALISM AND AMERICAN DECLINE 166 (1996). Judge Bork also gave interviews in 1989 and 1991 in which he commented on the Second Amendment to the same effect. 1989: "[The Second Amendment's] intent was to guarantee the right of states to form militias, not for individuals to bear arms." JOSEPH BLOCHER & DARRELL MILLER, POSITIVE SECOND AMENDMENT: RIGHTS, REGULATION, AND THE FUTURE OF *HELLER* 60 (2018) (quoting Claudia Luther, *Lectures at UCI with Rose Bird: Bork Says State Gun Laws Constitutional*, L.A. TIMES, Mar. 15, 1989, at 5); Jill Lepore, *The Commandments*, THE NEW YORKER, Jan. 10, 2011, https://www.newyorker.com/magazine/2011/01/17/the-commandments (same). 1991: "The National Rifle Association is always arguing that the Second Amendment determines the right to bear arms. But I think it's really

people's right to bear arms in a militia. The NRA thinks that it protects their right to have Teflon-coated bullets. But that's not the original understanding." Blocher & Miller, *supra*, at 60 (quoting Miriam Bensimhorn, *Advocates: Point and Counterpoint, Laurence Tribe and Robert Bork Debate the Framers' Spacious Terms*, LIFE, Fall 1991 (Special Issue), at 96, 98); MARK TUSHNET, IN THE BALANCE: LAW AND POLITICS IN THE ROBERTS COURT 148 (2013) (same).

16. Robert H. Bork, *Neutral Principles and Some First Amendment Problems*, 47 IND. L.J. 1, 20 (1971).

17. Rex E. Lee, *Conference on the Office of the Solicitor General of the United States*, 2003 BYU L. REV. 1, 32 (2003).

18. *Id.*

19. RALPH WALDO EMERSON, *History, in* ESSAYS 3, 8 (1841).

20. Kimel v. Fla. Bd. of Regents, 528 U.S. 62 (2000) (limiting application of the money-damages provisions of the Age Discrimination in Employment Act to the states); Bd. of Tr. of the Univ. of Ala. v. Garrett, 531 U.S. 356 (2001) (same for the Americans with Disabilities Act); and Alexander v. Sandoval, 532 U.S. 275 (2001) (limiting the federal courts' authority to create implied private rights of action to enforce federal statutes and regulations against the states).

21. *See* Lee Epstein, William Landes & Richard Posner, *Why (and When) Judges Dissent*, 3 J. LEGAL ANALYSIS 101, 106 & n.9 (2011).

22. According to the statistics published in the *Harvard Law Review*'s annual Supreme Court Issue, the Court has decided between 30% and 40% of cases unanimously every Term between 2010 and 2019, with the exception of the OT 2013, when the Court decided 48.6% of cases unanimously. *Statistics*, 128 HARV. L. REV. 401, 406 (2014). *See also* Epstein et al., *supra* note 21, at 106, which found that the Court decided 62% of cases without dissent 1990–2007.

23. CLARENCE THOMAS, MY GRANDFATHER'S SON 286 (Harper 2007).

Chapter 2

1. 5 U.S. (1 Cranch) 137, 177 (1803). *Marbury* was not the first time the Supreme Court discussed judicial review. It had considered the concept before. Cooper v. Telfair, 4 U.S. (4 Dall.) 14, 19 (1800) (Chase, J.). *See also* Calder v. Bull, 3 U.S. (3 Dall.) 386, 387, 392–93 (1798) (Chase, J.); *id.* at 399 (Iredell, J.); Hylton v. United States, 3 U.S. (3 Dall.) 171, 175 (1796) (Chase, J.); KEITH WHITTINGTON, REPUGNANT LAWS: JUDICIAL REVIEW OF ACTS OF CONGRESS FROM THE FOUNDING TO THE PRESENT 65–85 (2019); William Michael Treanor, *Judicial Review before* Marbury, 58 STAN. L. REV. 455, 541–54 (2005); Larry Kramer, *We the Court*, 115 HARV. L. REV. 5, 81–83 (2001). It is not even clear that *Marbury* was the first time the US Supreme Court exercised the power. Its claim to being first depends on a narrow definition of what counts as a "case" and what qualifies as

a "holding," and on the reality that the Court did not always keep good records in its earliest cases. In *Hayburn's Case*, the justices riding circuit invoked the Constitution to justify their refusal to adjudicate pension cases for the secretary of war as directed by a statute of Congress. *See* DAVID P. CURRIE, THE CONSTITUTION IN THE SUPREME COURT: THE FIRST HUNDRED YEARS, 1789–1888, 6–9 (1985). And in *United States v. Yale Todd*, the Supreme Court appears to have held that the same statute was "invalid and that any actions taken under it were void." WHITTINGTON, *supra*, at 66; *see also id.* at 67–69; Treanor, *supra*, at 533–38, 537 n. 423; CURRIE, *supra*, at 10–22. But no opinion from *Yale Todd* survives, and Congress mitigated the effects of the Court's decision. Some scholars doubt whether *Yale Todd* involved judicial review. The pleadings, they say, suggest the Court avoided, or at least could have avoided, the constitutional issue. *See, e.g.*, WHITTINGTON, *supra*, at 68–69.

Over the years, lawyers and legal scholars have re-evaluated, re-interpreted, and even re-invented *Marbury*. They have held it up to stand for one view of judicial review or another, as the hero or as the villain. *See, e.g.*, James Bradley Thayer, *The Origin and Scope of the American Doctrine of Constitutional Law*, 7 HARV. L. REV. 129, 130 n.1 (1893) (criticizing judicial review and suggesting that "*Marbury v. Madison* . . . has been overpraised"); ALEXANDER BICKEL, THE LEAST DANGEROUS BRANCH: THE SUPREME COURT AT THE BAR OF POLITICS 1 (1962); Sanford Levinson, *Why I Do Not Teach* Marbury *(Except to Eastern Europeans) and Why You Shouldn't Either*, 38 WAKE FOREST L. REV. 553 (2003); Larry Kramer, Marbury *and the Retreat from Judicial Supremacy*, 20 CONST. COMMENT. 205 (2003); Michael Stokes Paulsen, *The Irrepressible Myth of* Marbury, 101 MICH. L. REV. 2706 (2003). *Compare also* Cooper v. Aaron, 358 U.S. 1, 18 (1958) (unanimous opinion for the Court) ("*Marbury v. Madison* . . . declared the basic principle that the federal judiciary is supreme in the exposition of the law of the Constitution . . . as a permanent and indispensable feature of our constitutional system."), *with* Josh Blackman, *The Irrepressible Myth of* Cooper v. Aaron, 107 GEO. L.J. 1135 (2019) (criticizing the use of *Marbury* to support claims to judicial supremacy).

2.   WHITTINGTON, *supra* note 1, at 38–59 (describing the path to federal judicial review and showing how little *Marbury* had to do with much of it).

3.   *Id.* at 44 ("The newly formed states of the independent United States were the first to experiment with horizontal judicial review—courts' constitutional review of the coordinate legislatures of the same government.").

4.   MASS. CONST., Part I, art. 30.

5.   Jack Rakove, *The Origins of Judicial Review: A Plea for New Contexts*, 49 STAN. L. REV. 1031, 1037 (1997).

6. *See generally* ALLISON LACROIX, THE IDEOLOGICAL ORIGINS OF AMERICAN FEDERALISM (2010); Allison LaCroix, *What If Madison Had Won? Imagining a Constitutional World of Legislative Supremacy*, 45 IND. L. REV. 41 (2011).

7. Gordon Wood, *The Origins of Judicial Review Revisited, or How the Marshall Court Made More out of Less*, 56 WASH. & LEE L. REV. 787, 795 (1999).

8. PHILIP HAMBURGER, LAW AND JUDICIAL DUTY (Harvard Univ. Press 2008).

9. Mary Sarah Bilder, *The Corporate Origins of Judicial Review*, 116 YALE L.J. 502 (2006). Scott Gerber shows how a separate judiciary arose from the experiences of the colonies and original thirteen states. *See* SCOTT DOUGLAS GERBER, A DISTINCT JUDICIAL POWER: THE ORIGINS OF AN INDEPENDENT JUDICIARY, 1606–1787 (Oxford Univ. Press 2011).

10. Wood, *supra* note 7, at 794.

11. *Id.* at 798.

12. GORDON WOOD, CREATION OF THE AMERICAN REPUBLIC 155 (1998 ed.) (1969).

13. Wood, *supra* note 7, at 790.

14. AKHIL R. AMAR, AMERICA'S CONSTITUTION: A BIOGRAPHY 207 & 569 n.2 (2006).

15. *Id.* at 569 n. 2.

16. *Id.* at 207.

17. *Id.* at 237.

18. PA. CONST. of 1776, Decl. of Rights, § 11.

19. *See* THE FEDERALIST NO. 83 (Alexander Hamilton) ("In Connecticut . . . the trial by jury extends in PRACTICE further than in any other State yet mentioned. Rhode Island is, I believe, in this particular, pretty much in the situation of Connecticut.").

20. William E. Nelson, *The Eighteenth-Century Background of John Marshall's Constitutional Jurisprudence*, 76 MICH. L. REV. 893, 904 (1978).

21. *Id.*

22. *See id.* at 912–17.

23. *See id.* at 904–17.

24. MASS. CONST. of 1780, pt. 1, art. 1; *Massachusetts Constitution and the Abolition of Slavery*, MASS.GOV, https://www.mass.gov/guides/massachusetts-constitution-and-the-abolition-of-slavery#slavery-in-colonial-and-revolutionary-massachusetts.

25. Jon Swan, *The Slave Who Sued for Freedom*, 41 AM. HERITAGE 51, 54 (Mar. 1990).

26. *Id.*

27. *Id.*

28. *Id.*

29. John D. Cushing, *The Cushing Court and the Abolition of Slavery in Massachusetts: More Notes on the "Quock Walker Case,"* 5 Am. J. Legal Hist. 118, 118–19 (Apr. 1961).

30. *Id.*

31. *See id.* 119–30.

32. *See* Cushing, *supra* note 29, at 122–26; Arthur Zilversmit, *Quok Walker, Mumbet, and the Abolition of Slavery in Massachusetts*, 25 Wm. & Mary Q. 614, 615–17 (Oct. 1968).

33. Cushing, *supra* note 29, at 130–31.

34. A panel of high court appellate judges oversaw the trial. In the late eighteenth century, the Massachusetts Supreme Judicial Court regularly held jury trials as part of its duties. *See* Frank Washburn Grinnell, *The Constitutional History of the Supreme Judicial Court of Massachusetts from the Revolution to 1813*, 2 Mass. L.Q. 359, 437–38, 474–79 (1917).

35. Cushing, *supra* note 29, at 131. The state made several non-constitutional arguments as well. *Id.* at 130–31.

36. *Id.* at 133.

37. *See* Nelson, *supra* note 20, at 911 (noting that judges' instructions were ineffective because they were often contradictory).

38. Zilversmit, *supra* note 32, at 623.

39. *See* Nelson *supra* note 20, at 910–13 (noting the respect given to juries to be "good lawmen" as well as a judge's inability to supersede the will of the juries regardless of their interpretation of the law).

40. Cushing *supra* note 29, at 143.

41. *See, e.g.*, Zilversmit, *supra* note 32, at 614; Cushing, *supra* note 29, at 118, 134.

42. Zilversmit, *supra* note 32, at 617 ("There is, of course, no evidence that any of the freedom suits established that slavery *per se* was illegal.").

43. *See* Cushing *supra* note 29, at 139.

44. *See* Zilversmit, *supra* note 32, at 624 ("the decision of Ashley to confess judgment marked a formal recognition of the abolition of slavery in Massachusetts").

45. Georgia adopted a new constitution in 1789. At that point, the charter sorted the three branches of government into three articles. Before 1787, only Massachusetts did this. Amar, *supra* note 14, at 207. In its article on the judiciary, the new Georgia Constitution allowed the legislature to fix a "mode of correcting errors and appeals," and allowed "judges to direct a new trial by jury . . . which shall be final." Ga. Const. of 1789, art. III, § 2. It also introduced three-year terms for judges and protected judges from diminutions in salary while in office, an idea imported from the new federal constitution. *Id.* § 5; Albert B. Saye, A Constitutional History of Georgia, 1732–1945, 145 (1948) (2010 reprint). But the overall structure of the court system did not change much. All but a handful of cases, mostly civil claims involving small dollar amounts, were heard by courts of final jurisdiction in each county. *See* Ga. Const.

of 1789, art. III, § 1; Saye, *supra*, at 179–80 (describing how the state Judiciary Act of 1789 created inferior courts in each county that handled small civil claims and performed administrative functions like collecting taxes and licensing taverns).

46. Georgia historian Albert Saye suggests that "[t]he colonial practice of having the Governor and Council serve as a court of appeals appears . . . to have continued temporarily," although the practice does not appear anywhere in the constitution. *See* Saye, *supra* note 46, at 178. Under the 1777 constitution, the state legislature selected the governor, and legislators elected out of their own body the executive councilors. *See* Ga. Const. of 1777, art. II. In this way, the extra-constitutional appellate court also represented the people. The state also held a Convention of Judges, an annual rule-making conference, that sometimes informally decided legal issues "reserved" by judges from the supreme (later called "superior") courts. A lot of mist surrounds this body. But there's one thing it was not, a court of appeals that had the final say over the meaning of laws and the constitution. *See generally* Beverly Bates, *Two Courts for the Price of One: The Superior Courts of Georgia and the Convention of Judges, 1797–1845*, 2 Ga. J.S. Legal Hist. 219 (1993).

47. *See* Ga. Const. of 1777, arts. 40, 44, 46.

48. *Id.* at art. 40.

49. Saye, *supra* note 46, at 178. This was also a common practice in New England around the time of the Revolution. *See, e.g.*, Hendrik Hartog, *The Public Law of a County Court: Judicial Government in Eighteenth-Century Massachusetts*, 20 Am. J. Legal Hist. 282 (1976). But Georgia appears to have taken the practice further than any other state at the founding by including it in its constitution.

50. Ga. Const. of 1777, art. 40.

51. *Id.*

52. *Id.* arts. 41, 42.

53. *Id.* art. 42.

54. *See* Amar, *supra* note 14, at 237–42.

55. *Id.* at 239.

56. *See generally* Akhil Amar, America's Unwritten Constitution: The Precedents and Principles We Live By (2012); Laurence H. Tribe, The Invisible Constitution (2008).

57. Hamburger, *supra* note 8, at 620.

58. Jack N. Rakove, *The Origins of Judicial Review: A Plea for New Contexts*, 49 Stan. L. Rev. 1031, 1034–35 (1997) (cited in Hamburger, *supra* note 8, at 15 n.35).

59. *See* Hamburger, *supra* note 8, at 255–80; Mary Sarah Bilder, The Transatlantic Constitution: Colonial Legal Culture and the Empire (2004).

60. *See* John O. McGinnis, *The Duty of Clarity*, 84 GEO. WASH. L. REV. 843, 867–76 (2016).

61. HAMBURGER, *supra* note 8, at 398.

62. *Id.*

63. *See* WOOD, *supra* note 12, at 148, 160; William F. Swindler, *Seedtime of an American Judiciary: From Independence to the Constitution*, 17 WM. & MARY L. REV. 503, 507 (1976).

64. Two minor exceptions existed for a time. Connecticut entered the Union with some locally elected lower-court judges, a practice left over from the colony's early days. The short-lived Vermont Republic also elected some of its judges, a topic covered briefly in Chapter 3.

65. HAMBURGER, *supra* note 8, at 2, 585–86. Not until 1792 does Kentucky become the first American government to make a premise of judicial review explicit, saying that any law "contrary to the constitution is void." KY. CONST. of 1792, art. XII; *see* Thayer, *supra* note 1, at 129. The Supreme Clause of the US Constitution comes close with respect to judicial review and state laws, saying that federal law "shall be the supreme Law of the Land," "and the Judges in every State shall be bound thereby, any Thing in the Constitution or Laws of any State to the Contrary notwithstanding." U.S. Const. art. VI, § 2.

66. MASS. CONST. Part I, art. 30.

67. *Id.* Chapter 6 elaborates on the historical context of express separation-of-powers clauses like this one.

68. Elbridge Gerry, by the way, approved of judicial review. In his words, it would provide "a sufficient check [against] encroachments on their own department by their exposition of the laws, which involved a power of deciding on their constitutionality." 1 THE RECORDS OF THE FEDERAL CONVENTION OF 1787, at 97 (Max Farrand ed., 1911) (quoted in Treanor, *supra* note 1, at 470).

69. *See* GORDON S. WOOD, POWER AND LIBERTY: CONSTITUTIONALISM IN THE AMERICAN REVOLUTION (forthcoming Oxford Univ. Press 2021).

70. *See* VA. CONST. of 1776, form of government, para. 29.

71. *See* William M. Treanor, *The* Case of the Prisoners *and the Origins of Judicial Review*, 143 U. PA. L. REV. 491, 501–03 (1994); Commonwealth v. Caton, 8 Va. (4 Call) 5, 5–7 (1782).

72. *See* Treanor, *supra* note 72, at 501–02.

73. THOMAS HUNTER, *The Teaching of George Wythe*, *in* THE HISTORY OF LEGAL EDUCATION IN THE UNITED STATES: COMMENTARIES AND PRIMARY SOURCES 143, 160 (Steve Sheppard ed., 1999).

74. *See* Treanor, *supra* note 72, at 507–08.

75. Rough Draft of Randolph's Argument to the Court, *quoted in* Treanor, *supra* note 72, at 510.

76. Treanor, *supra* note 72, at 522 (quoting Tucker's notes). *Cf. Marbury*, 5 U.S. (1 Cranch) at 177 ("Those who apply the rule to particular cases,

must of necessity expound and interpret that rule."); THE FEDERALIST 78 (Alexander Hamilton) ("[I]n determining between two contradictory laws . . . it is the province of the courts to liquidate and fix their meaning and operation.").

77. *See* Treanor, *supra* note 72, at 522–23.
78. *Id.* at 527 (quoting Tucker's notes) (emphasis in original).
79. *Id.* at 530.
80. *Id.* at 536 (quoting from Pendleton's notes *in* 2 THE LETTERS AND PAPERS OF EDMUND PENDLETON, 1734–803, 422 (David J. Mays ed., 1967)).
81. *Caton*, 8 Va. (4 Call) at 8.
82. *Id.*
83. Treanor, *supra* note 72, at 537–38.
84. *Id.* at 517 & n.101, 538.
85. *Caton*, 8 Va. (4 Call) at 10–11.
86. Treanor, *supra* note 72, at 540.
87. Kamper v. Hawkins, 3 Va. (1 Va. Cas.) 20 (1793).
88. *Id.* at 36, 39.
89. *Compare id.* at 38–39, *with Marbury*, 5 U.S. (1 Cranch) at 177–78.
90. McGinnis, *supra* note 60, at 900.
91. *Kamper*, 3 Va. (1 Va. Cas.) at 74.
92. *Id.* at 78.
93. *Id.* at 77–78.
94. *Id.* at 78–79.
95. *Id.* at 81.
96. *See id.* at 61 ("[T]he violation must be plain and clear, or there might be danger of the judiciary preventing the operation of laws which might be productive of much public good.").
97. *Id.* at 65.
98. *Id.* at 30–31.
99. *Id.* at 32.
100. *Id.* at 47–48; *cf. id.* at 36–38 (Roane, J.).
101. *Id.* at 53; *see* Treanor, *supra* note 1, at 516–17.
102. Bayard v. Singleton, 1 N.C. (Mart.) 5 (1787).
103. Treanor, *supra* note 1, at 478 (citing *Bayard*, 1 N.C. (Mart.) 5).
104. David P. Currie, *The Most Insignificant Justice: A Preliminary Inquiry*, 50 U. CHI. L. REV. 466, 479 (1983).
105. N.C. CONST. of 1776, art. I, § 25.
106. *Bayard*, 1 N.C. (Mart.) at 6.
107. *Id.* at 6–7.
108. *Id.* at 7; *see* Treanor, *supra* note 1, at 479.
109. *See* Treanor, *supra* note 1, at 479–80.
110. 1 THE LAW PRACTICE OF ALEXANDER HAMILTON: DOCUMENTS AND COMMENTARY 292–93 (Julius Goebel ed., 1964).

111. HENRY B. DAWSON, *The Case of Elizabeth Rutgers versus Joshua Waddington* vi, viii–x (1866).

112. 1 THE LAW PRACTICE OF ALEXANDER HAMILTON, *supra* note 110, at 291.

113. FORREST MCDONALD, *Alexander Hamilton: A Biography* 65 (1982). *But see* 1 THE LAW PRACTICE OF ALEXANDER HAMILTON, *supra* note 110, at 291 n.26.

114. 1 THE LAW PRACTICE OF ALEXANDER HAMILTON, *supra* note 110, at 289–90.

115. *Id.* at 290.

116. *Id.*

117. *Id.*

118. *Id.* at 282.

119. *See* Act of March 17, 1783 ("An Act for granting more effectual relief in cases of certain trespasses"), *reprinted in* 1 LAWS OF NEW YORK 552 (Weed, Parsons & Co. ed., 1886); *see also* 1 THE LAW PRACTICE OF ALEXANDER HAMILTON, *supra* note 110, at 295–97; Treanor, *supra* note 1, at 480.

120. ALAN NEVINS, AMERICAN STATES DURING AND AFTER THE REVOLUTION 269 (1969).

121. 1 THE LAW PRACTICE OF ALEXANDER HAMILTON, *supra* note 111, at 292–93.

122. *Id.* at 302 (quotation omitted).

123. *See id.* at 291–92.

124. WOOD, *supra* note 12, at 458.

125. *See* Def. Br., Draft No. 4, *in* 1 THE LAW PRACTICE OF ALEXANDER HAMILTON, *supra* note 1110 at 367–68, 374–75.

126. THE FEDERALIST No. 78 (Alexander Hamilton).

127. Opinion, *in* 1 THE LAW PRACTICE OF ALEXANDER HAMILTON, *supra* note 110, at 393 (quotation omitted).

128. *Contra* McGinnis, *supra* note 60, at 843, 917–18 (arguing that the "judicial duty of clarity also suggests that the judiciary can engage only in interpretation, not construction during the course of judicial review").

129. Opinion, *in* 1 THE LAW PRACTICE OF ALEXANDER HAMILTON, *supra* note 110, at 415; *see* Kramer, *supra* note 1, at 56 (noting the application of Blackstone's tenth rule of construction). *Cf.* 1 WILLIAM BLACKSTONE, COMMENTARIES ON THE LAWS OF ENGLAND 61–62 (1765).

130. 1 THE LAW PRACTICE OF ALEXANDER HAMILTON, *supra* note 110, at 412.

131. NEVINS, *supra* note 120, at 271.

132. Treanor, *supra* note 1, at 487.

133. *Id.*; 1 THE LAW PRACTICE OF ALEXANDER HAMILTON, *supra* note 111, at 312–13 (reproducing and discussing the resolution); NEVINS, *supra* note 120, at 271–72 (discussing same).

134. NEVINS, *supra* note 120, at 272.

135. *Founders Online, From George Washington to James Duane, 10 April 1785,* NAT'L ARCHIVES, https://founders.archives.gov/documents/Washington/04-02-02-0347.

136. *Rutgers* became many things to many scholars. Some read it as evidence that Americans saw their constitutions as judicially enforceable fundamental law from the start. *See, e.g.*, Saikrishna Prakash & John Yoo, *Questions for the Critics of Judicial Review*, 72 GEO. WASH. L. REV. 354, 362–63 (2003). Others emphasize that the binding effect of fundamental law on the legislature was better understood than the judicial role in enforcing it. *See, e.g.*, Treanor, *supra* note 1, at 487. Still others take the case to represent an unremarkable application of Blackstone's widely accepted interpretive rules. *See* Kramer, *supra* note 1, at 56.

137. I say relatively quickly because some states were skeptical of judicial review at the outset, such as Vermont, and some citizens, lawyers, and legislatures were critical of it in specific cases, Thayer, *supra* note 1, at 132–34, as we will see in the next chapter.

138. HAMBURGER, *supra* note 8, at 180; *see also id.* at 309–16 (discussing the English idea of "manifest" contradiction or error and its coming to American law, especially in the Virginia cases, *Kamper v. Hawkins* (1793) and *The Case of the Prisoners* (1782)). See more generally MARY SARAH BILDER, THE TRANSATLANTIC CONSTITUTION: COLONIAL LEGAL CULTURE AND THE EMPIRE (Harvard Univ. Press 2008) (describing a colonial tradition in which the laws of the colonies could not be repugnant to the laws of England).

139. "In an early review of these state court decisions, Charles Grove Haines concluded that the search for a single decisive case that established the power of judicial review and drove subsequent developments was misguided. 'It seems rather that a series of precedents with a cumulative effect, along with a common sentiment in practically all of the colonies, led men to the acceptance of certain ideas and consequences,' and this resulted in judicial review's emergence . . . by the time of the federal convention in 1787." WHITTINGTON, *supra* note 1, at 45 (quoting CHARLES GROVE HAINES, THE AMERICAN DOCTRINE OF JUDICIAL SUPREMACY 82 (Macmillan 1914)).

140. The founding generation was focused on prohibiting the legislature, not the judiciary, from altering constitutional guarantees. In the words of Justice Roane from the *Kamper* case: "If the legislature may infringe this Constitution, it is no longer fixed; it is not this year what it was the last; and the liberties of the people are wholly at the mercy of the legislature." WHITTINGTON, *supra* note 1, at 48 (quoting Kamper v. Hawkins, 3 Va. 20, 31 (1793)). If the founding generation was wary of giving American legislators authority to update an unwritten constitution, it would have been doubly wary of giving that same authority to American judges with respect to written constitutions.

141. McGinnis, *supra* note 60, at 869–76 (describing the Founding generation's interpretive tools); *id.* at 881–85 (describing how state courts applied those tools to clarify constitutional language); *see also* John O. McGinnis

& Michael B. Rappaport, *Unifying Original Intent and Original Public Meaning*, 113 Nw. L. Rev. 1371, 1401–18 (2019) (showing that cabinet members and legislators debating the validity of the Bank of the United States shared interpretive methods even as they disagreed over the right answer to the question).

142. For these reasons, I do not address the ubiquitous schools of modern thought for interpreting constitutions, usually focused on the federal constitution. *See, e.g.*, RICHARD EPSTEIN, THE CLASSICAL LIBERAL CONSTITUTION (2014) (urging an interpretation based on Enlightenment ideas about liberty); CLARK M. NEILY III, TERMS OF ENGAGEMENT: HOW OUR COURTS SHOULD ENFORCE THE CONSTITUTION'S PROMISE OF LIMITED GOVERNMENT (2013) (urging courts to police the size and reach of government); JACK BALKIN, LIVING ORIGINALISM (2011) (arguing that evolving constitutional interpretations do not always conflict with the Constitution's original meaning); STEPHEN BREYER, ACTIVE LIBERTY (2005) (urging a flexible and pragmatic approach to constitutional interpretation that emphasizes participation in collective self-government); RANDY E. BARNETT, RESTORING THE LOST CONSTITUTION (2003) (arguing that courts should adopt a "presumption of liberty" to reinvigorate limits on government); JOHN HART ELY, DEMOCRACY AND DISTRUST: A THEORY OF JUDICIAL REVIEW (1980) (proposing a democracy-reinforcing reading of the Constitution); RONALD DWORKIN, TAKING RIGHTS SERIOUSLY (1977) (urging a moral reading of the constitution); David Strauss, *Common Law Constitutional Interpretation*, 63 U. CHI. L. REV. 877 (1996) (suggesting that the Constitution's text plays a relatively small role in constitutional interpretation compared with the evolving body of judge-made law); WHITTINGTON, *supra* note 1, (compiling and analyzing all of the US Supreme Court's cases undertaking judicial review of federal laws). My modest goal is to identify insights from the early state court decisions that bear on judicial review today in the state and federal courts.

143. It may be true that there is a "paucity of evidence," a small number of cases, to show how the federal Framers would have conceived of judicial review. EDWARD S. CORWIN, *What Kind of Judicial Review Did the Framers Have in Mind? in* CORWIN'S CONSTITUTION: ESSAYS AND INSIGHTS OF EDWARD S. CORWIN 71 (Kenneth D. Crews ed., 1986). But that may confirm that judges did not exercise that power lightly at the outset, as I am inclined to think. And it may suggest, as Hamburger thinks and I think, that the search for evidence is too one-sided and looks only at federal cases or state high court cases. HAMBURGER, *supra* note 8, at 14–15.

144. HAMBURGER, *supra* note 8, at 15–16.

145. *See* John Manning, *Textualism and the Equity of the Statute*, 101 COLUM. L. REV. 1, 8 (2001).

146. *Id.*

147. *Id.* at 61.

148. HAMBURGER, *supra* note 8, at 15. For like reasons, the idea is not, in Caleb Nelson's words, to avoid constitutional questions; it is to avoid unconstitutionality. *See* Caleb E. Nelson, *Avoiding Constitutional Questions Versus Avoiding Unconstitutionality*, 128 HARV. L. REV. F. 331 (2015).

149. Thayer, *supra* note 1, at 140–43 (mentioning many state and federal cases requiring a clear error before invalidating a statute).

150. HAMBURGER, *supra* note 8, at 618.

151. *See, e.g.*, Cooper v. Telfair, 4 U.S. (4 Dall.) 14, 19 (1800) (Paterson, J.); Calder v. Bull, 3 U.S. (3 Dall.) 386, 399 (1798) (Iredell, J.); Hylton v. United States, 3 U.S. (3 Dall.) 171, 175 (1796) (Chase, J.); Kamper v. Hawkins, 1 Va. 20, 39 (1793) (Roane, J.); *id.* at 61 (Tyler, J.). *See* McGinnis, *supra* note 60, at 881–85, 887–93, 898–901, for discussion of "clarity" in early judicial decisions.

152. VanHorne's Lessee v. Dorrance, 2 U.S. (Dall.) 304, 309 (C.C.D. Pa. 1795) (Paterson, J.); *see also, e.g.*, Marbury v. Madison, 5 U.S. (1 Cranch) 137, 177 (1803); *Kamper*, 3 Va. at 40 (Roane, J.); Correspondence, PROVIDENCE GAZETTE, Oct. 7, 1786, *quoted in* HAMBURGER, *supra* note 8, at 443 (summarizing the opinions of the judges in Trevett v. Weeden (R.I. 1786)).

153. THE FEDERALIST No. 81 (Alexander Hamilton).

154. McGinnis, *supra* note 60, at 883 n.194 (quoting St. George Tucker's argument notes from the *Case of the Prisoners* (Va. 1782), *in* 3 ST. GEORGE TUCKER'S LAW REPORTS AND SELECTED PAPERS, 1782–1895, 1744 (Charles F. Hobson ed., 2013)).

155. *See, e.g.*, Byrne's Adm'rs v. Stewart's Adm'rs, 3 S.C. Eq. (3 Des. Eq.) 466, 476 (S.C. App. Eq. 1812); Commonwealth ex rel. O'Hara v. Smith, 4 Binn. 117, 123 (Pa. 1811). For discussion of the English antecedent, "manifest contradiction," see HAMBURGER, *supra* note 8, at 309–16.

156. Letter from James Iredell to Richard Dobbs Spaight (Aug. 26, 1787), *quoted in* McGinnis, *supra* note 60, at 885.

157. THE FEDERALIST No. 78 (Alexander Hamilton).

158. Hylton v. United States, 3 U.S. (3 Dall.) 171, 175 (1796) (Chase, J.).

159. Cooper v. Telfair, 4 U.S. (4 Dall.) 14, 19 (1800) (Paterson, J.).

160. *Id.* at 18 (Washington, J.).

161. 5 U.S. (1 Cranch) at 177.

162. McGinnis, *supra* note 60, at 894–95 (citing HAMBURGER, *supra* note 8, at 312–13).

163. CURRIE, *supra* note 1, at 55.

164. Treanor, *supra* note 1, at 496.

165. McGinnis and Rappaport respond, for example: "We are skeptical of Treanor's claim that the interpretive rules for constitutions at the time

of the Framing required the courts to aggressively protect entities not involved in the legislative process, such as judges and juries, but to defer to legislatures in other circumstances." John McGinnis & Michael Rappaport, *Original Methods Originalism: A New Theory of Interpretation and the Case Against Construction*, 103 Nw. L. Rev. 751, 795 (2009).

166. Kramer, *supra* note 1, at 79.

167. *Id.* In contrast to John McGinnis and Philip Hamburger, Kramer claims that "[c]ourts exercising judicial review" in the early Republic "made no claim to treat fundamental law as ordinary law." *Id.* Instead, he says, "They justified their refusal to enforce laws as a 'political-legal' act on behalf of the people." *Id.* In the early nineteenth century, "the conceptual and linguistic framework shifted as the Constitution was 'legalized' and came to be seen more and more as ordinary positive law" with decisions like *Marbury v. Madison* (1803). *Id.* at 13. That change, however, was judicial review's second act. The first, argues Kramer, "was a successful bid by judges to an equal place in [a] scheme" of government where "[e]ach branch could express its [constitutional] views as issues came before it in the ordinary course of governing" but where "[n]one of the branches' views" was "final or authoritative." *Id.* at 87. Judges, he says, first had to achieve "status as members of a coordinate branch capable of making and acting upon independent judgments about the meaning of the Constitution" as a political document before they could claim it as a legal one that they should decipher. *Id.*

168. William E. Nelson, *Changing Conceptions of Judicial Review: The Evolution of Constitutional Theory in the States, 1790–1860*, 120 U. Penn. L. Rev. 1166, 1167–69 (1972) (discussing early cases); Sylvia Snowiss, *The Marbury of 1803 and the Modern Marbury*, 20 Const. Comment. 231, 233 (2003). *See also* Sylvia Snowiss, Judicial Review and the Law of the Constitution (1990). In this sense, perhaps the practice of restraint itself became liquidated. William Baude, *Constitutional Liquidation*, 71 Stan. L. Rev. 1 (2019).

169. 28 U.S.C. § 453; *see also, e.g.*, Cal. Const. art. 20, § 3 (constitutional oath of office); Mich. Const. art. 11, § 1 (oath of public officers); Mich. Comp. Laws §§ 168.400, 409h, 420, 467j (requiring the judges and justices of Michigan's supreme, appellate, circuit, and district courts to take the constitutional oath of office); Ohio Const. art. XV, § 7 (requiring an oath or affirmation to support the United States and Ohio constitutions); Ohio Rev. Code § 3.23 (judicial oath); Utah Const. art. 4, § 10 (constitutional oath of office).

170. Thayer, *supra* note 1, at 129.

171. *Id.* at 139.

172. *Id.* at 149–51.

173. *Id.* at 137 n.1.

174. *Id.* at 151–56.

175. Jeffrey S. Sutton, 51 Imperfect Solutions 149 (2018) (quoting an unsigned editorial written by Frankfurter in a 1925 edition of the *New Republic*).

176. Learned Hand, The Spirit of Liberty 189–90 (Irving Dillard ed., 1953).

177. Thayer, *supra* note 1, at 152.

178. *Id.* at 154–55.

179. Oliver Wendell Holmes, Collected Legal Papers 295–96 (1920).

180. Of course, one could embrace a deferential approach to judicial review for all state court decisions with respect to all laws before a given state court.

181. To the extent that people premise their approach to federal judicial review on the political responsiveness of the government under scrutiny, the contrast between the highly democratic state governments and the far-less-democratic national government should favor more rigorous review of federal laws.

182. *Federal Bureau of Prison Statistics*, Fed. Bureau of Prison, www.bop.gov/about/statistics (last visited Nov. 29, 2020).

183. Whittington, *supra* note 1, at 15 (citing *Brutus, No. 11, in* Howard Gillman, Mark A. Graber, & Keith E. Whittington, 1 American Constitutionalism, 57 (Oxford Univ. Press, 2d ed. 2017)).

184. Thayer, *supra* note 1, at 138.

185. *Cf.* David E. Bernstein, Rehabilitating Lochner: Defending Individual Rights Against Progressive Reform (2011).

186. *See* McGinnis, *supra* note 60, at 881–85 (cases before the U.S. Constitution), 887–901 (state and federal cases after 1789).

187. *See* Hamburger, *supra* note 8, at 256–74, 309–16.

188. Justice Tom Lee, a member of the Utah Supreme Court, has done yeoman's work in developing corpus linguistics as an interpretive tool. *See* Thomas R. Lee & Stephen C. Mouritsen, *The Corpus and the Critics*, U. Chi. L. Rev. (forthcoming 2021); Thomas R. Lee & James C. Phillips, *Data-Driven Originalism*, 167 U. Pa. L. Rev. 261 (2019); Thomas R. Lee & Stephen C. Mouritsen, *Judging Ordinary Meaning*, 127 Yale L.J. 788 (2018).

189. Jeffrey S. Sutton, *The Role of History in Judging Disputes About the Meaning of the Constitution*, 41 Tex. Tech L. Rev. 1173, 1191 (2009).

190. 28 U.S.C. § 453; *see also, e.g.*, N.C. Gen. Stat. § 11–11; Ohio Rev. Code § 3.23.

191. Even those inclined toward a narrow separation-of-personnel, rather than separation-of-powers, interpretation of this provision presumably would not relish judges who effectively exercise legislative powers by issuing decisions ungrounded in existing laws, whether statutes or constitutions.

192. Evan Caminker, *Thayerian Deference to Congress and Supreme Court Supermajority Rule: Lessons from the Past*, 78 Ind. L.J. 73, 79 (2003) (describing "political component" and "value choices" implicated by judicial review).

193. *Kamper*, 3 Va. (1 Va. Cas.) at 39.

194. *Id.*

195. Antonin Scalia, *The Rule of Law as a Law of Rules*, 56 U. Chi. L. Rev. 1175, 1178–79 (1989).

Chapter 3

1. One caveat is that the Seventeenth Amendment, by permitting the direct election of US senators, made the confirmation process more directly accountable to the people in the states, not to the legislatures in the states.

2. Jed Handelsman Shugerman, The People's Courts 276–77 (2012).

3. Before 1776, Connecticut and Rhode Island were "corporate colonies" that "had elected their governors and were in fact already republics." Instead of writing new constitutions at the start of the revolution, they "revised their existing colonial charters by simply eliminating all references to the Crown." Gordon S. Wood, Power and Liberty: Constitutionalism in the American Revolution (forthcoming Oxford Univ. Press 2021).

4. *See* Akhil Reed Amar, America's Constitution: A Biography 207, 218, 233, 569 n. 2 (2006).

5. Gordon S. Wood, Creation of the American Republic, 1776–1787, 135 (1969).

6. *Id.* at 160.

7. Mass. Const. of 1780, part II, ch. II, § 1, art. IX; N.Y. Const. of 1777, art. XXIII. In Maryland, the governor appointed judges with the advice and consent of his executive council. Md. Const. of 1776, art. XLVIII. But the legislature chose the governor and the council. *Id.* at arts. XXV, XXVI. Unlike Massachusetts and New York, where the people elected their governors directly, the Maryland legislature remained in control of judicial appointments. Pennsylvania had a similar arrangement. The legislature named the state's president, the head of the executive branch, and Pennsylvania's counties selected other executive councilors directly. Pa. Const. of 1776, § 19. And they in turn selected the judges. *Id.* § 20. Delaware had its governor and legislature appoint Supreme Court justices "by joint ballot," Del. Const. of 1776, § 12, and New Hampshire adopted a model like Massachusetts in 1784; at the Founding, however, the legislature chose judges there too. *Compare* N.H. Const. of 1776 (providing that "all public officers . . . be appointed by the Council and Assembly"), *with* N.H. Const. of 1784, pt. II (providing that "all judicial officers . . . shall be nominated and appointed by the president and council").

8. Wood, *supra* note 5, at 160.

9. *See, e.g., id.* at 150–59, 449–52, 603–04 (describing the functional separation of governmental powers during the Founding era and its significance); Steven G. Calabresi & Joan L. Larsen, *One Person, One*

Office: Separation of Powers or Separation of Personnel, 79 CORNELL L. REV. 1045, 1057–61 (1994) (same for separation of personnel).

10. WOOD, *supra* note 5, at 160–61.

11. While tenure during "good behavior" initially freed judges from executive control, in many states legislatures retained the power under their first constitutions to remove judges more or less at will and to control judicial salaries, thus blunting the effect of indefinite terms. *See* WOOD, *supra* note 5, at 161; David P. Currie, *Separating Judicial Power*, 61 LAW & CONTEMP. PROBS. 7, 9–10 (1998). Judicial independence in the immediate aftermath of the American Revolution was for these reasons rather "asymmetrical." Jack N. Rakove, *Original Justifications for Judicial Independence*, 95 GEO. L.J. 1061, 1065 (2007).

12. WOOD, *supra* note 5, at 155–56.

13. *See, e.g.*, N.J. CONST. of 1776, art. IX ("The Governor & Council (seven whereof shall be a quorum) [shall] be the Court of Appeals in the last resort in all causes of law, as heretofore . . ."); ALBERT B. SAYE, A CONSTITUTIONAL HISTORY OF GEORGIA, 1732–1945, 178 (1948) (2010 reprint) (describing Georgia's informal continuation of the colonial practice in the first decades after independence based on reports of it in the *Georgia Gazette* from 1787 to 1788). A few more states replaced the colonial practice of appealing to the governor and Council with new appellate tribunals that consisted in whole or in part of executive or legislative officials. *See, e.g.*, DEL. CONST. of 1776, art. 17 (governor and six legislative appointees, three selected by each house); N.Y. CONST. of 1777, art. XXXII (supreme court judges, chancellor, and senators); *see also* S.C. CONST. of 1778, art. XXIV (lieutenant-governor and privy council may serve as court of chancery).

14. Gordon S. Wood, *The Origins of Judicial Review Revisited, or How the Marshall Court Made More out of Less*, 56 WASH. & LEE L. REV. 787, 791 (1999).

15. PHILIP HAMBURGER, LAW AND JUDICIAL DUTY 526 (2008); *see generally id.* at 522–29.

16. *Id.* at 528.

17. THE FEDERALIST No. 81 (Alexander Hamilton).

18. *See generally* Amasa M. Eaton, *The Development of the Judicial System in Rhode Island*, 14 YALE L.J. 148 (1905); AMAR, *supra* note 4, at 207.

19. Connecticut, which like Rhode Island did not frame a new, written constitution after 1776, appointed judges annually. William F. Swindler, *Seedtime of an American Judiciary: From Independence to the Constitution*, 17 WM. & MARY L. REV. 503, 507 (1976). Under Georgia's 1777 constitution, which did not specify terms of office, the chief justice served a one-year term and the rest of the state's judges served at the legislature's pleasure. SAYE, *supra* note 13, at 112; Joseph H. Smith, *An Independent Judiciary: The Colonial Background*, 124 U. PA. L. REV. 1104, 1155 (1976).

20. Charles Warren, *Earliest Cases of Judicial Review of State Legislation by Federal Courts*, 32 YALE L.J. 15, 16–17 (1922) (describing the background of *Trevett v. Weeden*); HAMBURGER, *supra* note 15, at 436–37 (same).

21. Warren, *supra* note 20, at 17.

22. *Id.* at 18; HAMBURGER, *supra* note 15, at 437–39.

23. HAMBURGER, *supra* note 15, at 440.

24. Warren, *supra* note 20, at 18.

25. HAMBURGER, *supra* note 15, at 439.

26. *See* Warren, *supra* note 20, at 16; HAMBURGER, *supra* note 15, at 437.

27. HAMBURGER, *supra* note 15, at 440 (quoting JAMES M. VARNUM, THE CASE, TREVETT AGAINST WEEDEN 4 (1787)).

28. *Id.* at 439–40.

29. Warren, *supra* note 20, at 19.

30. *Id.*; HAMBURGER, *supra* note 15, at 441. Rhode Island, as noted, continued to operate under its former royal charter.

31. WOOD, *supra* note 5, at 460 (quoting VARNUM, *supra* note 27, at 29).

32. VARNUM, *supra* note 27, at 29 (quoting the Rhode Island judicial oath).

33. WOOD, *supra* note 5, at 460. For more on James Varnum's judicial duty argument, see HAMBURGER, *supra* note 15, at 442–43, and William Michael Treanor, *Judicial Review Before* Marbury, 58 STAN. L. REV. 455, 476–77 (2005).

34. VARNUM, *supra* note 27, at 15, *quoted in* Treanor, *supra* note 33, at 477.

35. HAMBURGER, *supra* note 15, at 442; *see also* Treanor, *supra* note 33, at 477 (quoting Varnum's argument that the statute "was not creative of a new law, but declaratory of the rights of all the people, as derived from the Charter [and] from their progenitors, time out of mind").

36. HAMBURGER, *supra* note 15, at 442. Hamburger notes that "the record simply stated that 'the said Complaint do[es] not come under Cognizance of the Judges here present, and . . . it is hereby dismissed.'" *Id.* at 443 n.133 (quoting the court record found in the archives of the Rhode Island State Judicial Center at Pawtucket).

37. Correspondence, PROVIDENCE GAZETTE, Oct. 7, 1786, *quoted in* HAMBURGER, *supra* note 15, at 443; Treanor, *supra* note 33, at 478. About one of the judges, the *Gazette* said in full: "Judge Tillinghast took notice of the striking repugnancy in the expressions of the act, '*Without trial by jury, according to the laws of the land*'—and on that ground gave his judgment the same way [as the two judges who found the act unconstitutional]." Correspondence, *supra* (emphasis in original). William Treanor reads this passage to say that Tillinghast thought the law to be unconstitutional. Treanor, *supra* note 33, at 478. But Philip Hamburger reads the passage differently. He suggests that Judge Tillinghast "held the act repugnant to itself," that is, self-contradictory and "[its] intent[] so difficult to discern that the act could not be executed." HAMBURGER, *supra* note 15, at 444. Whichever view is right,

the essential point is that Tillinghast found a reason to declare the law void.

38. Warren, *supra* note 20, at 20 (quoting the Assembly resolution as reproduced *in* 10 RECORDS OF THE STATE OF RHODE ISLAND AND PROVIDENCE PLANTATION 215 (John Russell Barlett ed. 1865)).

39. *Id.*

40. HAMBURGER, *supra* note 15, at 445.

41. *Id.*

42. *Id.* (quoting the judges' memorial in VARNUM, *supra* note 27, at 45–46).

43. VARNUM, *supra* note 27, at 42–43.

44. *Id.* at 43.

45. *See generally id.* at 38-46.

46. *Id.* at 46; *see* HAMBURGER, *supra* note 15, at 445; Warren, *supra* note 20, at 20–21.

47. VARNUM, *supra* note 27, at 51.

48. *Id.* at 53.

49. HAMBURGER, *supra* note 15, at 445–46; Warren, *supra* note 20, at 21.

50. HAMBURGER, *supra* note 15, at 444, 446. Hamburger wryly observes that Mumford's "affliction," which prevented him from appearing before the Assembly, "seems to have been of the same sort that had already rendered [him] almost speechless on the bench." *Id.* at 444.

51. Jed Handelsman Shugerman, *Economic Crisis and the Rise of Judicial Elections and Judicial Review*, 123 HARV. L. REV. 1061, 1147 (2010).

52. Treanor, *supra* note 33, at 477.

53. 2 THE RECORDS OF THE FEDERAL CONVENTION OF 1787, 28 (Max Farrand, ed., rev. ed. 1937).

54. *See, e.g.,* Irving R. Kaufman, *The Essence of Judicial Independence*, 80 COLUM. L. REV. 671, 685–86 (1980).

55. Theodore W. Ruger, *"A Question Which Convulses a Nation": The Early Republic's Greatest Debate About the Judicial Review Power*, 117 HARV. L. REV. 826, 829 (2004).

56. Letter from Thomas Jefferson to George Thomson (June 22, 1825), *quoted in* Ruger, *supra* note 55, at 883.

57. Ruger, *supra* note 55, at 830.

58. *Id.*

59. KEITH E. WHITTINGTON, REPUGNANT LAWS: JUDICIAL REVIEW OF ACTS OF CONGRESS FROM THE FOUNDING TO THE PRESENT 49 (2019) (quoting KY. CONST. of 1799, art. XII, § 28).

60. Ruger, *supra* note 55, at 840 (quoting remarks by Senator Henry Clay as carried by Kentucky newspapers in 1822).

61. *Id.* at 841.

62. *Id.* at 842 (quoting an 1824 anti-court pamphlet).

63. *Id.* at 845.

64. *Id.* at 839–40; *see also id.* at 843–44. The United States Supreme Court
confirmed the harsh consequences of the compact, and of constitutional
adjudication by courts, in *Green v. Biddle* in 1823. 21 U.S. (8 Wheat.) 1. It
invalidated a set of Kentucky statutes that gave tenants and squatters
additional rights and protections in ejectment actions, commonly known
as "occupying claimant laws," under the Federal Constitution's Contracts
Clause. It held that the Clause protected the rights of landholders frozen
in place by the interstate compact and that the occupying claimant laws
infringed on those rights. *Id.* at 92–93; *see* Ruger, *supra* note 55, at 843–44.
The laws, however, made some sense in Kentucky, where land titles could
be untrustworthy and "not only intentional squatters but also those who
built homes and farms fully believing they owned the land upon which
they lived were at risk of eviction." Ruger, *supra* note 55, at 843. *Green*
showed that the democratic decisions of Kentucky's citizens, however
sensible they might be, could be undone by judges the Commonwealth's
people did not choose and whom they could not hold accountable.

65. Ruger, *supra* note 55, at 845.

66. *Id.* at 847 (quoting Governor Joseph Desha, Message to the Kentucky
Legislature (Nov. 7, 1825)). Ruger observes that the court rejected
invitations by the defendant's counsel to defer to the legislature's
judgment and "declared its own supremacy in determining whether an act
indeed transcended constitutional limits." *Id.* at 846–47. Whether or not
the law impaired the obligation of contract was a close question, and the
request for deference rested on "reliable rhetorical tropes of Jeffersonian
republicanism," if nothing else. *Id.* at 846.

67. *Id.* at 847 (quoting Governor Joseph Desha, Message to the Kentucky
Legislature (Nov. 7, 1825)).

68. *See* the Rhode Island story as discussed in this chapter and a summary of
a similar 1807 court controversy in Ohio in Ruger, *supra* note 55, at 839.
Ted Ruger observes that, because "Ohio judges served only for seven-year
terms, . . . after immediate impeachment efforts narrowly failed to garner
the requisite supermajority, the legislature simply waited until it could
appoint more desirable judges." *Id.* Kentucky's legislators did not have
that luxury.

69. KY. CONST. of 1792, art. IV, § 3; *see* Ruger, *supra* note 55, at 849.
Kentucky's procedure for removing judges sat somewhere between the
simple-majority "address" of some states and full-blown impeachment,
authorized by Article V, § 1 of the state's 1792 constitution. It allowed
removal "for any reasonable case" on a two-thirds vote of both houses. *Id.*

70. *See* WOOD, *supra* note 5, at 161; Swindler, *supra* note 19, at 507.

71. *See* Currie, *supra* note 11, at 10; Swindler, *supra* note 19, at 507.

72. Ruger, *supra* note 55, at 849.

73. *Id.*

74. *Id.* (quoting a placard at Governor Joseph Desha's victory banquet after the 1824 election).
75. *Id.*
76. *Id.* at 850.
77. *Id.* at 850–51.
78. *Id.* at 851.
79. *Id.*
80. Ky. Const. of 1792, art. IV, §1.
81. Ky. Const. of 1792, art. IV, § 3.
82. Ruger, *supra* note 55, at 851–52 (quoting *Liberty Saved* (Louisville, Ky., William Tanner ed. 1825).
83. *Id.* at 848.
84. *Id.* at 853–54.
85. *Id.* at 854.
86. *Id.*
87. *Id.* at 854–55.
88. Letter from John Marshall to Martin P. Marshall (Dec. 27, 1825), *quoted in* Ruger, *supra* note 55, at 881–82; Ruger, *supra* note 55, at 866.
89. Ruger, *supra* note 55, at 882–83. Lincoln was not yet active in politics but he expressed sympathy for the old court fifteen years later, after he entered the Illinois legislature. *Id.* at 882.
90. Shugerman, *supra* note 2, at 3.
91. *Id.* at 5.
92. *See id.* at 60–65.
93. *See id.* at 66–77.
94. See *id.* at 276–77. Georgia began electing superior court judges as well in 1835. Virginia adopted judicial elections in 1850 but that lasted only until 1864. Connecticut and Vermont, two early pioneers, adopted judicial elections for some courts but not others. Maryland followed for all courts a year later. Massachusetts, New Hampshire, New Jersey, North Carolina, and Rhode Island rejected proposals to elect judges even as they made other changes to their state courts. Finally, there were no changes to judicial selection in Delaware or South Carolina during this period. These states continued to select judges as before. *Id.* The methods of "judicial selection ha[ve] a regional character" today as well, with gubernatorial appointment restricted to "New England and upper Mid-Atlantic states." Jessica Bulman-Pozen & Miriam Seifter, *The Democracy Principle in State Constitutions*, 119 Mich. L. Rev. (forthcoming 2021).
95. Glenn R. Winters, *Selection of Judges—An Historical Introduction*, 44 Tex. L. Rev. 1081, 1082 (1966). Although some scholars dispute the significance of New York's adoption of judicial elections in 1846 for the nationwide trend, *see* Caleb Nelson, *A Re-Evaluation of Scholarly Explanations for the Rise of the Elective Judiciary in Antebellum America*, 37 Am. J. Legal Hist. 190, 192–93 (1993), every state to join the Union

between 1846 and the start of the Civil War in 1861 did so electing all of its judges, with the exception of Iowa (which elected only its lower court judges). Contrast that with the experience before 1846, when no new state started off electing all of its judges. SHUGERMAN, *supra* note 2, at 276–77. Even Iowa, which at first glance might seem to be an exception, supports taking New York's adoption of judicial elections in 1846 as a turning point. Although the Hawkeye State joined the Union the same year, it held its first constitutional convention while still a territory two years earlier, in 1844. The proper method for selecting the state's judges was a topic of considerable debate at the convention, and the delegates had few models ready at hand. By adopting a "divided approach" like Indiana and Michigan before it—popular election for lower court judges and appointment for justices of the supreme court—delegates hoped that Iowa could "learn through experience whether one was preferable to the other." TODD E. PETTYS, THE IOWA STATE CONSTITUTION 14–15 (2d ed. 2018). In 1858, Iowa joined 17 other states in electing all judges. *See* SHUGERMAN, *supra* note 2, at 276–77. For a discussion of how Iowa's territorial experience affected the state's judiciary in the 1850s and 1860s, see Chapter 4.

96. *See* HAW. CONST. of 1959, art. V, § 3.

97. Roy A. Schotland, *Iowa's 2010 Judicial Election: Appropriate Accountability or Rampant Passion?*, 46 CT. REV. 118, 118–19 (2009–2010) [hereinafter Schotland, *Iowa's 2010 Judicial Election*]; Roy A. Schotland, *New Challenges to States' Judicial Selection*, 95 GEO. L.J. 1077, 1104 (2007).

98. *Id.*

99. *See* Schotland, *Iowa's 2010 Judicial Election, supra* note 97, at 119, 120 n.7. For a current breakdown of which states use retention elections, see *Judicial Selection: An Interactive Map*, BRENNAN CTR. FOR JUSTICE, http:// judicialselectionmap.brennancenter.org (last visited Dec. 14, 2020).

100. GEORGE WINCHESTER, THE NATCHEZ, Nov. 9, 1832, *quoted in* Nelson, *supra* note 95, at 190.

101. Nelson, *supra* note 95, at 193.

102. *Id.* at 191 (quoting Learned Hand, *The Elective and Appointive Methods of Selection of Judges*, 3 PROCEEDINGS ACAD. POL. SCI. N.Y. 82, 82 (1913)).

103. GA. CONST. of 1798, amend. X (1835); SUP. CT. GA., *Supreme Court of Georgia History*, https://www.gasupreme.us/court-information/history/ (last visited Dec. 14, 2020).

104. SHUGERMAN, *supra* note 2, at 67.

105. *Id.* at 66.

106. *Id.*

107. *Id.* at 69.

108. *Id.*

109. June Term 1818, *Walker's Mississippi Reports 36, reproduced in* SHUGERMAN, *supra* note 2, at 69.

110. June Term 1820, *Walker's Mississippi Reports* 83, *cited in* SHUGERMAN, *supra* note 2, at 69, 315 n.58.

111. SHUGERMAN, *supra* note 2, at 69.

112. *Id.* at 70.

113. *Id.*

114. NATCHEZ GAZETTE, Jan. 22, 1825, *quoted in* SHUGERMAN, *supra* note 2, at 70.

115. SHUGERMAN, *supra* note 2, at 70.

116. WOODVILLE REPUBLICAN, July 23, 1825, *quoted in* SHUGERMAN, *supra* note 2, at 70.

117. SHUGERMAN, *supra* note 2, at 70 (quoting NATCHEZ GAZETTE, Jan. 22, 1825).

118. *Id.*

119. *Id.* at 66, 74–75.

120. *Id.* at 66.

121. *Id.*

122. *Id.* at 74.

123. *Id.* at 70.

124. Nelson, *supra* note 95, at 201.

125. *Id.* at 192; *see also* SHUGERMAN, *supra* note 2, at 75.

126. Nelson, *supra* note 95, at 199 (quoting DUNBAR ROWLAND, COURTS, JUDGES, AND LAWYERS OF MISSISSIPPI, 1798–1935, 89, 92 (1935)); *see also* SHUGERMAN, *supra* note 2, at 175–76.

127. *See generally* Harry L. Witte, *Judicial Selection in the People's Democratic Republic of Pennsylvania: Here the People Rule?*, 68 TEMP. L. REV. 1079 (1995).

128. PA. CONST. of 1776, §§ 19, 20.

129. *Id.* § 23.

130. PA. CONST. of 1790, art. V, § 2.

131. *Id.* art. II, § 8; Swindler, *supra* note 19, at 507.

132. Witte, *supra* note 127, at 1104 (quoting G. S. Rowe, *Judicial Tyrant and Vox Populi: Pennsylvanians View Their State Supreme Court*, 118 PA. MAG. HIST. & BIOGRAPHY 33 (1994)).

133. *Id.* at 1006 (quoting William Duane, AURORA, Mar. 31, 1805, *in* Glenn L. Bushey, *William Duane, Crusader for Judicial Reform*, 5 PA. HIST. 141, 145 (1938)).

134. *Id.*

135. PA. CONST. of 1838, art. V, § 2. Associate judges on the Courts of Common Pleas served five-year terms, and "president," or presiding, judges on that court served for ten years, as did judges on other "courts of Record." *Id.* For a discussion of the debate about judicial independence in the 1837 constitutional convention, see generally Witte, *supra* note 127, at 1106–11; Roy H. Akagi, *The Pennsylvania Constitution of 1838*, 48 PA. MAG. HIST. & BIOGRAPHY 301 (1924).

136. SHUGERMAN, *supra* note 2, at 278.

137. Shugerman, *supra* note 51, at 1103.

138. *Debate in the House of Representatives on the Proposed Amendment to the Constitution, Remarks of Mr. Biddle of Philadelphia, February 8, 1850*, PA. TELEGRAPH, Feb. 20, 1850, *quoted in* Shugerman, *supra* note 51, at 1104.

139. *Election of Judges*, 8 AM. L.J. 481, 481 (1849), *quoted in* Shugerman, *supra* note 51, at 1104 (alteration by Shugerman).

140. ROSCOE POUND, THE FORMATIVE ERA OF AMERICAN LAW 3–4, 30 n. 2 (1938).

141. Eakin v. Raub, 12 Serg. & Rawle 330, 347 (Pa. 1825) (Gibson, J., dissenting).

142. *Id.* at 348.

143. *Id.* at 349.

144. William E. Nelson, *Changing Conceptions of Judicial Review: The Evolution of Constitutional Theory in the States, 1790–1860*, 120 U. PA. L. REV. 1166, 1181 (1972) (quoting *Eakin*, 12 Serg. & Rawle at 355).

145. *Id.* at 1182.

146. *Id.* (quoting De Chastellux v. Fairchild, 15 Pa. 18, 20 (1850)) (alteration by Nelson).

147. Roger K. Newman, *John Bannister Gibson*, *in* THE YALE BIOGRAPHICAL DICTIONARY OF AMERICAN LAW 219 (Roger K. Newman ed., 2009).

148. William A. Porter, *John Bannister Gibson, as a Lawyer, a Legislator and a Judge*, *in* MEMOIRS OF JOHN BANNISTER GIBSON: LATE CHIEF JUSTICE OF PENNSYLVANIA 135 (Thomas P. Roberts ed., 1890).

149. SHUGERMAN, *supra* note 2, at 136.

150. Shugerman, *supra* note 51, at 1127–28.

151. *See generally* Paul A. Freund, *Appointment of Justices: Some Historical Perspectives*, 101 HARV. L. REV. 1146 (1988).

152. *See generally id.* at 1147–57.

153. *See, e.g.*, Beverly Bates, *Two Courts for the Price of One: The Superior Courts of Georgia and the Convention of Judges, 1797–1845*, 2 GA. J.S. LEGAL HIST. 219, 222–23 (1993) (describing how Georgia judges' controversial exercise of judicial review touched off a factional conflict within the state's Democratic-Republican Party over the judges' reappointment by the legislature).

154. In a sign of things to come, the Senate in 1986 confirmed William Rehnquist to be chief justice by a relatively close 65–33 vote.

155. Paul Reidinger, *The Politics of Judging*, 73 A.B.A.J. 52, 52 (Apr. 1, 1987).

156. *See* Paul D. Carrington, *Judicial Independence and Democratic Accountability in Highest State Courts*, 61 L. & CONTEMP. PROBS. 79, 81 (Summer 1998).

157. KATHLEEN A. CAIRNS, THE CASE OF ROSE BIRD: GENDER, POLITICS, AND THE CALIFORNIA COURTS 102 (2016).

158. *Id.* at 124.

159. *Id.* at 177.

160. *Id.* at 179; *see* also Reidinger, *supra* note 155, at 56.

161. CAIRNS, *supra* note 157, at 176.

162. *Id.* at 197.

163. *Id.* at 198.

164. Reidinger, *supra* note 155, at 54.

165. *Id.*

166. *See* Proposition 8 (codified as amended at CAL. CONST., art I, § 28(f)
    (2)); David Aram Kaiser & David A. Carrillo, *California Constitutional
    Law: Reanimating Criminal Procedural Rights After the "Other" Proposition
    8*, 56 SANTA CLARA L. REV. 33, 37 (2016).

167. 763 N.W.2d 862 (Iowa 2009).

168. In re Ralph, 1 Morris 1 (Iowa Terr. 1839).

169. *See Varnum*, 763 N.W.2d at 877 (citing *Admission of Women to the Bar*, 1
    CHI. LAW TIMES 76, 76 (1887)).

170. Mark Curriden, *Judging the Judges: Landmark Iowa Elections Send Tremor
    Through the Judicial Retention System*, A.B.A.J. (Jan. 1, 2011), https://
    www.abajournal.com/magazine/article/landmark_iowa_elections_send_
    tremor_through_judicial_retention_system.

171. *Id.*

172. *Id.*

173. Schotland, *Iowa's 2010 Judicial Election*, *supra* note 97, at 123.

174. CHARLES GARDNER GEYH, WHO IS TO JUDGE? THE PERENNIAL DEBATE
    OVER WHETHER TO ELECT OR APPOINT AMERICA'S JUDGES 5–6 (2019).

175. TOM WITOSKY & MARC HANSEN, EQUAL BEFORE THE LAW: HOW IOWA
    LED AMERICANS TO MARRIAGE EQUALITY 188 (2015).

176. *Id.* at 165–66.

177. *Id.* at 163.

178. *Id.* at 179.

179. Schotland, *Iowa's 2010 Judicial Election*, *supra* note 97, at 120.

180. Martin H. Redish & Jennifer Aronoff, *The Real Constitutional Problem
    with State Judicial Selection: Due Process, Judicial Retention, and the
    Dangers of Popular Constitutionalism*, 56 WM. & MARY L. REV. 1, 53 (2014);
    see also Jeff Eckhoff, *Retention Vote Shows Shift in Iowa's Same-Sex Marriage
    Views*, DES MOINES REG. (Nov. 8, 2012), http://perma.cc/W45C-3DEJ.

181. James Parker Hall, *The Selection, Tenure and Retirement of Judges*, 37 J.
    AM. JUD. SOC'Y 37, 43 (1919). See Nelson, *supra* note 95, at 190–91, for a
    summary of the "Jacksonian" view held by many scholars.

182. Nelson, *supra* note 95, at 224.

183. *Id.*

184. *Id.*

185. *Id.*

186. Shugerman, *supra* note 51, at 1142–43.

187. *Id.* at 1142.

188. *Id.* at 1144; *see also* SHUGERMAN, *supra* note 2, at 57–83 (arguing that judicial elections took root first in states where separation of powers was an express goal of constitutional reform).

189. Shugerman, *supra* note 51, at 1144.

190. Kermit Hall, *The Judiciary on Trial: State Constitutional Reform and the Rise of an Elected Judiciary, 1846–1860*, 45 THE HISTORIAN 337, 348, 350 (1983).

191. *Id.* at 354.

192. *See* Shugerman, *supra* note 51, at 1139–41, 1142–45.

193. *See* Neal Devins, *Public Opinion and State Supreme Courts*, 13 U. PA. J. CONST. L. 455, 494–95 (2010); *id.* 485 & n. 133, 503 (discussing Ohio's Norwood v. Horney decision).

194. *See, e.g.*, Michael S. Kang & Joanna M. Shepherd, *Judging Judicial Elections*, 114 MICH. L. REV. 929, 943–44 (2016); Gregory A. Huber & Sanford C. Gordon, *Accountability and Coercion: Is Justice Blind When It Runs for Office?*, 48 AM. J. POL. SCI. 247, 258 (2004). Some studies suggest that judges become tougher on criminal defendants as the election nears. *See* Melinda Gann Hall, *Electoral Politics and Strategic Voting in State Supreme Courts*, 54 J. POL. 427, 438–43 (1992); Huber et al., *supra*, at 253–62.

195. *See* Joanna Shepherd, *Are Appointed Judges Strategic Too?*, 58 DUKE L.J. 1589, 1594 (2009). I can't say the studies all go one way. One of them suggests elected judges in some settings are more likely to engage in judicial review. *See* Stefanie A. Lindquist, *Judicial Activism in State Supreme Courts: Institutional Design and Judicial Behavior*, 28 STAN. L. & POL'Y REV. 61, 71 (2017).

196. John H. Culver & John T. Wold, *Rose Bird and the Politics of Judicial Accountability in California*, 70 JUDICATURE 81, 85–87 (1986).

197. Curriden, *supra* note 170.

198. Sarah Boden, *State Supreme Court Justices Win Retention*, IOWA PUB. RADIO (Nov. 9, 2016), https://www.iowapublicradio.org/post/state-supreme-court-justices-win-retention.

199. *See* JEFFREY S. SUTTON, 51 IMPERFECT SOLUTIONS: STATES AND THE MAKING OF AMERICAN CONSTITUTIONAL LAW 210–11 (2018).

200. D. Moran, *Kaus to Retire from State Supreme Court*, L.A. TIMES (July 2, 1985).

201. *See* Brian T. Fitzpatrick, *Judicial Selection and Ideology*, 42 OKLA. CITY U.L. REV. 53 62–64 (2017).

202. I know of one exception: Judge Harry Pregerson's confirmation hearing. When asked what he would do "if a decision in a particular case was required by case law or statute . . . [but] offended [his] own conscience," Judge Pregerson replied, "I would follow my conscience." *Hearings on the Selection and Confirmation of Federal Judges Before the S. Comm. on*

the Judiciary, Part 4, 96th Cong. 450 (1979) (statements of Sen. Alan K. Simpson and Judge Harry Pregerson).

203. Brutus, No. 11, in 1 AMERICAN CONSTITUTIONALISM 57 (Oxford Univ. Press 2d ed. 2017).

Chapter 4

1. Caleb Nelson, *A Re-Evaluation of Scholarly Explanations for the Rise of the Elective Judiciary in Antebellum America*, 37 AM. J. LEGAL HIST. 190, 224 (1993).

2. Jessica Bulman-Pozen & Miriam Seifter, *The Democracy Principle in State Constitutions*, 119 MICH. L. REV. 859, 884 (2021). New York was a conspicuous exception when it comes to the election of judges. For an account of the rise of voter initiatives in territorial states, see Nathaniel A. Persily, *The Peculiar Geography of Direct Democracy: Why the Initiative, Referendum, and Recall Developed in the American West*, 2 MICH. L. & POL'Y REV. 11 (1997).

3. THE DECLARATION OF INDEPENDENCE (U.S. 1776).

4. *See* Act of Dec. 31, 1862, ch. 6, 12 Stat. 633–34 (admitting forty-eight named loyal counties of Virginia as the state of West Virginia); Act of Mar. 3, 1820, ch. 19, 3 Stat. 544 (admitting the Maine district of Massachusetts as the state of Maine); Act of Feb. 4, 1791, ch. 4, 1 Stat. 189 (admitting the Kentucky district of Virginia as the state of Kentucky).

5. VT. CONST. of 1777, pmbl.; *see also* JED HANDELSMAN SHUGERMAN, THE PEOPLE'S COURTS 58–59 (2012) (describing the conflict with New York that led to Vermont's independence and motivated its desire to establish local control of government institutions, including courts).

6. Vermont settlers criticized the New York judiciary as inefficient and beholden to "the wealthy and well-connected," who invoked the courts and the state's ejectment laws to remove settlers from their land. *See* SHUGERMAN, *supra* note 5, at 58–59. The Vermont Republic's judges were less prone to delay and more flexible about collecting court fees through in-kind ways or through payment schedules timed by the harvest. *Id.* at 59–60. What's more, they turned to local judicial elections for trial judges to ensure that these courts would be responsive to local custom and opinion. *See id.* at 58–60; VT. CONST. of 1777, ch. 2, § 27.

7. Stanley E. Siegel, A Political History of the Texas Republic, 1836–1845, at vii–viii (1956) (Ph.D. dissertation, The Rice Institute); *see generally id.* at 3–32 (describing the experience of American settlers in Texas from the Austin land grant in 1821 through Texas's declaration of independence in March 1836).

8. American colonists who settled the land north of the Rio Grande in the 1820s had difficulties with distant Mexican appellate courts in the mid-1820s through 1830s as their settlements grew. In particular, settlers wanted to import jury trials to administer justice locally. *See* Siegel, *supra*

note 7, at 10, 17. The concern about the ability to obtain justice from Mexican officials motivated the push for self-government in Texas; *see id.* at 9–10, 17, just as distrust of British judges had motivated the colonists before 1776, and just as distrust of federal officials in the US territories would motivate residents of the territories to call for statehood in the latter half of the nineteenth century.

9.   When the United States occupied California at the start of the Mexican-American War, American settlers' calls for representation and civilian constitutional government grew. The military authorities followed the custom of preserving the existing system of civilian government in foreign occupied territory, which meant appointing local magistrates to govern the province's settlements. The Golden State's territorial phase was overtaken by events when the population grew from around 10,000 to nearly 100,000 in two years, between 1848 and 1850, after the discovery of gold. California held a constitutional convention in 1849 and joined the Union a year later. *See generally* SHUGERMAN, *supra* note 5.

10. JOSEPH R. GRODIN ET AL., THE CALIFORNIA STATE CONSTITUTION 5–6 (2d ed. 2015) (1993); *see generally* Joseph Ellison, *The Struggle for Civil Government in California, 1846–1850*, 10 Q. CAL. HIST. SOC'Y 3 (1931) (Parts I & II); *id.* at 129 (Part III); NEAL HARLOW, CALIFORNIA CONQUERED: THE ANNEXATION OF A MEXICAN PROVINCE, 1846–1850 (1989).

11. GRODIN ET AL., *supra* note 10, at 6; HARLOW, *supra* note 10, at 265. For a discussion of the *alcalde* system and its contribution to calls for civil government and home rule, see Ellison, *supra* note 10, at 12–25, 144.

12. Ordinance of July 13, 1787 [Northwest Ordinance of 1787], *reprinted in* DOCUMENTS ILLUSTRATIVE OF THE FORMATION OF THE UNION OF THE UNITED STATES, H.R. Doc. No. 69-398, at 47–54 (Charles Callan Tansill ed., 1927).

13. Act of Aug. 7, 1789 [Northwest Ordinance of 1789], ch. 8, 1 Stat. 50; LAWRENCE M. FRIEDMAN, A HISTORY OF AMERICAN LAW 127–28 (2019); *see* Ohio Enabling Act, ch. 40, 2 Stat. 173 (1802); Indiana Enabling Act, ch. 57, 3 Stat. 289 (1816); Illinois Enabling Act, ch. 67, 3 Stat. 428 (1818); Act of Jan. 26, 1837, ch. 6, 5 Stat. 144 (admitting the state of Michigan); Act of May 29, 1848, ch. 50, 9 Stat. 233 (admitting the state of Wisconsin); Act of May 11, 1858, ch. 31, 11 Stat. 285 (admitting the state of Minnesota); AKHIL R. AMAR, AMERICA'S UNWRITTEN CONSTITUTION 262 (2012) (describing how these six states were carved from the Northwest Territory). One wrinkle accompanied Ohio's entry into the Union. Although Congress authorized the people of Ohio to write a constitution for their new state and to ask Congress for admission into the Union, *see* Ohio Enabling Act, *supra*, the national legislature never formally ratified the new state charter or voted on admission, STEVEN H. STEINGLASS & GINO J. SCARSELLI, THE OHIO STATE CONSTITUTION 19 (2011). Congress

acknowledged Ohio's existence on February 19, 1803, when it passed a law providing for the enforcement of federal law in the new "State," *id.*, and the Senate seated Ohio's first member later that year, *200th Anniversary of Ohio Statehood*, NAT'L ARCHIVES, https://www.archives.gov/legislative/features/ohio-statehood (last reviewed July 15, 2019). In 1902, the Ohio General Assembly declared March 1, 1803—the day the new state's legislature first assembled—to be the official "birth of the state." STEINGLASS & SCARSELLI, *supra*, at 19. And in 1953, Congress formally recognized Ohio as the nation's seventeenth state and retroactively fixed March 1, 1803, as the date of admission. *Id.*; Act of Aug. 7, 1953, Pub. L. No. 83-204, ch. 337, 67 Stat. 407 ("Joint resolution for admitting the State of Ohio into the Union").

14. DAVID MCCULLOCH, PIONEERS 29 (2019).
15. Dred Scott v. Sandford, 60 U.S. (19 How.) 393 (1857).
16. Northwest Ordinance of 1789, pmbl.; Northwest Ordinance of 1787, arts. I–III; Gregory Ablavsky, *Administrative Constitutionalism and the Northwest Ordinance*, 167 PA. L. REV. 1631, 1632 (2019).
17. *Id.* (quoting the Northwest Ordinance).
18. *Id.* at 1631–32.
19. *Id.* at 1665 (quoting H.R.J. Res. 208, 74th Cong., ch. 249, 49 Stat. 511 (1935)).
20. Northwest Ordinance of 1787, pmbl., § 1, 1 Stat. at 51–53 (acknowledging the continuing legal effect of the Northwest Ordinance of 1787 and adopting a new procedure for appointing territorial officers consistent with the new federal constitution); Northwest Ordinance of 1787 §§ 3–5, at 48; *see* Ablavsky, *supra* note 16, at 1633.
21. Northwest Ordinance of 1787 §§ 5, 9, at 48–50; *see* FRIEDMAN, *supra* note 13; Ablavsky, *supra* note 16, at 1633.
22. Northwest Ordinance of 1787 §§ 9–11, at 49–51.
23. *Id.*
24. *Id.*
25. Ablavsky, *supra* note 16, at 1634.
26. Northwest Ordinance of 1787 § 7–11, at 49–51.
27. *Id.*; Ablavsky, *supra* note 16, at 1654.
28. Ablavsky, *supra* note 16, at 1654.
29. *Id.*
30. *Id.* (quoting Letter from James Monroe to Thomas Jefferson (May 11, 1786), *in* 2 THE PAPERS OF JAMES MONROE 298 (Daniel Preston & Marlena C. DeLong eds., 2006)).
31. Northwest Ordinance of 1787, art. 5, at 53–54.
32. Kermit L. Hall, *Hacks and Derelicts Revisited: American Territorial Judiciary, 1789–1959*, W. HIST. Q., 275 (Jul. 1981).
33. *Id.* at 284.
34. *Id.*

35. *Id.* at 284–85.
36. *Id.* at 284 (quoting FRIEDMAN, *supra* note 13, at 326, and disputing his characterization of territorial judges).
37. *Id.* at 286.
38. Ablavsky, *supra* note 16, at 1633 n.12; *see* Act of March 3, 1805, ch. 38, 2 Stat. 338, 338–39.
39. Vitruvius, CENTINEL OF THE NORTH-WESTERN TERRITORY (Cincinnati Oct. 4, 1794), *cited in* Ablavsky, *supra* note 16, at 1631.
40. Ablavsky, *supra* note 16, at 1660.
41. *Id.*
42. *Id.* at 1660–61 (quoting EVERETT SOMERVILLE BROWN, THE CONSTITUTIONAL HISTORY OF THE LOUISIANA PURCHASE: 1803–1812, 131 (2000)).
43. *Id.* at 1661 (quoting Sanford Levinson & Bartholomew Sparrow, *Introduction* to THE LOUISIANA PURCHASE AND AMERICAN EXPANSION, 1803–1898, at 1, 13 (Sanford Levinson & Bartholomew Sparrow eds., 2005)).
44. *Id.* at 1634.
45. *Id.*
46. *Id.* at 1667.
47. *Id.* at 1636.
48. *Id.* at 1636–37 (quoting letter from Monroe to Thomas Jefferson (May 11, 1786), in 2 THE PAPERS OF JAMES MONROE, *supra* note 30, at 298–99).
49. *Id.* at 1654 (quoting letter from William Goforth to President (January 5, 1802), *in* 3 THE TERRITORIAL PAPERS OF THE UNITED STATES 198 (Clarence Edward Carter ed., 1934)).
50. Clark C. Spence, *The Territorial Officers of Montana, 1864–1889*, 30 PAC. HIST. REV. 123, 124 (1961).
51. Carleton W. Kenyon, *Legal Lore of the United States: A Bibliographical Essay*, 56 CAL. L. REV. 681, 682 (1968) (Arizona); *see also* Andrew P. Morriss, *Judicial Removal in Western States and Territories, in* LAW IN THE WESTERN UNITED STATES 86, 88 (Gordon Morris Bakken ed., 2000) (noting that Arizona's residents called the territorial supreme court the "Supreme Court of Affirmance" because it rarely reversed the trial-court decisions of the justices riding circuit).
52. Kenyon, *supra* note 51, at 694.
53. Spence, *supra* note 50, at 127.
54. Address of R. M. Clarke, Attorney General, 3 NEV. REPORTS 17 (1868), *quoted in* David A. Hardy, The Nevada Territorial Supreme Court: A Transitional Influence from Frontier Lawlessness to Statehood 104 (2015) (Ph.D. dissertation, University of Nevada, Reno).
55. *Territorial Courts*, FED. JUD. CTR., fjc.gov, https://perma.cc/V8JN-NANZ; *Brief History of Montana*, MONTANA.GOV, https://perma.cc/2C9L-8KVS.

56. Spence, *supra* note 50, at 134.

57. Hall, *supra* note 32, at 284–85. Kermit Hall explains that, at three-quarters, the proportion of "foreign" appointees was highest between 1828 and 1889. Pull back the lens and about three-fifths, or 57%, of territorial judges came from outside the territory they served between 1789 and 1959. *Id.* at 284. The appointment of locals was most common in the United States' Pacific territories at the turn of the twentieth century, largely due to the "exigencies of obtaining cooperation from colonial populations that resisted quick destruction or assimilation." *Id.* at 285.

58. Spence, *supra* note 50, at 134.

59. *Id.* at 132 (quoting *Inter-Mountains Freeman* (Butte Apr. 9, 1882), on the appointment of a new territorial secretary).

60. *Id.* (quoting *Daily Herald* (Helena Mar. 27, 1879)).

61. Section 12 of the Northwest Ordinance of 1787 provided that once the Territory had 5,000 free male residents and had elected a territorial legislature, that legislature would choose a non-voting delegate to represent territorial interests in Congress. *See* Northwest Ordinance of 1787, §§ 9, 12. The 1789 Ordinance retained the provision and Congress extended the right to elect a non-voting delegate to the Southwest Territory in 1790, *see* Act of May 26, 1790, ch. 14, 1 Stat 123, which became the first to actually do so. Montana elected delegates to Congress under its organic act beginning in 1864. *See* Act of May 26, 1864, ch. 95, § 13, 13 Stat. 85, 91.

62. *See* Spence, *supra* note 50, at 133–34 & nn. 30–32.

63. *Id.* at 133.

64. *Id.* at 134.

65. *Id.*

66. *Id.*

67. W. Turrentine Jackson, *Montana Politics During the Meagher Regime 1865–1867*, 12 Pac. Hist Rev. 139, 139–40 (1943).

68. Henry N. Blake, *Memoirs of a Many-Sided Man: The Personal Record of a Civil War Veteran, Montana Territorial Editor, Attorney, Jurist in* Mont. Mag. W. Hist., 39 (Vivian A. Paladin, ed. Autumn 1964). http://www.dorchesteratheneum.org/pdf/BlakeMemoirs.pdf.

69. Jackson, *supra* note 67, at 141, 153.

70. *Id.* at 146–47.

71. *Id.* at 148.

72. *Id.*

73. *Id.*

74. *Id.* at 148, 152.

75. *Id.* at 152.

76. *Id.* at 152–53.

77. Spence, *supra* note 50, at 135.

78. *See* Friedman, *supra* note 13, at 359.

79. Spence, *supra* note 50, at 132–33 (quoting Delegate Maginnis).

80. *Id.* at 132.

81. *Id.* at 129 & n.18.

82. *Id.* at 135; *see also* Llewellyn L. Callaway, *Something About the Territorial Judges*, 4 Mont. L. Rev. 5, 7–9 (1943).

83. Spence, *supra* note 50, at 125.

84. *Id.* at 126.

85. *Id.*

86. Callaway, *supra* note 82, at 11.

87. *Id.* at 11–12.

88. *See* Gordon Morris Bakken, *Lawyers in the American West, 1820–1920: A Comment*, 1 Nev. L.J. 88, 89, 91–92 (2001).

89. Callaway, *supra* note 82, at 12.

90. *See generally* Mont. Const. of 1889, arts. V–VII.

91. *See generally* Howard R. Lamar, The Far Southwest, 1846–1912: A Territorial History 275–80 (2000 ed.) (1966) (describing the Mormon settlement of the Great Basin and the government of the state of Deseret before 1850); *id.* at 285 (describing the appointment of Mormon leaders to key territorial posts).

92. *Id.* at 286.

93. *Id.* at 292.

94. Utah Organic Act, c. 51, § 6, 9 Stat. 453, 454 (1850).

95. Dale D. Goble, *Theocracy vs. Diversity: Local vs. National in Territorial Utah*, in Law in the Western United States, *supra* note 51, at 293, 296.

96. *Id.* (quoting An Act in Relation to the Judiciary, Feb. 4, 1852, Utah Territorial Laws 38, 43); *see also* Lamar, *supra* note 91, at 288.

97. Goble, *supra* note 95, at 296.

98. Lamar, *supra* note 91, at 294.

99. *Id.*

100. *Id.* at 307.

101. *Id.* at 308.

102. *Id.*

103. *Id.*

104. *Id.*

105. *Id.* at 317.

106. Goble, *supra* note 95, at 297.

107. 87 U.S. (20 Wall.) 375, 382–84 (1874).

108. *See id.* at 382.

109. Poland Act, ch. 469, § 3, 18 Stat. 253, 254 (1874).

110. *Id.* §§ 1–2, 18 Stat. at 253.

111. Lamar, *supra* note 91, at 333.

112. Edmunds-Tucker Act, ch. 397, 24 Stat. 635 (1887); *see* Lamar, *supra* note 91, at 344; Goble, *supra* note 95, at 298.

113. Lamar, *supra* note 91, at 344.

114. *Id.*

115. *Id.*

116. Goble, *supra* note 95, at 298.

117. *See* Ariz. Const. art. XX, par. 2; N.M. Const. art. XXI, § 1; Okla. Const. art. I, § 2; Utah Const. art. III, § 1; Arizona Enabling Act, 36 Stat. 569 (1910); New Mexico Enabling Act, 36 Stat. 558 (1910); Oklahoma Enabling Act, 34 Stat. 269 (1906); Utah Enabling Act, 28 Stat. 108 (1894).

118. Kathleen Flake, The Politics of American Religious Identity: The Seating of Senator Reed Smoot, Mormon Apostle 2 (2005).

119. *Id.* at 5.

120. *Id.* at 146.

121. Paul B. Beers, Pennsylvania Politics Today and Yesterday: The Tolerable Accommodation 51 (2010); *see also* Flake, *supra* note 118, at 146.

122. Patrick M. Garry, The South Dakota State Constitution 12 (Oxford Univ. Press 2014).

123. Morriss, *supra* note 51, at 86, 87.

124. *Id.* at 86.

125. *Id.* at 86–87 (quoting historian Doane Robinson).

126. Elwyn B. Robinson, History of North Dakota 198 (2017).

127. Bernard Floyd Hyatt, A Legal Legacy for Statehood: The Development of the Territorial Judicial System in the Dakota Territory, 1861–1889 (May 1987), at 214–21 (dissertation, Texas Tech University).

128. Howard Roberts Lamar, Dakota Territory, 1861–1889: A Study of Frontier Politics 130 (1956), *quoted in* James E. Leahy, The North Dakota State Constitution 7 (Oxford Univ. Press 2014).

129. *Id.*

130. Leahy, *supra* note 128, at 7.

131. Robinson, *supra* note 126, at 198.

132. *Id.* at 199.

133. 1 George W. Kingsbury, History of the Dakota Territory 635 (1915).

134. *Id.*

135. Thomas E. Simmons, *Territorial Justice Under Fire: The Trials of Peter Wintermute, 1873–1875,* 31 S.D. Hist. 91, 98 (2001).

136. *Id.* at 102; 1 Kingsbury, *supra* note 133, at 639.

137. 1 Kingsbury, *supra* note 133, at 639.

138. *Id.*

139. Simmons, *supra* note 135, at 107.

140. *Id.* at 108, 110.

141. *Id.* at 112.

142. 2 Kingsbury, *supra* note 133, at 1182.

143. Morriss, *supra* note 51, at 87.

144. Earl Martin, Clark v. Board of School Directors: *Reflections After 150 Years,* 67 Drake L. Rev. 169, 171 (2019) (symposium introduction).

145. Russell E. Lovell, II, *Shine On, You Bright Radical Star:* Clark v. Board of School Directors *(of Muscatine)—The Iowa Supreme Court's Civil Rights Exceptionalism*, 67 DRAKE L. REV. 175, 179 (2019).

146. Robert G. Allbee, *Alexander G. Clark*, 67 DRAKE L. REV. 203, 204–05 (2019).

147. *Id.* at 205.

148. Lovell, *supra* note 145, at 179.

149. *Id.* at 180.

150. Goodwin Liu, *State Courts and Constitutional Structure*, 128 YALE L.J. 1304, 1345–46 (2019) (internal citations included in the article).

151. Lovell, *supra* note 145, at 210.

152. *Id.*

153. *See* AKHIL R. AMAR, AMERICA'S CONSTITUTION: A BIOGRAPHY 421–22 (2006) (observing that in the 1890s and 1900s "merely by voting on a routine basis in the Rocky Mountain West, women pioneers were proving by their daily example that equal suffrage was an eminently sensible and thoroughly American way of life suitable for adoption in sister states," and noting that the first ten or so states to adopt equal suffrage were former territories of the West or Midwest).

154. *See* Liu, *supra* note 150, at 1352–60.

155. JEFFREY S. SUTTON, 51 IMPERFECT SOLUTIONS 208–12 (2018).

156. Michigan v. Long, 463 U.S. 1032 (1983).

157. Jean Edward Smith, JOHN MARSHALL: DEFINER OF A NATION 403 n.* (1996) (quoting JOSIAH QUINCY, FIGURES OF THE PAST 189–90 (1883)).

158. Jeffrey S. Sutton, San Antonio Independent School District v. Rodriguez *and Its Aftermath*, 94 VA. L. REV. 1963, 1979 (2008); Jamison E. Colburn, *Rethinking Constitutionalism*, 28 RUTGERS L.J. 873, 898 (1997) (book review); *see* Lawrence Gene Sager, *Fair Measure: The Legal Status of Underenforced Constitutional Norms*, 91 HARV. L. REV. 1212, 1218 (1978).

159. There are exceptions. For example, as noted earlier, the constitutions of Colorado and New Mexico each start with the latitude and longitude lines of the area covered by the states. COLO. CONST. art. I; N.M. CONST. art. I. Perhaps there is something to be said for identifying the area covered by a charter before announcing the rules for governing it. Or perhaps, and far more likely, the two new states simply had a disagreement about their shared border. *See* New Mexico v. Colorado, 267 U.S. 30 (1925); DALE A. OESTERLE & RICHARD B. COLLINS, THE COLORADO STATE CONSTITUTION 33–34 (2011). Either way, both constitutions quickly move on to individual rights, found in Article II in both of them. COLO. CONST. art. II; N.M. CONST. art. II.

160. *See, e.g.*, Ohio v. Robinette, 519 U.S. 33, 40 (Ginsburg, J., concurring) (describing the "unique vantage point" of state supreme court justices regarding traffic-stop searches).

161. A qualification or two is in order. In some areas of federal constitutional law, take obscenity as one, the United States Supreme Court has permitted the law to account for local community standards. *See, e.g.,* Miller v. California, 413 U.S. 15, 32 (1973) ("It is neither realistic nor constitutionally sound to read the First Amendment as requiring that the people of Maine or Mississippi accept public depiction of conduct found tolerable in Las Vegas, or New York City."). And some scholars have argued for local tailoring in other areas. *See, e.g.,* Joseph Blocher, *Firearm Localism*, 123 YALE L.J. 82 (2013).

162. *See, e.g.,* Robert F. Williams, *Forward: Looking Back at the New Judicial Federalism's First Generation*, 30 VAL. U. L. REV. i, xxiv (1996).

163. New State Ice Co. v. Liebmann, 285 U.S. 262, 311 (1932) (Brandeis, J., dissenting) ("It is one of the happy incidents of the federal system that a single courageous state may, if its citizens choose, serve as a laboratory; and try novel social and economic experiments without risk to the rest of the country.").

164. *See, e.g.,* Sutton, *supra* note 158, at 1981.

165. *See, e.g.,* RICHARD A. POSNER, HOW JUDGES THINK (2008). *See also* Jeffrey S. Sutton, *A Review of Richard A. Posner, How Judges Think*, 108 MICH. L. REV. 859 (2010) (responding to Judge Posner's criticism of the political nature of judging).

166. R. Randall Kelso, *Standards of Review Under the Equal Protection Clause and Related Constitutional Doctrines Protecting Individual Rights: The "Base Plus Six" Model and Modern Supreme Court Practice*, 4 U. PA. J. CONST. L. 225, 195 n.14 (2002).

167. Am. Energy Corp. v. Rockies Exp. Pipeline LLC, 622 F.3d 602, 606 (6th Cir. 2010).

168. *See* Craig v. Boren, 429 U.S. 190, 211–13 (1976) (Stevens, J., concurring).

169. SUTTON, *supra* note 155, at 115; *see id.* at 92–108 (describing state court decisions before *Buck v. Bell*).

170. *Id.* at 194–95; Jeffrey S. Sutton, *Why Teach—and Why Study—State Constitutional Law*, 34 OKLA. CITY U.L. REV. 165, 166 (2009).

171. *See, e.g.,* David E. Pozen, *The Irony of Judicial Elections*, 108 COLUM. L. REV. 265, 271–72 (2008) (describing how the conventional account of judicial elections is often "distilled to a single trade-off: independence versus accountability"); Paul J. De Muniz, *Politicizing State Judicial Elections: A Threat to Judicial Independence*, 38 WILLAMETTE L. REV. 367 (2002); Erwin Chemerinsky, *Preserving an Independent Judiciary: The Need for Contribution and Expenditure Limits in Judicial Elections*, 74 CHI.-KENT L. REV. 133, 135 (1998) (lamenting that "state court judges are being targeted for particular rulings and are being ousted from office for their decisions").

172. Yale Law Professor David Schleicher might push back on this point. In his thought-filled piece, "Federalism and State Democracy," 95 TEX.

L. Rev. 763 (2017), he argues that local elections often turn on national political debates and the positions of the national political parties. He may be right. But I doubt the success rate of candidates for local office who openly admit that they presumptively rely on the insights of officials based in Washington, DC, rather than their own state, to resolve new or complex problems.

173. Other possibilities exist for these tendencies—that the press of work at the state courts makes it easier to stick with the volumes of federal precedent on many matters, that most law schools still do not teach state constitutional law, or that many lawyers do not brief the state constitutional claims independently of the federal doctrine. But these considerations do not turn on the election of state court judges.

174. *See* Sutton, *supra* note 155, at 203–12.

175. Home Building & Loan Ass'n v. Blaisdell, 290 U.S. 398 (1934) (holding that Minnesota's suspension of banks' contractual rights did not violate the impairment-of-contract clause in the United States Constitution).

176. Rucho v. Common Cause, 139 S. Ct. 2484 (2019) (treating as a political question, unresolvable by the federal courts, a federal constitutional challenge to legislative districts created by partisan gerrymandering). Chapter 8 returns to this topic and the state and federal responses to gerrymandering claims.

177. *Compare* Philip Hamburger, Is Administrative Law Unlawful? (2014), *with* Adrian Vermeule, *No*, 93 Tex. L. Rev. 1547 (2015) (book review).

178. *See* discussion *infra* Chapter 6.

179. John Hart Ely, Democracy and Distrust (Harvard Univ. Press 1980).

180. Joseph Blocher makes a related federal-state dialogue point in his trenchant article about "reverse incorporation." Joseph Blocher, *Reverse Incorporation of State Constitutional Law*, 84 S. Cal. L. Rev. 323, 347–49 (2011).

181. Citizens United v. FEC, 558 U.S. 310 (2010).

182. *Id.* at 339 (quoting Buckley v. Valeo, 424 U.S. 1, 19 (1976)).

183. *Id.* at 319.

184. *Id.* at 342, 347 (quoting First Nat'l Bank of Boston v. Bellotti, 435 U.S. 765, 766 (1978)).

185. W. Tradition P'ship v. Attorney General, 271 P.3d 1, 8–9 (2011) (citing K. Ross Toole, Montana, An Uncommon Land (1959) and C. B. Glasscock, The War of the Copper Kings (1935)).

186. *Id.* at 8.

187. *Id.*

188. *Id.*

189. *Id.* at 9.

190. *See* Bradford Clark, *Supremacy Clause as a Constraint on Federal Power*, 71 Geo. Wash. L. Rev. 91, 99–103 (2003).

191. Am. Tradition P'ship v. Bullock, 567 U.S. 516, 516 (2012).

192. *Id.*

193. SUTTON, *supra* note 155, at 178–90.

194. *W. Tradition P'ship*, 271 P.3d at 11.

195. Although the Montana Supreme Court's opinion is less than clear, it does
       not seem that the plaintiffs took two constitutional shots (state and federal)
       rather than just one (federal) in challenging the law. Either way, state
       constitutional law could affect the meaning of the statute, and the Montana
       attorney general was free to argue as much. In a state court system like
       Oregon that determines whether state action removes the federal problem,
       moreover, a state court on its own initiative would be free to consider the
       state claim anyway to avoid the federal constitutional issue. *See* SUTTON,
       supra note 155, at 178–82. Notably, Article III of the US Constitution
       does not restrict the state courts when it comes to the case or controversy
       requirement, standing, or the prohibition on advisory opinions. Many state
       courts have long provided advisory opinions, a key structural difference
       between the state and federal courts. But here's the key takeaway: No
       state constitution in the country, to my knowledge, would prohibit a state
       supreme court motivated to ignore the Supremacy Clause due to a US
       Supreme Court decision it did not like to first acknowledge that the state
       constitution did not have the same meaning as the federal constitution.
       That is exactly what the Montana Supreme Court could have done.

196. MKB Mgmt. Corp. v. Burdick, 855 N.W.2d 31 (N.D. 2014).

197. *Id.* at 45–46 (separate opinion of VandeWalle, C.J.) (concluding that the
       North Dakota constitution *does not* encompass a fundamental right to
       abortion); *id.* at 94–95 (separate opinion of Sandstrom, J.) (same); *id.* at
       64 (separate opinion of Kapsner, J., joined by Maring, S.J.) (concluding
       that the North Dakota construction *does* guarantee a fundamental
       right to abortion); *id.* at 91 (separate opinion of Crothers, J.) (arguing
       that resolving the state-law question was "unnecessary and doctrinally
       improper").

198. 564 N.W.2d 104, 110–11 (Mich. Ct. App. 1997).

199. *See generally* PAUL BENJAMIN LINTON, ABORTION UNDER STATE
       CONSTITUTIONS (Carolina Academic Press, 3d ed. 2020). Thirteen state
       courts have ruled that their state constitutions protect a right to abortion
       independent of what the federal constitution requires: Alaska, California,
       Florida, Hawaii, Iowa, Kansas, Massachusetts, Minnesota, Mississippi,
       Montana, New Jersey, New Mexico, and New York. The rest are largely
       silent. *Id.*

200. State v. Brown, 930 N.W.2d 840, 857–58 (Iowa 2019) (concurring
       specially) (quotations omitted). Others have echoed the point. *See,
       e.g.,* Hans Linde, *E Pluribus—Constitutional Theory and States Courts,*
       18 GA. L. REV. 165, 179 (1984); Ronald K. L. Collins, *Reliance on State
       Constitutions—Away from a Reactionary Approach,* 9 HASTINGS CONST.

L.Q. 1, 10 (1981); Earl M. Maltz, *False Prophet—Justice Brennan and the Theory of State Constitutional Law*, 15 HASTINGS CONST. L.Q. 429, 443–44 (1988); 1 JENNIFER FRIESEN, STATE CONSTITUTIONAL LAW: LITIGATING INDIVIDUAL RIGHTS, CLAIMS AND DEFENSES 44–45 (4th ed. 2008). *See generally* PAUL BENJAMIN LINTON, ABORTION UNDER STATE CONSTITUTIONS 13–17 (3d ed. 2020) (collecting these citations, among many others).

201. *See* Mapp v. Ohio, 367 U.S. 643, 657–60 (1961).

202. *See generally* SUTTON, *supra* note 155, at 42–84. Think of the point from another perspective, the stop-and-frisk doctrine created under federal law by *Terry v. Ohio*, 392 U.S. 1 (1968), which no state court, best I can tell, has consistently rejected under its own constitution. Ask yourself whether the *Terry* doctrine should be uniformly adopted under all fifty state constitutions. Here we have uniformity at a time when many wonder whether the stop-and-frisk doctrine has been hurtful to relationships between law enforcement and the communities they serve. *See* Nathaniel C. Sutton, *Lockstepping Through Stop-and-Frisk: A Call to Independently Assess* Terry v. Ohio *Under State Law*, 107 VA. L. REV. 639 (2021).

Part II

1. Sweezy v. New Hampshire, 354 U.S. 234, 255 (1957).

2. G. Alan Tarr, *Interpreting the Separation of Powers in State Constitutions*, 59 N.Y.U. ANN. SURV. AM. L. 329, 330 (2003).

Chapter 5

1. *See generally* G. ALAN TARR, UNDERSTANDING STATE CONSTITUTIONS 56–57 (1998).

2. *Id.* at 333.

3. *Id.*

4. U.S. CONST. art. II, § 1 (emphasis added).

5. GORDON S. WOOD, CREATION OF THE AMERICAN REPUBLIC, 1776–1787 138 (1998).

6. *Id.*

7. AKHIL REED AMAR, AMERICA'S CONSTITUTION: A BIOGRAPHY 133 (2012).

8. *Id.*

9. *See, e.g.,* MASS. CONST. pt. II, ch. II, § 1, art. IX (requiring the governor to have consent of the council to make judicial appointments).

10. William P. Marshall, *Break Up the Presidency? Governors, State Attorneys General, and Lessons from the Divided Executive*, 115 YALE L.J. 2446, 2450–51 (2006).

11. Marshall, *supra* note 10, at 2450–51; WILKINS UPDIKE, MEMOIRS OF THE RHODE ISLAND BAR 15–22 (1842). Because Rhode Island, unlike most states, initially continued to operate under its royal charter at the founding, the office of the attorney general did not become part of the

Rhode Island Constitution until the state's first constitution was ratified in 1842. *See* R.I. CONST. of 1842, art. VIII, § 1.

12. *See* N.J. CONST. OF 1776, art. XII (providing for the appointment of a provincial secretary and treasurer by the legislature); N.C. CONST. of 1776, Art. XXII ("the General Assembly shall . . . appoint a Treasurer or Treasurers for this State"); N.C. CONST. of 1776, Art. XXIV ("the General Assembly shall . . . appoint a Secretary for this State"); MD. CONST. of 1776, Art. X ("the House of Delegates may . . . appoint auditors").

13. Miriam Seifter, *Understanding State Agency Independence*, 117 MICH. L. REV. 1537, 1553 (2019).

14. *See* Caleb Nelson, *A Re-Evaluation of Scholarly Explanations for the Rise of an Elective Judiciary in Antebellum America*, 37 AM. J. LEGAL HIST. 190, 207 (1993) (discussing the concurrent rise of elected executive officers and elected judiciaries).

15. *See* Seifter, *supra* note 13, at 1553 ("In the mid-nineteenth century, and consistent with tenets of Jacksonian democracy, many states provided for the popular election, rather than appointment or legislative election, of their existing executive officials.").

16. *See* Nelson, *supra* note 14, at 207 ("The same conventions that stripped governors and legislatures of their powers to appoint judges stripped them of their powers to appoint many other officials as well.").

17. Marshall, *supra* note 10, at 2452 .

18. COUNCIL OF STATE GOV'TS, THE BOOK OF THE STATES 268 (2005); cited in Marshall, *supra* note 10, at 2448 n.3.

19. HAW. CONST. art V, § 6; N.H. CONST., pt. 2, arts. 46, 47, 73; N.J. CONST. art. V, § IV, paras. 3, 5; cited in Marshall, *supra* note 10, at 2448 n.3.

20. ALASKA CONST. art. III, § 25; WYO. STAT. ANN. § 9-1-601 (2005); cited in Marshall, *supra* note 10, at 2448 n.3.

21. Seifter, *supra* note 13, at 1552.

22. *Id.*

23. *Id.*

24. *Id.*

25. *See Adjutants General Terms and Qualifications Statutes*, NATIONAL CONFERENCE OF STATE LEGISLATURES (Feb. 8, 2013), https://www.ncsl.org/research/military-and-veterans-affairs/adjutants-general-qualification-statutes.aspx.

26. Christopher R. Berry & Jacob E. Gersen, *The Unbundled Executive*, 75 U. CHI. L. REV. 1385, 1400 (2008).

27. *Id.* (as of 2002).

28. *Id.*

29. *See* Caleb Nelson, *supra* note 14, at 207 ("As one disgruntled conservative at the Kentucky convention put it, 'We have provided for the popular election of every public officer save the dog catcher, and if the dogs could vote, we should have that as well.' ").

30.   AKHIL REED AMAR, AMERICA'S CONSTITUTION: A BIOGRAPHY 195 (2004).

31.   Morrison v. Olson, 487 U.S. 654, 661 (1988).

32.   *Id.* at 662.

33.   *Id.* at 663.

34.   *Id.* at 691–92.

35.   *Id.* at 698–99.

36.   *Id.* at 729.

37.   *See id.* at 729–31.

38.   *Id.* at 732.

39.   *Id.* at 731.

40.   *Id.* at 699.

41.   Nick Bravin, *Is* Morrison v. Olson *Still Good Law? The Court's New Appointments Clause Jurisprudence*, 98 COLUM. L. REV. 1103, 1106 (1998).

42.   Terry Eastland, *Scalia's Finest Opinion*, WASHINGTON EXAMINER (Mar. 11, 2016), https://www.washingtonexaminer.com/weekly-standard/scalias-finest-opinion.

43.   *Morrison*, 487 U.S. at 710.

44.   *Id.* at 699.

45.   Anthony Johnstone, *A State Is a "They," Not an "It": Intrastate Conflicts in Multistate Challenges to the Affordable Care Act*, 2019 BYU L. REV. 1471, 1477 (2020) (citing EMILY MYERS, STATE ATTORNEYS GENERAL: POWERS AND RESPONSIBILITIES 7 (4th ed. 2018)).

46.   *See* State of Kansas ex rel. Stephan v. Finney, 836 P.2d 1169 (Kan. 1992) (attorney general sued the governor at the legislature's direction in a mandamus action seeking a determination whether the governor had the constitutional authority to enter into a binding gaming compact with an Indian tribe without approval of the legislature).

47.   *See* Peter M. Shane, *The Originalist Myth of the Unitary Executive*, 19 U. PA. J. CONST. L. 323, 345–49 (2016) (discussing diverging approaches to the appointment of administrative officials in state constitutions, including many state constitutions that "say nothing at all about the appointment of state civil officers not named in the constitution").

48.   States following the Missouri plan, for example, have "eliminat[ed] the requirement that the Governor's pick be confirmed by the senate or a similar popularly elected body." Stephen J. Ware, *The Missouri Plan in National Perspective*, 74 Mo. L. REV. 751, 759 (2009).

49.   *See generally* John M. Coles, *Preserving Integrity: Why Pennsylvania's Independent Counsel Law Is Working*, 104 DICK. L. REV. 707 (1999).

50.   PA. CONST. art. IV, § 4.1.

51.   *Id.*

52.   *See* Coles, *supra* note 49, at 721. Coles notes that, prior to the independent counsel statute, there was no clear way to avoid the conflict-of-interest problem. The "special deputy" provided for in Pennsylvania

law was appointed by the attorney general, and county district attorneys typically had a working or political relationship with the attorney general.

53. 18 Pa. Cons. Stat. § 9512(b) (2018).

54. 18 Pa. Cons. Stat. § 9543(a)(1) (2018).

55. *See* 18 Pa. Cons. Stat. (2018).

56. Coles, *supra* note 49, at 724. In a decision written by Judge Garcia, the New York Court of Appeals invalidated a law that created a special prosecutor, appointed by the governor, to investigate certain crimes, reasoning that it unconstitutionally withdrew core prosecutorial authority from local district attorneys. See The People v. Viviani, Nos. 15–17 (Mar. 30, 2021).

57. I thank Richard Cordray, the former attorney general and solicitor general of the state of Ohio, for telling me about this incident.

58. Cal. Const. art. V, § 11.

59. Cal. Const. art. V, § 10, cl. 2.

60. In re Comm'n on the Governorship of California, 603 P.2d 1357, 1360 (Cal. 1979).

61. Wallace Turner, *California's Lieutenant Governor: An Adversary in Brown's Shadow*, N.Y. Times, Sec. A, at 14 (May 15, 1979).

62. Cal. Const. art. VI, § 16(d)(2).

63. *In re Comm'n on the Governorship of Cal.*, 603 P.2d at 1362.

64. *Id.*

65. *Id.*

66. *Id.* at 1363.

67. *Id.* at 1364.

68. *Id.* at 1365.

69. 586 S.E.2d 606 (Ga. 2003).

70. *Id.* at 607.

71. Reynolds v. Sims, 377 U.S. 533 (1964).

72. Section 5 of the Voting Rights Act is no longer enforceable. *See* Shelby County v. Holder, 570 U.S. 529 (2013).

73. *Baker*, 586 S.E.2d at 607.

74. *Id.*

75. *Id.* at 608.

76. *Id.* at 609.

77. *Id.* at 609; Ga. Const. art. V, § 2, para. I.

78. *Baker*, 586 S.E.2d at 609; Ga. Const. art. V, § 2, para. II.

79. Ga. Const. art. V, § 2, para. I.

80. *Id.*

81. Ga. Const. art. V, § 3, para. IV.

82. Ga. Code Ann. § 45-15-35 (2020).

83. *Baker*, 586 S.E.2d at 609.

84. *Id.* at 609; Ga. Code Ann. § 45-15-3 (2020).

85. *Baker*, 586 S.E.2d at 609.

86. *Id.*

87. *Id.*

88. *Id.* at 610.

89. *Id.*

90. *Id.*

91. *Id.* at 611.

92. Ga. Const. art. V, § 3, para. IV.

93. *Baker*, 586 S.E.2d at 612.

94. *Id.* at 612.

95. *Id.*

96. *Id.* at 613.

97. *Id.*

98. *Id.* at 613–14.

99. *Id.* at 614.

100. *Id.*

101. *Id.*

102. *Id.* at 615.

103. *Id.*

104. *Id.*

105. *Id.* at 615–16.

106. *Id.* at 616.

107. *Id.*

108. *Id.*

109. Margaret H. Lemos & Ernest A. Young, *State Public-Law Litigation in an Age of Polarization*, 97 Tex. L. Rev. 43, 6566 (2008). *See generally* Margaret H. Lemos, *Aggregate Litigation Goes Public: Representative Suits by State Attorneys General*, 126 Harv. L. Rev. 486 (2012).

110. Four states obtained independent settlements prior to the multi-state settlement, which involved the remaining forty-six states and four major tobacco companies. *See* Richard A. Daynard et al., *Implications for Tobacco Control of the Multistate Tobacco Litigation*, 91 Am. J. Pub. Health 1967, 1967–68 (2001).

111. Lemos & Young, *supra* note 109, at 46, 66.

112. *Id.* at 66.

113. *Id.*

114. The other states were South Carolina, Nebraska, Texas, Utah, Louisiana, Alabama, Michigan, Colorado, Pennsylvania, Washington, Idaho, South Dakota, Indiana, North Dakota, Mississippi, Arizona, Nevada, Georgia, Alaska, Ohio, Kansas, Wyoming, Wisconsin, Maine, and Iowa. *See, e.g.*, Brief for Petitioners on Severability, Nat'l Fed'n of Indep. Bus. v. Sebelius, 567 U.S. 519 (2012).

115. Johnstone, *supra* note 45, at 1475 n.18.

116. *Health Care Lawsuit*, WASHINGTON STATE OFFICE OF THE ATTORNEY GENERAL (last visited Dec. 10, 2020), https://www.atg.wa.gov/health-care-lawsuit.

117. Daniel Himebaugh, *Can the Attorney General Sue over Healthcare?*, PACIFIC LEGAL FOUNDATION (Mar. 24, 2010), https://pacificlegal.org/can-the-attorney-general-sue-over-health-care/.

118. *See* City of Seattle v. McKenna, 259 P.3d 1087, 1093 (Wash. 2011).

119. WASH. CONST. Art. III, § 2.

120. *McKenna*, 259 P.3d at 1092.

121. *See* Horne v. Flores, 557 U.S. 433, 438–39 (2009).

122. Joseph Kanefield & Blake W. Rebling, *Who Speaks for Arizona: The Respective Roles of the Governor and Attorney General When the State Is Named in a Lawsuit*, 53 ARIZ. L. REV. 689, 695 (2011).

123. *Id.* at 696.

124. Although Brewer did not challenge Goddard at the time, she did allege that he had "usurped" her authority. *See id.*

125. *Id.* at 697.

126. *Attorney General's Statement on Governor's Health Care Lawsuit Sign-On*, IOWA DEPARTMENT OF JUSTICE, OFFICE OF THE ATTORNEY GENERAL (Jan. 18, 2011), https://www.iowaattorneygeneral.gov/newsroom/attorney-general-s-statement-on-governor-s-health-care-lawsuit-sign-on.

127. *Id.*

128. *See, e.g.*, Brief for Respondents on Severability, , Nat'l Fed'n of Indep. Bus. v. Sebelius, 567 U.S. 519 (2012).

129. Johnstone, *supra* note 45, at 1485–86.

130. *See* United States v. Texas, 136 S. Ct. 2271 (2016).

131. *See* DHS v. Regents of the University of California, 140 S. Ct. 1891 (2020).

132. 524 U.S. 417 (1998). I say one case. A discerning reader might say two, *Clinton* plus *Immigration and Naturalization Service v. Chadha*, 462 U.S. 919 (1983). That's a fair point when it comes to vetoes and separation of powers more generally. *Chadha* concerned a provision of the Immigration and Nationality Act, 8 U.S.C. § 1254(a)(1), that authorized the immigration agency to halt deportation of an alien living in the United States for seven years if the attorney general found that the deportation would create "undue hardship." If the attorney general took such action, he or she had to report the decision to Congress, giving either house of the national legislature the power to veto the decision. When the House of Representatives exercised this authority against Jagdish Raj Chadha, he sued—and won. The Court, through an opinion by Chief Justice Burger, ruled that Congress could not give itself a legislative veto over actions by the executive branch that violated bicameralism and the Presentment Clause. Because this section concerns executive branch vetoes, it is one branch removed from *Chadha*.

133. *Clinton*, 524 U.S. at 439.

134. *Id.* at 439–40 (quoting INS v. Chadha, 462 U.S. 919, 951).

135. *Id.* at 440.

136. *Id.* at 471.

137. *Id.*

138. *Id.*

139. Richard Briffault, *The Item Veto in State Courts*, 66 TEMPLE L. REV. 1171, 1175 (1993).

140. *See* WASH. CONST. art. III, § 12. In Washington, the state supreme court has interpreted the state constitution to allow for the veto of "sections" of non-appropriation bills, but what constitutes a section remains a subject of litigious debate. *See* Washington State Motorcycle Dealers Ass'n v. State, 763 P.2d 442, 448 (Wash. 1998). The Oregon Constitution provides that "the Governor shall have power to veto single items in appropriation bills, and any provision in new bills declaring an emergency." OR. CONST. Art. V, § 15a.

141. For helpful discussions of these issues, *see* Winston D. Holliday, Jr., *Tipping the Balance of Power: A Critical Survey of the Gubernatorial Line Item Veto*, 50 S.C.L. REV. 503 (1999) (discussing South Carolina's experience and comparing it with Iowa, Wisconsin, and Virginia); Richard Briffault, *The Item Veto in State Courts*, 66 TEMPLE L. REV. 1171 (1993).

142. St. John's Well Child & Family Center v. Schwarzenegger, 239 P.3d 651 (Cal. 2010).

143. *Id.* at 655.

144. *Id.*

145. *Id.* at 658.

146. *Id.* at 659.

147. *Id.* at 660.

148. *Id.*

149. *Id.* at 664.

150. *Id.*

151. *Id.*

152. *Id.*

153. *Id.* at 669.

154. Jackson v. Sanford, 731 S.E.2d 722 (S.C. 2011).

155. *Id.* at 723.

156. S.C. CONST., art. IV, § 21.

157. *Id.* at 724–25.

158. *Id.* at 725.

159. *Id.* at 725–26.

160. WIS. CONST. art. V, § 10(1)(b).

161. State ex rel. Wisconsin Telephone Co. v. Henry, 260 N.W. 486 (Wis. 1935).

162. *Id.* at 491.

163. *Id.* at 492. *See, e.g.,* State ex rel. Sundby v. Adamany, 237 N.W.2d 910, 916 (Wis. 1976).

164. *Henry*, 260 N.W. at 491.

165. Mary E. Burke, *The Wisconsin Partial Veto: The Past, Present, and Future*, 1989 WIS. L. REV. 1395, 1396 (1989).

166. State ex rel. Wisconsin Senate v. Thompson, 424 N.W.2d 385 (Wis. 1989).

167. *Id.* at 387.

168. *Id.* at 388.

169. *See* WIS. LEGIS. COUNCIL INFO. MEMORANDUM, GOVERNOR'S PARTIAL VETO AUTHORITY, docs.legis.wisconsin.gov/misc/lc/information_memos/2020/im_2020_12 (last visited Dec. 14, 2020); *see* WIS. CONST. art. V, § 10(1)(c).

170. *Id.*

171. Steven G. Calabresi, *The Fatally Flawed Theory of the Unbundled Executive*, 93 MINN. L. REV. 1696, 1697 (2009).

172. Marshall, *supra* note 10.

173. Christopher R. Berry & Jacob E. Gersen, *The Unbundled Executive*, 75 U. CHI. L. REV. 1385, 1387 (2008) (arguing that "unbundling executive authority enhances democratic accountability and government performance").

174. Calabresi served in the Reagan administration, while Marshall served in the Obama and Clinton administrations and was the solicitor general of Ohio.

175. RON CHERNOW, ALEXANDER HAMILTON 107–13 (Penguin 2004).

176. THE FEDERALIST NO. 70 (Alexander Hamilton).

177. Marshall, *supra* note 10, at 2454.

178. *Id.* at 2452.

179. Lemos & Young, *supra* note 109, at 65.

180. *Id.* at 48.

181. *See* Dan Schweitzer, *The Modern History of State Attorneys Arguing as Amici Curiae in the U.S. Supreme Court*, 22 GREEN BAG 2D 143 (2019).

182. Lemos & Young, *supra* note 109, at 70.

183. *Id.* at 69.

184. *See* PAUL NOLETTE, FEDERALISM ON TRIAL: STATE ATTORNEYS GENERAL AND NATIONAL POLICYMAKING IN CONTEMPORARY AMERICA 198–219 (2015).

185. *See, e.g.*, Massachusetts v. EPA, 549 U.S. 497, 518–20 (2007) (treating the Article III standing requirements for "a suit by a State for an injury to it in its capacity" as a sovereign differently from those "between two private parties").

186. Daryl J. Levinson & Richard H. Pildes, *Separation of Parties, Not Powers*, 119 HARV. L. REV. 2311 (2006) (noting the growing tendency

of competition between political parties, not political branches, to characterize the operations of American government).

187. Lemos & Young, *supra* note 109, at 55. What Larry Baum and Neal Devins claim has caused divisions in the courts—the formal and informal organizations with which judges affiliate—may cause something similar with state attorneys general. *See* LAWRENCE BAUM & NEAL DEVINS, THE COMPANY THEY KEEP (2019).

Chapter 6

1. Robert A. Schapiro, *Contingency and Universalism in State Separation of Powers Discourse*, 4 ROGER WILLIAMS U.L. REV. 79, 92–93 (1998) ("Federal separation of powers doctrine does not apply directly to the states.").

2. In addressing these topics, I have benefited from the work of several scholars, who have written incisively about state administrative law. *See, e.g.*, Miriam Seifter, *Understanding State Agency Independence*, 117 MICH. L. REV. 1537 (2019); Miriam Seifter, *Further from the People? The Puzzle of State Administration*, 93 N.Y.U. L. REV. 107 (2018); Miriam Seifter, *Gubernatorial Administration*, 131 HARV. L. REV. 483, 521–23 (2017); Aaron Saiger, Chevron *and Deference in State Administrative Law*, 83 FORDHAM L. REV. 555 (2014); Michael Pappas, *No Two-Stepping in the Laboratories: State Deference Standards and Their Implications for Improving the* Chevron *Doctrine*, 39 MCGEORGE L. REV. 977 (2008); Jim Rossi, *Politics, Institutions, and Administrative Procedure: What Exactly Do We Know from the Empirical Study of State-Level APAs, and What More Can We Learn?*, 58 ADMIN. L. REV. 961 (2006); Jim Rossi, *Dual Constitutions and Constitutional Duels: Separation of Powers and State Implementation of Federally Inspired Regulatory Programs and Standards*, 46 WM. & MARY L. REV. 1343 (2005); Daniel Ortner, *The End of Deference: How States (and Territories) Are Leading a (Sometimes Quiet) Revolution Against Administrative Deference Doctrines* (March 11, 2020), https://papers.ssrn.com/sol3/papers.cfm?abstract_id=3552321; D. Zachary Hudson, *A Case for Varying Interpretive Deference at the State Level*, 119 YALE L.J. 373 (2009).

3. *See* James Rossi, *Institutional Design and the Lingering Legacy of Antifederalist Separation of Powers Ideals in the States*, 52 VAND. L. REV. 1167, 1191–201 (1999); *see also* Jason Iuliano & Keith E. Whittington, *The Nondelegation Doctrine: Alive and Well*, 93 NOTRE DAME L. REV. 619 (2017); Douglas H. Ginsburg & Steven Menashi, *Our Illiberal Administrative Law*, 10 N.Y.U. J.L. & LIBERTY 475, 492–93 (2016).

4. Iuliano & Whittington, *supra* note 3, at 635.

5. Cass R. Sunstein, *Nondelegation Canons*, 67 U. CHI. L. REV. 315, 322 (2000).

6. Cynthia R. Farina, *Deconstructing Nondelegation*, 33 HARV. J.L. & PUB. POL'Y 87, 87 (2010) (quoted in Jason Iuliano & Keith E. Whittington, *supra* note 3, at 620).

7.   293 U.S. 388 (1935).

8.   295 U.S. 495 (1935).

9.   Pub. L. No. 73-67, 48 Stat. 195 (1933) (repealed 1966).

10. *Id.* at 195–96.

11. *Compare* AMITY SHLAES, THE FORGOTTEN MAN: A NEW HISTORY OF THE GREAT DEPRESSION 214–45 (2007) (giving a historical overview of the *Schechter* prosecution and arguing that the prosecution singled out the Schechters' business for compliance with kosher customs), *and* Amity Shlaes, *What Gorsuch's Critics Get Wrong About the Administrative State,* NAT. REVIEW (July 30, 2019), https://www.nationalreview.com/2019/07/administrative-state-what-neil-gorsuch-critics-get-wrong/ (defending this thesis from attack), *and* Josh Blackman, *Amity Shlaes Responds on* Schechter Poultry, VOLOKH CONSPIRACY (July 31, 2019), https://reason.com/2019/07/31/amity-shlaes-responds-on-schechter-poultry/ (same), *with* Mark Tushnet, *Epistemic Closure on the Supreme Court,* BALKINIZATION (July 5, 2019), https://balkin.blogspot.com/2019/07/epistemic-closure-at-supreme-court.html (questioning the accuracy of some of Shlaes's historical arguments and suggesting that the Schechters were likely committing health violations), *and* Mark Tushnet, *Epistemic Closure and the* Schechter *Case* (Harvard Public Law, Working Paper No. 19-42, 2019), https://papers.ssrn.com/sol3/papers.cfm?abstract_id=3436689## (same).

12. *See* SHLAES, *supra* note 11, at 241.

13. A.L.A. Schecter Poultry Corp. v. United States, 295 U.S. 495, 529–530 (1935).

14. *Id.* at 523, 530, 534.

15. *Id.* at 537–38, 542.

16. SHLAES, *supra* note 11, at 245.

17. 531 U.S. 457 (2001). The Court relied on *J. W. Hampton, Jr. & Co. v. United States,* 276 U.S. 394 (1928), as establishing the "intelligible principle" test.

18. 42 U.S.C. § 7409 (2018).

19. *See* Whitman v. Am. Trucking Ass'ns, 531 U.S. 457, 462–463 (2001)a (quoting 42 U.S.C. §§ 7408–7409).

20. *See id.* at 472 (quoting 42 U.S.C. § 7409(b)(1)).

21. *Id.* at 474.

22. 139 S. Ct. 2116 (2019).

23. 34 U.S.C. § 20913(d) (2018).

24. Gundy v. United States, 139 S. Ct. 2116, 2144 (2019) (Gorsuch, J., dissenting).

25. *Id.* at 2130–31 (Alito, J., concurring in the judgment).

26. *Id.* at 2131–32 (Gorsuch, J., dissenting).

27. *Id.* at 2135–37.

28. *Id.* at 2143–44.

29.   Steven G. Calabresi & Joan L. Larsen, *One Person, One Office: Separation of Powers or Separation of Personnel?*, 79 Cornell L. Rev. 1045, 1070 n.116 (1994).

30.   *See id.*

31.   Mass. Const. art. XXX.

32.   Rossi, *Institutional Design, supra* note 3, at 1190 (citing Bernard Schwartz, *Curiouser and Curiouser: The Supreme Court's Separation of Powers Wonderland*, 65 Notre Dame L. Rev. 587, 588 (1990)).

33.   *See id.* at 1190–91.

34.   Tex. Const. art. II, § 1.

35.   Gordon S. Wood, Power and Liberty: Constitutionalism in the American Revolution (Oxford Univ. Press 2021), at Ch. 2.

36.   *Id. See* Gordon S. Wood, The Creation of the American Republic 152–61 (1969); *see also id.* at 430–63 (observing that there was a "second wave" of state constitutionalism in the 1780s that focused on strengthening the executive against the legislature after an era of legislative supremacy in the state constitutions of the 1770s).

37.   Conn. Const. amend. XVIII.

38.   Iuliano & Whittington, *supra* note 3, 620.

39.   *See* Rossi, *supra* note 3 at 1990–93. Rossi's work appears to be the most up-to-date categorization of state non-delegation doctrines. *See* Brenner M. Fissell, *When Agencies Make Criminal Law*, 10 U.C. Irvine L. Rev. 855, 869 n.82 (2020) ("Rossi's remains the most current assessment [of state non-delegation doctrines].").

40.   *See* Rossi, *supra* note 3, at 1191–201. Even within these categories, there is substantial diversity, as Rossi goes on to explain. For example, strong non-delegation states have distinct limiting principles. Some, like Montana and Kentucky, use the federal non-delegation "intelligible principle" test but enforce it more rigorously. *See* Williams v. Bd. of Cnty. Com'rs, 308 P.3d 88, 99 (Mont. 2013); In re Petition to Transfer Territory from High Sch. Dist. No. 6 to High Sch. Dist. No. 1, 15 P.3d 447, 451 (Mont. 2000); Bacus v. Lake Cnty., 354 P.2d 1056, 1061 (Mont. 1960); Flying J Travel Plaza v. Transp. Cabinet, Dep't of Highways, 928 S.W.2d 344, 350 (Ky. 1996); Legis. Res. Comm'n v. Brown, 664 S.W.2d 907, 914–915 (Ky. 1984); Miller v. Covington Dev. Auth., 539 S.W.2d 1, 4 (Ky. 1976). Others, like Texas, Illinois, and Florida, limit delegation to distinct categories. *See* Hous. Auth. v. Higginbotham, 143 S.W.2d 79, 87 (Texas 1940); Stofer v. Motor Vehicle Cas. Co., 369 N.E.2d 875, 878–79 (Ill. 1977); B.H. v. State, 645 So.2d 987, 992 (Fla. 1994).

41.   Rossi, *Dual Constitutions, supra* note 2, at 1359; *see* Rossi, *Institutional Design, supra* note 3; *see also* Harold H. Bruff, *Separation of Powers Under the Texas Constitution*, 68 Tex. L. Rev. 1337, 1340 (1990).

42. Michael Asimow, Arther Earl Bonfield & Ronald M. Levin, State and Federal Administrative Law 413 (2d ed. 1998); *see also generally id.* at 413–19.
43. McNeill v. Nevada, 375 P.3d 1022 (Nev. 2016).
44. *Id.* at 1023–24.
45. *Id.* at 1025.
46. *Id.* at 1025–26 (quoting Clark Cnty. v. Luqman, 697 P.2d 107, 110 (Nev. 1985)).
47. *Id.* at 1026–27.
48. Fla. Stat. § 380.05(2) (1975).
49. *See* Askew v. Cross Key Waterways, 372 So. 2d 913, 915–16 (Fla. 1978) (citing Fla. Stat. § 380.05 (1975)).
50. 372 So. 2d 913 (Fla. 1978).
51. *Id.* at 918 (citing Fla. Const. art. II, § 7).
52. *Id.* (quoting Fla. Const. art. II, § 3).
53. *Id.* at 918–19.
54. *Id.* at 922–24.
55. *See id.* at 925–26 (England, C.J., concurring).
56. 645 So. 2d 987 (Fla. 1994).
57. *Id.* at 989–90 (quoting Fla. Stat. § 39.061 (1990)).
58. *See id.* at 992 (quoting Chiles v. Children A, B, C, D, E, & F, 589 So. 2d 260, 264 (Fla. 1991)).
59. 885 So. 2d 321 (Fla. 2004).
60. *Id.* at 334 (quoting the circuit court opinion).
61. Mich. Const. Art. III, § 2.
62. Florida became the first state court to codify a law allowing for such certifications, now codified at Fla. Stat. ch. 25.031. *See* Rebecca A. Cochran, *Federal Court Certification of Questions of State Law to State Courts: A Theoretical and Empirical Study*, 29 J. of Legis. 157, 159 n.12 (2013). By the way, state courts do not have the same power in the other direction—to certify federal law questions to federal courts. *Id.* at 160.
63. MCL 10.31(1).
64. *Id. See also* In re Certified Questions, No. 161492, 28-29 (Mich. Decided Oct. 2, 2020) (for descriptions of orders).
65. In re Certified Questions, No. 161492 (Mich., decided Oct. 2, 2020). The certification request involved two questions. The first was whether the governor had authority to re-declare an emergency after April 30 under a separate "state of disaster" statute, twenty-eight days after the first emergency order ended. All seven justices agreed that the governor could not re-declare an emergency in this way under the statute without new support by the legislature. Justice Markman's opinion rejected the main argument in response by the governor—that the twenty-eight-day limitation amounted to a "legislative veto" and should be invalidated under Michigan law for reasons comparable to those used by the United

States Supreme Court in holding that a legislative veto violated separation of powers. *See* INS v. Chadha, 462 U.S. 919 (1983). The state court concluded that Governor Whitmer "did not possess authority . . . to renew her declaration of a state of emergency" based on the COVID-19 pandemic under MCL 30.403 after April 30, 2020. *In re Certified Questions*, No. 161492, at 12.

66. *Id.* at 48.

67. *Id.* at 20.

68. *Id.* at 20–21.

69. *Id.* at 5 (quoting People v. Skinner, 502 Mich. 89, 100 (2018)).

70. MICH. CONST. art. III, § 2.

71. In re Certified Questions, at 22 (quoting COOLEY, CONSTITUTIONAL LIMITATIONS 92, 116–17 (1886)).

72. *Id.*(quoting JOHN LOCKE, TWO TREATISES OF GOVERNMENT 408–09 (Peter Laslett ed., 1963). A series of recent articles offers thrusts and parries over the original meaning of the US Constitution when it comes to its authorization, or not, of delegation of powers among the three branches. *Compare* Julian Davis Mortenson & Nicholas Bagley, *Delegation at the Founding*, COLUM. L. REV. (forthcoming 2021), *with* Ilan Wurman, *Nondelegation at the Founding*, YALE L.J. (forthcoming 2021); *see also* Nicholas R. Parrillo, *A Critical Assessment of the Originalist Case Against Administrative Regulatory Power: New Evidence from the Federal Tax on Private Real Estate in the 1790s*, YALE L.J. (forthcoming 2021).

73. In re Certified Questions, at 23 (quoting Osius v. St. Clair Shores, 344 Mich. 693, 698 (1956)).

74. *Id.* at 24–27 & n.18.

75. *Id.* at 27.

76. *Id.* at 28–29.

77. *Id.* at 31–35.

78. *Id.* at 35.

79. *Id.* at 2, 47–48.

80. *Id.* at 3.

81. Dissent, at 1–3.

82. 503 A.2d 838 (N.H. 1986).

83. *Id.* at 839.

84. *Id.* at 839–40.

85. N.H. CONST. pt. I, art. 37.

86. *See* Act of June 1, 1993, 73rd Leg., R.S., ch. 8, § 1, 1993 Tex. Gen. Laws 29, 30, repealed by Act of May 30, 1997, 75th Leg., R.S., ch. 463, § 1.30, 1997 Tex. Gen. Laws 1769, 1783.

87. Tex. Boll Weevil Eradication Found., Inc. v. Lewellen, 952 S.W.2d 454, 465 (Tex. 1997) (quoting Mistretta v. U.S., 488 U.S. 361, 371 (1989)).

88. *Id.* at 466 (quoting Brown v. Humble Oil & Refin. Co., 83 S.W.2d 935, 941 (1935)).

89. *Id.* at 466–67.

90. *Id.* at 469–71.

91. *Id.* at 473–75.

92. *Id.* at 475 (quoting A.L.A. Schechter Poultry Corp. v. United States, 295 U.S. 495, 553 (1935) (Cardozo, J., concurring)).

93. *See* 1997 Tex. Gen. Laws 1769; 1999 Tex. Sess. Law Serv. Ch. 286 (West); *see also* Robert A. Ewert, *Delegations to Private Entities: The Application of the Boll Weevil Eight Factor Test*, 2 Tex. Tech. J. Tex. Admin. L. 275, 283 (2001).

94. Press Release, Sid Miller, Commissioner, Texas Department of Agriculture, Commissioner Miller Announces Successes for Boll Weevil Eradication in Texas (Sept. 22, 2015), https://www.texasagriculture.gov/NewsEvents/NewsEventsDetails/tabid/76/Article/3021/Commissioner-Miller-Announces-Successes-for-Boll-Weevil-Eradication-in-Texas.aspx.

95. *See, e.g.*, Erik Luna, *Rage against the Machine: A Reply to Professors Bierschbach and Bibas*, 97 Minn. L. Rev. 2245, 2246 (2013).

96. 1 Kenneth Culp Davis, Administrative Law Treatise § 2.07 (1st ed. 1958) (quoted in Rossi, *supra* note 2, at 1364). To his credit, Professor Davis included a brief section on the state courts' treatment of the non-delegation doctrine in his original treatise. He noted that many state courts already were enforcing the non-delegation doctrine more robustly than their federal counterparts, writing that "the nondelegation doctrine in the state courts continues to have a good deal of force during the nineteen-fifties." But he incorrectly went on to say that "one may confidently predict" a permissive attitude toward delegation would "gradually become the prevailing state law of the future." *Id.* at 72–73.

97. Justice Marshall, then-Justice Rehnquist, and Justice O'Connor did not participate.

98. Chevron, U.S.A., Inc. v. Nat. Res. Def. Council, Inc., 467 U.S. 837 (1984).

99. 5 U.S.C. § 706 (2018).

100. Skidmore v. Swift & Co., 323 U.S. 134, 140 (1944).

101. Bowles v. Seminole Rock & Sand Co., 325 U.S. 410, 414 (1945).

102. Aditya Bamzai, *The Origins of Judicial Deference to Executive Interpretation*, 126 Yale L.J. 908, 916 (2017). *See also Pittston Stevedoring Corp. v. Dellaventura*, 544 F.2d 35 (1976) (Friendly, J.) (offering his views on the state of agency deference eight years before *Chevron*).

103. *See* Gary Lawson & Stephen Kam, *Making Law Out of Nothing at All: The Origins of the* Chevron *Doctrine*, 65 Admin. L. Rev. 1, 29–33 (2013) (arguing no one understood *Chevron* to be a landmark decision at the time it was decided); *see also id.* at 1–28 (placing *Chevron* in the context of DC Circuit developments of administrative law), *id.* at 33–75 (detailing how *Chevron* became a landmark decision and expressing skepticism about the evolution).

104.   46 Fed. Reg. 50,766 (Oct. 14, 1981).

105.   *Chevron*, 467 U.S. at 840.

106.   *Id.* at 842–43.

107.   *Id.* at 843–44.

108.   *Id.* at 857–58 (quoting 46 Fed. Reg. 16281 (Mar. 12, 1981)).

109.   *Id.* at 866.

110.   *Id.* at 865–66.

111.   *See* Antonin Scalia, *Judicial Deference to Administrative Interpretations of Law*, 1989 DUKE L.J. 511, 516–17. *See also* ANTONIN SCALIA, THE ESSENTIAL SCALIA: ON THE CONSTITUTION, THE COURTS, AND THE RULE OF LAW 283–92 (Jeffrey S. Sutton & Edward Whelan eds., 2020) (containing excerpts from article).

112.   United States v. Mead Corp., 533 U.S. 218, 236 (2001). *See* Antonin Scalia, *On* Chevron *Deference Twenty Years Later*, 66 ADMIN. L. REV. (Spring 2014). *See also* SCALIA, *supra* note 111 (containing excerpts from article).

113.   Justice Elena Kagan, The Scalia Lecture: A Dialogue with Justice Kagan on the Reading of Statutes at 8:29 (Nov. 17, 2015), http://today.law. harvard.edu/in-scalia-lecture-kagan-discusses-statutory-interpretation. *See generally* Christopher J. Walker, *Attacking* Auer *and* Chevron *Deference: A Literature Review*, 16 GEORGETOWN JOURNAL OF LAW & POLICY 103 (2018).

114.   PHILLIP HAMBURGER, IS ADMINISTRATIVE LAW UNLAWFUL? (2014).

115.   Michigan v. EPA, 135 S. Ct. 2699, 2712 (2015) (Thomas, J., concurring).

116.   Baldwin v. United States, 140 S. Ct. 690 (2020) (Mem).

117.   *Id.* at 690–93 (Thomas, J., dissenting from the denial of certiorari).

118.   For then-Judge Gorsuch: *see* Gutierrez-Brizuela v. Lynch, 834 F.3d 1142, 1149–58 (10th Cir. 2016) (Gorsuch, J., concurring) (arguing that *Chevron* and *Brand X* should be overturned); United States v. Nichols, 784 F.3d 666, 667–677 (10th Cir. 2015) (Gorsuch, J., dissenting from denial of rehearing en banc). For then-Judge Kavanaugh: *see, e.g.,* Loving v. I.R.S., 742 F.3d 1013, 1016 (D.C. Cir. 2014) (emphasizing that *Chevron* step one should employ all rules of statutory construction before deferring to an agency); Brett M. Kavanaugh, *Fixing Statutory Interpretation*, 129 HARV. L. REV. 2118 (2016) (expressing skepticism about legal doctrines— including *Chevron*—that require judges to determine whether a statute is "ambiguous"); The Heritage Foundation, *The Joseph Story Distinguished Lecture: Judge Brett M. Kavanaugh*, at 28:00, YouTube (Oct. 25, 2017), https://www.youtube.com/watch?v=s_rR6518w3I.

119.   Ortner, *supra* note 2; *see also* Pappas, *supra* note 2.

120.   Ortner, *supra* note 2. *See generally* ASIMOW, ET AL., STATE AND FEDERAL ADMINISTRATIVE LAW 557–70 (comparing federal and state approaches to administrative deference); Saiger, *supra* note 2, at 557–60 (noting different approaches and citing additional literature about the various state approaches).

121.   *See* Ortner, *supra* note 2, text accompanying notes 43–51.

122. Fla. Const. art. V, § 21.
123. Ariz. Rev. Stat. Ann. § 12-910(E) (2018); *see also* Ortner, *supra* note 2, text accompanying notes 52–56.
124. Wis. Stat. Ann. § 227.10(2g) (2018); *see also* Ortner, *supra* note 2, text accompanying notes 57–58.
125. *See* Ortner, *supra* note 2, text accompanying notes 32–36, 58.
126. Tetra Tech v. Wis. Dep't of Rev., 914 N.W.2d 21 (Wis. 2018).
127. *Id.* at 28 (Kelly, J.) (lead opinion).
128. *Id.* at 40 (quoting Wis. Const. art. VII, § 2).
129. *Id.* at 41.
130. *Id.* at 41–42.
131. *Id.* at 43–44 (quoting Perez v. Mortg. Bankers Ass'n, 135 S. Ct. 1199, 1217 (2015) (Thomas, J., concurring)).
132. *Id.* at 45.
133. *Id.* at 45, 54.
134. *Id.* at 29 n.4.
135. *See id.* at 67–74 (Ziegler, J., concurring).
136. *See id.* at 74–76 (Gableman, J., concurring).
137. *See id.* at 63–67 (A. Bradley, J., concurring).
138. *See id.* at 28 n.3, 29 n.4 (lead opinion).
139. Wis. Stat. Ann. § 227.10(2g) (West 2018); *see also* Ortner, *supra* at note 2, text accompanying notes 57–58.
140. King v. Miss. Mil. Dep't, 245 So. 3d 404 (Miss. 2018).
141. *Id.* at 407.
142. *Id.* at 407–08 (citing Miss. Const. art. 1, § 1).
143. *Id.* at 408 (quoting Miss. Const. art. 1, § 2).
144. *Id.*
145. *Id.* (quoting Gutierrez-Brizuela v. Lynch, 834 F.3d 1142, 1156 (10th Cir. 2016) (Gorsuch, J., concurring)).
146. Pub. Water Supply Co., Inc. v. Dipasquale, 735 A.2d 378 (Del. 1999).
147. *Id.* at 378–80.
148. *Id.* at 382–83 (footnote omitted).
149. Saiger, *supra* note 2, at 582. *See id.* at 557–60 (including citations to other studies to like effect); Ortner, *supra* note 2.
150. *See* Cobb v. Bd. of Counseling Pros. Licensure, 896 A.2d 271, 275 (Me. 2006); Goldberg v. Bd. of Health of Granby, 830 N.E.2d 207, 213 (Mass. 2005). It's not even clear that the Massachusetts High Court consistently follows this approach. As for other states, some use similar approaches to *Chevron*. *See* Kokochak v. West Virginia State Lottery Comm'n, 695 S.E.2d 185, 190 (W.Va. 2010) (applying the *Chevron* test but only for legislative rules that are independently determined to be valid); Jou v. Hamda, 201 P.3d 614, 621 (Haw. Ct. App. 2009) (describing a test in which the agency's interpretation will bind a court unless the interpretation is "palpably erroneous"); Seeton v. Pennsylvania Game Com'n, 937 A.2d 1028, 1037 n.12 (Pa. 2007) (claiming that—even though

Pennsylvania has never adopted the two-step *Chevron* test—"the *Chevron* approach . . . is indistinguishable from our own approach to agency interpretations of Commonwealth statutes"); Bernard W. Bell, *The Model APA and the Scope of Judicial Review: Importing* Chevron *into State Administrative Law*, 20 WIDENER L.J. 801, 818–20 (2011) (describing these and other states with approaches similar to *Chevron*).

151. J. M. Balkin & Sanford Levinson, *The Canons of Constitutional Law*, 111 HARV. L. REV. 963, 970 (1998).

152. *See* Rossi, *Institutions*, *supra* note 2, at 1190–1201. Rossi's twenty "strong delegation" states use an approach that is more robust than the federal non-delegation doctrine. He concedes that, as a formal doctrinal matter, many of his twenty-three "moderate delegation" states look similar to the federal doctrine. *Id.* at 1200. Even so: "Despite the doctrinal similarities . . . [moderate non-delegation] state courts are much more likely to strike down statutes as unconstitutional [for overdelegating] than their federal counterparts." *Id.*

153. Iuliano & Whittington, *supra* note 3, at 636–45. In the first non-delegation case identified by them, Respublica v. Philip Urbin Duquet, 2 Yeates 493, 494, 500–01 (Pa. 1799), the Pennsylvania Supreme Court rejected the claim that its legislature "cannot confer" on a local government authority to criminalize infringements of property rights that affect the public welfare.

154. Rossi, *Institutional Design*, *supra* note 3, at 1189 (noting that the approach of most state courts to the non-delegation doctrine "contrasts starkly" with the approach of the federal courts).

155. *See* Sanford Levinson, *Courts as Participants in "Dialogue": A View from American States*, 59 U. KAN. L. REV. 791, 805–06 & nn.67–68 (2011) (stating that he "strongly suspect[s]" that "more state supreme court justices have had some kind of political career prior to joining the judiciary" than their federal counterparts).

156. U.S. Term Limits, Inc. v. Thornton, 514 U.S. 779 (1995) (holding that states may not adopt term limits for their federal representatives).

157. Rossi, *Dual Constitutions*, *supra* note 2, at 1375.

158. *See* MONT. LEGIS. SERVS. DIV., *A Guide to the Montana Legislature* (Jan. 2019), https://leg.mt.gov/content/About-the-Legislature/2019guide-montana-legislature.pdf.

159. *See* NAT. CONF. OF STATE LEGIS., *Full- and Part-Time Legislatures* (June 14, 2017), https://www.ncsl.org/research/about-state-legislatures/full-and-part-time-legislatures.aspx.

160. *See* U.S. TERM LIMITS, *How Many States Have Term Limits on Their Legislatures?* (June 8, 2018), https://www.termlimits.com/state-legislative-term-limits/.

161. Rossi, *Dual Constitutions*, *supra* note 2, at 1375.

162. Saiger, *supra* note 2, at 570.

163. *Id.* at 567.

164. *See* Felicetti v. Secretary of Communities & Development, 386 Mass. 868, 873 (Mass. 1982) (reasoning that in the face of "contrary interpretations" "within the executive branch" over the meaning of the same statute, "deference to agency construction of a statute . . . loses much of its usefulness"). Note that the source of this exception, the Massachusetts Supreme Judicial Court, is one of the state courts most likely to defer to agency interpretations.

165. Saiger, *supra* note 2, at 568.

166. One can wonder, I acknowledge, how much accountability flows from a separate election for, say, the insurance commissioner. That's not a top-of-the-ticket race. And the idea that many citizens will gauge their vote based on administrative decisions or rules issued by the commissioner has a fairyland quality to it. *See* David Schleicher, *Federalism and State Democracy*, 95 Tex. L. Rev. 763 (2017) (noting lack of voter knowledge about second-order state and local elections). Plus, any agency can still create an aggregation of power problem that offends liberty by announcing an aggressive rule, interpreting it, and enforcing it against a hapless citizen. Either way, the broader point, the one that matters, is that the plural executive offers considerable ground for state variation in administrative law.

167. Saiger, *supra* note 2, at 561.

168. Saiger, *supra* note 2, at 562.

169. *Gundy*, 139 S. Ct. at 2144 (Gorsuch, J., dissenting).

170. Bd. of Tr. of Judicial Form Ret. Sys. v. Attorney General, 132 S.W.3d 770, 784 (Ky. 2003).

171. Ginsburg & Menashi, *supra* note 3, at 483, 498. Plenty of academics, for what it is worth, continue to defend *Chevron* and the administrative state. *See, e.g.*, Cass R. Sunstein & Adrian Vermeule, Law and Leviathan: Redeeming the Administrative State (2020); Adrian Vermeule, Law's Abnegation: From Law's Empire to the Administrative State (2016).

172. Ginsburg & Menashi, *supra* note 3, at 479 n.12 (citing Separation of Powers Restoration Act, S. 2724, 114th Cong. (2016); H.R. 4768, 114th Cong. (2016)).

173. 5 U.S.C. § 706 (2018).

174. Rossi, *Institutions, supra* note 2, at 976–80.

175. *Compare* Bell, *supra* note 150, at 836–40 (2011) (arguing that some state APAs have limited their states' delegation and deference compared to the federal level) *with* Pappas, *supra* note 2 at 1008 (arguing that state APAs "have had little effect on doctrinal development" of delegation and deference); *and compare* Saiger, *supra* note 2, at 570–74 (analyzing Pappas and Bell and identifying a degree of incompatibility between *Chevron*-style deference and most state APAs); *with* Rossi, *Institutions, supra*

note 2, at 972–75 (emphasizing the lack of empirical study on the effect of state APAs). *See also* William D. Araiza, *In Praise of a Skeletal APA*, 56 ADMIN. L. REV. 979 (2004) (noting that the "judiciary, not legislature," should "evolve specific standards for review, because of [the] great variety of approaches to judicial review).

176. *See, e.g.*, Mistretta v. United States, 488 U.S. 361, 415–16 (1989) (Scalia, J., dissenting) (concluding that the creation of the federal Sentencing Commission did not violate the non-delegation doctrine but did violate other separation–of-powers principles).

177. United States v. Nichols, 784 F.3d 666, 671 (10th Cir. 2015) (Gorsuch, J., dissenting from the denial of rehearing en banc).

178. Alexander Bickel put this last point well: "Delegation without standards short-circuits the lines of responsibility that make the political process meaningful." Alexander Bickel, *The Constitution and the War*, COMMENTARY 52 (July 1972).

179. Antonin Scalia, *A Note on the Benzene Case*, AEI JOURNAL ON GOVERNMENT AND SOCIETY 28 (July/August 1980). Justice Scalia was commenting on then-Justice Rehnquist's efforts to reinvigorate the non-delegation doctrine in Indus. Union Dep't v. Am. Petrol. Inst., 448 U.S. 607, 685–86 (1980) (Rehnquist, J., concurring).

180. Williamson v. Lee Optical Inc., 348 U.S. 483 (1955).

181. Oliver v. Okla. Alcoholic Beverage Control Bd., 359 P.2d 183, 187 (Okla. 1961).

182. Democratic Party of Okla. v. Estep, 652 P.2d 271, 277–78 (Okla. 1982).

183. Tex. Antiquities Comm'n v. Dallas Cnty. Cmty. Coll. Dist., 554 S.W.2d 924, 927 (Tex. 1977). In this case, the court used vagueness as a tool in striking down a law that gave an agency power to identify "all buildings and locations of historical interest." *Id.*

184. Kwik Shop, Inc. v. City of Lincoln, 498 N.W.2d 102, 108–09 (Neb. 1983).

185. Guillou v. Div. of Motor Vehicles, 503 A.2d 838, 840 (N.H. 1986).

186. Bacus v. Lake Cnty., 354 P.2d 1056, 1061 (Mont. 1960).

187. Opinion of the Justices to the House of Representatives, 471 N.E.2d 1266, 1273–74 (Mass. 1984).

188. Montoya v. O'Toole, 610 P.2d 190, 191 (N.M. 1980).

189. State ex. rel. Barker v. Manchin, 279 S.E.2d 622, 631 (W.Va. 1981).

190. Rogers v. Watson, 594 A.2d 409, 414 (Vt. 1991).

191. 529 U.S. 120 (2000).

192. *See id.* at 159–61.

193. *See* 135 S. Ct. 2480, 2488–89 (2015).

194. Ginsburg & Menashi, *supra* note 3 ("We see no principled distinction for this purpose between major and non-major questions."); Cass R. Sunstein, Chevron *Step Zero*, 92 VA. L. REV. 187, 245 (2006) (noting the absence of a "metric" distinguishing major from non-major questions).

It's a different question whether a major-questions inquiry might help courts when it comes to identifying non-delegation problems.

195. *Chevron*, 484 U.S. at 843–44.
196. Abramski v. United States, 134 S. Ct. 2259, 2274 (2014).
197. *Cf.* The Federalist No. 47, at 297–99 (James Madison) (Clinton Rossiter ed., 1961).
198. United States v. Wiltberger, 18 U.S. (5 Wheat.) 76 (1820).
199. Carter v. Welles-Bowen Realty, Inc., 736 F.3d 722, 729 (6th Cir. 2013) (Sutton, J., concurring); Esquivel-Quintana v. Lynch, 810 F.3d 1019, 1027 (2016) (Sutton, J., concurring in part and dissenting in part).
200. Louisiana v. Carr, 761 So. 2d. 1271, 1274 (La. 2000).
201. *Carter*, 736 F.3d at 730.
202. Clark v. Martinez, 543 U.S. 371, 380 (2005); *see also, e.g.*, Maracich v. Spears, 133 S. Ct. 2191, 2209 (2013); Kasten v. Saint-Gobain Performance Plastics Corp., 563 U.S. 1, 16 (2011); Leocal v. Ashcroft, 543 U.S. 1, 11 n.8 (2004); Scheidler v. Nat'l Org. for Women, 537 U.S. 393, 408–09 (2003).
203. 515 U.S. 687 (1995).
204. *Id.* at 691–93.
205. *Id.* at 703–04.
206. *Id.* at 704 n.18.
207. *Carter*, 736 F.3d at 734 (Sutton, J., concurring); *see also, e.g.*, United States v. Grimaud, 220 U.S. 506, 519 (1911); Touby v. United States, 500 U.S. 160, 165–67 (1991); *cf. Leocal*, 543 U.S. at 11 n.8; Whitman v. United States, 135 S. Ct. 352, 354 (2014) (Scalia, J., statement respecting denial of certiorari).
208. *See* Bill Bryson, The Mother Tongue 14–15 (2001).
209. Only a few state court judges have identified this problem. *See, e.g.*, Moriarity v. Ind. Dep't of Natural Resources, 113 N.E.3d 614, 625–26 (Ind. 2019) (Slaughter, J., dissenting); Healthscript, Inc. v. Indiana, 770 N.E.2d 810, 814 n.6 (Ind. 2002); Lineberger v. North Carolina Dep't of Corr., 657 S.E.2d 673 (N.C. Ct. App. 2008). That may turn on the reality that so few state courts incorporate a rigid *Chevron* regime into state law. And it may turn on the reality that the state courts show more care when a statute has a criminal application, prompting them to apply the rule of lenity, not administrative deference.
210. John S. Baker, *Revisiting the Explosive Growth of Federal Crimes*, Heritage Foundation (June 16, 2008), https://www.heritage.org/report/revisiting-the-explosive-growth-federal-crimes.
211. United States v. Baldwin, 745 F.3d 1027, 1031 (10th Cir. 2014).
212. Another problematic area of deference arises in tax law and goes beyond *Chevron* deference. Called the substance over form doctrine, it originally rested on a useful and practical insight—that what parties label something in legal transactions does not control its tax consequences.

But over time it grew into a doctrine that permitted the IRS to defy the *legislative* label that Congress put on permitted transactions to impose taxes on transactions structured in reliance on the U.S. Code. *See* Summa Holdings, Inc. v. Comm'r of the IRS, 848 F.3d 779 (6th Cir. 2017). The substance-over-form doctrine allows the agency to construe statutes broadly when it believes taxpayers are paying fewer taxes than they should, even when their calculations are anchored in statutory text. What's most jaw-dropping about the substance-over-form doctrine is that it exceeds *Chevron*. From the IRS's perspective, it receives deference even when its interpretation of a statute would not get beyond step one of *Chevron*, even in other words when the statute unambiguously does not apply. I have yet to come across a state court that uses the substance-over-form doctrine in the way the federal government currently does. Many states, to the contrary, require a strict construction of tax laws. *See, e.g.*, Sorg v. Iowa Dep't of Revenue, 269 N.W.2d 129, 131–33 (Iowa 1978); Maas Bros. v. Dickinson, 195 So.2d 193, 198 (Fla. 1967); Hawaiian Trust Co. v. Borthwick, 35 Haw. 429 (Haw. 1940); Stone v. Rogers, 189 So. 810, 812 (Miss. 1939). The non-delegation doctrine also has had "considerable success over the years" in state tax cases, from an 1830 Tennessee case that prohibited the legislature from delegating property tax authority to the judiciary to a 1965 North Dakota case that prohibited the legislature from delegating power to set an excise tax on potatoes to the Potato Development Commission. Iuliano & Whittington, *supra* note 3, at 644 (citing Marr v. Enloe, 9 Tenn. 452 (Tenn. 1830) and Scott v. Donnelly, 133 N.W.2d 418 (N.D. 1965)).

213. Gary Fields & John R. Emshwiller, *The Many Efforts to Count Nation's Federal Criminal Laws*, WALL STREET JOURNAL (July 23, 2011), https://www.wsj.com/articles/SB10001424052702304319804576389601079728920.

214. Saiger, *supra* note 2, at 560.

215. Ginsburg & Menashi, *supra* note 3, at 478.

216. *See generally* Kent Barnett & Christopher J. Walker, Chevron *in the Circuit Courts*, 116 MICH. L. REV. 1 (2017).

217. John F. Manning, *The Nondelegation Doctrine as a Canon of Avoidance*, 2000 SUP. CT. REV. 223, 223; *see also* Cass R. Sunstein, *Nondelegation Canons*, 67 U. CHI. L. REV. 315, 315–16 (2000); Aditya Bamzai, *Delegation and Interpretive Discretion: Gundy, Kisor, and the Formation and Future of Administrative Law*, 133 Harv. L. Rev. 164 (2019).

218. *See McNeil*, 375 P.3d at 1025.

219. *See Tetra Tech*, 914 N.W.2d at 74–76 (Gableman, J., concurring).

220. *See, e.g.*, Minn. Stat. Ann. § 14.125.

221. SEC v. Chenery Corp., 332 U.S. 194 (1947) (requiring reviewing courts, when assessing the validity of agency action, to look only at the grounds invoked by the agency); *see* Kristin E. Hickman & Aaron L. Nielson, *Narrowing* Chevron's *Domain*, 70 DUKE L.J. 931 (2021) ; Jonathan

H. Adler & Christopher J. Walker, *Delegation and Time*, 105 Iowa L. Rev. 1931 (2020).

222. *Garcia v. San Antonio Metro. Transit Auth.*, 469 U.S. 528, 552 (1985).

223. *Gregory v. Ashcroft*, 501 U.S. 452 (1991).

Chapter 7

1. JED HANDELSMAN SHUGERMAN, THE PEOPLE'S COURTS 105 (2012).

2. *Id.* at 72 (quoting Letter from Thomas Jefferson to William Charles Jarvis (Sept. 28, 1820)).

1. *Fletcher v. Peck*, 10 U.S. (6 Cranch) 87, 88 (1810).

2. Jane Elsmere, *The Notorious Yazoo Land Fraud Case*, 51 GA. HIST. Q. 425, 426 (1967).

3. *Id.*

4. *Id.*

5. *Id.*

6. *Id.* at 427.

7. *Id.* at 428.

8. *Fletcher*, 10 U.S. at 87.

9. *Id.* at 87–88.

10. FEDERAL JUDICIAL CENTER, *Cases That Shaped the Federal Courts:* Fletcher v. Peck, at 5 (2020), https://www.fjc.gov/sites/default/files/cases-that-shaped-the-federal-courts/pdf/Fletcher.pdf.

11. *Id.*

12. *Id.*

13. DAVID P. CURRIE, THE CONSTITUTION IN THE SUPREME COURT: THE FIRST HUNDRED YEARS 130 (1985).

14. *Fletcher*, 10 U.S. at 131.

15. *Id.* at 130.

16. *Id.*

17. *Id.*

18. *Id.* at 131.

19. *Id.*

20. *Id.* at 135.

21. *Id.* at 133, 135.

22. U.S. CONST. Art. I, § 10, cl. 1.

23. *Fletcher*, 10 U.S. at 137.

24. *Id.* at 139.

25. CURRIE, *supra* note 13, at 128, 136 n.81; 1 C. WARREN, THE SUPREME COURT IN UNITED STATES HISTORY 392 (rev. ed. 1926); James W. Ely Jr., *The Marshall Court and Property Rights: A Reappraisal*, 33 J. MARSHALL L. REV. 1023, 1034 (2000).

26. *Fletcher*, 10 U.S. at 136.

27. CURRIE, *supra* note 13, at 128; Ely, *supra* note 25, at 1034; Joseph M. Lynch, Fletcher v. Peck: *The Nature of the Contract Clause*, 13 SETON HALL

L. REV. 1, 1 (1982) ("The well-known case of *Fletcher v. Peck*, in which for the first time a state statute would expressly be held invalid as conflicting with the Federal Constitution.").

28. 3 U.S. (3 Dall.) 199 (1796).

29. 2 U.S. (2 Dall.) 304 (1795).

30. Martha J. Dragich, *State Constitutional Restriction on Legislative Procedure: Rethinking the Analysis of Original Purpose, Single Subject, and Clear Title Challenges*, 38 HARV. J. ON LEGIS. 103, 103–04 (2001).

31. *Id.* at 103.

32. *Id.*

33. Michael E. Libonati, *State Constitutions and Legislative Process: The Road Not Taken*, 89 B.U. L. REV. 863, 865 (2009).

34. *Id.* (quoting G. ALAN TARR, UNDERSTANDING STATE CONSTITUTIONS 95 (1998)).

35. Dragich, *supra* note 30, at 103.

36. *Id.* at 103–04.

37. Millard H. Ruud, *"No Law Shall Embrace More Than One Subject,"* 42 MINN. L. REV. 389, 391 (1957).

38. *Id.*

39. Daniel N. Boger, *Constitutional Avoidance: The Single Subject Rule as an Interpretive Principle*, 103 VA. L. REV. 1247, 1249 (2017).

40. *Id.*; Richard Briffault, *The Single-Subject Rule: A State Constitutional Dilemma*, 82 ALB. L. REV. 1629, 1633 (2019) (noting that single-subject and clear-title requirements appear "almost always in the same sentence").

41. GA. CONST. Art. III, § V, para. III.

42. Savannah v. State, 4 Ga. 26, 38 (Ga. 1848).

43. Fletcher v. Peck, 10 U.S. (6 Cranch) at 88.

44. GA. CONST. OF 1798, Art. I, § 17.

45. *Savannah*, 4 Ga. at 38; *see* Elsmere, *supra* note 2, at 426.

46. N.J. CONST. OF 1844, Art. IV, § 7, cl. 4.

47. Thornton Sinclair, *The Operation of a Constitutional Restraint on Bill-Styling*, 2 U. NEWARK L. REV. 30 (1937).

48. Ruud, *supra* note 37, at 389.

49. ILL. CONST. OF 1848, Art. III, § 22.

50. MI. CONST. OF 1835, Amend. II.

51. *Id.*

52. The New Jersey constitution of 1844 was ratified in June of that year. N.J. Const. of 1844, preamble. *See* John E. Bebout & Joseph Harrison, *The Working of the New Jersey Constitution*, 10 WM. & MARY L. REV. 337, 339 (1968).

53. N.J. CONST. OF 1844, Art. IV, § 7, cl. 4.

54. ROBERT LUCE, LEGISLATIVE PROCEDURE: PARLIAMENTARY PRACTICES AND THE COURSE OF BUSINESS IN FRAMING OF STATUTES 548 (1922).

55. *Id.* at 549.

56. *Id.*

57. *Id.*

58. *Id.* at 550.

59. Founders Online National Archives, *Board of Trade: Report on Pennsylvania Laws, 24 June 1760*, https://founders.archives.gov/documents/Franklin/01-09-02-0045.

60. Michael D. Gilbert, *Single Subject Rules and the Legislative Process*, 67 U. PITT. L. REV. 803, 812 (2006).

61. Boger, *supra* note 39, at 1249.

62. Gilbert, *supra* note 60, at 812. While Massachusetts does not have a single-subject rule for legislation, the constitution requires constitutional initiatives to contain only subjects "which are related or which are mutually dependent." MASS. CONST., Articles of Amendment, Art. XLVIII, II, § 3.

63. State v. Elvins, 32 N.J.L. 362, 364 (N.J. 1867).

64. THEODORE SEDGWICK, A TREATISE ON THE RULES WHICH GOVERN THE INTERPRETATION AND APPLICATION OF STATUTORY AND CONSTITUTIONAL LAW 570 (1857).

65. Washington v. Page, 4 Cal. 388 (Cal. 1854).

66. *See* Ruud, *supra* note 37, at 393. At the time Ruud was writing, Ohio was the only state that still treated its single-subject rule as directory. That has since changed. *See, e.g.,* State ex rel. Ohio Acad. of Trial Lawyers v. Sheward, 715 N.E.2d 1062, 1099 (Ohio 1999) (describing the historic reluctance of Ohio courts to enforce the single-subject rule and acknowledging that the stance of the Ohio courts has changed).

67. 723 N.E.2d 265 (Ill. 1999).

68. *Id.* at 268.

69. *Id.*

70. *Id.*

71. *Id.*

72. *Id.* at 270.

73. *Id.* at 271.

74. *Id.* at 272.

75. *Id.* at 273.

76. *Id.* at 274.

77. *Id.*

78. 668 A.2d 1370 (Del. 1995).

79. DEL. CONST. Art. II, § 16.

80. Turnbull v. Fink, 668 A.2d 1370, 1378 (Del. 1995).

81. *Id.*

82. *Id.* at 1379.

83. *Id.* at 1382.

84. *Id.*

85. *Id.*

86. *Id.*
87. *Id.*
88. *Id.* at 1385.
89. *Id.*
90. *Id.* at 1386.
91. *Id.*
92. ILL. CONST. art. VIII, § 1.
93. State ex rel. Warren v. Nusbaum, 208 N.W.2d 780, 795 (Wis. 1973).
94. *See* Brian Libgober, *The Death of Public Purpose (And How to Prevent It)*, at 19, John M. Olin Center (March 2016), http://www.law.harvard.edu/ programs/olin_center/fellows_papers/pdf/Libgober_63.pdf (stating that the public purpose doctrine is "a principle recognized in every state of the country"); *see also* Dale F. Rubin, *The Public Pays, the Corporation Profits: The Emasculation of the Public Purpose Doctrine and a Not-For-Profit Solution*, 28 U. RICH. L. REV. 1311, 1313 n.15 (1994) ("All fifty states either have amended their constitutions to include the doctrine or the doctrine has received judicial sanction."). States that do not include the prohibition in their constitutions have implied it. *See, e.g.,* Hopper v. City of Madison, 256 N.W.2d 139, 142 (Wis. 1977) ("Although not established by any specific clause in the state constitution, the public purpose doctrine is a well-established constitutional tenet.").
95. 467 S.E.2d 615 (N.C. 1996).
96. *Id.* at 618.
97. *Id.* at 619.
98. N.C. CONST. Art. V, § 2(1).
99. *Maready,* 467 S.E.2d at 618.
100. *Id.* at 620–21.
101. *Id.* at 624–25.
102. *Id.* at 624–26.
103. *Id.* at 624–27.
104. *Id.* at 631–33.
105. *Id.* at 634–36.
106. 256 N.W.2d 139 (Wis. 1977).
107. *Id.* at 142.
108. *Id.*
109. *Id.* at 143.
110. *Id.*.
111. *Id.* at 144–45.
112. *Id.* at 145.
113. *Id.* at 146.
114. 546 N.W.2d 424 (Wis. 1996).
115. *Id.* at 440.
116. 657 N.W.2d 344 (Wis. 2003).
117. *Id.* at 346.

118. *Id.* at 351.
119. *Id.* at 353.
120. *Id.* at 355.
121. *Id.*
122. *Id.* at 357–58.
123. *Id.* at 358–59.
124. *Id.* at 359–60.
125. Michael P. Malone, The Battle for Butte: Mining and Politics on the Northern Frontier, 1864–1906 (1981); *see also* Michael P. Malone, et al., Montana: A History of Two Centuries 224 (rev. ed. 1991).
126. *Id.*
127. Gilbert, *supra* note 60, at 832.
128. *Id.*
129. *Id.*
130. *Id.* at 837.
131. *Id.*
132. *Id.*
133. McIntire v. Forbes, 909 P.2d 846, 857 (Or. 1996) (holding that the proposed subject "relating to the activities of State government" was too broad to qualify under Oregon's single-subject rule).
134. *See* Boger, *supra* note 39, at 1249 ("Out of the forty-three states that have enacted [the single-subject] rule, forty also contain a title requirement.").
135. *See* Simmons-Harris v. Goff, 711 N.E.2d 203 (Ohio 1999).
136. Iowa Const. art III, § 29; Or. Const. art. IV, § 20.
137. 877 S.W.2d 98 (Mo. 1994).
138. *Id.* at 103.
139. See, e.g., William H. Pryor Jr., *The Importance of State Constitutions*, National Review (Jun. 7, 2018), https://www.nationalreview.com/2018/06/state-constitutions-important-components-of-federalism/.
140. Burns v. Cline, 382 P.3d 1048 (Okla. 2016).
141. Simmons-Harris v. Goff, 711 N.E.2d 203 (Ohio 1999).
142. James A. Gardner, *State Courts as Agents of Federalism: Power and Interpretation in State Constitutional Law*, 44 Wm. & Mary L. Rev. 1725, 1745–46 (2003); Briffault, *supra* note 40, at 1629–30. Briffault notes the difficult of enforcing single-subject rules, *id.* at 1636, 1659, as does Daniel Lowenstein, Daniel H. Lowenstein, *California Initiatives and the Single-Subject Rule*, 30 UCLA L. Rev. 936, 940–41 (1983).
143. *See* Libgober, *supra* note 94, at 23 (noting that "there is not a single instance of a Court invalidating economic incentives to private individuals or corporations" using the public-purpose doctrine from 1994 to 2014, and that "cases involving the public-purpose doctrine are both rare and decreasing over the last twenty years.").

144. Jennifer Friesen, 4 State Constitutional Law: Litigating
Individual Rights, Claims, and Defenses § 7.07[3] (2006). Similar to
the US Constitution, the New Jersey Constitution provides that "private
property shall not be taken for public use without just compensation."
Hon. Peter G. Sheridan, Kelo v. City of New London: *New Jersey's Take
on Takings*, 37 Seton Hall L. Rev. 307, 325 (2007) (citing N.J. Const.
art. I, § 20).

145. Bd. of County Comm'rs v. Lowery, 136 P.3d 639, 651 (Okla. 2006) ("To
the extent that our determination may be interpreted as inconsistent
with the U.S. Supreme Court's holding in *Kelo v. City of New London*,
today's pronouncement is reached on the basis of Oklahoma's own special
constitutional eminent domain provisions."); City of Norwood v. Horney,
853 N.E.2d 1115, 1141 (Ohio 2006) ("We find that the analysis by . . . the
dissenting justices of the United States Supreme Court in *Kelo* [is a] better
model[] for interpreting Section 19, Article I of Ohio's Constitution.").

146. One state court decision comes close. In Goldstein v. New York State
Urban Dev. Corp., 879 N.Y.S.2d 524 (2009), the New York Court of
Appeals upheld an exercise of eminent domain as part of a redevelopment
anchored by a new stadium for the Brooklyn Nets and treated it as a
permissible public use under the New York Constitution.

Chapter 8

1. *See* Stanley L. Engerman & Kenneth L. Sokoloff, *The Evolution of Suffrage
Institutions in the New World*, 65 J. Economic Hist. 891, 896–99 (2005).

2. *Id.* at 904.

3. *See* Akhil Reed Amar, America's Constitution: A Biography 421–22
(2006).

4. In 1776, New Jersey permitted anyone with £50 to vote. N.J. Const. of
1776 art. V. In 1797, the state made clear that women could vote through
"An Act to regulate the election of members of the legislative council
and general assembly, sheriffs and coroners, in this State." Section XI
of the act allowed "all free inhabitants of this State, of full age, who are
worth fifty pounds, . . . and have resided within the county in which they
claim a vote, for twelve months immediately preceding the election," and
provided that "no person shall be entitled to vote in any other township
or precinct, than that in which he or she doth actually reside at the
time of the election." Special Collections/University Archives, Rutgers
University Libraries. But this explicit permission was revoked in 1807,
and the 1844 New Jersey Constitution explicitly limited the right to vote
to men. And that's where things stayed until the Nineteenth Amendment
in 1920 and, more formally in the Garden State, the 1947 New Jersey
Constitution.

5. U.S. Const. Art. I, § 2, cl. 3.

6. 369 U.S. 186 (1962).

7. *Id.* at 187–92, 237–41.

8. *Id.* at 245 (Douglas, J., concurring).

9. 328 U.S. 549 (1946).

10. *Baker,* 369 U.S. at 217, 222.

11. *Id.* at 198–237.

12. *Id.* at 244–45 (Douglas, J., concurring).

13. *Id.* at 253, 258 (Clark, J., concurring).

14. *Id.* at 258–59.

15. *Id.* at 259 & n. 9.

16. *Id.* at 265 (Stewart, J., concurring) (quotation omitted).

17. *See* Cody S. Barnett & Joshua A. Douglas, *A Voice in the Wilderness: John Paul Stevens, Election Law, and a Theory of Impartial Governance,* 60 WM. & MARY L. REV. 335, 353 (2018) (citing *More Perfect—The Political Thicket,* RADIOLAB (June 10, 2016), http://radiolab.org/story/the_political_ thicket/).

18. Barnett & Douglas, *supra* note 17, at 354.

19. *Baker,* 369 U.S. at 267–330 (Frankfurter, J., dissenting).

20. *Id.* at 267.

21. *Id.* at 270.

22. *Id.* at 297.

23. *Id.* at 300–01.

24. *Id.* at 300.

25. *Id.* at 323–24.

26. *Id.* at 330–40 (Harlan, J., dissenting).

27. *Id.* at 336.

28. *Id.* at 333.

29. *Id.* at 339–40.

30. 376 U.S. 1 (1964).

31. *Id.* at 5–6.

32. *Id.* at 7–8.

33. 377 U.S. 533 (1964).

34. *Id.* at 589 n. 1 (Harlan, J., dissenting).

35. *Id.* at 562, 568, 577.

36. *Id.* at 562.

37. *Id.* at 562, 584.

38. *Id.* at 537–87.

39. *Id.* at 587–88 (Clark, J., concurring in the affirmance). Justice Stewart also authored a brief concurrence. *See id.* at 588–89 (Stewart, J., concurring).

40. *Id.* at 588 (Clark, J., concurring).

41. *Id.* at 588 (Stewart, J., concurring).

42. *Id.* at 590–91 (Harlan, J., dissenting).

43. *Id.* at 591.

44. *Id.* at 606–11 & n. 69.

45. *Id.* at 623–24.

46. *Id.* at 589–625.

47. *See generally* Kirkpatrick v. Preisler, 394 U.S. 526 (1969); Wesberry v. Sanders, 376 U.S. 1 (1964). It's worth adding that decennial redistricting sometimes arises from congressional reapportionment. Under Art. 1, § 2, Cl. 3: "Representatives and direct Taxes shall be apportioned among the several States which may be included within this Union, according to their respective Numbers. . . . The actual Enumeration shall be made within three Years after the first Meeting of the Congress of the United States, and within every subsequent Term of ten Years, in such Manner as they shall by Law direct." Prior to the 1920s, the House of Representatives would increase in size with population, meaning states would usually gain congressional seats every ten years. Congress failed to reapportion within ten years only once, in the 1920s, due to the new capping of the size of the House and the fear of some states that they would lose congressional seats as a result. *See Reapportionment and Redistricting*, CQ PRESS ENCYCLOPEDIA OF AMERICAN GOVERNMENT, http://library.cqpress.com/cqresearcher/document. php?id=cqresrre1927120600. With a fixed pie of 435 representatives today, all that matters is relative population among states, not overall population. Whenever a state gains or loses a congressional seat, it thus has to draw new maps, something it would have to do with or without a "one person, one vote" rule. In 2010, ten states lost seats and eight states gained seats. *See 2010 Apportionment of the U.S. House of Representatives Map*, UNITED STATES CENSUS BUREAU (December 2010), https://www.census.gov/library/visualizations/2010/dec/2010-map.html. The same was true in 2000. *See 2000 Apportionment Results Map*, UNITED STATES CENSUS BUREAU (December 2000), https://www.census.gov/library/visualizations/2000/dec/2000-map.html. A similar projection is in order for 2020. *See Projected 2024 Electoral Map Based on New Census Population Data*, 270TOWIN (December 30, 2019), https://www.270towin.com/news/2019/12/30/projected-2024-electoral-map-based-on-new-census-population-data_925.html. Because there are seven states that have only one seat, that means about 40% of multi-member states suffer/benefit from a delegation change every ten years.

48. Pamela S. Karlan, *The Rights to Vote: Some Pessimism About Formalism*, 71 TEX. L. REV. 1705, 1705, 1707 (1993).

49. 52 U.S.C. § 10301 (2018).

50. 478 U.S. 30 (1986).

51. *Id.* at 50–51.

52. 507 U.S. 25 (1993).

53. 509 U.S. 630, 649, 653 (1993).

54. For one analysis of the relationship between *Thornburg v. Gingles* and *Shaw v. Reno*, *see* Richard H. Pildes & Richard G. Niemi, *Expressive*

Harms, "Bizarre Districts," and Voting Rights: Evaluating Election-District Appearances After Shaw v. Reno, 92 MICH. L. REV. 483 (1993).

55. Davis v. Bandemer, 478 U.S. 109 (1986) (*abrogated by* Rucho v. Common Cause, 139 S. Ct. 2484 (2019)).

56. 541 U.S. 267 (2004).

57. *Id.* at 305 (plurality opinion).

58. *See id.* at 317 (Stevens, J., dissenting); *id.* at 343 (Souter, J., dissenting); *id.* at 355 (Breyer, J., dissenting).

59. *See id.* at 306–16 (Kennedy, J., concurring in the judgment).

60. *See, e.g.*, Gill v Whitford, 138 S. Ct. 1916 (2018); League of United Latin American Citizens v. Perry, 548 U.S. 399 (2006).

61. 139 S. Ct. 2484 (2019).

62. *Id.* at 2491–93.

63. *Id.* at 2491.

64. *Id.* at 2494 (quoting 2 Records of the Federal Convention of 1787, at 430 (Max Farrand ed., 1966)) (additional internal quotation omitted).

65. *Rucho*, 139 S. Ct. at 2494 (quoting Vieth v. Jubelirer, 541 U.S. 267, 277 (2004) (plurality opinion)).

66. *Id.* at 2496.

67. *Id.* at 2497.

68. *Rucho*, 139 S. Ct. at 2496 (quoting LULAC v. Perry, 548 U.S. 399, 420 (2006) (opinion of Kennedy, J.)).

69. *Rucho*, 139 S. Ct. at 2499 (quoting Davis v. Bandemer, 478 U.S. 109, 159 (1986) (opinion of O'Connor, J.)).

70. *Rucho*, 139 S. Ct. at 2499.

71. *Id.*

72. *Id.* at 2500.

73. *Id.*

74. *Id.*

75. *Id.* at 2501.

76. *Id.* at 2493–508.

77. *Id.* at 2501.

78. *Id.* at 2502.

79. *Id.* at 2506.

80. *Id.* at 2507–08.

81. *Id.* at 2509 (Kagan, J., dissenting).

82. *Id.* at 2517 (Kagan, J., dissenting).

83. *Id.* at 2524 (Kagan, J., dissenting).

84. Laura Royden & Michael Li, Extreme Maps, Brennan Center 6 (2017). https://www.brennancenter.org/sites/default/files/publications/Extreme%20Maps%205.16_0.pdf.

85. *See, e.g.*, No. 159 MM 2017 (November 9, 2017) (per curiam) (order granting extraordinary jurisdiction); 175 A.3d 282 (Mem) (per curiam) (2018); No. 159 MM 2017 (January 26, 2018) (per curiam) (order

appointing Professor Nathaniel Persily as an advisor to the court); 178 A.3d 737 (2018); 181 A.3d 1083 (Mem) (per curiam) (2018).

86. *See* 42 Pa. C.S.A. § 726 (2020).

87. *See League of Women Voters*, No. 159 MM 2017 at 2 (November 9, 2017).

88. *League of Women Voters*, 175 A.3d at 284.

89. *Id.*

90. *Id.* at 285–86 (Baer, J., concurring and dissent).

91. *See id.* at 286–87 (Saylor, C.J., dissenting).

92. *Id.* at 287–88 (Mundy, J., dissenting).

93. *League of Women Voters*, No. 159 MM 2017, at 2 (January 26, 2018).

94. Letter from Brian S. Paszamant to the Supreme Court of Pennsylvania, January 31, 2018, brennancenter.org/sites/default/files/legal-work/ LWV_v_PA_Scarnati-Response-to-01.26.18-Order.pdf; *see also* Sam Levine, *Top Pennsylvania Republican Says He'll Ignore Court Order to Help Fix Gerrymandering*, HuffPost (Jan. 31, 2018), https://www. huffpost.com/entry/joseph-scarnati-gerrymandering-pennsylvania_n_ 5a723db6e4b05253b27550c2.

95. *See* Memorandum from Representative Cris Dush to All House Members (Feb. 5, 2018), https://www.legis.state.pa.us/cfdocs/Legis/CSM/ showMemoPublic.cfm?chamber=H&SPick=20170&cosponId=25163; *see also* Sam Levine, *Pennsylvania GOP Moves to Impeach Supreme Court Democrats for Gerrymandering Ruling*, HuffPost (Mar. 21 2018), https://www.huffingtonpost.ca/entry/pennsylvania-republicans-move- to-impeach-supreme-court-democrats-for-gerrymandering-ruling_n_ 5ab16875e4b0decad044deeo.

96. *League of Women Voters*, 178 A.3d at 741–42.

97. Pa. Const. Art. 1, § 5.

98. *League of Women Voters*, 178 A.3d at 814.

99. *Id.* at 815–16 (citing Pa. Const. Art. 2, § 16).

100. *Id.* at 818–20.

101. *Id.* at 824.

102. *Id.* at 825–31 (Baer, J., concurring and dissenting).

103. *Id.* at 831–34 (Saylor, C.J., dissenting).

104. *Id.* at 834–38 (Mundy, J., dissenting).

105. *League of Women Voters*, 181 A.3d at 1084–121.

106. *See id.* 1121–22 (Saylor, C.J., dissenting); *see also id.* at 1122 (Baer, J., dissenting); *id.* (Mundy, J., dissenting).

107. *See* Nate Cohn, *Democrats Didn't Even Dream of This Pennsylvania Map. How Did It Happen?*, New York Times (Feb. 21, 2018), https:// www.nytimes.com/2018/02/21/upshot/gerrymandering-pennsylvania- democrats-republicans-court.html.

108. Jonathan Lai & Liz Navratil, *Pa. Gerrymandering Case: State Supreme Court Releases New Congressional Map for 2018 Elections*, Philadelphia Enquirer (Feb. 19, 2018), https://www.inquirer.com/philly/news/politics/

pennsylvania-gerrymandering-supreme-court-map-congressional-districts-2018-elections-20180219.html.

109. Editorial, *Pennsylvania's Redistricting Coup*, WALL STREET JOURNAL (Feb. 20, 2018), https://www.wsj.com/articles/pennsylvanias-redistricting-coup-1519170870?mod=article_inline.

110. *Pennsylvania Election Results*, NEW YORK TIMES, Election 2016 (Last updated Sept. 3, 2017), https://www.nytimes.com/elections/2016/results/pennsylvania.

111. *Pennsylvania Election Results*, NEW YORK TIMES, Election 2018 (Last updated May 15, 2019), https://www.nytimes.com/interactive/2018/11/06/us/elections/results-pennsylvania-elections.html.

112. Cooper v. Harris, 137 S. Ct. 1455 (2017).

113. *See* Royden & Li, *supra* note 84, at 6. R.

114. Harper v. Lewis, 19 CVS 012667, 191028 (N.C. Super. Ct. Oct. 28, 2019) (order granting preliminary injunction).

115. *Id.* at 3–4 (citing *Rucho*, 139 S. Ct. at 2507).

116. *Harper*, 19 CVS 012667, at 6–7 (citing N.C. CONST. Art. 1 § 10).

117. *Harper*, 19 CVS 012667, at 7–8 (citing N.C. CONST. Art. 1 § 19).

118. *Harper*, 19 CVS 012667, at 8–11 (citing N.C. CONST. Art. 1 § 14).

119. *Harper*, 19 CVS 012667, at 8–11 (citing N.C. CONST. Art. 1 § 12).

120. *Harper*, 19 CVS 012667, at 12–14, 18.

121. *Id.* at 17.

122. *See* Michael Wines, *Republicans Redrew a Gerrymandered Map. Try Again, Say Democrats*, NEW YORK TIMES (Nov. 15, 2019), https://www.nytimes.com/2019/11/15/us/north-carolina-maps-gerrymander.html.

123. Harper v. Lewis, 19 CVS 012667, 191202 (N.C. Super. Ct. Dec. 2, 2019) (order on prior injunction and BOE filing); *see also* Gary D. Robertson, *Judges: New North Carolina Congress Map Will Be Used in 2020*, ABC NEWS (Dec. 2, 2019), https://abcnews.go.com/Politics/wireStory/judges-north-carolina-congress-map-2020-67443331.

124. *See* David Leonhardt, Opinion, *A Win for Gerrymandering*, NEW YORK TIMES (Dec. 3, 2019), https://www.nytimes.com/2019/12/03/opinion/north-carolina-gerrymander-map.html; Stephen Wolf (@PoliticsWolf), TWITTER (Dec. 2, 2019, 1:26 PM), https://twitter.com/PoliticsWolf/status/1201568455486517248.

125. *See, e.g.*, Michael Gentithes, *Gobbledygook: Political Questions, Manageability, & Partisan Gerrymandering*, 105 IOWA L. REV. 1081, 1098–99 & nn. 97, 100 (2020) (providing a sampling of both legal scholarship and investigative journalism into the development of re-districting technology and its likely effect on partisanship); Ronald A. Klain, *Success Changes Nothing: The 2006 Results and the Undiminished Need for a Progressive Response to Political Gerrymandering*, 1 HARV. L. & POL. REV. 75, 80–86 (2007).

126. *Rucho*, 139 S. Ct. at 2502–04.

127. *Id.* at 2518 (Kagan, J., dissenting).

128. *Id.* at 2505.

129. *Id.*.

130. *See* Baker v. Carr, 369 U.S. 186, 188–91 (1962) (quoting TENN. CONST. art. II).

131. 369 U.S. at 259 n. 9 (Clark, J., concurring) (citing Scholle v. Secretary of State, 360 Mich. 1 (1960)).

132. *See* Transcript of Oral Argument at 16–17, Rucho v. Common Cause, 139 S.Ct. 2484 (2019) (No. 18-442) (question from Justice Gorsuch about state efforts to limit gerrymandering via initiatives and legislative actions); *id.* at 68–71 (questions from Justice Gorsuch and Justice Kavanaugh about initiatives and state supreme court decisions); *Rucho*, 139 S.Ct. at 2507 (discussing state supreme court decisions, commissions, and state restrictions on permissible re-districting criteria as potential paths forward).

133. 478 U.S. 186 (1986).

134. Powell v. Georgia, 510 S.E.2d 18 (Ga. 1998).

135. 539 U.S. 558 (2003).

136. 409 U.S. 810 (1972) (dismissing an appeal from a Minnesota Supreme Court case that held the federal constitution did not require states to permit same-sex marriages for "want of a substantial federal question").

137. Obergefell v. Hodges, 576 U.S. 644 (2015).

138. *Rucho*, 139 S.Ct. at 2507.

139. FL. CONST. art. III, § 20(a).

140. League of Women Voters of Florida v. Detzner, 172 So.3d 363 (2015).

141. Iowa Code § 42.4(5) (2016).

142. Del. Code Ann., Tit. xxix, § 804 (2017); Va. Code Ann. § 24.2-304.4 (West 2020).

143. *Independent and Advisory Citizen Redistricting Commissions*, COMMON CAUSE, https://www.commoncause.org/independent-redistricting-commissions/ (last accessed July 23, 2020).

144. COLO. CONST. art. V, sec. 44.

145. N.J. CONST. art. II, sec. 2.

146. Alexander M. Bickel, *The Durability of* Colegrove v. Green, 72 YALE L.J. 39, 43 (1962).

147. OHIO CONST. art. XIX; Jessie Balmert, *Ohio Voters Just Approved Issue 1 to Curb Gerrymandering in Congress*, CINCINNATI ENQUIRER (May 8, 2018), https://www.cincinnati.com/story/news/politics/elections/2018/05/08/ohio-issue-1-gerrymandering/580679002/.

148. *See* Annie Lo, *Citizen and Legislative Efforts to Reform Redistricting in 2018*, BRENNAN CENTER FOR JUSTICE (Nov. 7, 2018), https://www.brennancenter.org/our-work/analysis-opinion/citizen-and-legislative-efforts-reform-redistricting-2018.

149. Jessie Balmert, *Ohio Voters Just Approved Issue 1 to Curb Gerrymandering in Congress*, Cincinnati Enquirer (May 8, 2018), https://www.cincinnati.com/story/news/politics/elections/2018/05/08/ohio-issue-1-gerrymandering/580679002/.

150. Rebecca Powell and Nick Coltrain, *Colorado Election: Amendments Y and Z Pass, Changing the Way Colorado Does Redistricting*, Coloradoan (Nov. 6, 2018), https://www.coloradoan.com/story/news/politics/elections/2018/11/06/colorado-election-results-amendments-y-and-z-pass-changing-redistricting-process/1894902002/.

151. Lisa Riley Roche, *Utah Proposition to Battle Gerrymandering Passes as Final Votes Tallied*, DeseretNews (Nov. 20, 2018), https://www.deseret.com/2018/11/20/20659293/utah-proposition-to-battle-gerrymandering-passes-as-final-votes-tallied; Mori Kessler, *"Better Boundaries" Ballot Initiative Would Create Independent Redistricting Commission*, St George News (July 24, 2017), https://www.stgeorgeutah.com/news/archive/2017/07/24/mgk-better-boundaries-ballot-initiative-would-create-independent-redistricting-commission#.XxmMjVVKi71.

152. U.S. Const. art. I, § 4.

153. Emanuel Celler, *Congressional Apportionment—Past, Present, and Future*, 17 Law & Contemp. Probs. 268, 272 (1952).

154. *Id.* at 271–72; *see also* Wood v. Broom, 287 U.S. 1, 6–7 (1932) (holding that the requirements included in the 1911 Reapportionment Act were abrogated by the 1929 reapportionment act).

155. *See* Colegrove v. Green, 328 U.S. 549, 554–56 (1946) ("The short of it is that the Constitution has conferred upon Congress exclusive authority to secure fair representation by the States in the popular House. . . . If Congress failed in exercising its powers, whereby standards of fairness are offended, the remedy ultimately lies with the people. . . . Courts ought not to enter this political thicket. The remedy for unfairness in districting is to secure State legislatures that will apportion properly, or to invoke the ample powers of Congress"); *Rucho*, 139 S.Ct. at 2508 ("The Framers gave Congress the power to do something about partisan gerrymandering in the Elections Clause.").

156. H.R. 1, 116th Cong., §§ 2401–21 (1st Sess. 2019).

157. *See, e.g.*, Francesca Lina Procaccini, *Partisan Gerrymandering: State Courts Come to Bat on the Free-Speech Issue of Our Day*, 2 Md. B.J. 128 (2020); Steven Shepard & Scott Bland, *The Nationwide Battle over Gerrymandering Is Far from Over*, Politico (June 27, 2019), https://www.politico.com/story/2019/06/27/supreme-court-gerrymandering-1385960.

158. Six states also guarantee that elections be "free and open." An additional twelve states simply guarantee that they be "free." And fifteen states protect elections from improper influence or interference by "civil or military powers." *See Free and Equal Election Clauses in State Constitutions*, National Conference of State Legislatures (Nov. 4, 2019), https://

www.ncsl.org/research/redistricting/free-equal-election-clauses-in-state-constitutions.aspx.

159. Bickel, *supra* note 147, at 40 (quoting Jaffe, *Standing to Secure Judicial Review: Public Actions*, 74 HARV. L. REV. 1265, 1303 (1961)).

160. Bickel, *supra* note 147, at 41.

161. Wechsler, *The Political Safeguards of Federalism*, in PRINCIPLES, POLITICS AND FUNDAMENTAL LAW 49, 50 (1961) (quoted in Bickel, *supra* note 147, at 41).

162. Bickel, *supra* note 147, at 42.

163. *Id.* at 43.

164. *Id.* at 44.

165. *See* Bush v. Gore, 531 U.S. 98, 111–22, (2000) (Rehnquist, C.J., concurring, joined by Scalia and Thomas, JJ.); Republican Party of Pennsylvania v. Boockvar, No. 20-542, 2020 WL 6304626, at *1 (U.S. Oct. 28, 2020) (Statement of Alito, J.); Moore v. Circosta, No. 20A72, 2020 WL 6305036 (U.S. Oct. 28, 2020) (Gorsuch, J., dissenting).

Chapter 9

1. ROBERT F. WILLIAMS, THE LAW OF AMERICAN STATE CONSTITUTIONS 40–41 (2009) (citing CARL L. BECKER, THE HISTORY OF POLITICAL PARTIES IN THE PROVINCE OF NEW YORK, 1760–1776 (1909)).

2. Bond v. United States, 564 U.S. 211, 221 (2011) (quotation omitted).

3. Richard Briffault, *The Challenge of the New Preemption*, 70 STAN. L. REV. 1995, 2008 (2018).

4. *Id.*; David J. Barron, *The Promise of Cooley's City: Traces of Local Constitutionalism*, 147 PENN. L. REV. 487 (Jan. 1999) ("The text of the Constitution does not mention local governments, and black-letter constitutional law formally deems them to be the mere administrative appendages of the states that 'create' them.").

5. Williams v. Mayor & City Council, 289 U.S. 36, 40 (1933); *see also, e.g.*, Holt Civic Club v. City of Tuscaloosa, 439 U.S. 60, 71 (1978) (States have "extraordinarily wide latitude . . . in creating various types of political subdivisions and conferring authority upon them").

6. Briffault, *supra* note 3, at 2020.

7. *Id.*

8. Barron, *supra* note 4, at 493.

9. 517 U.S. 620 (1996) (invalidating a Colorado initiative that barred local laws designed to prohibit discrimination based on sexual orientation under the Fourteenth Amendment's Equal Protection Clause).

10. 458 U.S. 457 (1982) (invalidating a Washington initiative that ended local school assignment plans designed to increase racial integration under the Fourteenth Amendment's Equal Protection Clause). *But see* Schuette v. Coalition to Defend Affirmative Action, 572 U.S. 291 (2014)

(upholding constitutional initiative that prohibited state and local governments from using affirmative action).

11. 521 U.S. 898 (1997).

12. *Id.* at 903 (quoting 18 U.S.C. § 922(s)(2)).

13. *Id.* at 905.

14. 505 U.S. 144 (1992).

15. *Printz*, 521 U.S. at 905–10.

16. *Id.* at 910–15.

17. *Id.* at 918–20(quotations omitted).

18. *Id.* at 920–21 (quotations omitted).

19. *Id.* (quotations omitted).

20. *Id.* at 921–22.

21. *Id.*

22. *Id.* at 935.

23. 138 S. Ct. 1461 (2018).

24. KELSEY Y. SANTAMARIA, CONG. RSCH. SERV., LSB10386, IMMIGRATION ENFORCEMENT & THE ANTI-COMMANDEERING DOCTRINE: RECENT LITIGATION ON STATE INFORMATION-SHARING RESTRICTIONS (2020).

25. 521 U.S. 507 (1997).

26. 426 U.S. 833 (1976), *overruled* by Garcia v. San Antonio Metro. Transit. Auth., 469 U.S. 528 (1985).

27. Heather K. Gerken, *The Supreme Court, 2009 Term—Forward: Federalism All the Way Down*, 124 HARV. L. REV. 4, 6 (2010).

28. Briffault, *supra* note 3, at 2019.

29. *Id.* at 2008 (citing Williams v. Mayor of Baltimore, 289 U.S. 36, 40 (1933)).

30. JOHN DINAN, STATE CONSTITUTIONAL POLITICS 40 (Chicago 2018).

31. *Id.* (quoting MICH. CONST., art. IV, § 23 (1850)).

32. *Id.* (quoting IND. CONST., art. IV, § 22 (1851)).

33. *Id.* (citing HOWARD LEE MCBAIN, THE LAW AND THE PRACTICE OF MUNICIPAL HOME RULE 68–92 (Columbia Univ. Press 1916)).

34. *Id.* (quoting MCBAIN, *supra* note 33, at 92).

35. *Id.* at 40–41.

36. *Id.* at 41.

37. *Id.*

38. *Id.* (quoting David O. Porter, *The Ripper Clause in State Constitutional Law: An Early Urban Experiment: Part I*, 1969 UTAH L. REV. 307 (1969)).

39. *Id.* (quoting Michael E. Libonati, *Local Government, in* 3 STATE CONSTITUTIONS FOR THE TWENTY-FIRST CENTURY, 123–24 (G. Alan Tarr & Robert Williams eds., 2006)).

40. I thank Harvard Law Professor Nikolas Bowie for telling me about this episode of the NPR podcast "This American Life," from which many of the facts of this story are drawn. *See* THIS AMERICAN LIFE, *Episode 629: Expect Delays*, NPR (Oct. 20, 2017), https://www.thisamericanlife.org/629/transcript.

41. According to the 2010 Census. *Id.*
42. Village of Linndale v. State, 706 N.E.2d 1227, 1229 (Ohio 1999).
43. OHIO CONST. Art. XVIII, § 3.
44. West Jefferson v. Robinson, 205 N.E.2d 382, 386 (Ohio 1965).
45. Garcia v. Siffrin Residential Ass'n, 407 N.E.2d 1369, 1377–78 (Ohio 1980).
46. *Village of Linndale*, 706 N.E.2d at 1230.
47. *Id.*
48. Linndale's challenge to the bill appeared to be based in part on Ohio's single-subject provision. *See* Village of Linndale v. State, 19 N.E.3d 935 (Ohio Ct. App. 2014) (reversing the trial court's grant of summary judgment to the state on the grounds that the bill may violate Ohio's single-subject rule, but holding that the dissolution of mayor's courts can stand if other parts of the bill are severed).
49. *See* Oh. Rev. Stat. § 1905.01 (2020).
50. *See* City of Dayton v. State, 87 N.E.3d 176, 184 (Ohio 2017) (referring to 4511.093(B)(1) as it was written in 2017).
51. *Id.*
52. *Id.* at 182 (citing City of Canton v. State, 766 N.E.2d 963 (Ohio 2002)).
53. *Id.* at 184.
54. *Id.* at 184–85.
55. *See* Oh. Rev. Stat. § 4511.093.
56. 24 Iowa 455 (1868). *See* Patricia D. Cafferata, *Back Story: John Forrest Dillon, the Man Behind Dillon's Rule*, NEVADA LAWYER (June 2013), https://www.nvbar.org/wp-content/uploads/NevLawyer_June_2013_BackStory.pdf
57. *Id.* at 461, 475.
58. *Id.*
59. 1 JOHN F. DILLON, THE LAW OF MUNICIPAL CORPORATIONS 173 (2d rev. ed. James Cockroft & Co. 1873).
60. Barron, *supra* note 4, at 508; *see* Merriam v. Moody's Ex'rs, 25 Iowa 163, 170 (1868).
61. Barron, *supra* note 4, at 508.
62. Adam Coester, *Dillon's Rule or Not?* NATIONAL ASSOCIATION OF COUNTIES (Jan. 2004). The alert reader may wonder how Dillon's Rule could be the law in thirty-one states when forty-plus states have home rule. That is because Dillon's Rule, a principle of limited delegation, is a background norm that a state may replace with home rule or leave in place. When a state rejects Dillon's Rule, that makes it easier for local governments to act in the first instance, but it does not by itself protect the locality when a state wishes to displace a local action or reassert authority over a matter.
63. Jon D. Russell & Aaron Bostrom, *Federalism, Dillon Rule and Home Rule*, AMERICAN CITY COUNTY EXCHANGE (Jan. 2016), https://www.alec.org/app/uploads/2016/01/2016-ACCE-White-Paper-Dillon-House-Rule-Final.pdf.

64. 24 Mich. 44 (1871).

65. *Id.* at 95.

66. *Id.* at 95–96.

67. *Id.* at 96.

68. *Id.* at 97.

69. *Id.* at 98.

70. *Id.*

71. *Id.* at 108.

72. *Id.*

73. *Id.* at 109.

74. *Id.* at 111.

75. *Id.* at 107.

76. Thomas M. Cooley, A Treatise on the Constitutional Limitations Which Rest upon the Legislative Power of the States of the American Union 459 (Little, Brown & Co. 3d ed. 1874) (quoted in Barron, *supra* note 4, at 513).

77. Barron, *supra* note 4, at 513.

78. *Id.* at 521.

79. *Id.* at 513–14.

80. Dinan, *supra* note 30, at 44 (quoting McBain, *supra* note 33, at 15).

81. City of Taylor v. Detroit Edison, 715 N.W. 2d 28 (Mich. 2006) ("reconcil[ing] [city's] constitutional authority to exercise 'reasonable control' over its streets with the Michigan Public Service Commission's broad regulatory control over public utilities").

82. Associated Builders and Contractors v. Lansing, 880 N.W.2d 765, 770 (2016) (quotation omitted).

83. Morrow v. Kansas City, 186 Mo. 675 (1905) (quoting Mo. Const. of 1875 art. IX § 16).

84. St. Louis v. Western Union Tel. Co., 149 U.S. 465, 468 (1893).

85. Dinan, *supra* note 30, at 42 (quoting George Bradfield, *from* 12 Debates of the Missouri Constitutional Convention of 1875, 495 (Isidor Loeb & Floyd C. Shoemaker eds., State Historical Society of Missouri, 1930–44)).

86. *Id.* at 41–42.

87. *Id.* at 42.

88. *Id.*

89. Briffault, *supra* note 3, at 2011 n.111 (citing Dale Krane et al., *Home Rule in America: A Fifty-State Handbook* app. at 476 tbl.A1, 477 tbl.A2 (2001)).

90. *Id.*

91. Dinan, *supra* note 30, at 44.

92. *Id.* (quoting Robert Crosser, *from* 2 Proceedings and Debates of the Constitutional Convention of the State of Ohio 1483 (F. J. Heer Printing 1912)).

93. *Id.* (quoting Crosser, *supra* note 93, at 1484).

94. *See generally* Nestor M. Davidson, *Localist Administrative Law*, 126 YALE L.J. 564 (2017). That separation of powers sometimes operates at the local level in the same way it operates at the state and national levels does not mean it always does so. Some local governments, particularly smaller ones, are governed by commissions of one sort or another, which merge legislative and executive functions. Something similar happens with some council-manager systems of government. Thus, while some of the same assumptions of federal and state administrative law apply at the local level, as the New York City case illustrates, that is not always true.

95. N.Y. Statewide Coal. of Hispanic Chambers of Commerce v. N.Y.C. Dept. of Health & Mental Hygiene, 16 N.E.3d 538 (N.Y. 2014).

96. *Id.*

97. Robert F. Williams, *State Constitutional Law: Teaching and Scholarship*, 41 J. LEGAL EDUC. 243, 243 (1991).

98. Barron, *supra* note 4, at 487.

99. *Id.,* at 612; Briffault, *supra* note 3, at 2017–21; Michael Q. Cannon, *The Dual-Faceted Federalism Framework and the Derivative Constitutional Status of Local Governments*, 2012 B.Y.U. L. REV. 1585, 1591–95 (2012).

100. People ex rel. Le Roy v. Hurlbut, 24 Mich. 44, 107–08 (Mich. 1871).

101. *See generally* Barron, *supra* note 4 (exploring the foundations of Cooley's thinking in *Hurlbut* and other writings and raising possibilities of judicial enforcement of these implied constitutional norms).

102. Briffault et al., Principles of Home Rule for the Twenty-First Century NATIONAL LEAGUE OF CITIES 13 (Feb. 12, 2020).

103. *See generally* Briffault, *supra* note 3; Richard C. Schragger, *The Attack on American Cities*, 96 TEX. L. REV. 1163 (2018); Paul Diller, *Intrastate Preemption*, 87 B.U.L. REV. 1113 (2007).

104. David J. Barron, *Reclaiming Home Rule*, 116 HARV. L. REV. 2257, 2276 (2003).

105. Briffault, *supra* note 102, at 103. The authors are Richard Briffault, Nestor Davidson, Paul Diller, Sarah Fox, Laurie Reynolds, Erin Scharff, Richard Schragger, and Rick Su.

106. Briffault, *supra* note 102, at 35.

107. *Id.*

108. RUSSELL & BOSTROM, *supra* note 63, at 4.

109. Hunter v. City of Pittsburgh, 207 U.S. 161, 178–79 (1907).

Chapter 10

1. *Jefferson to Samuel Kercheval*, July 12, 1816, *in* THOMAS JEFFERSON, WRITINGS 1402 (Library of America 1984).

2. THE FEDERALIST No. 49, at 340 (Jacob E. Cooke ed., Wesleyan 1961); JAMES A. BAYARD, A BRIEF EXPOSITION OF THE CONSTITUTION OF THE UNITED STATES 3, 135–36, 160 (2d ed. 1838) (echoing the need for "stability" in the federal constitution).

3. The Federalist No. 49, *supra* note 2, at 340.

4. Anne Permaloff, *Methods of Altering State Constitutions*, 33 CUMB. L. REV. 217, 219 (2002).

5. G. Alan Tarr, *Interpreting the Separation of Powers in State Constitutions*, 59 N.Y.U. ANN. SURV. AM. L. 329, 334 (2003).

6. *Id.*

7. JOHN DINAN, STATE CONSTITUTIONAL POLITICS 23 (2018).

8. *Id.*

9. *Id.* at 11.

10. Tarr, *supra* note 5, at 334–36.

11. RICHARD B. BERNSTEIN & JEROME AGEL, AMENDING AMERICA xii (Times Books 1993).

12. DINAN, *supra* note 7, at 23.

13. *Id.*

14. *Id.* at 26, Table 1.3.

15. Donald S. Lutz, *Toward a Theory of Constitutional Amendment*, 88 AM. POL. SCIENCE REV. 355, 355–70, Tbl. C-1 (1994). For those who think blame or praise for innovative US Supreme Court decisions rests at the feet of Article V, it's worth examining the Australian experience. That constitution, as Lutz notes, has been amended less frequently than the US Constitution, and yet the Australian High Court seems to engage in far less inventive constitutional interpretation. As one marker, it required marriage equality through legislation rather than judicial interpretation.

16. 2 U.S. (2 Dall.) 419 (1793).

17. LIBRARY OF CONGRESS, THE CONSTITUTION OF THE UNITED STATES OF AMERICA: ANALYSIS AND INTERPRETATION, *Centennial Edition* 28 n. 3 (2013), https://web.archive.org/web/20140225114303/http:/www.gpo.gov/fdsys/pkg/GPO-CONAN-2013/pdf/GPO-CONAN-2013.pdf.

18. Dred Scott v. Sandford, 60 U.S. (19. How.) 393 (1857).

19. 158 U.S. 601 (1895).

20. 88 U.S. 162, 178 (1874).

21. 302 U.S. 277 (1937). Two years after the Twenty-Fourth Amendment, *Harper v. Virginia State Board of Elections*, 383 U.S. 663 (1966), reversed *Breedlove*, holding that the Fourteenth Amendment prohibited poll taxes in connection with state elections, too.

22. 400 U.S. 112 (1970).

23. John Dinan says that only four amendments overrule US Supreme Court decisions: the Eleventh, Fourteenth, Sixteenth, and Twenty-Sixth. DINAN, *supra* note 7, at 109. I think it's fair to add that the Thirteenth and Fifteenth Amendments overrule *Dred Scott* as well. That takes us to six. He does not count the Nineteenth Amendment as effectively overruling the *Minor* or *Breedlove* decisions. I do. Either way, whether it's four amendments that overrule Court decisions or eight, that's a paltry figure after 232 years.

24. In the words of Donald Lutz: "It is possible that the great difficulty faced in amending the US Constitution led to heavy judicial interpretation as a virtue in the face of necessity." Lutz, *supra* note 15, at 364.

25. GOODWIN LIU, PAMELA S. KARLAN & CHRISTOPHER H. SCHROEDER, KEEPING FAITH WITH THE CONSTITUTION (Oxford Univ. Press 2010); MICHAEL J. KLARMAN, BROWN v. BOARD OF EDUCATION AND THE CIVIL RIGHTS MOVEMENT (Oxford Univ. Press 2007); DAVID STRAUSS, THE LIVING CONSTITUTION (Oxford Univ. Press 2010).

26. JoEllen Lind, *Dominance and Democracy: The Legacy of Women Suffrage for the Voting Right*, 5 UCLA WOMEN'S L.J. 103, 161–62 (1994).

27. Akhil Reed Amar, *How Women Won the Vote*, 29 WILSON QUARTERLY 30, 32 (2005).

28. DAVID E. KYVIG, EXPLICIT AND AUTHENTIC ACTS 408 (Univ. Press of Kan. 2016).

29. Thirteen, I can't resist adding, is a number associated with Chief Justice John Marshall, our thirteenth justice and the justice most associated with giving us federal judicial review.

30. Five states (Idaho, Kentucky, Nebraska, South Dakota, and Tennessee) rescinded their approval, though the effectiveness of those rescissions remains to be seen. KYVIG, *supra* note 28, at 409, 415.

31. 518 U.S. 515 (1996).

32. *Id.* at 518, 531.

33. 83 U.S. 130 (1872) (upholding Illinois's refusal to allow Myra Bradwell to practice law under the Fourteenth Amendment).

34. Tarr, *supra* note 5, at 332.

35. *Id.*; *see also* G. ALAN TARR, UNDERSTANDING STATE CONSTITUTIONS 201–05 (1998).

36. Permaloff, *supra* note 4, at 219.

37. *State I&R*, INITIATIVE AND REFERENDUM INSTITUTE, http://www.iandrinstitute.org/states.cfm (last visited Sept. 25, 2020).

38. Lutz, *supra* note 15, at 356. Lutz notes that William Penn first referred to an amendment process in his 1678 treatise, *Frame of Government*, "which may explain why Pennsylvania was the first state to adopt one." *Id.* at 356 n.1.

39. *Id.* at 356.

40. DINAN, *supra* note 7, at 12.

41. *Id.* at 13.

42. *Id.*

43. *Id.*

44. *Id.*

45. *Id.*

46. *Id.* at 13, 15.

47. TARR, *supra* note 35, at 23 (cited in Robert F. Williams, *Evolving State Constitutional Processes of Adoption, Revision, and Amendment: The Path Ahead*, 69 ARK. L. REV. 553, 554 (2016)).

48. Kermit L. Hall, *Mostly Anchor and Little Sail: The Evolution of American State Constitutions, in* TOWARD A USABLE PAST: LIBERTY UNDER STATE CONSTITUTIONS, 394–95 (Paul Finkelman & Stephen E. Gottlieb eds., U. Ga. Press 1991).

49. DINAN, *supra* note 7, at 23; G. ALAN TARR, CONSTITUTIONAL POLITICS IN THE STATES: CONTEMPORARY CONTROVERSIES AND HISTORICAL PATTERNS 3 (Greenwood 1996).

50. TOWARD A USABLE PAST: LIBERTY UNDER STATE CONSTITUTIONS, 14 n.19 (Paul Finkelman & Stephen E. Gottlieb eds., U. Ga. Press 1991); DINAN, *supra* note 7, at 23.

51. TARR, *supra* note 35, at 19; ROBERT F. WILLIAMS, STATE CONSTITUTIONAL LAW: CASES AND MATERIALS 18–19 (2d ed. 1993).

52. DINAN, *supra* note 7, at 23.

53. Hall, *supra* note 48, at 393–95; Goodwin Liu, *State Courts and Constitutional Structure*, 128 YALE L.J. 1304, 1350–51 (2019) (reviewing Jeffrey S. Sutton, *51 Imperfect Solutions: States and the Making of American Constitutional Law* (Oxford Univ. Press 2018)).

54. Permaloff, *supra* note 4, at 217.

55. *Id.* at 226–27.

56. *Id.* at 227–28.

57. DINAN, *supra* note 7, at 17 tbl.1.2.

58. Permaloff, *supra* note 4, at 229–30.

59. *Annotation, Construction and Application of Constitutional or Statutory Requirement as to Short Title, Ballot Title, or Explanation of Nature of Proposal in Initiative, Referendum, or Recall Petition*, 106 A.L.R. 555 (2019).

60. Permaloff, *supra* note 4, at 231.

61. *See generally id.*

62. MASS. CONST., amend. art. XLVIII, pt. 2, §2; MISS. CONST. art. XV, sec. 273, §5. Note that Mississippi adopted the initiative for the *second* time in 1992. It's the only state to create and remove an initiative process. The state supreme court voided the initiative in 1922. *See Mississippi*, INITIATIVE AND REFERENDUM INSTITUTE (2020), http://www.iandrinstitute.org/states/state.cfm?id=13.

63. Citizens Protecting Michigan's Constitution v. Secretary of State, 921 N.W.2d 247 (2018).

64. Permaloff, *supra* note 4, at 225 (citing G. Alan Tarr, *For the People: Direct Democracy in State Constitutional Tradition*, INITIATIVE & REFERENDUM INSTITUTE, http://www.iandrinstitute.org/docs/Tarr-DD-in-the-State-Constitutional-Tradition-IRI.pdf.)

65. *See* ARIZ. CONST. art. IV, § 1; ARK. CONST. art. V, § 1; CAL. CONST. art. II, §§ 8, 10; COLO. CONST. art. V, § 1; IDAHO CONST. art. III, § 1; MO.

CONST. art. III, §§ 50–51; MONT. CONST. art. III, § 4; NEB. CONST. art. III, §§ 1–2, 4; N.D. CONST. art. III; OKLA. CONST. art. V, §§ 1–3, 6–8; OR. CONST. art. IV, § 1; S.D. CONST. art. III, § 1; UTAH CONST. art. VI, § 1; WASH. CONST. art. II, § 1.

66.   *See* ALASKA CONST. art. XI, §§ 1–7; ME. CONST. art. IV, Init., pt. 3, § 18; MASS. CONST. amend. art. XLVIII, pt. 5, § 1; MICH. CONST. art. II, § 9; NEV. CONST. art. XIX, § 2; OHIO CONST. art. II, § 1b; WYO. CONST. art. III, § 52.

67.   Permaloff, *supra* note 4, at 236–43.

68.   Steven H. Steinglass, Opinion, *Legislature Undercut Work of Constitutional Panel*, COLUMBUS DISPATCH, Nov. 16, 2017.

69.   Peter J. Galie & Christopher Bopst, *The Constitutional Commission in New York: A Worthy Tradition*, 64 ALB. L. REV. 1285, 1316 (2001).

70.   FLA. CONST. art. XI, § 2–4 (1968) (permitting initiative, convention, and revision commission).

71.   Permaloff, *supra* note 4, at 243.

72.   Mary E. Adkins, *What Florida's Constitution Revision Commission Can Teach and Learn from Those of Other States*, 71 RUTGERS U.L. REV. 1177, 1181 (2019).

73.   Galie & Bopst, *supra* note 69, at 1316.

74.   Permaloff, *supra* note 4, at 228.

75.   *Id.* at 228–29.

76.   *Id.* at 229.

77.   *Id.* at 237.

78.   *See generally Constitution Revision Commission 2017–2018*, FLORIDA STATE UNIVERSITY (2018), https://crc.law.fsu.edu/.

79.   Adkins, *supra* note 72, at 1213.

80.   *Id.* at 1216 (citing P. K. Jameson & Marsha Hoscak, *Citizen Initiatives in Florida: An Analysis of Florida's Constitutional Initiative Process, Issues, and Alternatives*, 23 FLA. ST. U.L. REV. 417, 426 (1995)).

81.   Armstrong v. Harris, 773 So.2d 7, 11 (Fla. 2000). In this fascinating case, the Florida Supreme Court invalidated an amendment that passed with 72% support and that would have linked interpretations of Florida's "cruel or unusual punishment" clause to the US Supreme Court's interpretation of the federal "cruel and unusual punishment" clause. *See* Adkins, *supra* note 72, at 1218.

82.   Detzner v. Anstead, 256 So.3d 820, 824 (Fla. 2018).

83.   Jim Saunders, *Florida Supreme Court Asked to Block Constitutional Amendments*, ORLANDO WEEKLY (Aug. 15, 2018. 11:50 AM), https://www. orlandoweekly.com/Blogs/archives/2018/08/15/florida-supreme-court-asked-to-block-constitutional-amendments; Brendan Rivers, *Bill Filed to Ban Bundled Amendments from Constitution Revision Commission*, WJCT (Nov. 26, 2018), https://news.wjct.org/post/bill-filed-ban-bundled-amendments-constitution-revision-commission; James Call, *Former*

Lawmakers Urge Voters to Reject All 8 CRC Amendments, TALLAHASSEE DEMOCRAT (Aug. 21, 2018), https://www.tallahassee.com/story/news/2018/08/21/former-lawmakers-urge-voters-reject-all-crc-amendments/1050133002/.

84. Detzner v. League of Women Voters of Florida, 256 So.3d 803 (Fla. 2018).

85. Note, *Judicial Approaches to Direct Democracy*, 118 HARV. L. REV. 2748, 2756 (2005) (cited in Adkins, *supra* note 72, at 1213).

86. Adkins, *supra* note 72, at 1229. Notably, Florida placed Amendment 4 on the ballot for 2020, which would have required the people to approve an amendment in two successive general elections, each by a 60% supermajority vote. The amendment failed by a margin of 5%. *November 3, 2020 General Election Official Results*, FLORIDA DEPARTMENT OF STATE, https://results.elections.myflorida.com/Index.asp?ElectionDate=11/3/2020 (last visited Dec. 14, 2020).

87. *2020 Constitutional Amendments*, League of Women Voters of Florida, https://www.lwvfl.org/amendments-2020-2/ (last visited Mar. 8, 2021); *see also* Gary Blankenship, *Abolishing the CRC Passes House, Moving to Senate*, THE FLORIDA BAR (Jan. 27, 2020), https://www.floridabar.org/the-florida-bar-news/abolishing-the-crc-passes-house-moving-in-senate/.

88. "A study of the constitutional history of New York reveals that the constitutional commission has a long and vital history"—used ten times in the state's history—"as a means of proposing meaningful and necessary reform within the state. Some of the most significant constitutional revision in New York has been the product of such commissions, and the most successful commissions were held in the aftermath of constitutional convention defeats." Galie & Bopst, *supra* note 69, at 1287. They point out that other states have used commissions, even when lacking the authority to propose amendments directly to the people, in productive ways. Take the Georgia Constitution of 1945, which "represents the first time in American history that a constitution was written by a commission and ratified by popular vote. This action was taken following several unsuccessful attempts to pass a resolution that would have convened a constitutional convention and represents a method for obtaining a complete revision of the constitution while avoiding the negatives of the convention process." *Id.* at 1323.

89. Kim Robak, *The Nebraska Unicameral and Its Lasting Benefits*, 76 NEB. L. REV. 791, 793 n.9 (1997).

90. *Id.*

91. *Id.*

92. *Id.* at 794.

93. *Id.*

94. *Id.*

95.   *Id.*; see George W. Norris, *A Model State Legislature*, reprinted in *One Branch Legislature for States Would Improve Results*, N.Y. TIMES, Jan. 28, 1923, at 12).

96.   Robak, *supra* note 89, at 796.

97.   *Id.* (quoting RICHARD L. NEUBERGER & STEPHEN B. KAHN, INTEGRITY: THE LIFE OF GEORGE W. NORRIS 278 (1937)).

98.   *Id.* at 798.

99.   *Id.* at 798 n. 38.

100. *Id.* at 797 n. 35.

101. *Id.* at 799.

102. SANFORD LEVINSON, IS THE UNITED STATES CONSTITUTION SUFFICIENTLY DEMOCRATIC: HOW WOULD WE KNOW AND DO WE REALLY CARE? 14 (March 21, 2013) (quoting John Roche), https://amc.sas.upenn.edu/sites/www.sas.upenn.edu.andrea-mitchell-center/files/uploads/Levinson_DCC.pdf.

103. Robak, *supra* note 89, at 799 n. 47.

104. *Id.* at 805 (quoting *Nebraska R.F.D. to F.D.R.*, 17 TIME MAGAZINE, Jan. 11, 1937, at 16).

105. *Id.* at 805 (quoting *Nebraska: Unicameral Body Legislates Alone and Likes It*, NEWSWEEK, May 22, 1937, at 12).

106. *Id.* at 796 n. 27.

107. Paula Abrams, *The Majority Will: Case Study of Misinformation, Manipulation, and the Oregon Initiative Process*, 87 OR. L. REV. 1025, 1025–26 nn. 2–3.

108. Burton J. Hendrick, *The Initiative and Referendum and How Oregon Got Them*, 37 MCCLURE'S MAGAZINE, 235, 240 (1911).

109. ALLEN EATON, THE OREGON SYSTEM 3 (1912).

110. JEFFREY S. SUTTON, 51 IMPERFECT SOLUTIONS: STATES AND THE MAKING OF AMERICAN CONSTITUTIONAL LAW, 178–90 (Oxford Univ. Press 2018); *see generally* Hans A. Linde, *First Things First: Rediscovering the States' Bill of Rights*, 9 U. BAL. L. REV. 379 (1980). As it happens, Linde was not a proponent of the initiative. *See* Hans Linde, *When Initiative Lawmaking Is Not "Republican Government": The Campaign Against Homosexuality*, 72 OR. L. REV. 19, 43–44 (1993).

111. David Schuman, *The Origin of State Const. Direct Democracy, William Simon U'Ren and the Oregon System*, 67 TEMP. L. REV. 947, 952 n. 38 (1994).

112. *Id.* at nn. 40–42 & n. 57.

113. *See Oregon*, INITIATIVE AND REFERENDUM INSTITUTE (2020), http://www.iandrinstitute.org/states/state.cfm?id=23; DAVID SCHMIDT, CITIZEN LAWMAKERS: THE BALLOT INITIATIVE REVOLUTION 6–8 (Temple Univ. Press 1989).

114. *History of Initiative & Referendum in Oregon*, BALLOTPEDIA, https://ballotpedia.org/History_of_Initiative_%26_Referendum_in_Oregon (last

visited Sept. 25, 2020); Schuman, *supra* note III, at n. 9 (citing SCHMIDT, *supra* note 113).

115. Pacific States Tel. & Tel. Co. v. Oregon, 223 U.S. 118, 133–34 (1912).

116. LINCOLN STEFFENS, UPBUILDERS 287–88 (Doubleday 1909).

117. *Id.*

118. *Initiative, Referendum and Recall*, OREGON BLUE BOOK 4 (2019–20), https://sos.oregon.gov/blue-book/Documents/elections/initiative.pdf.

119. *Pacific States Tel.*, 223 U.S. at 137.

120. *Id.* at 149–50.

121. *Id.* at 150.

122. *Id.*

123. 517 U.S. 620 (1996) (invalidating an initiative that prohibited Colorado local governments from enacting measures that protected gay citizens from discrimination).

124. 576 U.S. 787 (2015) (upholding Arizona ballot initiative's creation of a commission to regulate redistricting in the face of a claim that it violates Article I's requirement that the "Legislature" be responsible for election regulations).

125. Comment, *Reforming Direct Democracy: Lessons from Oregon*, 93 CALIF. L. REV. 1191, nn. 33–34 (2005).

126. *Gorky's Opinion on America*, OREGONIAN, July 17, 1906, at 8, https://oregonnews.uoregon.edu/lccn/sn83025138/1906-07-17/ed-1/seq-8/.

127. *Republican Party Comes Back*, OREGONIAN, Nov. 5, 1914, at 10, https://oregonnews.uoregon.edu/lccn/sn83025138/1914-11-05/ed-1/seq-10/.

128. SCHMIDT, *supra* note 113, at 265–66.

129. For more scholarship about state constitutional amendments in general and initiatives in particular, *see* Jon M. Philipson, *Second-Order Logrolling: The Impact of Direct Legislative Amendments to State Constitutions*, 41 NOVA L. REV. 23 (2016); John Dinan, *State Constitutional Amendments and American Constitutionalism*, 41 OKLA. CITY U.L. REV. 27 (2016); and Robert F. Williams, *Evolving State Constitutional Processes of Adoption, Revision, and Amendment: The Path Ahead*, 69 ARK. L. REV. 553 (2016).

130. Ronald M. George, *The Perils of Direct Democracy: The California Experience*, Speech to the Am. Acad. of Arts & Scis. (Oct. 10, 2009).

131. CAL. CONST., art. II, § 10a.

132. JEFFREY S. SUTTON, RANDY J. HOLLAND, STEVEN R. MCALLISTER & JEFFREY M. SHAMAN, STATE CONSTITUTIONAL LAW: THE MODERN EXPERIENCE 895 (3rd ed. West 2020) (quoting George, *The Perils of Direct Democracy*). Arizona has something similar. The legislature may amend an initiative but only if it "furthers the purposes of such measure" and is approved by three-quarters of the members of both houses. ARIZ. CONST., Art. 4, § 1.

133. *Summary of Data, History of California Initiatives*, CALIFORNIA SECRETARY OF STATE, https://elections.cdn.sos.ca.gov/ballot-measures/pdf/summary-data.pdf (last visited September 7, 2020).

134. *Initiatives Voted Into Law, History of California Initiatives*, CALIFORNIA SECRETARY OF STATE, https://www.sos.ca.gov/elections/ballot-measures/resources-and-historical-information/history-california-initiatives (last visited Mar. 8, 2021).

135. JOE MATHEWS & MARK PAUL, CALIFORNIA CRACKUP: HOW REFORM BROKE THE GOLDEN STATE AND HOW WE CAN FIX IT 37 (Univ. Cal. Press 2010).

136. *Id.* at 64.

137. Serrano v. Priest, 18 Cal. 3d 728, 776–77 (1976).

138. William A. Fischel, *Did "Serrano" Cause Proposition 13?*, 42 NAT. TAX J. 465, 469 (1989).

139. MATHEWS & PAUL, *supra* note 135, at 55.

140. CALIFORNIA CONSTITUTION REVISION COMMISSION, FINAL REPORT AND RECOMMENDATIONS TO THE GOVERNOR AND THE LEGISLATURE 43 (1996), http://www.californiacityfinance.com/CCRCfinalrpt.pdf.

141. MATHEWS & PAUL, *supra* note 135, at 64.

142. *Id.*

143. The Honorable J. Harvie Wilkinson III, *Toward One America: A Vision in Law*, 83 N.Y.U. L. REV. 323, 327–28 (2008).

144. SUTTON ET AL., *supra* note 132, at 896.

145. *Id.*

146. *Id.*; *see generally* Rudy Klapper, *The Falcon Cannot Hear the Falconer: How California's Initiative Process Is Creating an Untenable Constitution*, 48 LOY. L.A. L. REV. 755 (2015).

147. Maimon Schwarzschild, *Popular Initiatives and American Federalism, or, Putting Direct Democracy in Its Place*, 13 J. CONTEMP. LEGAL ISSUES 531, 546 (2004). The outlier was Utah, which allows initiatives and referenda.

148. SUTTON ET AL., *supra* note 132, at 897.

149. Richard J. Ellis, Symposium: *Signature Gathering in the Initiative Process: How Democratic Is It?*, 64 MONT. L. REV. 35, 76 nn. 130–31 (2003).

150. SUTTON ET AL., *supra* note 132, at 897.

151. *Id.* at 898.

152. *Id.* at 897.

153. Tarr, *supra* note 5, at 333.

154. MARK A. GRABER, A NEW INTRODUCTION TO AMERICAN CONSTITUTIONALISM, 158–59 (Oxford Univ. Press 2013) (quoted in DINAN, *supra* note 7, at 5).

155. Williams, *supra* note 47, at 553 n.2 (citing Jonathan L. Marshfield, *Dimensions of Constitutional Change*, 43 RUTGERS L.J. 593, 598 (2013)).

156. Permaloff, *supra* note 4, at 235.

157. *Id.* at 220 (citing G. Alan Tarr, *For the People: Direct Democracy in the State Constitutional Law Tradition*, INITIATIVE & REFERENDUM INSTITUTE at 3, http://www.iandrinstitute.org/docs/Tarr-DD-in-the-State-Constitutional-Tradition-IRI.pdf).

158. *Id.* at 235–36.

159. *Id.* at 229.

160. *Id.*

161. Galie & Bopst, *supra* note 69, at 1323–24.

162. SANFORD LEVINSON, OUR UNDEMOCRATIC CONSTITUTION: WHERE THE CONSTITUTION GOES WRONG (AND HOW WE THE PEOPLE CAN CORRECT IT) (Oxford Univ. Press 2006); SANFORD LEVINSON, FRAMED: AMERICA'S 51 CONSTITUTIONS AND THE CRISIS OF GOVERNANCE (Oxford Univ. Press 2012).

163. Galie & Bopst, *supra* note 69, at 1324.

164. Robert F. Williams, *Should the Oregon Constitution Be Revised, and If So, How Should It Be Accomplished?*, 87 OR. L. REV. 867, 874 (2008).

165. James A. Henretta, *Foreword: Rethinking the State Constitutional Tradition*, 22 RUTGERS L.J. 819, 829 (1991).

166. *Id.* at 388.

167. Jeffrey S. Sutton, *The Role of History in Judging Disputes About the Meaning of the Constitution*, 41 TEX. TECH. L. REV. 1173, 1177 (2009).

168. Cf. Akhil Reed Amar, *The Consent of the Governed: Constitutional Amendment Outside Article V*, 94 COLUM. L. REV. 457 (1994).

Epilogue

1. Cass R. Sunstein, *Foreword: Leaving Things Undecided*, 110 HARV. L. REV. 4, 7 (1996). A modern example of democracy-forcing action, based on federal judicial engagement *and* restraint, is the death penalty. Whether through the judicial, executive, or legislative branches, the states have responded forcefully to federal judicial intervention and federal hands-off decisions. *See* Maurice Chammah, Let the Lord Sort Them: The Rise and Fall of the Death Penalty (Crown 2021); Anand Giridharadas, *Why the Death Penalty Is Dying: A New Book Tells the Surprising Story*, N.Y. TIMES (Jan. 26, 2021) (noting, in a review of the book, that after 1999 "the death penalty began again to die. This time, it wasn't a high edict [like the 1972 US Supreme Court decision] that doomed it, but the unsung, helter-skelter, hydra-headed, revolution-by-a-thousand-cuts process through which real change often comes").

2. Do not accept too easily the assumption that difficult-to-amend constitutions invariably demand amendment by interpretation. Recall that Australia has the hardest constitution to amend of Western democracies. And yet it has a firm tradition of using legislation to deal with new circumstances.

3. GORDON S. WOOD, POWER AND LIBERTY: CONSTITUTIONALISM IN THE AMERICAN REVOLUTION (Oxford Univ. Press 2021).
4. *Id.*
5. Sanford Levinson, *Is the United States Constitution Sufficiently Democratic: How Would We Know and Do We Really Care?*, 1 (UNIV. PENN., 2013); *see* SANFORD LEVINSON, OUR UNDEMOCRATIC CONSTITUTION: WHERE THE CONSTITUTION GOES WRONG (AND HOW WE THE PEOPLE CAN CORRECT IT) (2006); SANFORD LEVINSON, FRAMED: AMERICA'S 51 CONSTITUTIONS AND THE CRISIS OF GOVERNANCE (2012).
6. Levinson, *Is the United States Constitution Sufficiently Democratic?*, *supra* note 5, at 10.
7. Jessica Bulman-Pozen & Miriam Seifter, *The Democracy Principle in State Constitutions*, 119 MICH. L. REV. 859, 904 (2021).

Appendix

1. "Judicial Selection, An Interactive Map," The Brennan Center for Justice, http://judicialselectionmap.brennancenter.org/?court=Supreme&state=CA (last accessed July 23, 2020).
2. Virginia Division of Legislative Services, *A Legislator's Guide to the Judicial Selection Process* 1, available at http://dls.virginia.gov/pubs/legisguidejudicselect.pdf.
3. 2 S.C. Code Ch. 19, §§ 20, 80, 90.
4. *Id.*
5. *Supra* note 1.
6. *Id.*
7. CAL. CONST., art. II, § 15.

INDEX

———◆———

For the benefit of digital users, indexed terms that span two pages (e.g., 52–53) may, on occasion, appear on only one of those pages.